Kafū the Scribbler

Nagai Kafū
Self-Portrait, 1932

Michigan Classics in Japanese Studies, Number 3

Center for Japanese Studies
The University of Michigan

Kafū the Scribbler

The Life and Writings of Nagai Kafū, 1879–1959

Edward Seidensticker

Center for Japanese Studies, The University of Michigan
Ann Arbor, Michigan

Library of Congress Cataloging in Publication Data

Seidensticker, Edward, 1921–
    Kafū the Scribbler : the life and writings of Nagai Kafū,
1879–1959 / Edward Seidensticker.
        p.   cm.—(Michigan classics in Japanese studies : no. 3)
    Reprint. Originally published: Stanford, Calif. : Stanford
University Press, 1965.
    Includes bibliographical references (p. 350–52).
    ISBN 0-939512-46-7
    1. Nagai, Kafū, 1879–1959—Criticism and interpretation.
I. Nagai, Kafū, 1879–1959.   II. Title.   III. Series.
PL812.A4Z88   1990
895.6'342—dc20   90-1385
                                                              CIP

Reprinted by arrangement of Stanford University Press

Reprinted in 1990 by the Center for Japanese Studies, 108 Lane Hall, The University of Michigan,
Ann Arbor, MI 48109-1290

Printed in the United States of America

Preface

This book is based upon two assumptions: that it is possible for an author to be better and more important than any one of his works; and that it is possible for an author to have a certain universal appeal and yet be so firmly attached to a particular setting as to make a knowledge of that setting essential to a complete awareness of the appeal. It follows that a general survey of the writing, together with representative bits and snatches from it, and a description of the setting are necessary if the new reader is to be properly introduced. No single book may seem worthy of translation, and yet the author and his setting may seem worthy of a book.

It is my feeling that Nagai Kafū is such an author. This book is therefore an introduction to the man and his city, accompanied by a fairly generous sampling from his works. It is neither pure biography nor pure criticism nor yet a pure anthology, but a blending of the three. The result will probably seem satisfactory to almost no one, for almost everyone will wish to have had one of the three in a less adulterated form. I doubt, however, if Kafū would have accommodated himself to any other sort of introduction, and I have long thought him one of the fine writers of modern Japan.

It might be argued that the rather fragmentary and in-between form I have chosen is more appropriate for introducing a lyric poet than a novelist. I would reply only that Kafū is a very discursive sort of novelist. Excerpt treatment does not damage the dramatic unity of his works, for there is little dramatic unity in the first place.

Annotation has been limited to identification of obscure persons, works, and places, and again no one is likely to be satisfied. It is hoped that the Bibliographical Note will cover the sources well enough to make sentence-by-sentence attribution unnecessary. Anyone who wishes to inquire about the sources of particular items will be speedily answered.

Photographs, paintings, and line drawings are reproduced through the courtesy of the Iwanami Publishing Company, the Chūō Kōron Publishing Company, and Nagai Nagamitsu, who holds original rights to all works by Kafū. The self-portrait facing the title page is taken from Kafū's diary, entry of February 21, 1932. The drawings by Kafū on pp. 1, 179, and 345 are also taken from the diary. Permission for complete retranslation of *The River Sumida* and partial retranslation of *Rivalry* and "Hydrangea" has been granted by the Grove Press and the Charles E. Tuttle Company, respectively.

The Japanese name order has been followed throughout the book, with the family name first. When a single element of a name is used, Japanese custom requires that it be a writer's "elegant sobriquet" if he has one. If he has none, the family name is most commonly used. Again, Japanese custom has been respected in this book: Tanizaki (who has no sobriquet), but Kafū.

E. S.

Contents

Eight pages of photographs follow p. 136.

Part one The Life

Chapter one Beginnings

Tokyo in 1879 was a smaller city than it had been a decade earlier, when the Tokugawa Shogunate was overthrown and the young Emperor Meiji took up residence in the city. The mansions and barracks of the military class that had circled the Shogun's castle and sprawled over the hills to the south and west were falling into ruin. The hilly aristocratic regions of the city had always been grim and somber, however, and the changes of the decade had not yet had much effect on the Shitamachi, the flat crescent to the north and east of the castle. The Shitamachi was the land of the artisans and merchants who thought themselves the true sons of Edo, the Shogun's city. To be sure, a new ruling class had moved in from the rustic clans of the far southwest, but the son of Edo could still look around him and see no one approaching him in dash and urbanity.

Yet change was coming, and there was little the Shitamachi could do about it, or even tried very hard to do. "Enlightenment" and "Culture" were in the air. They meant inviting in upon the insular warmth a chilly flood of influences from the Occident. Although the son of Edo may have been a sentimental partisan of the old regime, it was not he, but a dissident group of rustics from the southwest, who presently took arms against the Westernizing Meiji government. The last overt resistance had been put down by 1879, and the city, aristocratic hills and plebeian lowlands alike, was poised on the edge of Enlightenment. The population of Tokyo more than trebled in the next four decades. An occasional rumor that red bricks caused beriberi could, it is true, bring a brief return to the traditional, but red bricks were taking over the Ginza district, the commercial heart of Tokyo. Shimbashi Station and the foreign settlement at Tsukiji were already in existence, windows on the world. In short, the city was ready for the great leap, whatever its native sons may have thought about the prospect.

Nagai Kafū (or Sōkichi) was born on December 3, 1879, in the Koishikawa district of Tokyo. That day, according to the almanacs, was the unluckiest in the whole Chinese cycle of sixty days, a circumstance in which Kafū was later to take some pride. In those days still on the outskirts of Tokyo, Koishikawa was soon to have the city spilling all around it, and today it is quite engulfed. Urbanization has been able to do little to change its steep hills, but the "pebble brook," the *koishikawa* that gave the district its name, has been driven underground, and the willows and arched bridges of the old guidebooks to Edo are gone. The greatest estate in old Koishikawa, the Kōrakuen of the Mito Tokugawa family, now houses a baseball stadium and an amusement park, and the greatest temple, the Denzūin, mortuary chapel of the mother of the first Tokugawa Shogun, has crumbled away to dusty insignificance. Meanwhile Koishikawa has become a sort of Inner Queensborough, neither in nor yet away from the heart of the city.

Kafū was born almost within throwing distance of the Denzūin and the Kōrakuen. While he was growing up, there were still holdouts from Edo to be observed on the grounds of the Denzūin, most notably a young carpenter known as Demon Tome: "He had a demon mask tattooed all across his back, and his head, save for the topknot, was always a freshly shaven blue-black. He was a handsome and awesome young man. In those days many people still wore topknots, but most of them were over forty. I shall always be grateful to Demon Tome, who gave me a last, fleeting glimpse of the Edo craftsman with all his verve, the sort of artisan who was kept alive on the stage by Kikugorō." (v, 325-26.)*

As for the Kōrakuen, even after being turned into a military arsenal, it was a place to stir the childish imagination: "The blue skies, the roofs of the houses, the trees by the road—everything along the way gave rise to vague, indefinable fears," he was to write later of trips to his grandmother's house. "In particular, the road down Tomisaka Hill from the Denzūin, past the earthen wall of the arsenal and

* Except when otherwise indicated, all references are to the Chūō Kōron edition of Kafū's works.

the deep, dark groves inside, seemed truly terrifying.... Today a streetcar runs down the hill. That laminated gray wall of tile and earth and the high stone embankment from which it rose have disappeared, and most of the trees seem to have been cut down. Whenever I pass on a streetcar, I look out at it, but nothing is left to call back the old darkness and terror." (v, 330–31.)

There were strange and mysterious spots immediately at hand, too, such as the Nagai garden, which contained dark groves and much wild life. At one time it even harbored a fox, most sinister and non-urban of creatures. Then there were slopes with sinister names, such as Christian Hill, suggesting to the true child of Edo outlandish conspiracies against Lord Tokugawa. And these various mysteries were but a beginning, for Koishikawa lay on the outermost circle of the Tokugawa city, the circle of temples and cemeteries. Kafū was still a child when his family left Koishikawa, but he was to continue going for walks through the district and to write about them long after the groves had been cut down and most of the cemeteries moved. When he died, his brother found a map of the Koishikawa house and grounds in his desk.

Although love for the old city and anger at the Enlightenment that was destroying it were to be the controlling passions of Kafū's life, he could not claim to be a real Edo man. He suffered from a twofold handicap: Koishikawa was not a part of the Shitamachi; nor was his family a part of Edo—the true child of Edo was not made in a generation. Kafū's family was from the Nagoya region. It belonged to the prosperous landowning class and not, strictly speaking, to the military class proper; but its affinities were with the latter rather than with the merchants and artisans of Edo. One sometimes detects, in among Kafū's ill-tempered remarks about the rustic Meiji bureaucrat and entrepreneur, a note of envy at the purer pedigree of such colleagues as Tanizaki Junichirō, born in the Shitamachi to an Edo merchant family.

Rebellion against the family was common enough among sensitive young people of the day, but the conflict was generally a rather simple one between up-to-date liberation and old-fashioned restraints. In Kafū's case, the rebellion, when in due course it came, was of a more ambiguous nature. His family was simultaneously too new and too old for him. His father, Nagai Kagen (or Hisaichirō) was in many

ways one of the new men, a successful businessman and bureaucrat.
Educated in the West and an admirer of the West, Kagen was an
important functionary in the Ministry of Education and later an ex-
ecutive of Nippon Yūsen Kaisha (Japan Mail Lines), and so a servant
of the entrepreneurs who were redoing the country. He also seems
to have admitted elements of the new in the methods he chose for
educating his children. In imitation of Western ways, Kafū wore short
pants and short hair to primary school. The Japanese convention
called for covered legs and a bare scalp.

Yet Kafū's father was also on the side of Confucian restraints.
Thoroughly trained in the Chinese classics, he was able to turn out
a passable Chinese poem. He was among the drafters of the Imperial
Education Rescript, the definitive statement that Japanese education
would be authoritarian, and similar biases seem to have affected his
behavior toward his children. He would not allow melons in the
house, to cite one minor piece of willfulness, for he thought them
vulgar. Kafū was the eldest son, and so the child most heavily bar-
raged with Confucian notions of family responsibility. Kagen, then,
was on the side of newness without liberation, and Kafū's rebellion
aimed at oldness without restraints. The Edo of his dreams became a
place of beauty without fathers; and his father, neither wholly new
nor wholly old, a sort of distillation of what he most disliked in the
Meiji Period. Had Kagen found it possible to be more completely
the Tokugawa authoritarian, matters might have been easier.

There were also ambiguities on his mother's side. His maternal
grandfather was a well-known Confucian scholar, whose biography
Kafū was to write. Yet his grandmother and mother were both Chris-
tians, and the older of his two brothers, adopted into the mother's
family, became a Protestant minister. Kafū's father was given Christian burial, though he died too suddenly to have had any say in the
matter. The mother had other exotic tastes, too. One day, when still
a very small boy, Kafū came home from school to find guests whom
he, the family heir, was required to greet. They proved to be two
large, pale British ladies, and they gave him a real start. In general,
though, Kafū's writing indicates that this adventuresome convert to
the new was a model Japanese housewife, frugal and self-effacing,
and not one to oppose the Confucian edicts of her husband.

The grandmother was perhaps the deepest enigma of all. She took care of Kafū during a considerable part of his childhood, and it was from her house, in the Shitaya district of Tokyo, that he started going to school. The trip from the Koishikawa house to Shitaya was mysterious, leading past the Kōrakuen, and the Shitaya house was even more mysterious, a dark, empty place with suits of armor in the niches and crows cawing on the roof. Its destruction in the earthquake of 1923 was to be the occasion for Kafū's biography of his grandfather, which was written as much in memory of the house as in memory of his grandfather. The grandmother combined a most Christian manner toward Kafū (who seems to have been excessively grandmothered) with a core of old-world sternness.

Kafū was to write of the enigma later, in an essay called "The House in Shitaya": "I shall not go into the details of my grandmother's funeral. I shall only say that the Shitaya house, where I first saw those two incompatible forces, the sword and the cross, has come to seem indescribably strange." (v, 342–43.) How, he asks, could his grandmother, who had once taken a sword from the wall and defended her house in a most dramatic samurai fashion, have embraced the sweet, apparently permissive alien religion?

It was not always easy for sensitive young minds to accept the delicate mating, effected by their elders, of new methods to old restraints, and Kafū was not in every way the sort of eldest son to delight a Confucian father. There were early signs that he was not concentrating on his studies. As a middle-school student he once sold his overcoat to buy a *shakuhachi* flute, and he went for his *shakuhachi* lessons to the Yanagibashi geisha quarter. His fellow students included such austere persons as Marshal Terauchi, who was to lead the Japanese advance into Southeast Asia in 1942. He seems to have found them unsympathetic, and several decades later he stayed away from the funeral of an admired teacher for fear of meeting some of them. His great friend, one of the few men of whom he was to write with any affection, was a boy named Inoue Seiichi (his pen name was Aa), something of an authority on Edo erotic literature and customs. Inoue was later to affect the ways of the déclassé Edo writer and to die of drink. Kafū himself early read the amatory works of Tamenaga Shunsui, an important fiction writer of late Edo, disguising them as textbooks; and he made trips to the public library to copy out "secret" passages of Saikaku, the great seventeenth-century storyteller.

To the pull of the Edo past was added the sensuous pull of the present city, and new pleasures in which Inoue acted as guide and companion. While still in their teens, the two of them would go off together to the Yoshiwara, the most venerable of the pleasure quarters. Inoue seems to have sold parts of his family library to help pay for the excursions. Kafū later pleaded illness as the excuse for these happenings: "I have been used to illness since my early youth. Illness was so frequent from my teens to my mid-twenties that I may call myself lucky to have survived. Thinking that later regrets would be bad compensation for a youth not properly savored, I first visited the North Quarter at the age of eighteen, all by myself, on my way back from a call on an acquaintance at Ryūsenji." (XI, 92.)*

The moods of Shunsui were still to be found in the daytime city, too. Kafū was later to recall how he made excuses to stay behind while the family was off summering on the Shōnan coast. He would go boating on the Sumida River, and there, in sight of the banks so dear to Shunsui, read the forbidden books. "However violent the assaults of new ideas," he said, "I shall never be able to see the banks of the Sumida apart from the literature of Edo." (V, 280.) Despite the factory chimneys that were already going up on the far bank, sensuous, unthinking Edo still came back on the summer air, for "it is the summer that makes life in Tokyo most beautiful. . . . Bamboo cages with singing insects, painted fans, mosquito nets, sweet-smelling reed blinds and awnings, bells tinkling in the night breeze, lanterns, dwarf plants set into miniature landscapes—where else are there appurtenances of such delicacy? . . . Sometimes, walking along a canal of a summer evening, I have found myself drunk with a mood as of hearing a samisen somewhere—in a courtesan's room, perhaps, in a scene from Mokuami's 'The Robbers.'" (V, 287–88.)

Illness may be blamed in part for his failure to follow the most admired academic course. An intestinal ailment kept him in bed through much of 1895, and he spent long months at a seaside hospital in Odawara and at the family's villa in Zushi, south of Tokyo.

In 1897 he entered the Chinese department of the School of Foreign

---

* The Yoshiwara was known as "the North Quarter."

Studies. He had earlier taken lessons in Chinese poetry, and in the same year, 1897, he had spent some months in Shanghai, where his father, having left the Ministry of Education, was branch manager for the Japan Mail Lines. The family had already left Koishikawa, tentatively in 1890 and finally in 1896. One of the houses they occupied conjured up all kinds of sinister forms of life: "My father once had an official house in Kōjimachi.... The garden gave way abruptly to a cliff on which grew bamboo thickets, and these I must describe as quite terrifying. Late on summer evenings, scores of toads would come crawling out and lie like rocks strewn over the garden. Beyond the garden and a narrow street was a rise, on which the back of the German Legation could be seen, again through heavy groves. Having been nourished on Japanese superstition as a child, I would think on cold nights of ghosts and the like, and forcing myself out alone over the pitch-black veranda to the privy, I would look through the torn paper of the window and see, deep in the trees on the cliff, the brightly lighted windows of that Occidental mansion. I would hear piano music, and think what an inconceivably strange thing the life of a foreigner was." (x, 215-16.)

Of Kafū's career in the School of Foreign Studies there is little to say except that he scarcely went near the place and failed to graduate. Other things occupied his attention. He had written his first short stories while still in middle school. They seem to have been in the manner of Tamenaga Shunsui, stronger on incident than character, and they do not survive. The very first was about a nurse who attended him during his long illness, and who, it is said, was his first love. She, too, was responsible for his "elegant sobriquet" or pen name, Kafū (his legal name was Sōkichi). She was called O-hasu, "Miss Lotus," and Kafū means "Lotus Breeze." His literary efforts were concealed from his family. The art of fiction had been frowned upon by the Tokugawa Shogunate and was still not admired in conservative families.

These efforts began in earnest after the return of the family from Shanghai. Japanese practice required that he enroll himself as the disciple of some literary elder, and so, armed with four or five stories, he went knocking at the gate of Hirotsu Ryūrō, and was admitted. This was in 1898.

Ryūrō was not precisely an elder, being at the time in his late thirties, but he was one of the more distinguished writers of the day. It was a rather tentative day, when a flirtation with European realism had led to little but a warming-over of Tokugawa romanticism and a debate on literary language. The literary language of Edo, full of sinicisms and antiquated verbs, did not seem up to the demands of modern realism, and something very close to colloquial speech was coming into its own for literary uses. Ryūrō was among the experimenters with the vernacular, but his matter was familiar, merchant and courtesan torn by the contradictory pulls of duty and feeling. When Kafū came asking to be admitted to the profession, Ryūrō was fresh from his greatest success, *Double Suicide at Imado*. About the drowning of a Yoshiwara courtesan and a merchant who was her customer, this work belongs to the genre in which Ryūrō specialized, the "distressing novel." Distressing novels deal with sordid and sensational events, frequently of the demimonde, and do not, on the whole, fear being accused of a certain improbability in plot and characterization. They derive from the amorous literature of late Tokugawa, as does Ryūrō's favorite technique, a reliance on dialogue at the expense of description.

Kafū's earliest published stories could have been written by Ryūrō. Indeed some of them appeared either as joint works of the two or as Ryūrō's alone, and it has been suggested that when, as shortly happened, Kafū began edging away from Ryūrō to place himself under the tutelage of Iwaya Sazanami, a writer known chiefly for juvenile fiction, his reason had to do with Ryūrō's habit of pocketing manuscript money.

"Misty Night" (*Oboroyo*), written in late 1898 or early 1899, almost completely in dialogue, is Kafū's first surviving story, although others were published earlier. It tells of a courtesan and her mother, the latter a contrite woman who admits early mistakes and now hopes only that her daughter may be prevailed upon to pursue a more seemly calling. It is touching in a slight way, but the issue is never really in doubt, for daughter and calling seem beautifully matched. "Flower Basket" (*Hanakago*), which Kafū called his "virgin work," apparently with reference to date of publication and not date of composition, won a prize in 1899 in a contest sponsored by a newspaper. It tells of a young lady who through no fault of her own fails to maintain her purity for her bridegroom; and, with didactic intent, it shakes a finger at well-to-do rapists in such loaded lines as this: "Ah, poor Shizue, who had awaited this day to be decorated with beautiful roses and violets—ah, her name was a sad one, in all the papers, a raped woman, and her father, who was in the service of the evil count, could do nothing!" (XXIII, 34.)

The year of his first published fiction, 1899, was the year of another enterprise that had to be kept from his family. He apprenticed himself to a professional monologuist, a teller of *rakugo* comic stories. *Rakugo* men were, if anything, in worse repute with proper Confucian families than novelists. For more than a year Kafū frequented the variety theaters, going first to the master's house in Shitaya; then, in late afternoon, proceeding to the theater with the master's paraphernalia on his back; and, finally, crossing the city once more to sneak in the back door of his father's house. It was a strenuous life, but it had its little idylls, as when, one winter night, he and a pretty girl, a fellow disciple, saw with a simultaneous insight that they could not make it back across the city in the snow, and put up together at an inn. The episode, said Kafū, who was to recount it more than once, was like something out of a *ninjōbon,* a romantic novel of the Tokugawa Period. It was from Fukagawa that the two set out on their interrupted journey, and Fukagawa, on the left bank of the Sumida River, was one of the places in which Culture and Enlightenment had not yet awakened the unlettered masses from their Edo slumber. So one may assume that Kafū enjoyed himself; but not for long. A family retainer chanced one night to see a performance at which Kafū was in attendance, and he was led home by the ear.

The next year he had another try at giving himself to Edo. He entered the Kabuki Theater (Kabukiza) as apprentice to Fukuchi Ochi, the chief playwright. This episode, too, had to be kept secret. Although it was no longer improper for the better sort of people to see Kabuki, it was very improper indeed for them to be associated with it. And even in Kabuki circles, the playwright was not an honored figure. Traditionally he was a sort of craftsman, rather like a property man or stagehand, and it was his function, like that of the cameraman today, to show off the great actor to best advantage.

Ochi himself was representative of a new sort of playwright. A distinguished journalist and once a fairly distinguished politician, he was close to the management of the new Kabuki Theater, which opened in 1889. He was also close to the ninth Danjūrō, the greatest of Meiji actors, and therefore in a stronger position than most playwrights.

Kafū's own position was more conventional. "My duty as an apprentice playwright was to clap twice with wooden clappers at the opening of each act (the process was described as practice in using the clappers), and to clap again each time the revolving stage came into position or drums signaled the end of an act. I also kept the theater records, noting down curtain times and the like; and when there was an urgent notice to be passed around backstage, I was charged with making sure that no one missed it. I went from dressing room to dressing room, I saw the property men and stagehands and custodians of wardrobes and wigs, and I saw the flutists and drummers. From the first welcoming drum to the end of the day's performance I sat stiffly at attention in the playwrights' room, cloakless even in the dead of winter, forbidden to smoke; and if the head of the company appeared, or any notable guest, I was charged with making tea for him and disposing of the sandals he had stepped out of. When the chief playwright came in, I had to help him out of his cloak and fold it for him and see to all his needs and follow him around until he left again." (XI, 146-47.) Ochi made it clear that Kafū need expect no modern informality. He did not once look at the younger man in the course of their first meeting.

Kafū's career as a playwright lasted not quite a year. It is not recorded that he wrote any plays. In the spring of 1901 he left the Kabukiza to become a reporter for the *Yamato Shimbun,* an important daily. He specialized in the miscellaneous pieces, vaguely gossipy and scandalous, that in Japan go by the name "social reports," and he serialized a romance about the Yoshiwara, for which he also wrote the advance notices. "Kafū's subtle and delicate pen," these notices said, "will call up for the reader all the voluptuous treasures of Utamaro's lovely women." (XXIII, 326.) The title of the work was borrowed from Tamenaga Shunsui, as was the plot, and the technique came largely from Ryūrō. Despite its distinguished parentage, it was never finished. Early in 1902, Kafū was selected out, as the management of the newspaper described the process.

Brief though it was, the experience had its rewards. While working on the *Yamato,* Kafū came to know Jōno Saigiku, one of the last true

Edo dilettantes, in the last months of the old man's life—he died in 1901 at the age of seventy. Saigiku was an Edo-style *gesakusha,* a "frivolous writer" of fiction and fugitive essays. A true townsman, he had been the chief clerk at an Edo dry-goods store, and had descended from there into the disreputable world of fiction, his particular genre being rather like Ryūrō's "distressing novels." For Kafū, he was a man who had had the fortune to be part of a balanced, harmonious Edo composition. "After the death of Kanagaki Robun," wrote Kafū later, "there was but one man in Meiji to make us see what the plebeian writer had been in Edo. That man was Saigiku. I feel tears coming when I think how we sat there at our desks day after day and listened to him talk." (xi, 129.) Kanagaki Robun was a *gesakusha* who died in 1894.

If Kafū was looking back to Edo, he was also aware of new winds. As early as 1901 he was reading Zola in English, and the following year he entered night school to learn French.

Zola's position in the development of modern Japanese letters is a curious, contradictory one. With Ibsen, he was early in this century proclaimed the leader of a band of Japanese writers who called themselves naturalists, and from whom the "main current" of modern Japanese literature is generally said to flow. Whether or not he would have recognized his followers is another matter, for banners and standards have a way of getting turned upside down when they are imported into Japan. It is enough here to say that efforts to throw off the didacticism, the eroticism, and the excessive decoration of late Tokugawa fiction became a concerted literary movement at about the time of the Russo-Japanese War; that its more active participants, self-appointed disciples of Zola, turned in their quest for unadorned, impersonal truth to their own experience; and that virtually undisguised autobiography thereupon became the orthodox medium for Japanese prose naturalism.

Meanwhile certain other writers and scholars were doing what the naturalists proper never quite got around to, studying Zola in the original. At least one of them, Kafū, emerged from the study to produce fiction that would probably have been more acceptable to Zola than that which called itself naturalist. Yet when Kafū presently came into his own as a power in the literary world, he was called anti-naturalist—for he never admitted that flat, shapeless household reports were the ultimate in fiction. The categories of Japanese literary history are sometimes very curious.

In 1902 and 1903, at the height of his Zola fever, Kafū published three medium-length novels: *Ambition (Yashin)*, *Hell Flowers (Jigoku no Hana)*, and *The Woman of the Dream (Yume no Onna)*. His most famous statement of what he thought himself up to is in the epilogue to the second: "There can be no doubt that a part of man is beast.... He has built up religious and moral concepts from customary practices and from the circumstances in which he has found himself, and now, at the end of long discipline, he has come to give the darker side of his nature the name sin.... I wish to set down quite without reserve the whole of this darker side—the lust, the violence, the naked force that we have from our surroundings and from our ancestors." (XVIII, 448.) The first edition of *The Woman of the Dream* carries on its cover a picture of a naked lady with much in it suggesting "the darker side."

It is easy to make fun of these early exercises in Darwinism that shake tremulous, irritable fingers at Meiji hypocrisy and threaten to end up didactic after all. The male beasts are rather bloodless bourgeois sorts, unenthusiastic polygamists; and the women, despite the lure on that cover, are seldom caught in compromising positions except when they are victims not of heredity but of circumstance. All done up in white, they remind one more of Emily Dickinson than of Nana. In the first two of the three novels, Kafū simply does not go where the reader has been given every reason to expect him to go. The contrived plots—Kafū was not one to be apologetic about coincidence—and the wan characters are likely to call Ryūrō to mind before Zola.

But the third novel, given the age of the author and the time of writing, is a commendable work. Published in 1903, four years before the date at which literary historians generally place the beginning of the "naturalist" movement, *The Woman of the Dream* is an impersonal narrative with an illusion of independent life such as the naturalists were seldom able to manage. The impulse to preach sometimes comes very near the surface, but on the whole the work is a quiet, straightforward, and touching chronicle of a woman's life, a remarkable exercise for its day in setting forth without decoration or comment the essential facts about a fictitious person in real difficulties at a real moment in history. The fact that the person should be fictitious is important, for the writers who called themselves naturalists assumed that the only reality within their grasp was about real persons, themselves.

O-nami, the heroine, is the daughter of a provincial samurai lost in the new world of Meiji. To keep the family going, she indentures herself, first as a kept woman in Nagoya, and then, when her father has permitted himself to be swindled out of the money thus earned, as a prostitute in the Suzaki section of Tokyo. Despite bloodshed and scandal, she is eventually able to open an establishment of her own, and so to bring her family to Tokyo; but in the end her sacrifices come to nothing. Her sister runs away, and her father spends all his time asking why he ever left the provinces. As they bury him on a snowy afternoon, O-nami wonders what the point of it all has been:

"She heard her mother weeping, and she heard her daughter call 'Grandfather.' But O-nami herself was numb to sorrow. Sad things, painful things, they all had gone beyond a limit. She stood there blankly, as if wandering through some cold, aimless dream. Then, when she climbed into the carriage that was to take her home, and the temple gate was behind them, she was overcome by a sudden, indescribable wave of hopelessness and exhaustion. . . .

"Her dead heart, her hollow body, how would they get through the months and years stretching ahead? Behind her, in another carriage, were her mother and her fatherless little daughter. With dull, listless eyes O-nami looked out through the curtain. A wind had come up, and snow, swirling and twisting, was in process of burying everything, groves, houses, road, telegraph poles.

"Tonight the city, its countless lives, would lie silent under a blanket of white, like the cemetery. By the time the carriages had made their perilous way back to the house in Tsukiji, nothing was visible between snow and snow but lights like blood." (1, 424–25.)

So the book ends. It begins in November, and the mood is autumnal throughout: O-nami sitting alone in the gathering darkness, watching the charcoal embers glow, and trying to summon up courage for a visit to the widow of her keeper; O-nami on an autumn day passing the house where she was born and hearing a girl inside at a music lesson; O-nami arriving in Tokyo in a drizzling autumn rain; O-nami looking out over a wasted autumn garden in Suzaki, listening to the autumn insects, and getting drunk out of terror at the prospect of another night without customers—for her career has entered a slump.

The mood of the book is elegiac, a lament for a wasted life. Sometimes scene and emotion fuse in a manner far more Japanese than Zolaesque: "There were already lights on the railing of the long steel bridge, and there were a few stars dim in the ashen sky. The buildings on the islands that blocked the wide mouth of the river, the houses that lined the banks, were sinking into the shadow of night, and new lights were numberless upon the water. The sailboats anchored in the river sent up a forest of lights, some high and some low near the water, red and green in a disordered show of fireworks. Coming to the middle of the stream, O-nami leaned absently against the railing. She thought of how, years before, she had come the long road from the provinces, and had crossed this same long bridge to give herself to the Quarter. The sounds she had heard then were still in her ears: the waves, studded then and now with a confusion of lights, churned up in the sea wind and lapping at the stone piers; the whistles of the steamboats; and the rickshaw that had carried her across, its wheels grinding against the planks of the bridge....Each new crisis had brought her across the same long bridge. She looked over the railing, at the dark waters that would be flooding out to sea, and on to the far shores, and she wondered what strange power deep under the waters might be controlling her destiny, a destiny that had become so much a part of the view from this bridge." (1, 396–97.)

Against a background of autumnal landscapes, chilly houses, and feckless men incapable of love, sometimes incapable even of conversation, the life of a woman unfolds. She is alone in a world that eludes and defeats her, but the illusion that she has life is complete, as perhaps in no other novel of the period. The student of Kafū's career may suspect that he pulled back in astonishment and uncertainty at having accomplished so much, for it was rather a long time before he gathered himself for another such sustained effort at fiction, the art of creating memorable life.

If *The Woman of the Dream* as a work of fiction stands in somewhat frightened isolation, it is yet in comfortable company as the first of Kafū's elegies, and O-nami stands at the head of the parade of women upon whose shadowed lives the elegies were to center. She dominates the scene as few of the rest of them are able to, but the scene is always present, as if waiting to flood forward and absorb actor and emotion into a single lyrical solution. It takes but a small shift for the lament upon a wasted life to become a lament upon a despoiled city and a lost tradition. Before writing that lament, however, Kafū had to spend some corrective years abroad, penalty for his flirtation with the low life of Edo.

Chapter two Exile

In September 1903, Kafū was sent to the United States, where he remained until 1907. His own explanation for the exile is to be found in the romantic jottings that he called "Leaves from a Journal of a Western Voyage" (*Saiyū Nisshishō,* published in 1917). He says there that his father had given up hope of making a bureaucrat of him, and had decided that a degree from an American university might start him on a commercial career.

He first spent a year in Seattle and Tacoma, in theory learning English, although he was proud to be able to say, when finally he left the United States, that his French was better than his English. The "Leaves" for Seattle and Tacoma are brief, and remarkable chiefly for an absence of people, save Kafū himself, who is found reading Poe and apparently feeling like him. There are little tinges of homesickness, not without an element of contradiction in them. News of the death of a young novelist can bring cries of irritation at Meiji Japan, so unfriendly to artistic people; but they are presently followed by a suggestion that even Meiji Japan has something to recommend it: "The autumn is at length coming to a close. Morning and night, the trees along the streets shed their leaves like rain. At home the moonlight and the singing of insects would be beautiful as a poem; but here there is no such poem of nature. The days and the nights are silent and dreary, and only await the winter." (III, 379.) Perhaps the chief gain from his experience in America was a new awareness of the Japanese seasons.

Late in 1904 he moved to St. Louis, where he saw the fair. He wanted to go next to New Orleans, where he hoped to practice his French. People told him, however, that the climate was bad, and he went instead via Chicago to Kalamazoo, where he became a student of French and philosophy at Kalamazoo College. Again the "Leaves" have to do with books and nature, not people. On June 15, 1905, comes a farewell lyric: "And will I be back again when school begins in the autumn? If not, then I am saying good-bye forever to the grassy pastures and blossoming orchards to which have gone eight of these months of wandering. Good-bye, sweet Kalamazoo!" (III, 384.)

In July, in Pennsylvania, he decided that he had had enough of the United States, and must go on to France. But he had no money. Hearing that the Japanese Legation in Washington was shorthanded because of the Russo-Japanese War and the approaching negotiations, he applied for work, through a cousin who was on the staff of the New York consulate and who later became ambassador to Germany. By the end of the month he was in Washington, a janitor and messenger in the legation, with, according to the "Leaves," plenty of time for reading.

In August came a letter from his father, refusing to sponsor a trip to France under any circumstances. "Why should I be surprised?" the journal asks plaintively. "We never agree about anything." (III, 387.)

The only journal entries for August, the month of the Portsmouth negotiations, deal with the weather, French literature, and his obtuse father. Then one night while he is having a cocktail, a young lady strikes up a conversation. They go walking along the Potomac, and off to her lodgings. Her name is Edyth, and she is the first person to break the silence of the "Leaves," their exclusive concern, up to this point, with books (Huysmans, Musset, Maupassant, Loti, Poe) and nature. With her appearance, the journal changes into a sort of *künstler-roman,* a description of a young artist trying to throw off trammels —including, presently, the trammel imposed by Edyth herself.

There are moments of despondency, when not even art seems sufficient. On September 23 another inflexible letter comes from home, and Kafū is thrown into a mood by it. "As I had expected, Father still does not agree with my plans to go to France. Am I then to care about literature and health? I want dissipation. I want to destroy myself in dissipation. I visited the lady I have become acquainted with, and we drained the champagne bottles, and shouted for joy." (III, 388.)

So, if the journal is to be trusted, he and Edyth became friendly, and the story of their affair is the best reported such affair in Kafū's life. The young *künstler* emerges from it as a rather cold and unaffectionate person, quite prepared to enjoy Edyth and move on, in the name of art. It becomes clear, despite the romantic apostrophes, that she is fonder of him than he of her. The point is worth making because although Kafū had less to say about subsequent affairs, one follows the long parade of women through his life—most of them, like Edyth, of doubtful reputation—feeling that they were more used than loved. Love is an element rather wanting both in Kafū's life and in his work.

Still, he liked having Edyth around, it would seem. Late in the year he left Washington to return via New York to Kalamazoo, but meanwhile his father had arranged a position for him in the New York office of the Yokohama Specie Bank. So, with a flourish, farewell forever to Kalamazoo: "In tears, I kissed the snows of Michigan my last good-bye." To leave Kalamazoo is to leave solitude and art for the distractions of the city, and yet—New York is not far from Washington, where Edyth is, waiting to make him "drunk with her hot kisses" (III, 392–93).

Off to New York he goes, "an emotional young man who has only the dream of beauty." He sees Sarah Bernhardt, he goes to the opera, he has evenings in Chinatown, but in his heart there is "not a speck of light," for he does not like his work or his colleagues (III, 394). He prefers the dope-ridden ladies of Chinatown, whom he always goes to see after he has paid his Sunday call upon the branch manager. "I do not hesitate to call them my own dear sisters. I do not ask for light or help. I only await the day when I, too, shall be able to offer myself to a grain of opium." (III, 407–8.)

In June the journal records another stern letter from Tokyo, and Kafū decides that he will never go back. He will find a job somewhere washing dishes.

With the reappearance of Father, Edyth reappears as well. She comes to New York in July, and announces her intention to transfer her business from Trenton, to which she has already moved from Washington. She will find a pretty little apartment, and they will live together. Kafū's emotions are mixed. "In my heart a fierce battle goes on between love and the dream of art. Shall I stay in New York with Edyth forever and become an American? And if I do, when will I have a chance to visit the Paris I have longed to see all these years? I thought of the sorrowing Tannhäuser, weary of making love to the voluptuous goddess and eager to leave the cave of pleasure, and I looked disconsolately at her sleeping face." (III, 409–10.)

But then, again, it might work: "Maybe the best thing I could do would be to lose myself in some back street here, and never see another Japanese. Has Edyth not said that she will come to New York and that I am to live with her? Why should I be shy at becoming a menial in the house of a prostitute? It is the dark sort of life I have always been interested in." (III, 411.)

Edyth keeps her promise. First comes a silver cigarette case engraved "Love is All," and then comes Edyth, to establish herself in a room on Forty-ninth Street. Meanwhile, Kafū has begun studying French. "What pleasure can I expect, however long my life may be, if I allow myself to be sent back to a barbarous country in the Far East without once having set foot on the soil of France?" (III, 417.)

After more than a year in New York Kafū was transferred to the Lyon branch of the bank. The bank had already been patient enough with a most unpromising employee, and it is difficult to see why he should have been allowed a trip to Europe at its expense; but probably, as in the original New York appointment, his father's influence is to be noted.

Meanwhile Edyth was raising a great stir. On July 9, 1907, the journal finds him going around to say good-bye. She keeps him on and on, telling him that she has two or three business acquaintances in Paris ("women who made their floating way through the world as she did"), and she will join him and them there. "But there was room in my breast for literary aspirations and for them alone, and Edyth, with her tearful repetitiousness, might have been talking to herself." (III, 426.)

So ended the American episode. Of Edyth little more is known. An impassioned letter that Kafū wrote to her (in uncertain English) but never mailed has been preserved. He is said to have learned, after his return to Japan, that she found herself another Japanese patron.

Besides the "Leaves," the American years gave Kafū the material for a miscellany called *American Stories* (*Amerika Monogatari*). A collection of fourteen stories and ten essays, the *Amerika Monogatari* was begun in 1903, immediately after he reached Seattle, finished late in 1907, and published the following year. There has been much shifting and revising since, and a more accurate count today would be fourteen stories and seven essays, three of the original essays having been moved to the later *French Stories* (*Furansu Monogatari*).

During the year in the Pacific Northwest, he caught glimpses of life among the newly immigrated Japanese. The rawness of Seattle is evoked with considerable skill in the miscellany, and despite their dry, laconic style, the Seattle vignettes are sometimes very poignant: a barmaid transplanted from the old Shitamachi of Tokyo to a Seattle shantytown, a Kyushu folksong heard through the train whistles, fights over women among the predominantly male settlers. One senses the loneliness of a strange race in a hastily constructed world.

St. Louis became the setting for a Poe-like story about a Negro vampire who destroys a Frenchman. It contains some passing remarks about the unlikelihood that art will ever emerge from so businesslike a country. Chicago is the setting for an idyll enacted by two lovers, Stella and James, before the narrator, a Japanese known as "N." Stella and James play *Träumerei* and "Dixie" on piano and violin, and exchange passionate kisses when they are finished, and N. notes with envy that emotional fulfillment is possible in societies untroubled by Confucianism. Everything considered, however, love is not all. "I look into magazines, and I find no Daudet or Turgenev among the writers of the new continent. Perhaps the deep sadness of such writers is not to the taste of Americans." (III, 249.)

And other statements indicate that Japan had something to recommend it, too. Sexual freedom is better for men than for women, a letter from about the same period suggests, and Japan is aware of this truth. "Equality of the sexes is all very well as an ideal, but in practice American women are not very desirable. When a woman has really awakened, there is nothing for a man to enjoy dallying with."*

Some of the New York sketches and stories (though about people, not nature) are in the mood of the journal, romantic soliloquies: a young man wandering among the fallen leaves of Central Park, a book of verse in his hand; a very similar young man walking the city

---

* Quoted by Yoshida, p. 59 (see Bibliographical Note).

at night, drunk with its evil charms. In "Walking at Night" (*Yoa-ruki*), another French influence is to be detected, although Kafū had already been prey to the sinister poetry of the city before he found Baudelaire. "I love the gaudy lights of the city," says the young night-walker. "They show that man can rebel against the will of God, that he has the strength to resist the laws of nature. They bring salvation from the darkness of night, they bring awakening from death. . . .

"Ah, goddess of evil! When I lay my head upon your breast, your blood as cold as wine in the depths of some dark cellar, I feel not passion for a beloved, but rather affection for a sister, dependence upon a merciful mother." (III, 334, 341.)

Other New York sketches echo the same mood in a less declamatory fashion. Here, in "A Chronicle of Chinatown" (*Chinatown no Ki*), is a voluptuous swim through the district: "I stood quite overcome by the stench and the heat, and I thought to myself, What balance, what harmony! I thought I had never before heard so poignantly the music of human degradation and collapse. . . .

"Pulling around them rags that scarcely covered their twisted bodies, their oozing eyes like rotten oysters, their matted white hair like dirty cotton wadding, they existed only to feed fleas. They found shelter where they could, in corners of back halls, under floors, in toilets, and they lived, precariously, by doing laundry and odd jobs for the whores, who never asked such favors of them. . . .

"I love Chinatown. It is a treasury of 'Flowers of Evil.' I only fear that the people we are in the habit of calling humanitarians will one day tear down this world apart from the world." (III, 324, 327–28, 329.)

In others the impulse toward self-abasement is kept at slightly more of a remove. Thus in "Long Hair" (*Nagakami*), a narrative within a narrative, the central figure in the central narrative is a renegade Japanese nobleman who is kept by an ostrich-plumed American lady of advanced years. The gentleman wears his hair long, in what we are told is the style of Henry IV, the better for the lady to pull when she is in one of her moods.

In "New Year's Day" (*Ichigatsu Tsuitachi*), Kafū has a go at his father. This time the structure is unwieldiness itself, a narrative within a narrative within a narrative. The outermost of these layers is about an unusual young man who works for a Japanese bank in New

York. He cannot bear the sight of rice, and he cannot force sake down his throat, because they remind him of his dead mother. His father scarcely spoke to her save to reprimand her for something wrong with a meal; and she died of pneumonia, contracted one snowy night when she went out to bring in a dwarf pine to satisfy some whim of his.

Other sketches are quite unemotional, more in the realistic vein of *The Woman of the Dream*. Thus there is what would appear to be an authentic description of a bawdy house just off Sixth Avenue. It is run by Mrs. Stanton, and her boarding employees are Blanche, Iris, Louise (a Parisienne), Hazel, and Josephine. The house has a baroque decor reminiscent of Sister Carrie's rooms, and in Mrs. Stanton's own chambers are a Japanese umbrella, a Japanese lantern, and a two-panel brocade screen, eloquent little reminders that japonaiserie in interior decoration has something of a history behind it. We learn in great detail what each of the girls looks like, what her special forte is, and why she came upon this way of life. We follow them through their day, from early afternoon, when it begins, until just before dawn, when Mrs. Stanton has to pay off a plainclothesman, and Flora and Julia, who live out and commute, start for home. Kafū never seems other than beautifully informed.

In yet other stories, personal romanticism and straight realism are mixed. Thus the setting for "Dawn" (*Akatsuki*) is Coney Island, and the hero, or one of them, is a young Japanese who does what Kafū threatens in the journal, loses himself in the seedier part of America. Again there is a narrative within a narrative. The technique is found so frequently as to make one suspect that Kafū may be hoping to create an illusion of aesthetic distance by mechanical means. The first narrator, a Japanese who, like Kafū himself, is trying to earn money for a trip to Europe, has gone to work in a bowling alley. The dreariness of the place is nicely evoked: "The last of the stars had faded, but the sky, not yet completely light, was an undescribable murky color, and covered over with a thin haze, a warning that it would be another hot and muggy day." (III, 221.) As day breaks, the second narrator takes over, and he also turns out to be a projection of the author. He is a professor's son, and being a failure in Japan, has cut himself off from his family, and means never to go back. "I will work, drink, eat, and buy women until I no longer have the brains left to think of the future." (III, 232–33.)

It has been argued by Japanese critics and literary historians that the years abroad made Kafū a writer—that they aroused him to the possibilities of the lonely artist's life, and made him see the importance of the Japanese tradition and part company with the Japanese naturalists. It could be argued just as effectively, however, that the United States, at least, made almost no difference to him. There are occasional expressions of delight with the American landscape, and as high summer of the affair with Edyth approaches, there is a statement that he will never be able to leave, that every American tree, every blade of American grass, delights him; but for the most part the *American Stories* and the "Leaves" show a fondness for the demimonde and a wish to see France, both of which tendencies had been with him before he left Japan. As for the lyrical cries from the young artist's heart, they have less to do with America and the remoteness of home than with family problems by no means new, and with his reading in French literature, which by now included romantics and exotics as well as Zola and Maupassant. Various themes can be isolated in the search for a theme that unifies the collection: the absolute claims of art, the intransigence of the Japanese father, the joys of self-abasement. The young artist had shown his susceptibility to all of them, however, before he left Tokyo. He went through the United States like a tourist, picking up knickknacks to be had more cheaply in Japan. The only new acquisition, perhaps, was an awareness that nature plays a more subtle part in Japanese life than in American.

The *American Stories,* published piecemeal before his return to Japan, established Kafū as an antinaturalist, of the persuasion the Japanese commonly call "diabolical" or "decadent," terms that are not necessarily derogatory, and merely imply a wild romanticism as opposed to naturalistic prosiness. In fact, Kafū's romantic apostrophes seem strained and his agony histrionic, and he emerges from the *American Stories* as rather a slow burner. Anger at paternal authority and Meiji are not too remote from elegiac sadness at the trials of O-nami; and the tenet that fulfillment awaits in the lower reaches of society presently proves to be a good traveler. Back in Japan it is to become a quest for fine, disreputable relics of Edo.

Kafū left New York in July 1907, after persuading Edyth not to follow. He was able to sever relations with the bank almost as promptly. No more diligent in Lyon than he had been in New York, he was advised early in 1908 that it might be better if he were to resign, and on March 5 he was given notice of his release. There remained only the final word from his father, and that came on March 20. All the possibilities debated in New York were debated once again. "Even if I go back, I do not want to see him. Where, then, shall I hide? I have a little money left. Shall I go back to New York and dissipate with Edyth?" (III, 435.) Instead he went to Paris, where he took a room on the Left Bank. When his money had run out, he started back for Japan.

The *American Stories* had already been published by the time he returned from France, and shortly after his return he began offering the literary magazines short pieces with the subtitle *French Diary* (*Furansu Nikki*). In March 1909, a considerable collection of sketches, short stories, and essays, together with a play, was scheduled to be published as *French Stories* (*Furansu Monogatari*). It was banned, however, because the play, "Love in a Foreign Land" (*Ikyō no Koi*), and one of the stories, "Dissipation" (*Hōtō*), were found to be deleterious to the public morals. Eventually, by devious routes—almost no edition of *French Stories* is exactly like any other edition—the whole collection did reach the public, although not in exactly the original form. A somewhat abridged version of "Dissipation" was published in 1923. "Love in a Foreign Land" did not appear until 1947.

It is not easy to see why the censors leaped upon these works, unless perhaps they were determined to leap upon something and the two pieces were the most conspicuous, one the longest story and the other the only play in the collection. Neither is a very distinguished specimen of its genre, and some years later "Leaves from a Journal of a Western Voyage," a very similar work, was published without difficulty. "Dissipation," called "Clouds" (*Kumo*) in the 1923 version, is about a young Japanese diplomat in Paris. He has said goodbye (on C Street behind the post office—the detail is impeccable) to a passionate Washington prostitute named Erma, who gives him introductions to the girls around the Madeleine. He knows that to stay in Paris means to degrade himself more and more, yet the nearest thing he feels to real emotion is dislike for Japan. Erma was fond enough of him to wish to keep him in luxury, but he found Erma, though appealing in her way, irksome. Rose-Annette, who succeeds her in Paris, is downright loathsome. Disliking his work, disliking his country and countrymen, suspecting that the little troupe around the Madeleine really despises him, he considers drifting to South America and rotting. Moved briefly by news of Erma's death (in Panama, where she has followed the canal workers), he thinks it might be nice to jump into the Seine and have news of his death reported in beautiful French—and, inevitable adjunct, ugly Japanese. His is not the bravura manner, however, and we leave him hoping to be run down by a streetcar. The story is a very wordy one, and it must have been still wordier when the industrious censor pushed his way through it.

"Love in a Foreign Land" is equally diffuse, the sort of play one can scarcely imagine seeing performed. It has to do with a young Japanese who commits suicide with a young American lady, and another young Japanese who goes over the whole problem very articulately and finally returns to Japan, "where human emotions are killed" (xxiv, 347). There is a single good speech, a mocking one about the glories of the new Japan, and it may have caught the bureaucratic eye: "Ladies and gentlemen. I am grateful to be allowed the honor of introducing the up-to-date Japanese Empire to my dear American friends. . . . It is so peaceful a country that drunks sleep happily in gutters. The state and the police and the people are as close as parents and children. Wherever the people gather, therefore, at political meetings, at performances of various sorts, at athletic contests, there the police are in their grand uniforms, a source of boundless popular pride. . . . Wishing to make the earth in which their ancestors sleep as rich as possible, the Japanese decline to build sewers, but rather see to it that the last drop of sewage sinks into the earth and is not lost in the maws of fishes." (xxiv, 356.)

Most of the pieces set in France might be described as travel sketches, cries of delight with France and the French. Kafū was to say later that France confirmed him in his liking for Edo and dislike of Meiji, and demonstrated the possibility of a modernization that left the old, finished picture fairly well alone. It confirmed him in his belief, he said, that the enemy was not the twentieth century but rather the breathless, ill-considered Japanese twentieth century, turning the Sumida River into a sewer and knocking down all of Tamenaga Shunsui's little river-bank restaurants. "When we think of the relationship between the left bank of the Sumida and Edo literature, we see that the men of Edo were even quicker than Parisians to find beauties on the outskirts of their city. . . .

"Even now the people of Paris take their families to the suburbs on Sundays, and sit on the grass and drink wine. We, by contrast, seem driven by an urgent need to destroy the picture-like beauties of tradition in the interests of the new age." (v, 284.)

These remarks came slightly later, however, and the sketches in *French Stories* proper leave one feeling that Kafū's experience of France was essentially bookish. They are filled with worshipful addresses to the makers of French culture, "Ah, Berlioz!" and "Ah, Maupassant!" (and, for that matter, "Ah, Byron!" too). The French landscape is beautiful because it is where they walked. Kafū was prepared to love France, and perhaps would have loved it with equal intensity had he been refused a landing permit.

The stories laid in France generally take up themes already noticed in the *American Stories*. They are full of young artists, alternately languid and intense, who in some cases seem bent on parodying themselves. "Journey Alone" (*Hitoritabi*) is the most extreme example. The story takes the form of a letter from a Japanese art student to a noblewoman, also Japanese, whom he has undertaken to guide through Italy. He must ask to be excused, however, for he wishes to be alone. He loves solitude. "Even on my daily strolls, I see profit only in walking with my beloved. Even more is this true when I travel. A companion to talk with and laugh with serves but to prevent one from touching the live pulse of nature. Ah, my dear lady, excellency, have you ever heard the music that Berlioz, the romantic French composer who went through life weeping alone, composed for Lord Byron's 'Harold in Italy'? If you will but listen to it, you will have no trouble knowing what goes on in my breast." (IV, 172.) The lady and her husband understand perfectly, and think it a fine thing that Japan is not being outdone in the production of eccentrics.

Implicit, of course, in this extravagant romanticism is a rejection of Confucian sternness, of the Confucian notion that people are never happier, which is to say never more natural, than when acquitting themselves of their duties. A comparison with Japanese writers who went abroad a decade earlier suggests how rapidly Confucianism was breaking down. Thus Mori Ogai, a man who had enormous influence on the development of modern Japanese prose style, tasted of the West just as fully as Kafū did and but a scant twenty years before, yet went ahead to finish a distinguished army career. It had not taken long for Confucian obligations to become insupportable weights upon the soul of the striving young artist.

With the beginning of the journey home, the notion of Japan became even more oppressive. The gloom of the *French Stories* deepens as the ship moves east. In "Twilight on the Mediterranean" (*Tasogare no Chichūkai*), Kafū stands on deck in the gathering darkness and thinks about the joys of the country he has left and the defects of the country he must go back to. "My feelings at that moment: I was leaving behind the love and the art of France, and I was going to a remote edge of the East, where death would presently bring an end to a dull, monotonous life. I asked myself whether we Japanese had any music to which I might entrust the feelings of that moment. . . .

"There are Takemoto and Tokiwazu and the other dramatic ballad forms, which, to be sure, express complicated feelings with some success; but they are less music than accompanied recitatives, and hardly suited to express sudden onsets of emotion. There is Utazawabushi, but that is a survival from another day, a thin lament from the pleasure quarters. The Nō recitative is old and elegant and filled with Buddhist melancholy, but in the final analysis not the thing for a modern steamship. It should be heard, rather, on a rush-floored boat, with an oar lapping the water, and pine trees, like an ink wash, far away on the shore. Then there is the chanting of Chinese poetry, and there is the Satsuma lute, but they, too, belong with the bland colors so special to Japan. They stir a plain, sad sense of beauty, a mood that has about it a primitive monotony.

"I was left despairing. I was of a country that offered no music to suit my feelings, however violent, or the mood of the evening, however stormy. Was there, I wondered, another such country in the world?

"Just then, from below deck, two or three English railway workers who were going out to India and a girl of whom I knew only that she was going to Hongkong began singing. Their song was light and gay, the sort of thing, I should imagine, that one hears in East End variety halls. It had no value as music, but precisely because it had none, I caught in it something perfectly appropriate to the mood of the English laborer going out to the tropics, completely suited to the dirty deck and the steerage cabins.

"Are the English not a fortunate people? English culture has given to men of the lowest classes music with which to express their sadness as wayfarers. . . . We Japanese are already too far from our middle ages to turn back to their music, and we find, however intense our attachment to the West and its music, that differences of land and custom are not easily overcome. . . .

"As the evening wore on, the water darkened and took on a strange luminescence. . . . Ah, Mediterranean sky, off the mystic shores of Africa! Sadly the song of the English workers faded away into the enigmatic sky. . . . And how had I been able to leave Paris so heedlessly?" (IV, 261–64.)

By the time he reaches Port Said, Turkey has replaced France and England as the country with which Japan compares badly. Quite satisfied with its old ways, it makes no attempt at superficial imitation of the West. "I admire Turkey. At least it is not hypocritical. It is not the sort of hypocrite that takes a shallow pride in seeking admission to the brotherhood of the West, and to that end puts together a sham culture. Turkey! Turkey of polygamy! Autocratic Turkey! Mysterious Turkey! Savage Turkey! Turkey of the great irony and the boundless riddle!" (IV, 276.)

When he reaches Singapore, he is face to face with his own, and loathes what he sees. The ship's purser introduces him to a Japanese man, woman, and child who have been living in China and are on the way back to Japan after a trip through India. "For some seconds I stared at them dumfounded, quite unable to speak. Perhaps because I had seen only Westernized Japanese, these pure domestic products were indescribably odd, and I felt all my malice at contemporary Japan come boiling up again." (IV, 285.)

The man is loud and boastful, but the woman and child are worse. The child screams and wets its pants, and has sores all over an enormous shaven head that reminds Kafū of an octopus. The mother, thin-haired and mousy, is already seasick, in anticipation of the time when the ship will get under way, and too preoccupied with her problem to pay much attention to the child.

"The face of the wife, with her thin hair, her dirty teeth, and her bloodless complexion, came to me as a lesson about the East, which belittles the art of personal grooming, which forbids all comment upon physical beauty, which denies the pleasures of love, and which makes of women mere machines for the production of soldiers to subjugate rivals. And the broad, coarse face of the schoolteacher who was her husband, and his loud assertive voice demanding submission of everyone in sight—the land of Meiji was the land of the superior man, of his Confucian justice and his filial piety. A scant ten days more and I would be back in it." (IV, 289.)

Chapter three Return

In August 1908, Kafū was back with his family, then living in Okubo, in the western outskirts of Tokyo. The collection called *American Stories* was already published, and the beginnings of that to be called *French Stories* were parceled out among the literary magazines shortly after his return. The next few years were to be the most productive of his life, the years when he found himself at the very center of the Japanese literary world, one of the young lions. The drab autobiographers who called themselves naturalists were passing from vogue, and, whatever right Kafū may once have had to claim Zola as an ancestor, the emotional and highly colored prose of certain of the French and American sketches established him as an "antinaturalist."

As an antinaturalist he helped edit a leading magazine and taught in a leading university. Meanwhile he was exploring the world of high prostitution, in which, he was sure, were to be found remnants of an older, more harmonious order. He was twice married in the next few years, once to a famous geisha, and he wrote some of his loveliest elegies on the disintegrating old city. Then, a decade or so later, the spotlight having shifted, he was to find himself facing a lonely, crotchety middle age.

During the months after his return he was kept busy telling his countrymen how sorry he was to be back. "A Few Hours in Singapore" (*Shingapōru no Sūjikan*), the open letter to the unattractive Japanese quoted at the end of the last chapter, was published in January 1909 under the less equivocal title "Revulsion" (*Akkan*). The rest of 1909 was spent on stories and essays with a single theme, the horrors of Meiji Japan. Twice Kafū was forestalled by the censors,

once in March with *French Stories,* and again in September with a
wordy, diffuse story called "Pleasure" (*Kanraku*).

In December 1909, an anonymous writer in the poetry magazine
Subaru, since identified as the poet Ishikawa Takuboku, said of Kafū's most recent work: "He is like a wealthy provincial son who has
been enjoying himself in Tokyo on his father's money, and who, a
young man of leisure upon his return to the provinces, tells everyone
in sight about the shortcomings of rustic geisha."

But Takuboku was unusually sensitive. On the whole, Meiji Japan
seems to have enjoyed being pilloried, and one critic has said that the
young Kafū, back in Japan trailing clouds from France, collected followers as an overripe apple collects ants.

If, however, the writings of the year of the return are filled with
complaints, they also contain hints that a refuge from Meiji could still
be found. "A Song of Fukagawa" (*Fukagawa no Uta,* published in
February 1909) is mostly a description of a streetcar ride across the
city from west to east. The streetcar is crowded with unpleasant
people, including a geisha who noisily sucks a decayed tooth. The
confusion at transfer points is remarkable, telling of a city that is
splitting at the seams and has no tailor. Presently the streetcar clanks
to a stop, for the power supply has given out. Kafū has a transfer
thrust into his hand. It will take him to Fukagawa, he sees, and he
is seized with an intense nostalgia. "I would run away from the
wretched center of the city to Fukagawa. My longing to take refuge
in Fukagawa was irresistible." (v, 82.)

Fukagawa, on the left bank of the Sumida, was at the edge of and
yet a center of plebeian Edo. There the grand courtesan of late Edo
ruled, and there the "Shitamachi mood" of Tamenaga Shunsui and
the Edo townsman had its last ground. "Before I left Japan, Fukagawa
of the waters had long been the place that answered to my every
taste, longing, sorrow, and joy. Even then, before the streetcar tracks
were laid, the beauty of the city was being destroyed, and that sad,
lonely vista beyond the river still let one taste of decline and decay
and an indescribably pure and harmonious beauty." (v, 82.)

And so, unsolicited transfer in hand, Kafū goes to Fukagawa.

There he finds himself in the precincts of the Fudō Shrine, listening to a mendicant musician, whose song is in a thin, melancholy

style dismissed as unenlightened by the new city. Kafū has a vision of the man's past: "I felt that he had not been born blind. He learned his geography and arithmetic in elementary school, and perhaps he even got a smattering of English in the upper grades. But he could not bring himself into harmony with the vulgar clutter of 'Meiji,' managed by ignorant foot-soldiers from Kyushu, and he lost his eyesight as he lost his money. Presently he found salvation in these pathetic circumstances, through an art that in its days of glory had had about it a certain verve and bravado. His eyes, filled with the bustle of the theater teahouses, the crimson carpets of rehearsal halls, the flowered hats and lanterns of festival days, were spared the horrid streetcars and power lines and all the rest of our superficial Westernization. . . .

"The evening sun over the plum groves to the left lighted the man's profile. The sad, squatting shadow fell on the stone fence behind, how faintly! On every stone the name of a donor to the temple was incised in red. Geisha, singers, carpenters, theater guides, gamblers—they all pursued callings left behind by our age. . . .

"I wanted to stay on and on in the fading light of Fukagawa, beneath the stones that fenced the shrine of the superstitious, listening to an Utazawa ballad. The thought of going back across Eitai Bridge was unbearable." (v, 87–89.)

The geisha going "chew-chew" as she sucks on her tooth is not an attractive figure, but it is she and her colleagues who nonetheless emerge from this and other peevish little essays as custodians of the past. Although Kafū is much admired by his countrymen as a "social critic," his criticism of Meiji is seldom profound or moving. At best it is amusing: "We went into a beer hall to sit down for a moment. There were no other customers. A sleepy waitress took an enormous amount of time bringing us beer. Finally, her sandals dragging sluggishly across the floor, she appeared. We were silent, our elbows on the dirty gray tablecloth. We looked out through the dirty window, the paint flecking from the sash, at the confusion in the street. The place shook each time a streetcar went past." (v, 148–49.) The hero of one story, thinking to choose something poignantly Western to perform at a charity concert, hits upon Chopin's funeral march.

What can be truly moving, however, is an emotion that goes with the querulousness, a sense of deprivation and a longing for the world

that geisha and blind musician manage, in a perilous fashion, to preserve. From these years come some very effective reminiscences about
his childhood, about the mysteries of the Koishikawa garden and its
fox, the darker mysteries of his grandmother's house, and the grounds
of the Denzūin, frequented by such stirring characters as the tattooed,
top-knotted young carpenter. The longing for the past often seems
ambivalent and contradictory, for it is not a reasoned position. How,
one wishes to know, can the young individualist rebelling against his
father so admire the world of the blindly superstitious and submis-
sive? The realm of the Edo courtesan is also the realm of the domi-
neering Edo father, and resentment at paternal authority constantly
seems to teeter on the edge of a longing to submit absolutely. "Why
am I not able to live in unquestioning docility like the slave of old?
That person is happiest who has not the strength to be resentful."
(v, 122.)

The merits of these pieces are to be found more in their lyrical
overtones than in intellectual profundity or reasoned argument. It
must be added that they do not, on the whole, give much evidence of
dramatic gifts. Nowhere does a character emerge who is the equal
of "the woman of the dream." After listening to all the complaining
about Meiji, one comes to wish that Meiji might be brought on stage
to speak for itself. The characters too obviously speak for the novelist,
and there is none of the give-and-take that a novelist with more talent
for the dramatic would have produced.

Kafū's performance was sufficiently respectable all the same to win
the approval of Natsume Sōseki, the foremost literary journalist of
the time. At Sōseki's behest, Kafū wrote a serial for the newspaper
Asahi in 1909 and 1910. It shares the defects of the shorter pieces, however. All the characters (there are five major ones) speak with a single
voice, and that voice is Kafū's.

The work was criticized at the time of publication as irresponsibly
fleshly and voluptuous. It is true that a great deal is said about aban-
donment to the dear, dirty world of Edo; but the essential fact about
the book is how unpeopled it seems. A landscape occupied by puppets,
their words too obviously breathed into them, can scarcely seem
fleshly at all, nor can its espousal of Edo seem very impassioned.

"I do not place much emphasis on action or dramatic variation,"
chants one of the puppets, who is in the guise of a novelist. "I want

rather to see to what point unhealthy human desires and pleasures can be pushed." (VI, 25.) This touches upon the heart of the matter. *Sneers* is essentially not dramatic but expository. Drama falls victim to the demands of exposition.

But even if it is not a good novel, it contains some charming prose lyrics. Far from being hotly voluptuous, it is elegiac, the geisha being important not for her body but for associations with the past. Here one of the five, the novelist, gives forth with a lyric upon a woman who is now married to another of the five, and who was once a Fukagawa geisha:

"Because I had O-kimi, this Fukagawa of the many waters, already beautiful, was yet more beautiful. Sometimes it stirred in me poetic impulses almost unbearable.... There was a certain sophistication about her, and with it an indescribable freshness, a childlike quality ...like an Edo maiden in a play. Setting out for an *ikebana* lesson, she would get into our boat with us as we returned from Fukagawa in the morning, and, floating in a cool morning breeze fragrant with resin from logs in the canals, I would glance at her as she sat half reclining on the mats of the open cabin, her chin in her hand and her arm against the bulwark.* How sweet were the dreams I lost myself in! A child of the district, O-kimi knew most of the boatmen by name. She would listen undisturbed to the most improper jokes, though now and then, smiling to show a gold tooth, she would give one of the rough fellows a dressing down. Indeed the memory is a dream, of young O-kimi there on the shore with flowers in her hand, the earthen walls of the warehouses a pure white in the morning sun behind her, the image rolling and swelling on the morning tide. We would move off, swaying slightly to the sound of oars, and O-kimi would call from above: 'I'll see you again tomorrow.' She would watch until our boat disappeared under the decaying bridge.... To me O-kimi was merely beautiful, not a woman to be loved.... Even now that she is the wife of another, I can see her face and be happy, and talk about her without wearying, because I still see, from long ago, O-kimi the girl, because she was the last beautiful vision I had of the land and city in which I was born.... If now, high in a house by the Suzaki canals, I let escape a sigh as I hear samisen and song in the dead of night, it is not at the

---

* *Ikebana* is the art of flower-arranging.

story, highly decorated and told in measures, of the lives of courtesans, as helpless as bamboo in a flooded marsh; I am thinking rather of myself as I was ten years ago." (VI, 52, 54–56.)

The speaker has had experiences remarkably like Kafū's: a period abroad, an unsympathetic father, a period of revulsion upon his return to Japan. And again like Kafū, he has begun finding survivals that Meiji has not yet ruined:

"Within six months or a year, as he began casually looking back over his youth, he found himself feeling a strong nostalgia for the relics of a vanished day, and seeing much that was admirable in the special qualities of his race....

"The first suspicion of this new mood came one day when he was walking through Shiba Park. He could see nothing in the bronze statue of Count Gotō that struck him as in any way beautiful, but asleep behind it, solitary and forgotten, lay the mortuary shrines of the Shoguns.* He stepped into the grounds and his astonishment grew. The memory had quite faded of days when his parents had brought him to this same park to see the cherry blossoms, and the surprise, as he found in a corner of the vulgar, ugly, accursed city a place yet reserved for art, was as if he had unearthed Pompeii.

"He listened to the young priest, who told him that the building was some two hundred years old, and who made much of every carved transom, painted door, and guilded lacunar. He was struck not only by these details but by the precise arranging of the buildings and grounds as a whole.

"First there was the gate with its curved, soaring roof, two menacing statues flanking the ornate doors. Flagstones led directly to a second gate. To the left and right the land was astonishingly level, and covered with uniform pebbles, each one as smooth as a jewel, and into the far corners of the rectangular enclosure, marked off by a fence, were ranged numberless lines of bronze lanterns. Inside the second gate was a higher level, the third and last, on which rested the shrine proper. Unlike the others, this last level was enclosed not by a simple fence but by roofed corridors. What a quiet dignity it had, the view from the shrine down over those corridors, hanging lanterns spaced among their lacquered pillars! Like the grounds, the floor of the

---

* Gotō Shōjirō (1838–97) was an important statesman.

shrine building itself was on different levels, and as one looked up from the third gate, the interior, dimly lighted and encased in decorations, seemed of an immeasurable depth.

"The design, in sum, was such as to raise to the highest possible intensity the sense of reverence and worshipfulness. It succeeded magnificently, the place was a masterpiece. As he sought to compare the complex with Parisian buildings he had believed to be the supreme aesthetic experiences of his life, he felt that the Shiba mausoleum, whether their superior or not, was in no way their inferior. Just as the acute angles of Gothic architecture communicated perfectly the spirit of the people that had created it, he thought in the intensity of his delight, so the rectangular lines of this shrine and the richness of its colors gave perfect expression to the proud and lonely and aloofly aristocratic bent of the East. . . .

"On another day, he and Nakatani went walking east of the river, through Mukōjima and on to Kameido. In all the Shinto shrines along the way, and there were many of them, the votive halls were hung with poetic epigrams. In Buddhist temples similar epigrams were carved in countless numbers on garden stones. He thought to himself that the pleasure, though it took a somewhat different form, was like that of roaming the parks and cemeteries of Paris and reading poetic inscriptions on old tombstones and memorials. He saw how heavily the man of Edo had depended upon art to break the monotony of his life." (VI, 72–75.)

Nakatani happens to be a playwright and another member of the quintet. But names and identifications do not really matter, the work being one long soliloquy. Lyrical or argumentative passages can be lifted from context and strung together without doing crucial damage to the mood of the whole.

Edo pulls in various ways, through music, dance, women, and neglected buildings; and almost always it is found under heavy shadows, and smelling of mold and decay. "From its very beginnings, our theater has had buried deep inside it an ineffable strength of darkness. Whatever the new theories of the learned, whatever the opinions of the powerful, whatever the calls for reform on the part of reckless journalistic gentlemen, their reforms are not reform but deracination and destruction. . . . The Kabuki is old and thoroughly rotten, and medical treatment is impossible. Attempts at treatment are equivalent to wringing the patient's neck." (VI, 68.)

In this world of shadows and decay, music has peculiarly evocative powers. It is not the wholesome, healthy, homey music of James, Stella, and Chicago, however. "Somewhat intoxicated, and more and more deeply moved at the thought that nothing could surpass a home with music in it, he watched the dance. Since his return to Japan he had been able to find this single example, the home of a Kabuki playwright, grievously infected by dying Edo and the corrupt world of the geisha. . . . Proper persons would no doubt make of it a home dirty to its very foundations; but in the society he was born to, only this degenerate place offered a harmonious beauty to compare with what he had seen in the healthy family life of the West. . . .

"O-kimi came back after putting the child to bed, and the conversation took a different turn. In the alley outside, the hour being late, he could hear a wandering musician, and the wooden clappers of a Kabuki mimic; and presently, from the second floor of a nearby house, there came a woman's voice singing a Shinnai ballad. Highly susceptible to the power of music, he was aroused this evening, by strains from another age, to a nostalgia so intense that he had to marvel at it himself. . . .

"And was it all Tokyo? Around him were the time and the life known as 'the present.' Once more he was filled with anger and loathing at the monster, the misbegotten monster, which, as became the adjective he had chosen to describe it, must presently disappear." (VI, 102, 105–6, 108.)

Music brings together the pleasure quarters and the Edo theater, the two hemispheres of this shadowy world. The importance of music is emphasized by the title of the finest chapter, apparently Kafū's own favorite, "The Samisen in the Night" (*Yoru no Samisen*). One of Kafū's five spokesmen (indeed somewhere along the way Kafū seems to begin speaking for himself, and eschews even a pretense at characterization) is out wandering the city; his thoughts as he hears a samisen call to mind another powerful evocation of darkness, Tanizaki Junichirō's "In Praise of Shadows" (*In-ei Raisan*):

"Kōu caught a note of deep sadness in it. At an hour when a child of good family would be asleep in her mother's arms, this young girl, an apprentice geisha, was sitting in the cold, her voice quavering and uncertain; and in it he felt not a straining to perfect her art, but a docility and resignation, and the pain that went with them, stemming from a fear of being scolded by some respected elder. Music of broken love in the Edo pleasure quarters was not something to be sung in the grand virtuoso manner, not a thing of great demands and high standards and massive auditoriums. It seemed to him, rather, that the true flavor of the music was to be appreciated here, sung in the girlish tones of one who, shrinking back into the shadows of these alleys, knew neither the anguish nor the rebelliousness of deep thought....It should be heard without reference to critics and standards, at just such an unfinished practice....

"The emotion that assailed him might have been likened to some such experience as this: after a view of green mountains towering into a clear sky, one looks into the murky depths of a swamp in the long, gloomy rains, and sees the colorless flowers of weeds in the dirty waters....In Japanese music, no matter what happiness it might sing of, he sensed a persistent sadness, as of a morning glory wilting in the bright morning sun with no one even to notice it....

"What was this Oriental darkness if not an heirloom shaped long ago and passed down through the generations? Born in this air and living in this air, he would be doing enough if he but acquiesced in the sadness. Why debate its merits? He could not, even if he wished, avoid breathing the air from the depths of the Oriental earth. Not only in music but in everything left by his ancestors, there was, as if upon conscious accord, a sadness not to be seen in the Occident. The difference was that between glad cathedral bells on Christmas Eve and the tolling from the bell tower of a Buddhist temple. Cathedrals and minsters have, to be sure, their various styles, Greek and Byzantine and Romanesque and Gothic. Yet all are alike in pushing up into the sky, sharper and lighter, from a firm hold on the ground. In Buddhist temples, by contrast, the heavy, heavy, tiled roof presses its terrible weight down from mid-heaven. One is made to look upward by Western churches, one bows to peer timorously into our temples. The statue of the Lord Amida sits there like a mummy and refuses to answer, while Christ stands with arms outstretched and looks to the heavens with living eyes....

"Our ancestors poured an almost supernatural ardor into concepts like patriotism, duty, and revenge; but for what is called love and should be an outpouring of the same emotions, they had only stern repression. It is not surprising that from the profound anguish of putting out flames with the cold water of ethics, a special Oriental sadness should have emerged. And for Kōu it appeared at its most perfect in Edo music, which sings the insubstantiality of love in the pleasure quarters....

"Today, along all the handsome main streets of the East, bells ring forth glad tidings of the age of liberation; but in the back streets, along the dirty waters of the canals, the whisper of the samisen is still there, wandering through the darkness. That voice of civilization, the locomotive, thunders past, but in the grass along the embankment insects are still singing. Listen for a moment. In the music of our ancestors, in Takemoto, Tomimoto, Itchū, Kiyomoto, frail notes from three thin strings are enough to call up emotions deep as the moment of death. Such music has no need for the complicated structures of Western music, harmony and polyphony and counterpoint. Kōu found it almost unbearable—the loneliness and sadness that were a part of Japanese music, that stemmed from its very inadequacy, its simplicity and its monotony." (VI, 178-85.)

If *Sneers* is studded with little lyrics, rather in the manner of the discursive genre known in Japan as the "poem story" (*utamonogatari*), the narrative falls short of coalescing into a novel. The characters are such ready spokesmen for the novelist that in the end they are nothing. Yet in another little lament for the changing city, an altogether less ambitious one, character and scene are so appropriate to each other that the elegy becomes adequate fiction. *The River Sumida* (*Sumidagawa*), written in the second half of 1909, is laid on the banks of that river where it passes Honjo and Fukagawa on the left and Asakusa on the right—the banks along which plebeian Edo had had its best days, and on which, a half century after its name was gone, traces of Edo were still to be found.

Such a deep nostalgia pervades the work that the reader might imagine its action to take place perhaps two decades earlier, when something dead in 1909 still survived. Not quite a decade after he wrote *The River Sumida,* however, Kafū was to say that he had had no such retrospection in mind. He was writing of the present, a time when progress was already filling in the canals of Edo and fouling its river, and pushing its culture back into a few melancholy, isolated pockets. The last of the old city was finally destroyed, he said, by the flood of 1910 and the fire of the following year.

Despite Kafū's assurances, it would be difficult to say that the novel —"novella" might be a more accurate characterization—is set at any precise point in time. For Kafū good things were always in the past, and this little work is a sort of evocation of a soft morning mist that the hot sun of the present is dispelling. If the scene, though of no particular time, is peculiarly Tokyo, that is because the mist in Tokyo seems unusually delicate and vulnerable, and the sun seems to be rising with an unusually cruel speed.

Four of the five characters in the story are likely to be burned: a boy who wishes to pursue his fondness for traditional music and give his life to it, his uncle and aunt, both of them graduates of the pleasure quarters, and his girl friend, destined to make a career in the degraded successors to those quarters. The fifth is the boy's mother, not a happy woman but a woman more at home in the new glare. She wants him to go to the university and become a bureaucrat.

It is quite possible to find Western parallels for and influences upon almost everything in *The River Sumida*. Its primitivism has much in common with the work of French regionalists, and it may be that Kafū was fully awakened to the charms of the old "nightless city," its sad music and its seasonal moods, when he read Baudelaire. Yet it is the "Shitamachi mood," that delicate blending of the city and the seasons, that dominates *The River Sumida,* and of this the French had little to teach him. The amatory writers of late Edo were his real masters. Here, from an essay on Tamenaga Shunsui written some decades later, are suggestions of the sort of thing they awakened him to:

"In *A Calendar of Plum Blossoms* (*Umegoyomi*), the unhappy O-chō and her ruined lover Tanjirō chance to meet in a quiet Fuka-gawa lane. They go into a little restaurant by the river, where they talk of the terrible changes that time has brought. Not a person, not a cart, passes. There is only the warm quiet of spring, flooding the river bank and the street, on and on. The thought of it to me is like a siren's song." (XIII, 338–39.)

"In *A Bounty of Love in the Springtime* (*Shunshoku Megumi no Hana*), the geisha Yonehachi steals away to a farmer's cottage in

Koume, east of the river, and as she is waiting on the veranda for her lover Tanjirō, she chances to look up at a plum tree, in bloom with the scent of very early spring. Twisting off a sprig, she bites it and tastes of the soft fragrance. The mood could not, I think, have been conveyed in an Ukiyoe print, or even in a plaintive Shinnai ballad." (XIII, 356.)

"Then there is *Spring Rain in the East Country* (*Azuma no Harusame*). A man is walking down a hedge-lined path in Negishi village, not far from the Yoshiwara. He hears the clear, high notes of a samisen. It is 'Eight Scenes of the Yoshiwara,' in the melancholy Itchū style. Scarcely thinking, he draws nearer to listen, and suddenly, from a sky overcast as it so often is in the time of the cherry blossoms, drops of rain begin to fall. The samisen stops. To the sound of garden sandals, a girl of perhaps twenty, with a verve that suggests her to be of a particular vocation, opens the gate and tells him that if the rain is troubling him he need not be shy about coming inside. They look at each other. They think they have met somewhere before, but cannot think where. As they talk idly of this and that, it transpires that the girl worked in the Yoshiwara at a time when the man was frequenting one of the houses, and that they saw each other from time to time at the teahouses. Sadness and happiness come over them at the thought of the days that are gone. The woman keeps the man on and on, and the man finds it harder and harder to leave." (XIII, 349–50.)

It was from such lyrical passages that Kafū learned, and they were to influence him to the end of his career, both for good and for bad. Neither Kafū nor Shunsui in the last example quoted was a writer to be suspicious of coincidences and improbable turns of plot; and if the fusion of background and character was sometimes a happy one for both writers, it sometimes had the effect for both of submerging character in argument or description. "I have occasionally fallen into the error of placing less emphasis on character than on background," Kafū himself once said (XVI, 132). And again, in describing one of his works, though not the one here under consideration: "What I have sought is . . . to make the words do what the colors of costume and setting do for the theater." (VIII, 4.)

It has already been pointed out that *Sneers* is so wanting in drama as to be hardly a novel at all, but rather a discursive essay interrupted now and then by a lyric. *The River Sumida* has equally little dramatic power. Though less given to complaint and declamation than the longer novel, the life it contains is scarcely more robust. The chapters follow a set pattern: a description of scene and season, moving from late autumn to early summer, and after the description a brief dialogue. Seldom is it more than a dialogue—Kafū seems shy of confronting any one character with more than one other. The characters presented so gingerly cannot be described as vivid. Chōkichi, the boy who wishes to play the samisen and would prefer not to go to the university, seems limp and watery. His limpness is particularly striking when one compares *The River Sumida* with Higuchi Ichiyō's *Growing Up* (*Takekurabe*), another picture of adolescence in the shadow of the Meiji pleasure quarters. Ichiyō's characters are little balls of fire in the Edo twilight. Chōkichi, by comparison, is tepid and uncertain. In the end we do not even know whether he will survive a bout of illness or not. It may seem wrong for *any* work of fiction to end on such an uncertain note, and it was not Kafū's intention so to end it. He meant to see Chōkichi through, and on into his samisen career.

Yet one cannot help being glad that he stopped where he did. An insubstantial wraith of a hero, left on the border of death, seems most appropriate for a sad, sweet, almost uninhabited little story. What makes it withal a beautiful little story is its success in evoking the moods of the old city, so soon to be blighted. In the end the irresolute Chōkichi does turn out to matter, and the glimpses of the vanishing city are the more poignant because, themselves so defenseless against the assaults of progress, they seem such a proper setting for his fecklessness. And *The River Sumida* has one crucial virtue that *Sneers* lacks: Chōkichi and his mother may not have a great deal to say, but when they do open their mouths they produce an illusion of speaking for themselves and not for Kafū. Though essentially the villain of the piece, the mother is treated with a fairness and impartiality that Kafū does not manage to summon up for most of his villains.*

In April 1910, Kafū became professor of French in Keiō University. Perhaps his strong-willed father made him feel uncomfortable about not having a fixed occupation, but Keiō had plans interesting enough to attract him in any case. Its chief rival among the private universi-

---

* A full translation of *The River Sumida* will be found in Part II of this book (pp. 181-218), to which longer translations have been relegated.

ties of Tokyo, Waseda, was an important literary center, and its magazine, *Waseda Literature* (*Waseda Bungaku*), a major vehicle for autobiographical "naturalism." Keiō must therefore have a literary magazine, too, and, of course, it should be "antinaturalist." It is a mark of the figure he cut in the years after his return from France that Kafū, not a university graduate, should have been invited, with professorial rank, to help edit the magazine. He was at the heart of the literary world, a leader of the antinaturalist camp. Two very eminent literary figures helped put him there: Mori Ogai, a novelist, critic, translator, poet, and playwright strongly under the influence of German idealism; and Ueda Bin, the translator who brought French symbolism to Japan. It was they who recommended him to Keiō.

The first issue of *Mita Literature* (*Mita Bungaku*) appeared in May.* The literary creed it espoused has been given a number of awkward names, such as "aestheticism" and "neoromanticism," and, of course, "antinaturalism." Actually its contributors were a motley lot, ranging from the austere Mori Ogai to the sybaritic Tanizaki Junichirō, and the Western reader is not likely to find such expressions as "romantic" very helpful in distinguishing naturalism from antinaturalism—for both naturalist and antinaturalist went in for Wertheresque straining and posing. Almost the only thing the antinaturalists had in common was a belief that telling all about himself was not the whole of an author's duty. A certain ability to shape and to produce pleasing cadences might also be asked of him. There seems, too, to have been an element of personal hostility in the conflict. In a famous essay encouraging the young Tanizaki, Kafū listed as one of Tanizaki's virtues his "urbaneness." In other words, he was a true son of Edo, and the naturalists were among the country bumpkins sacking the city.

The year 1910 was a busy and important one, then, but perhaps not quite as important as students of Kafū would have it. In 1910 came an incident that has been made much of in explaining Kafū's later withdrawal from the literary world, and his masochistic insistence that he was to be taken no more seriously than an Edo dabbler in erotica. Because of a plot, real or alleged, to assassinate the Emperor Meiji, several hundred radicals were rounded up and jailed in and

* Mita is the section of Tokyo in which the main Keiō campus is situated.

after May 1910, and twelve of them, including the anarchist Kōtoku Denjirō (or Shūsui), were put to death the following year. Kafū's own testimony is that the incident was a deep shock to him, and made him give up any notion of ever becoming a Zola.

The testimony is to be found in an essay called "Fireworks" (*Hanabi*), written in July 1919:

"In 1911, when I was teaching in Keiō University, I chanced on my way to class to see five or six police wagons go past Yotsuya on the way to the Hibiya courthouse. Of all the public incidents I had witnessed or heard of, none had filled me with such loathing. I could not, as a man of letters, remain silent in this matter of principle. Had not the novelist Zola, pleading the truth in the Dreyfus Case, had to flee his country? But I, along with the other writers of my land, said nothing. The pangs of conscience that resulted were scarcely endurable. I felt intensely ashamed of myself as a writer. I concluded that I could do no better than drag myself down to the level of the Tokugawa writer of frivolous and amatory fiction. Arming myself with the tobacco pouch that was the mark of the old-style dandy, I set out to collect Ukiyoe prints, and I began to learn the samisen. It was a matter of no interest to such inferior persons as the writer of light Edo fiction or the maker of color prints that Perry's Black Ships had arrived at Uraga, or that Ii Kamon no Kami, Great Minister of the Shogunate, was assassinated at the castle gate. They thought it better to know their place and remain silent. Quite as if nothing had happened, they went on writing their indecent books and making their indecent prints." (XII, 221–22.)

There is no reason to doubt that Kafū was upset by the Kōtoku case—for Kōtoku and his fellow defendants were the prisoners in the "five or six police wagons." Yet it is hard to believe that he emerged from the encounter significantly changed. Whatever his own views on the matter, he had never shown much sign of being a Zola. It is one thing to complain about the dirt and clutter of Meiji Japan, but quite another to fight for social justice. A liking for the things of Edo, on the other hand, including its more disreputable institutions, had been much in evidence before he left for the United States and France. It is important to remember, too, that Kafū did not get around to telling of the "crisis" until 1919, when he was in a slump and no doubt receptive to dramatic explanations for it. The common notion that the Kōtoku case was somehow crucial to Kafū's writing, then, has about it an ex-post-facto look.

Kafū's pupils have testified that he was a conscientious teacher, unusually punctual and regular. In other ways his behavior was not entirely professorial. The sympathy for geisha revealed in *The River Sumida* was more than an abstraction. In 1910 he took up with a geisha named Tomimatsu, a tattoo in whose memory he is said to have carried to his grave. When he lost her to a person with more money and determination, another geisha came along to console him. She was Yaeji of Shimbashi, later to be briefly his wife, and later yet, as Fujikage Shizue, one of the key figures in modernizing the Japanese dance.

In September 1911, Kafū was respectably married to a merchant's daughter, out of deference to his family. His relations with Yaeji were of such an intensity, however, that he was off in the Hakone Mountains with her, and not to be reached, when his father suddenly died early in January of the following year. This unfilial display seems to have bothered him, uneasy though his relations with his father had been. He was on the whole punctilious about visiting his father's grave, and was later to brood upon the unfortunate incident in his diary. That a geisha should have been the occasion for it, however, while his wife was ignorant of his whereabouts, does not seem to have troubled him in the least. His interests were not in bourgeois domesticity, but in the murky backwaters of the city, and that was that.

Of the wife little can be said. She was a fleeting and insubstantial figure, divorced in February 1913, and scarcely mentioned in his writing. She may perhaps be considered responsible for Kafū's many ill-natured references to wives and mothers. She appears in his writings only once: in a warning to young men that if they get mixed up with such women they may have to buy their way out. Always careful about his bank book and in his later years positively miserly, Kafū greatly resented the fact that his precipitous divorce cost him money.

The writings of 1910 and 1911, theoretically the years of the great crisis, show few signs of intensified suffering. Indeed things seem to go on much as always, the main themes being familiar enough, annoyance at Meiji and love for Edo. Most of the essays and sketches appeared in *Mita Literature,* and many of them were collected in 1911 under the title *After Tea* (*Kōcha no Ato*). The title suggests that Europe, too, continued to furnish occasions for nostalgia, the tea in question being black tea, the European sort. Once more the mood is elegiac, punctuated with sighs for the dying city.

Not ashamed of repeating himself, Kafū told once again, in *After Tea,* of the antique vision brought on by the Tokugawa tombs in Shiba Park and lightly coated with fiction in *Sneers.* And there are other views of those tombs:

"Once I visited the shrine in the middle of a snowstorm. I remember the astonishingly beautiful colors of the carvings that decorate the eaves, standing out from the white snow on the roof. The falling snow was like petals against the black lacquer of the gate; and the composition of the whole called up not associations with Western masterpieces but a reverie uniquely its own....

"And on one of those calm, clear, cold, windless nights when the white light of the moon and the deep translucence of the sky bring over our land a certain mood of the south, I climbed from the lake at the rear of the park up the heavily wooded hill, and, crossing a vermilion bridge, seated myself on a tree root and looked down from a small eminence over the tomb of the second Shogun.

"In the branches of an old tree, weaving a pattern against the darkly luminous sky, an owl was hooting. The moonlight turned the several roofs of the mortuary chapel into sheets of silver and the colors under the eaves into elfin fires. Beyond the roofs the level ground before the chapel was indescribably quiet and smooth, like the surface of a lake. The two and three rectangular fences enclosing it, the sharply erect lines of stone lanterns, and the stone pillars of the two purification fonts balancing each other to the left and right—all of these floated up sharply as if carved out by the mysterious light of the moon, and, if I may be permitted a slight exaggeration, it seemed to me that all of the symmetrical lines before me combined to give forth music. But it was of a nature wholly different from the forms of Wagner, the rules of Debussy. Rather, it was a whisper of a peculiar art transmitted in secrecy by the shapes of the land, audible only to the hearts of those born in the land.

"It is nearly a half century since a political revolution of sorts destroyed the great temple at Ueno. In the culture that has since been built in our capital, there have been trains and streetcars and factories, but that art of the people known as architecture has been quite destroyed. And with every moment that passes, our land takes on more completely the appearance of an Anglo-Saxon colony. The old and beautiful are disappearing before our eyes, and the new and good have not yet begun to send out shoots. If, wandering through a city as if wandering through huts put up on a burned-over waste, we may yet hope to come upon a corner where there remains a shade of past glory, where is that corner if not by these abandoned tombs?

"Let us be respectful of the past. The past is the mystical spring from which the future must always flow. It is the torch lighting the uncertain way of the present. From this place of the holy past let us drive out the ungainly monuments, the ugly bronze statues, all the other shoddy and inferior art objects that the new age has built, and let us instead keep our eyes on the great arts handed down to us in perpetuity from our ancestors. I say it unconditionally: our future has no road to proceed from save that of our past." (VI, 305–8.)

Today the Shiba mortuary shrines are gone, victims of the Second World War, and the tombs proper have been moved to make way for a luxury hotel. Overhead is the Tokyo Tower, grandest of monuments to modern electronics. One agrees with Kafū that it would have been nice if something could have been preserved. But not too well preserved, perhaps—had he seen them in their prime, he would probably have found the Shiba shrines altogether too robust and pushing. Buildings had to be decaying, cultures ill and dying, if not dead, before he could really like them.

Most of the stories collected in 1912 as *Night Tales from Shimbashi* (*Shinkyō Yawa*) were also written and published separately that year. One of the best, however, "The Peony Garden" (*Botan no Kyaku*), dates from 1909, the year after Kafū's return from France. It is among his best geisha stories, a disconsolate little piece about the changing landscape east of the river, and the tribulations of the geisha, whose work as a preserver of Edo was not all pleasure. It should be noted that the theme of self-abasement running through the story predates the Kōtoku incident, and can scarcely be attributed to it.*

The full melancholy of the story will not be appreciated, perhaps, unless it is pointed out that the geisha and her friend, like Chōkichi and his uncle in *The River Sumida*, make their way through an old plebeian district upon which the blight is descending. They set out from Yanagibashi, inferior modern successor to the elegant Fukagawa

---

* A translation of "The Peony Garden" will be found in Part II, pp. 219–25.

quarter of fifty years before. Across the river, in Honjo, the blight already seems incurable. Tatekawa, up which they are rowed, is the canal next south of that along which Chōkichi had that sad walk with his uncle, and the vicinity of the peony garden is today a large automobile graveyard, the abode of scrap dealers and hot-rodders. There is something prophetic about the act as, at the end of the story, the geisha Koren and the narrator turn back into the late-spring sunset, to be away from it all.

The other "night stories" are of uneven quality, some in the declamatory vein of *Sneers,* and, like it, not very satisfactory fiction. However, again like *Sneers,* they have their good moments. Thus "A Swirl of Pine Needles" (*Matsubadomoe*) is an improbable and very wordy story about a bank clerk who has a dreadful, club-joining, charity-driving wife, memories of an affair with a geisha, and a strong liking for Tokugawa music, which is for him "the repository of old dreams." (VII, 182.) At the end of the story, the wife, who has never recovered from her last baby, falls in love with Edo music too. For all its petulance and the arbitrariness of its plot, the story has nostalgic moments akin to the best in *The River Sumida.* Here we have the two lovers, geisha and hero, out for a walk: "Wandering through back streets quite at random, the two presently came out on the river. In a vacant lot by the river drive, full-branched willows, swaying in the quiet night wind, cast their shadows darkly on the street. Over an arched stone bridge, deserted by pedestrians, the lights of rickshaws passed bravely by on their way to the Yoshiwara. The late-night dews, telling of the approach of autumn, were chilly against skins covered still by the light cotton kimono of summer. The loneliness of the Milky Way seemed to flow down upon them. . . . Finally an empty rickshaw came up, and they decided to spend the night in Iriya. The voices of insects, like sudden showers in the night, there among the paddies at the edge of the city, and the sound of roistering in the Yoshiwara, just beyond the grove of the Tarō Inari Shrine, were memories of a dream that had gone on after waking." (VII, 173–74.) The Yoshiwara pleasure quarter, so decisively moved to the edge of town by the Tokugawa Shogunate that it was called "The Paddies," was already being separated from the nearest paddy by miles of factories and tenements.

The less declamatory stories run a considerable range, from the archly romantic to the dryly realistic. At one end of the spectrum is a story whose tone is set by the opening sentence: "Ah, my lover!" (vii, 229.) It suggests Kafū to be a highly eclectic writer, deriving at least as much from Musset as from Maupassant. At the other end is a provocative sketch about a Shimbashi geisha so omnivorous and undiscriminating that she will take even Chinese—even Occidentals—as guests. Kafū characterizes her as quite the incarnation of modernism.

Besides the story of the peony garden, the collection contains two most effective pieces. "The Bill Collector" (*Kaketori*) is about a little maid from a Shimbashi geisha house who makes her way across the city in an attempt to collect a worthless debt. If the promiscuous geisha just mentioned is the incarnation of the modern, the frightened little functionary in this story is quite the reverse, the child of Edo for whom exile begins the moment the flats of the old city are left behind. The trip across Tokyo is like a trip to the ends of the earth, and the girl finds herself becoming intensely homesick as she moves westward into the middle-class uplands. Here we start her on her way:

"She had a real streetcar ride only once or twice a year, when she went on holidays to visit her parents in Senjū, beyond Asakusa. A true daughter of the downtown flats, she knew, among the outlying parts of town, only Asakusa and Fukagawa to the north, and Shinagawa to the south. The very sound of the name 'Okubo,' off in the hills to the west—it was there that she had to collect the bill—made her feel as if she were off to the abode of foxes and badgers. She thought, too, that if she did not catch the first streetcar possible, she would not be back before dark." (vii, 72–73.)

It is midmorning, and Okubo is perhaps four miles away. Presently she boards her streetcar and moves into unknown western regions.

"She began to feel that every eye in the car was immovably fixed on her.... Suddenly she saw that no one else was dressed as she was.... She felt still more that she was off on an unknown road, among strangers. The conductor came to check transfers, and she asked him where it was that she had to get off—a little before Shinjuku, she thought— and her consternation and loneliness became yet more intense. . . . . .

"She had hoped that she could get there without transferring, and now she learned that she had to transfer not once but twice. She might as well have been cast out in some black forest or doorless maze from which she could not return. . . .

"Never again, however much her mistress might scold her, would she go on an errand over a distant, unknown road. Back in the house, she would just now be finished with the cleaning, and she would be at work airing the bedding and washing cotton kimonos for the customers to change into. How much better all that would be!" (VII, 77–78.)

The sense of being in an alien land has worked a considerable change on the poor girl. Earlier her duties have been described as not of a pleasant nature: "She had to wait upon the customers in their rooms, and then she was a sort of personal maid to the lady of the house. Busy though she was, she had to keep the lady's patron company (he was approaching sixty) while he had his evening drink. But that task was not the worst. The very worst was having to wash his false teeth for him when he had finished eating." (VII, 75.) That, viewed from the remoteness of perhaps two miles, this life should seem desperately attractive is testimony to the tightness of the little flatland world left over from Edo. In a manner half ironic, Kafū evokes it with considerably more success than in the forensic stories.

The best story of all, "Coming Down with a Cold" (*Kazagokochi*), is not only about a geisha but about an ailing geisha, a dying inhabitant of a dying world.* In her morbid person are the beauty and decay of Edo. The hero, whom she supports, has seen the pushing world of Meiji, and chosen entombment in preference to it, and the retreat into the past thus comes to be like a retreat from life itself, a flight into self-destruction. The useless and helpless hero, drowning himself in the dark waters of Edo, might seem like an effective dramatization of Kafū's own plight after the Kōtoku incident, were it not for the fact that similar figures are to be found earlier, in, for instance, "A Song of Fukagawa." It was a sort of degradation most attractive to Kafū, in any case. He was to create numbers of similar characters.

In 1912 the Emperor Meiji died, and literary historians generally aver that a new period began with the accession of Taishō. Whatever the virtues of the division for literature in general, the year 1912 may be taken as the beginning of a change in Kafū's career. New writers and schools were emerging, his position at the center of the literary world was less secure, and shortly he was to begin his withdrawal.

---

* The story is translated in Part II, pp. 226–36.

Chapter four Withdrawal

Although the death of the Emperor Meiji in 1912 is generally taken as marking the end of a literary period, the authors who were to dominate the first decade or so of the Taishō Period were already active in late Meiji. The naturalists, who had assumed that the ultimate duty of the novelist was to poke about in family closets for skeletons and then to describe them (along with such matters as what the novelist was in the habit of having for breakfast), were beginning to seem tiresome, and indeed were beginning to seem rather tired of themselves. The literary world was not wanting in people to reprove the naturalists: the rich young men of the Shirakaba school taxed them with a want of ideals and a failure to treat of the full man; the ponderous Mori Ogai had rather similar objections; Natsume Sōseki found them wanting in ideas and imagination; and such "decadents" as Kafū and Tanizaki Junichirō found their styles arid and awkward, and their persons rustic and boorish. Nothing very startling began for literature in 1912, then.

Yet in Kafū's career a change was coming. As editor of *Mita Literature* he was an important person in the literary world, and the early years of Taishō were years of withdrawal. He shortly left both *Mita Literature* and Keiō University, and with the emergence of such younger writers as Akutagawa Ryūnosuke, the rather simple Meiji view of reality, shared to a large extent by naturalists and antinaturalists alike, no longer enjoyed the vogue it once had. The assumption that facts were facts and that what happened happened gave way to the view that facts and incidents were fragmentary, ambiguous, and elusive. By the time of the great earthquake, when the reign of Taishō had lasted slightly more than a decade, Kafū had withdrawn from the literary world, to brood in near silence.

He waited a decent time after his father's death to leave Keiō University. One theory has it that he accepted appointment there in the first place only because his father made him uncomfortable. He pleaded illness, in any case, and resigned from both his positions there, as editor and as professor, in March 1916. Suffering from a chronic gastric ailment and fits of despondency, he was writing very little by the time he reached his fortieth birthday, and lamented in his diary that his productive days, and perhaps life itself, were near an end.

He was more hasty in ridding himself of that other burden acquired out of deference to father and family, his first wife. She was divorced in February 1913, only a few weeks after the father's death. In 1914 he was married a second time, to Uchida Yae, the lady whose professional name as a Shimbashi geisha was Yaeji, and as a dancer Fujikage Shizue—the lady, also, with whom he had been off in the Hakone Mountains when his father lay dying. Even before the marriage, it seems, she was visiting the Okubo house almost every day, and she and Kafū would go off together to take samisen and singing lessons in the old style called Utazawa. When he had a stomachache she would make him a comforting brew. This last is described in some detail in "Cowpeas" (*Yahazusō*, 1916), the plant in the title being the chief ingredient of the concoction.

The other members of Kafū's family were unenthusiastic. Yaeji was at least partly responsible (the division of the father's estate was also responsible) for a break between Kafū and the only brother who still bore the Nagai name—the middle of the three brothers, it will be remembered, had been adopted into the family of Kafū's mother. The break lasted almost to the end of Kafū's life, with Kafū apparently the more industrious of the two in making sure that it would not be repaired. In addition, the marriage and matters of property seem to have produced a distinct chill in relations between Kafū and his mother, who went to live with the brother, and whose funeral Kafū was one day to refuse to attend.

As described in "Cowpeas," the marriage seems to have been for a time a happy one, at least from Kafū's point of view. "I knew to the full the clean happiness of this world.... When there was a damaged screen in the bedroom or a torn door panel, we would get out old letters and papers we had kept hidden from each other, and read them as we pasted them over the holes—a pleasure unknown to the wealthy ones in their great, well-kept houses. When the fence beyond the chrysanthemums was in disrepair, or the bamboo lattice at the bathroom window, we would go cut our own bamboo and weave it to mend the damage—dalliance such as this is unknown to princes, public figures with white horses and silver saddles. Finding a spare moment from other pursuits, I would line my manuscript paper from a wood block, and Yae would kneel beside me with her sleeves tied up, not minding how inky her fingers got. This, surely, is a pleasure unknown to the modern scribbler, who does his polemics with a fountain pen on Western-style paper." (XI, 38–39.)

It may be that nostalgia made the marriage seem pleasanter than it was, for by the time the essay was written, Kafū had sold the Okubo house and was living in the lower part of the city. The association with Yae and Okubo, in any case, seems to have made autumn, the season in which they were married, a particularly attractive time of the year for Kafū: "There is no other time that makes me so long for that garden as late autumn. People may think that the hilly part of the city, with all its trees, is a place in which to pass the summer, but as a matter of fact it is much more pleasant to enjoy the cool of the summer in the middle of the city, to go for a walk through some street fair, where there are no thicket mosquitoes to torment you. It is in the middle of the city, too, that you raise the reed blind of a second-floor window and see the feather clouds of evening, and hear the sardinemongers along the river bank, and are suddenly hungry.

"In the winter, however, the fact that the houses are packed close together means that the short day is even shorter, and the breakfast room is in perpetual darkness. In the hilly uptown districts the fact that the trees have lost their leaves means that the garden is brighter and clearer than in the summer, and at the round window of the study the leaves of the banana tree have withered and fallen away, and so a soft light shines the whole day. As the sudden night showers become more frequent, the fallen leaves rot, and the earth is fragrant at the line of the shrubbery, and the titmice and wagtails and warblers are even livelier than in the summer. The hills of Tokyo are pleasant in November and December as at no other time of the year.

"Yae had finished her round of courtesy calls and was at home all the time. She repapered the doors. There is something quite delightful about the white of paper doors when the smell of paste has not yet gone, against the darkly shining wood of old pillars and verandas. The rooms were brighter than they had been, and the shadows of the leaves and the birds in the gentle evening sun made a person feel fresher and cleaner. At nightfall, with the rustling of bamboo in the evening wind at the back window, the lights on the new paper were again clean and bright. And yet another pleasure of winter was getting out the furnishings that had been put away since spring: the brazier, the hearth, the foot warmer, the low screens to break the draft. The brazier had been carefully dusted and polished every day through the winter and as long as the cold weather persisted into the spring, and now, in the dust of the closet through the summer, it had lost something of its sheen; and yet there it was, old and familiar, back in the usual spot, like a friend who had been away. 'And have you been well?' I wanted to ask. 'As you can see, I have managed to keep myself alive.' There is no other time, somehow, when memories come back as they do on the first morning the brazier is out. . . . And so all the furnishings and utensils I had known from childhood were taken out and cleaned when Yae came into the house, and the profligate who until yesterday had sought his pleasure outside now found domestic pleasures, and lost himself in the task of watching over the house left behind by his father." (xi, 42–44.)

But the pleasure would not seem to have been wholly shared. "The felicitous year passed, and the new year, too, had advanced to the time for warblers. One day I had business in Shiba, and on the way back I stopped to see Momiyama, my publisher, in Tsukiji. We talked of this and that until the evening was well along, and I called for a rickshaw to take me home. As I opened the gate, the dog was there as always, frisking at the skirt of my kimono, but the house seemed lonely. Yae was no longer there—she had left behind the one maid. A light was on in the breakfast room, and on the Chinese sandalwood table where we took our meals the keys were carefully laid out with a letter. The maid said that Madame had had her bath and gone out at about nine o'clock, and had presently telephoned, from where she had not said, that she would not be home that night. I was not particularly upset. I thought that she would be calling on some Shimbashi geisha, or perhaps a dancing pupil. It was only when I opened the letter that I realized the gravity of the matter." (XI, 48.)

Yaeji had in fact walked out on him.

In "Commuting to Tsukiji" (*Tsukijigayoi*), a short essay published in 1917, Kafū had this to say about his feelings upon realizing "the gravity of the matter": "In the Year of the Hare [1915], just when the voices of warblers were beginning to sound a bit tired, something happened that made the world a gloomy place. In my distress I said to myself that I would never again take a wife. I would live by myself, and not complain when the loneliness of old age caught up with me. The most urgent task facing me—how ridiculous it seems now!—was to learn the samisen. I would keep myself entertained by learning the samisen. I had already turned away from the world, and I knew that as I grew old I could expect no callers, and would have no one to call on.... Since then, there may have been days when the crows have not cawed, but there have been no days when I have not appeared at Tsukiji for my samisen lesson." (XI, 79–80.)

In "Cowpeas," Kafū gives no clear explanation of Yaeji's motives. He only suggests that the curious reader go off to Shimbashi and ask her, although he does not offer much hope for a detailed confession of the sort, he says, most modern ladies are given to. More than twenty years later, in *A Strange Tale from East of the River* (*Bokutō Kidan*), he was to offer an explanation, by implication at least—but an explanation not entirely consistent with what has been quoted above from "Cowpeas": "From my youth I had been making my way into the streets of the heavily painted, and even now I had not awakened to the evils of the practice. Under the pressure of circumstances, I had more than once followed the wishes of a woman and brought her into my house and set her at broom and dustpan. Always the experiment had been a failure. When such a woman leaves behind her old surroundings and no longer thinks herself lowly, she becomes unmanageable, either the slovenly wife or the fiery wife." (XVI, 205.) Perhaps there is more fiction than fact in this apparent reference to Yaeji, for besides being inconsistent with "Cowpeas," the passage reminds one of the marriage described, or alluded to, in "The Peony Garden," which was written before either of Kafū's own marriages.

After Kafū's death, Yaeji had her own explanation: "He was very fickle." Perhaps in that February of 1915 he stayed out once too often. Unlike most Japanese wives, Yaeji had a place of her own to go.

With her departure, and Kafū's alienation from his family, the big Okubo house was empty. Kafū himself departed in May, for rented quarters in Tsukiji, where he was within hearing distance of the professional samisen and the geisha's high titter.

Very early in the Taishō Period there came what may perhaps be called a sign of Kafū's wish to withdraw from the center of things, an excursion, the only extended one of his career, into historical fiction. Edo itself, and not merely Edo remains, gave him the setting for two medium-length novels published in 1913. The very titles, florid and not especially informative, suggest the world of late-Edo drama and fiction: *Willows Shedding Their Leaves at an Evening Window* (*Chiru Yanagi Mado no Yūbae*), and *Robe of Love under the Cherry Blossoms at Kasamori* (*Koigoromo Hana no Kasamori*). The two were later published together under the comprehensive title *Willow and Cherry* (*Yanagi Sakura*), apparently to signify two contrasting moods, autumnal and vernal. The willow piece, set in late summer and autumn, describes the last days of the Edo fiction-writer Ryūtei Tanehiko, who died in 1842, possibly (the circumstances are obscure) a victim of the harsh Tempō sumptuary edicts. The cherry-blossom piece, set in spring and early summer, describes the elopement of O-sen, a famous Edo beauty of a somewhat earlier day, immortalized in the prints of Suzuki Harunobu.

The two stories are mood pieces, attempts to convey an Ukiyoe-like harmony of color and line. They are therefore rather wanting in action. O-sen, in particular, always seems to be freezing into pretty poses, and waiting for Harunobu to come along and catch her at them. Here, in the introduction to *Willow and Cherry*, Kafū tells us what he thought he was about: "Puccini in his masterpiece captured 'Japan' as it appealed to the sensibilities of the West, and set it to music. Japan as it affects the sensibilities of the Japanese is quite another matter. What I wish to urge here—as I offer to the elders of Edo, its venerable and austere historians, and to the literary critics these two pieces set in Edo—has to do precisely with this matter of 'sensibilities.' Just as the tourist feels that he has seen something especially Japanese in the tombs at Nikkō and the shrine gate at Itsukushima and Mt. Fuji and cherry blossoms and geisha, so I feel that I have gained artistic awareness of a period now gone, a period known as Edo, through its poly-chrome prints and its popular literature. I am not interested in specific impressions. I am interested, rather, in what is necessary to bring them into harmony, ranged one beside another. And wherein lies this harmony? In the author's mood, ordering the whole of the work. One may think, for instance, of the Edo theater. . . . All the irregularities and eccentricities are melted into an exceedingly subtle harmony by the colors of the costumes and settings and by the music of the samisen. What I have sought in my *Willow and Cherry* is to make the author's mood have an effect similar to that of the samisen strain, to make the words do what the colors of costume and setting do for the theater." (VIII, 3-4.)

Sometimes, as when Tanehiko is out boating on the Sumida with friends, the verbal mood-music seems very near succeeding:

"From one of the boats in the dim light of the half moon the low voices of a man and a woman came to them, and a faint, subtle perfume of sachets, on a breeze that also brought, faintly, the rhythmical calls of night porters, along the earthen walls of a heavily wooded mansion on the bank; and an intermittent song to the plucked accompaniment of a samisen would be interrupted by the splash of a net, invisible somewhere out toward midstream. The wooden clappers of night watchmen on their rounds of the warehouses sounded out harsh and strident in the dew of the deepening night, and made one feel that, although it was still summer by the calendar, autumn was coming. One wanted others to be near.

"Perhaps worn out by the wanton thoughts that the scene called up, Tanehiko's two young disciples were standing disconsolately above him, their arms folded and their heads bowed. The sake that Kunisada had been drinking with his publisher had apparently been exhausted. As the torches of the anglers among the bridges far up the river became few enough to be counted, the revelry in the teahouses on the tree-lined embankment came over the water to them, and the songs of mendicant Shinnai singers; and the wall of the Komagata Temple stood out white in the moonlight." (VIII, 19-20.)

Or in this brief nocturne:

"The house was utterly quiet. Outside in the lane there had been the intermittent humming of passersby, the distant strain of a pair of Shinnai singers, the cries of hawkers; but all had suddenly been drowned out—for the night had grown late—by the clappers of the night patrols; and the great bell of Asakusa sounded through the sky of Edo, so grandly, yet so quietly. The round lantern, which every night had three and four wicks in it with no regard for the oil consumed, once again took possession of the writer's study, and, the light yet clearer and the shadows yet cooler, shone upon the half-finished manuscript on the Chinese desk, and the writing materials used so affectionately over the years. . . . The flowers bloomed and fell as the years passed, and his hair grew whiter and the wrinkles on his forehead deeper; but the round lantern went on casting its soft, seductive light, as if ten years were but a night." (VIII, 27–28.)

The days of the Tempō edicts that brought Tanehiko such discomfort must, despite their harshness, have had a peculiar poignancy for Kafū. When he wrote of them, they were just passing from living memory, as the days of Kafū's first Yoshiwara exploits are now about to pass from living memory. The devices to which he resorts in his attempts to "harmonize," however, seem bookish. He is able to describe the banks of the river with much precision as they would have looked to someone out boating in 1842, and he even manages to tell us what persons out boating might have talked about—what piece of erotic prose or art, for instance, was then the talk of Edo. Yet these careful reconstructions have a certain aridness about them. The fact that the author has not seen them but only read about them in books seems to make all the difference, and the banks of the river when observed by Tanehiko somehow do not compel as they do when observed by Chōkichi of *The River Sumida*. But it cannot be denied that Kafū's scholarship is impressive.

There is a sense in which the willow piece is not historical fiction at all. Tanehiko in trouble with the authorities is Kafū in trouble with the authorities, and Tanehiko's bouts of conscience are of a sort that Kafū would at least have *liked* to have had himself: "Tanehiko thought of his own position and that of Tōyama, and marveled that even in this sad day there could be so noble a thinker among the samurai.* And when he thought how he had consciously let himself slip to the level of the frivolous writer, he was filled with uneasiness and at

* Tōyama Saemonnojō, the date of whose death is uncertain, was one of the governors (*machibugyō*) of Edo.

the same time an indefinable self-contempt." (VIII, 15.) This sounds rather like the writer of "Fireworks," the Japanese Zola manqué.

It is not as a period piece at all that the willow story is most successful, but as a sort of elegy for artists who feel that the end is in sight. Kafū's works are soon to take on an autumnal mood themselves, a feeling that the end of a life and a culture has come. Certain of the best passages in his reconstruction of Tanehiko's last days are strikingly like descriptions he is presently to offer of his own loneliness, and, save for a few stage properties, they need hardly be set in Edo at all:

"By the calendar, at least, it was autumn, and the talk among the young people in the streets was already of the lanterns of the Yoshiwara. . . . It was Tanehiko's practice, when the calendar said that the hottest weather was past, to air all his books and possessions, and it was his practice on the night of the airing to invite in several close friends and disciples for a few cups of wine. There among his rare and much-loved books they would disport themselves with geisha and compose light poetry. But this year, under the stern new edicts, even the idea of taking out his books seemed frightening, and Tanehiko decided to let the worms have their way. . . .

"There seemed to be an ineradicable boundary line between yesterday, when the shock of the edicts had yet not broken in upon the calm beauty of the writer's life, and today, when there was only terror. And as he looked back across the line from the darkness of today to the brightness and gaiety on the other side, he could only feel that his own life was finished, that it belonged to the past. Suddenly weary, he found himself without strength to look into the future. Even his own works, piled on the shelves of his study, seemed less like his works than like those of good friends who had died—good friends about whom he had known everything, thoroughly and completely, while they lived. . . . He spent the day and night in reminiscence, thinking how old he had been when he wrote this, how old when he wrote that. His dissipated life, like the wild rose that has its fleeting color and scent and produces no seeds, had had its brief follies and infatuations, and now he had a childless old age to look forward to. He would try to forget, abandon himself to profitless memories of the past." (VIII, 38–40.)

If the mood of the Tanehiko story is autumnal, there is evidence from the same period that life for the degraded heir to Edo still had its pleasures. Beginning in the September 1913 issue of *Mita Literature,* Kafū serialized a journal called *Tidings from Okubo (Okubodayori)*, which in the end covered the year from July 1913 to June 1914. It is in one sense a highly impersonal sort of journal, saying nothing about family affairs or romantic affairs. Thus there is nothing about Kafū's estrangement from his family and nothing about his marriage and divorce. Yet in another sense it is very personal indeed, showing the sort of pursuits that can occupy the gentleman of leisure who has turned back to Edo.

There are occasional onsets of despondency and dyspepsia, but on the whole *Tidings from Okubo* is a rather happy work. Important and interesting people make their entrances and exits: the second Ichikawa Sadanji, a Kabuki actor with advanced ideas about his art, not on the whole approved of by the conservative Kafū; Osanai Kaoru, one of Sadanji's principal allies in trying to redo Kabuki; the people of the Mokuyōkai, the "Thursday Club," a literary group centering upon Iwaya Sazanami, Kafū's early mentor and benefactor; and the younger writers of the Mita group, notably the novelist and playwright Kubota Mantarō. The "tidings" have in them something of the hum of a thriving literary plant, and the smell of printer's ink. They also have geisha and plays and recitals, for Tokyo was already well on its way to becoming the city of all cities with the greatest variety of entertainment.

Although it is a relatively happy and well-populated little series of sketches, *Tidings from Okubo* is essentially about the pleasures of solitude, and, in true descent from discursive essays of the fifteenth century and before, it is dominated by a sense of decline. Autumn is more with it than spring, as it is to be with Kafū's novels, and the past is better than the present. A wearying Kafū, if we are to accept his description of himself, is in pursuit of a past that is a stronger runner than he, although on occasion it seems to turn and come back of its own accord, in a rather startling manner. Here is the entry for April 16, 1914: "Learning that there was to be a recital of traditional music in the Katō style, I set out to hear it—the place was a certain restaurant in one of the quarters. The sky was clear and the wind soft and warm, and it was the kind of day that makes one want to bring out a spring kimono; but just when, as an added attraction, the actor Sawamura

Sōjūrō had finished dancing *Musume Dōjōji* to the samisen of Kineya Rokuzaemon, the sky suddenly clouded over. Amid claps of thunder, rain came pouring down in sheets. I was less disturbed than moved, for I thought of Shokusanjin, and how, as he has recorded, he was in the Chōryūji Temple in Ichigaya, listening to *Dōjōji* from the samisen of Hara Budayū, a master of the day, when suddenly it clouded and there was a shower.* For a time I leaned against the railing and watched the rain fall on the river. When it showed no sign of stopping, I called a rickshaw and went to the special Kabuki performance at the Shintomiza." (x, 106.)

But generally the past is less agreeable about coming back of its own accord, and must be courted, through its disappearing relics. Thus an evening by the river brings memories of the proud Edo tradition: "There were, as always, fireworks for the midsummer river festival at Ryōgoku. It used to be that the geisha at Yanagibashi would take that night off, and to avoid the crowds, go hide somewhere on the outskirts of town, Negishi or Mukōjima perhaps; and on that night of all the year Yanagibashi would be a place without geisha. Such was the strong-minded Edo geisha, who thought it unseemly to appear at noisy parties on the night of the fireworks. This I have been told by a certain old gentleman." (x, 40.)

There are hunts for old books and old houses. "I walked along the narrow, winding back streets from below Yotsuya up the hill toward Onden. They had a worn, lonely look about them, with here and there an old temple or cemetery. Among the little houses were astonishingly large and venerable trees, to remind one that here had once stood quarters for lesser functionaries of the Shogunate. Delighted at noting that one such place had been recorded by Shokusanjin as the site of a meeting to compose light poetry, the first important meeting of the Temmei Period, I went out walking after dinner, partly also to see the new moon, then approaching first quarter.† I went into a shabby old second-hand book store. Chinese texts from the Tokugawa Period were scattered around in the greatest confusion.... I called for service,

---

* Shokusanjin, or Ota Nampo (1749–1823), was a writer of light poetry and fiction who had Edo verve in larger measure than most, and was extravagantly admired by Kafū.
† The Temmei era (1781–89) is associated with Shokusanjin and the rise of *kyōka* light verse.

and after a time an old man who apparently did not have the use of his limbs crawled painfully out from a mosquito net behind the tattered paper door, and, beating the dust from it, told me that the book I asked about was a collection of Matsudaira Sadanobu's essays copied by Prince Shirakawa. I guessed from his face and manner that he had once been a man of some position. In a heap that could have been taken for waste paper, I came upon a novel illustrated by Utamaro, and bought it at the price asked. Feeling sorry for the old man, I also bought a manuscript collection of Kikaku's poetry—it was in a remarkably good hand, on fine glazed paper. Then, from the badly lighted alley on which fell the light of the new moon, I went out to the main street. All the little houses had closed their shutters early, against the chilly autumn night." (x, 56–57.)

There is a certain amount of literary and dramatic criticism, highly conservative, as might be expected: "When we look about to decide which actors are worthy of notice in our day, we see that, with the single exception of Danshirō, they are all far from the main branch of the Ichikawa family, the thriving center of the theatrical world. In early Meiji, enjoying the patronage of the bureaucrats, Ichikawa Danjūrō created the specious art known as *katsureki* or 'living history.' We should be thankful that, by contrast, Kikugorō succeeded the great Kodanji, and so kept alive the tastes of the Edo townsman." (x, 91.)

"It may seem that I spend all my time talking about Mokuami, but, looking out over the garden, I have found myself thinking of a passage in the Kiyomoto ballad 'Call of the Wild Goose': 'Summer has passed, and autumn so swiftly, and already the sudden showers of winter are upon us.' Besides manners and emotions, Mokuami wove into his plays and librettos minute observations of the four seasons. His reality resembles that of Toyokuni and Hokusai. Impressionism is characteristic of all Edo art, but there are differences of degree depending on the period. That Toyokuni and Hokusai were extreme realists of Edo in its decline is apparent when we compare their works with those of the early nineteenth century and before. There is a predominance of detail urging a similar generalization when we compare the words and music of Mokuami with those of such earlier styles as Katō and Itchū. . . . Listening to Itchū, we think how very far it has receded into the past." (x, 77–78.)

There are observations about the changing city, harsh ones about the Ginza: "The Ginza at night is so bustling that it already suggests the end of the year.... As always, there are displays of decorated New Year's battledores in the window of the Tengadō. As always, too, there are gentleman and lady dolls inside the glass doors, the former in the latest Western mode, the latter in long coats. Let me list a few of the things I dislike about the Ginza: the enormous cupid dolls, the dolls of the Tengadō, and the girls of the Lion Café." (x, 84.)

Fond ones about Koishikawa: "We no longer know how it is to be startled by the call of the wild goose in the autumn twilight; but when as a child I played in our garden in Koishikawa, regretting the short-ness of the day, I would look up into the sky as the wild geese went by in the evening, and sing the little song that begins 'The last goose is first.' What a faraway world it now seems. Everything these days makes me feel the influence of my late father. It is because of his in-fluence, I think, that I am more interested in old things than most people my age. From that old house in Koishikawa you looked across the valley at Mejiro and Akagi on the next rise, and you could always see Mt. Fuji, while the clear waters of Edogawa Brook flowed at the foot of the hill. My father called our house, in Chinese fashion, 'The Hall of the Encircling Brook,' and sometimes 'The Hall of Advancing Green.' " (x, 58–59.)

And Asakusa: "Since there had been an Utazawa recital, I went with two or three others to have a drink in the Yoshiwara. On the way back, with the half moon in a sky that was just then clearing, the view over the great trees behind Kinryū Hill was like a stage setting. Since there are few lights above the main hall of the Asakusa Temple, the clash and clutter of the modern world disappears at night, and the lesser buildings, the Prayer Hall and the Hexagonal Hall and the rest, rise up among the old trees, and Asakusa is as it has always been, a delight to the eye. Tonight the row of lights leading away from the temple was like a picture, framed in the great gate and seen from the darkness of the temple precincts. I have always preferred pictures of famous buildings to exaggerated landscapes, and every detail seemed meant for a picture: the stairs of the great hall in the evening light, the towels of the purification font through a sudden rain, the great gargoyles of the ridge tiles biting at the half moon, the bronze eaves-troughs turned green-white in the moonlight. Back in the days be-fore it was frowned upon to hang out a shrine lantern before the archery stalls, the scene was hard to pull oneself away from, when, on an evening of sudden showers in early winter, the leaves of the nettle tree would blow against the little paper panels on which the name of the shop was written. I shall always remember how, as I was whiling away one such evening in the back room of one such establishment, the evening sky and the top branches of the great old trees were reflected from the bowl at my elbow." (x, 63–64.)

And of course the Sumida: "Mr. Iwaya is shortly to leave for Manchuria. The Mokuyōkai had a farewell party.... We first waited for everyone to assemble at the Garden of the Hundred Flowers, then proceeded to the Yaomatsu restaurant. The upstairs room to which we were shown was really too cheap and vulgar, and we asked if there might not be something better, perhaps in one of the outbuildings. It seemed, though, that all the rooms were fairly much the same, and we had to make the best of what we had. It being the night of 'the late moon,' the third night after the full moon, we all set out in a boat for Azuma Bridge. At night you cannot see the factories and bronze statues, and there is only the moon gently lighting the surface of the water, and, white in the mist beyond, the houses of Imado and Hashiba on the right bank, and the trees of Kanegafuchi and Komatsushima on the left. Ah, here it is, I thought, almost ready to weep—the Sumida! We put the geisha ashore at Mimeguri Landing, and as the boat tied up at Hanakawado, the drums and flutes of a festival came across the waters to us, as if opening a domestic tragedy on the Kabuki stage. And so we disbanded." (x, 62.)

What most impresses in *Tidings from Okubo* is the loving detail in which the seasons are reviewed as they pass over the garden and the city. Kafū's comments on the "realism" of Mokuami and Hokusai could almost have been made about his own "tidings." If, however, the manner is that of Edo in decline, it also has much in common with an earlier and fresher strain, the light verse (*kyōka*) of the late eighteenth century, as it emerged from the brushes of such masters as Shokusanjin. An awareness of the passing seasons was at the heart of it, an awareness so quick and subtle that the homelier manifestations of seasonal change—roasting fish, sandals drying after a rain—served it quite as well as the loftier. It is a way of observing and recording that can be something of a problem for the translator, Japanese nature not being Occidental nature, and yet, for all the strangeness of the flora, perhaps some suggestion of the results can be carried over into English. One paradoxical effect of *Tidings from Okubo,* so obsessed with and resentful of change, is to show that something, after all, has come through unchanged. The moods of the garden and the city are still, in a strange way, rather as they were a half century ago.*

In August 1914, a month after the last installment of *Tidings from Okubo* appeared in *Mita Literature,* Kafū began serializing another long essay, completed in the issue for June 1915. Thoroughly revised, and with the addition of an essay on Ukiyoe landscape prints, it came out as a book later in 1915. The title, *Hiyorigeta,* is a somewhat abstruse one, referring to a kind of footgear designed for bad weather. The first sentences explain it:

"I am unusually tall, and I am further distinguished by the fact that I always carry an umbrella and wear *hiyorigeta.* However bright the day, I never feel safe without my umbrella and *hiyorigeta*—for the weather of this perpetually soggy Tokyo is not to be trusted. The autumn sky and the masculine heart are commonly likened to each other as the most fickle of things, and the simile does more than just pamper the prejudices of wives. In the spring, at about the time when the cherries are in bloom, a day that starts out beautifully is certain to be a gale by two or three in the afternoon, or a rainstorm by evening. There is of course no need even to speak of the rainy season. In hot weather it is equally impossible to know when a torrent will come. To be sure, this changeability has had its advantages. Sudden showers could always be relied upon to bring together the gallants and beauties of old romances, and one likes to think that such happenings are not wholly things of the past. Is it not possible that somewhere, sheltered from prying eyes by an awning, a pair have taken advantage of a sudden after-theater shower to enact a romantic scene of their own? But the virtues of *hiyorigeta* are not in any case limited to their usefulness during sudden showers. When pleasant winter days have succeeded one another, the melting frosts turn the hilly districts of the city into a red mire, and downtown the muddy gutters splash over on the asphalt streets.

"And so I go out wearing *hiyorigeta* and carrying an umbrella." (x, 125–26.)

* Fairly long passages of seasonal description, translated in seasonal order, will be found in Part II, pp. 237–43.

The essay purports to describe a series of walks through Tokyo. Actually it is of a more fragmentary nature. Perhaps most of the material was indeed gathered while out walking, although the frequent complaints of ill-health make so much walking seem a touch unlikely; but the organization not by progressive observations but by subjects—temples, hills, cliffs, watery places—produces a jumpy, choppy effect. The progression of the seasons through the city, so important in *Tidings from Okubo,* is not wholly lacking. It tends to be more in evidence, however, when Kafū is reminiscing than when he is reporting, as for instance in a long description of a visit to the house of Mori Ogai, the giant of Meiji literature who has already been mentioned. Ogai lived behind Tokyo University, in a district rather remote from the heart of the old city, but not, like more recent suburbs, a whole space-voyage away. Negishi, the quiet retreat to which Yanagibashi geisha escaped in *Tidings from Okubo,* lies just beyond the next rise to the east.

"From the railing on the second floor you looked out over the roofs of the city to the distant sea. It was for this reason, I have heard, that Ogai named his house 'The Tower for Viewing the Tide.' I had the honor of being received there a number of times in a most friendly manner, but I never saw the tide. I did, however, once hear the sound, unforgettably deep, of the temple bell at Ueno. It was an evening in early autumn, when the days were still warm. Since the master appeared to be having dinner, I was shown to a room upstairs.... Save for the hanging and vase in the alcove, the room was quite bare. There were no inscriptions or knickknacks. I looked timidly into the room, through a sliding door, one of four, that had been left open. In the middle of it there was a desk, again bare, actually more like a table, a single board with four legs and no drawers, and no ornamentation.... Just then, on a wave of jasmine brought by the breeze that drove away the heat of the day, there came that sound, the bell of Ueno, to startle me as I sat alone waiting for the master of the Tide-viewing Tower to appear.

"I turned to look in the direction from which it had come. From the darkening mist that enveloped the vast expanse of city below the Sendagi cliff, countless lights were burning, and, as if in a dream, the last pale light of evening hung like a cloud over the groves of Ueno and Yanaka. I thought of the mysterious browns in the Chavannes mural for the Panthéon, the one of St. Genevieve looking quietly down over Paris at night.

"In the long, dying echo it struck again, and then again, and each time the shadows in the groves were deeper, and the lights in the low-lying city brighter; and the final echo was lost in the suddenly louder neighing of cart horses. Vacantly I looked around again at the bare, empty 'tower,' and I thought of the master quietly reading and writing in the bareness, and looking down at the lights and hearing in alternation the sound of the bells and the neighing of the horses. At no other time did the master himself seem so much like those mysterious browns of Chavannes.

"Brisk as a young student he came up the stairs, apologizing for his tardiness.... That evening I had in detail his views on the philosophy of Eucken, and it was after nine when I made my way down the hill past the Nezu Shrine, around the lake, and so out to the streetcar track. As I skirted the lake, I counted the stars among the great trees on the Ueno rise behind the Tōshōgū Shrine." (x, 206-9.)

There are other passages of reminiscence that go back to his boyhood and early youth, including some that have already been referred to—those, for instance, describing the mysteries of Christian Hill, and the "inconceivably strange" foreigners of whom he caught an occasional early glimpse. Mixed in among the memories new and old is an occasional philosophic reverie that touches upon an important truth about the changing, changeless city:

"Amid the squalor of the tenements along the smelly canals, with their rotting wooden bridges, and their fertilizer boats and garbage boats, you see the roof of a temple, and hear its wooden gong and its bell; and the mood is such as is to be found through all the poor, low-lying districts along the banks of the River Sumida. It seems to me that if such scenes of poverty can for a moment be separated from modern social problems and seen only for the poetry that is in them, the poorer districts of Tokyo, when compared with similar districts in London and New York, may be called squalid, just as the latter may; and yet in them there is a certain quiet, a hush, a tranquillity. It is true that a few sections are now so drowned in the smoke of factory chimneys and the noise of machinery as to be approaching the unrelieved squalor of the West; but in the poor back streets where this is not yet the case, a way of life handed down from the Tokugawa

Period survives among the shadows, with the superstitions of Buddhism to support it. . . . For better or for worse, modern culture has not yet come to these back streets. Hence you still sometimes hear the priestess's song, to the twanging of a bowstring. You hear other old music too, and see the lanterns and the fleeting smoke from fires welcoming the dead back to the midsummer festival. The vaguely sad resignation that is a legacy of Edo authoritarianism is being destroyed by the education of the new age, and when at length the awakening and the spirit of resistance come to these lower levels, then, I firmly believe, their real misery will begin." (x, 156–57.)

There is much about the passage that is not very pleasing, notably Kafū's apparent assumption that he knows better what is good for the masses than the masses know themselves. Yet it is true that not a great deal of Tokyo is merely sordid, as a great deal of London and New York is. And so the paradox presents itself once more: despite earthquakes, bombings, and Enlightenment, something fundamental resists change. Priestesses and twanging bows may no longer be very easy to come upon, but the street life of the poorer districts still leaves them as happy a working arrangement with poverty as any city has put together. Fifty years of change and catastrophe have somehow failed to produce the "unrelieved squalor" Kafū feared.

In 1913 and 1914 Kafū published a series of articles on the art and drama of the Edo Period, most of them in *Mita Literature*. Together with a 1918 article on the light poetry of the same period, they were collected in 1920 under the title *The Arts of Edo (Edo Geijutsuron)*. Several were originally written in the vernacular, but for the collection all were redone in the Edo literary style. Kafū's diary contains this entry for November 9, 1919: "The man from the Shunyōdō Publishing Company came around and kept pestering me for a new manuscript. Since my removal to Tsukiji, I have had little to do with writing; but fortunately I remembered some old articles on the Ukiyoe, and putting them in order, I offered them to him." (xix, 83.)

In large part the Ukiyoe essays are but a dry recounting of facts, compendious in nature, and we have it on eminent authority that as sources of information they are of no great value. True, they offer a convenient summary of a matter the Japanese tend to overlook, the pioneering investigations of such foreign connoisseurs as Ernest Fenollosa and Edmond de Goncourt; but their chief interest for the nonspecialist is in the occasional outbursts of lyricism, attempts to evoke the mood of Ukiyoe as a manifestation of the Edo spirit, and in the remarkably successful description of specific prints. To write an un-illustrated book about art and not have the reader constantly hanker-ing after illustrations is something of a tour de force.

Despite the dry manner, it is also a personal book, as a few passages from the first essay, "An Appreciation of Ukiyoe," should show:

"Admiration for Ukiyoe does not stop with me, as it seems to with foreigners, at Ukiyoe as art. It induces in me feelings almost religious. Ukiyoe was the special art form of the oppressed Edo plebeian, cre-ated in the face of constant harassment. The Kano line, or the Acade-my of the eighteenth century, which had the protection of the gov-ernment, failed to pass on to us the true artistic glories of its day. That task was performed instead by the despised artist of the town, virtually in shackles, even threatened with banishment. Is not Uki-yoe the triumphal song of the common man who refused to bow down? ...

"The painter's spirit shows itself in the strong, affirmative colors of an oil painting. If in the sleepy colors of the Ukiyoe wood-block print a similar manifestation is to be found, then the spirit must be one sagging under the burdens of an authoritarian age. It is impossible for me to forget these somehow sad and forlorn colors—their expres-sion of the fear, the sorrow, the weariness of a dark day, is like the low, muffled sound of a courtesan weeping. In my dealings with con-temporary society, I am sometimes outraged at the high-handed ways of the powerful, and I turn back to this art, to its forlorn, wavering colors. The darkness of the past comes back in the sad melody hidden there, to show me the arbitrary spirit that belongs to the Orient; and I know the profound futility of talking about righteousness. Greek art came from a land that had Apollo for its god, and the Ukiyoe came out of a rented shack in a dark alley, the work of a townsman whose status generally resembled that of a worm. It is said that times have changed. Only the surface has changed. When the cold, ra-tional eye penetrates deeper, it sees that our militarist politics have not changed in the slightest these hundred years. It cannot be by acci-dent that the sad colors of Ukiyoe seem very near as they whisper to me across the gulf of time. When I look at the strongly affirmative art of the West, it is as if I were looking vacantly up at some great mountain peak; but when I look at the weary, monotonous art and literature of the Edo Period, so wanting in individuality, I feel, both spiritually and physically, an almost numbing sense of repose. The feeling has no relation to anything so rigorously scholarly as to be called 'my studies in the Ukiyoe.' " (xi, 187–89.)

"When some inferior translated play is put on in our capital city and the cliques announce the birth of a new drama, when odious painters are vying for empty fame at the official art exhibit, and the spiteful and envious views of the vulgar roar forth—at such times, in the soft autumn rain, in my lonely house on the edge of town, as the voices of insects fade away with the autumn, I quietly take out an Ukiyoe print and sit alone looking at it, and Shunshō and Sharaku and Toyokuni bring the theater of high Edo before me, and Utamaro and Eishi lure me into the delights of the Nightless City, and Hokusai and Hiroshige give me tranquil views of Edo." (xi, 191.)

"How I love the Ukiyoe! The print of the courtesan who has sold herself to the cruel life for ten years so that she may help her parents—it makes me want to weep. The figure of the geisha at the bamboo-latticed window, looking absently at a flowing stream, fills me with delight. The night view of the river with only a noodle vendor left behind intoxicates me. The cuckoo calling out to the moon of a rainy night, leaves falling in a sudden autumn shower, the sound of a temple bell carried away on a wind of falling petals, snow on a mountain path at nightfall—everything in this dreamlike world, transitory, lonely, productive of sighs, is near me, and takes me back to the past." (xi, 195.)

Clearly, nostalgia for the cozy, self-contained world of Edo contributes quite as much to Kafū's love of Ukiyoe as artistic considerations do. Even inferior latter-day artists could work a powerful spell: "These illustrations are an endless fascination to me, not only because of the lovers themselves, but because of the clean, spruce, little houses that are the backgrounds, so in harmony with the human figures— the latticed doors, the little gardens, the delicately papered windows, the low screens, the long, low braziers, the stairways with closets under them, even the hearths. It is all very poor, all very clean ·and happy." (xi, 322.) This passage, from "The Ukiyoe in Decay" (*Suitaiki no Ukiyoe*), has to do with Kuninao, a rather minor practitioner of the art when the "decay" was well advanced.

Curiously, no mention is made of the erotic print that flourished beside staider forms. Kafū was something of an expert on this disreputable little genre, and was the owner of an extensive collection of erotica. It has been suggested that the eccentricities of his old age may have been brought on partly by the loss of the collection in the 1945 bombings.

Even when it is not the immediate subject, the Ukiyoe is seldom far in the background. Thus the only essay on literature in the collection is a discussion of *kyōka,* the light verse that frequently accompanied Ukiyoe prints and had its best days in eighteenth-century Edo. Kafū's admiration for its principal exponent, Shokusanjin, has already been noted. He particularly admired the alertness of the *kyōka* poet to the humbler signs of seasonal change, dried fish and drying sandals and the like. In the end his anthem to *kyōka* comes to seem a little shrill and exaggerated: "I have always thought the *Tales of Ise* [*Ise Monogatari*] to be the essential heart of Japanese literature, and I have thought the poetry of Bashō and Shokusanjin to be the purest of Edo literature." (xi, 344-45.) Or perhaps the praise is not so exaggerated after all. It is not clear whether the expression "Edo literature" refers to the literature of the Edo Period, or, more narrowly, to literature produced in the city of Edo.

Again in the final essay of the collection, "The Special Characteristics of the Edo Theater" (*Edo Engeki no Tokuchō*), the Ukiyoe keeps coming up: "As I examine the sources of my admiration for the mixed form known as the Kabuki, I note that its tendencies are very much like those of the Ukiyoe. The Ukiyoe arose from the desire to give pleasurable representation to the outward form of plebeian Edo life, but it departed from simple representation and presently become a special kind of decorative art. The Edo theater, too, is a realistic art seeking to represent the emotions of plain, vulgar people, but sometimes it takes on unbelievably strange forms.... The characteristics of both are, down to the very core, the characteristics of the time and race from which they sprang, and neither shows the slightest influence of foreign thought or the slightest attempt at imitation. Hence my fascination and admiration. Nor would I limit myself to Edo prints and paintings. In every branch of the arts—music, painting, sculpture—down to pleasures and the most ordinary, everyday attitudes, the period of isolation known as Edo saw its tendencies through to their own conclusions, free from outside interference, in a fashion that I would imagine to be without parallel in any foreign culture." (XI, 351–52.)

The essay concludes with a snarl at theater reformers, who are warned to keep their dirty hands off the Kabuki. The conclusion proved embarrassing, however, since Mori Ogai, Kafū's revered master and benefactor, was among those who advocated abandoning the Kabuki; and so a postscript had to be added: "I am filled with consternation to see that the master's views are in direct opposition to mine. I have said that there is something to be admired in the old theater as long as it is left unreformed. And why have I said so? When I see performances at the Kabuki Theater and the Imperial Theater, particularly of Gidayū pieces, I see the new realism quite destroying the true Kabuki mood; and by contrast the old-style actors still holding out at the Miyatoza manage to carry through every motion and gesture, never permitting one's attention to flag. So I think that if the old theater could be cut off from the new age and presented in the old manner, it could be ranged beside Nō comic interludes as something by no means valueless.... The arts and entertainments of the Edo Period, products of an authoritarian day, communicate to us (or at least to me), in our own authoritarian day, sometimes a biting irony, sometimes a warm affection, sometimes a sense of taking refuge in a world apart, a world bathed in spring radiance." (XI, 358.)

In April 1913, slightly earlier than the first installment of *Tidings from Okubo,* Kafū published a collection of translations from French poetry under the title *Coral Anthology (Sangoshū).* His principal work as a translator, the collection contains ten poems by de Régnier, seven each by Verlaine and Baudelaire, and one to three each by twelve other poets, some of whom, thanks to Kafū, are probably better remembered today in Japan than in their own land. The poems had been published separately in *Mita Literature* and other magazines from as early as 1909. The original collection also contained translations from and studies of such prose writers as Maupassant, Loti, and Prévost. These last have since been separated from the poems and assembled with other essays of a similar nature under the title *Studies of the Arts of the West (Taisei Bungei Ronshū).*

The most interesting essay, originally published in *Mita Literature,* is entitled "French Naturalism and the Reaction Against It" (*Furan-*

su no Shizenshugi to sono Handō), and may be read as a blast at the Japanese naturalists. It is remarkable for the sour view it takes of Zola, who, in contrast to Maupassant, is treated as a narrow sort of naturalist. The school of Zola, Kafū argues, which concentrated not on the whole of reality but on its meaner aspects, carried the seeds of its own destruction, and presently a return to "true" naturalism came in lands outside France, particularly in the Scandinavian countries. In other words: narrow Japanese naturalism is up a blind alley, and the future lies instead with the full naturalism of Nagai Kafū.

The *Coral Anthology* is much admired in Japan. Since it is a dangerous business to criticize translation from one foreign language to another, specimens of praise had best be recorded here without comment. Yoshida Seiichi, author of the most detailed single study of Kafū, has called the collection one of the two most important Japanese anthologies of translated poetry, the other being by Ueda Bin, one of Kafū's sponsors at Keiō. The novelist Uno Kōji, concluding that the collection is about seven-tenths Kafū and only three-tenths French, once placed it beside *The River Sumida* at the head of Kafū's masterpieces. When, in 1956, the magazine *Bungei* asked a number of writers and critics to list their favorites among Kafū's works, eight of them included the *Coral Anthology*. One important critic called it the only really good thing Kafū ever did, and a well-known poet said it was "the greatest achievement in the translation of poetry into Japanese." It is safe to conclude that the translations are striking, if perhaps more Kafū than France. Japanese symbolist poetry seems to have been greatly in debt to them, although it is usually Ueda Bin who is given credit for bringing symbolism to Japan.

The year 1915, when Kafū's second wife walked out on him and he was about to walk out on Keiō, was a gloomy one for another reason. He published a single piece of fiction during the year, the long story "Summer Dress" (*Natsusugata*), which was his first piece of fiction in a contemporary setting since *Night Tales from Shimbashi*. It was promptly found harmful to the public morals, and banned. Kafū had originally intended it for publication in *Mita Literature,* but, as he wrote later (in *Kakademo no Ki,* or *A Chronicle I Might Better Not Have Written,* 1918), decided himself that it might be a little risky. Then, at the urging of a friendly publisher, the Momiyama Shoten, he decided to have a try at publishing it in book form.

The authorities pounced and the publisher was severely reprimanded. "Summer Dress" finally came out, slightly revised, in March 1947.

The heroine is Kafū's first good slattern, a species to occupy his attention increasingly in his middle years. Although his slatterns frequently call themselves geisha, they are of a lower order than the ladies praised elsewhere as preservers of the arts, and the "summer dress" of the title is more a matter of undress. Perhaps the authorities who found the story dangerous were disturbed at having a too common sort of woman brought into the glare of publicity: the bawdy woman in whose habitat, the new "quarters" of the Tokyo hills, bawdiness was not overlaid with the ceremonial trappings and artistic pretensions of the old downtown quarters. The story has much to recommend it as a piece of well-researched realism, but the authorities were right: it is a touch salacious. The immaculate style is strangely at odds with the very maculate contents, especially in passages in which Kafū seems to be indulging his fondness for playing the voyeur.

The plot is simple. A sundries merchant named Keizō, approaching middle age, sets up a cheap "geisha" as his mistress, in rented lodgings. The setting is Kagurazaka, one of the new quarters in the Tokyo hills. He enjoys her and the quarter for a season, and then learns that when she abandoned her profession, she did not abandon the whole of her clientele. A man with a quick head for profits and losses, he disowns her, and later, when she has found a new "patron," goes off to see her again, and so has at the expense of the new patron what certain of her old customers formerly had at his expense. It is a story of easy carnal accommodations, quite unencumbered by notions of honor and romantic love, and it is also a story of the messy new city, which is generally contrasted unfavorably with the old. Yet Kafū's attitude toward the new is by no means consistent. In no other story is his fondness for the messy and unwashed more in evidence.

Here is O-chiyo (also, variously, Chiyo and Chiyoka), the bawdy geisha: "There was not in O-chiyo the slightest trace of the fastidious Edo geisha, whose teachers were professionals of venerable lineage. It did not bother O-chiyo in the least to wear a nightgown until the dirt at the neck was polished and shiny. Her hair was untidy, put up only once in three or four days after much badgering by the keeper of the house. When she was busy, she would go for days without a bath, taking her sweaty body with her from this teahouse and that house of assignation, only pausing to add a new coating to her flaky paint if she was called to entertain at some party. The more sensitive of her colleagues found her habits trying, and more than once told her so: 'Chiyo, you have to take better care of yourself. Old customers don't matter, but how is a new one to know you aren't sick?' Then, seeing that their advice did no good at all, they would begin grumbling behind her back. You couldn't find a dirtier girl than Chiyoka, they would say. If they were men, Chiyoka would be one girl they would not buy.

"But times were changing, and the fastidiousness of the child of Edo, jumping into his morning bath and emerging like a boiled octopus, was disappearing among customers, too.... Keizō found in O-chiyo a freedom and a certain fleshliness quite unlike the traditional geisha, and he was strangely aroused, as when, in a movie, he saw some naked Occidental model. What to the old geisha, with her insistence on neatness and her aplomb, would have been terrible shortcomings, therefore, were precisely the characteristics that made Chiyo a woman not easy for Keizō to give up.... Sometimes he would be tying his obi, almost ready to go home, and the naked O-chiyo, all in disarray among the bedding, would say that she was very lonely, and add, with a touch of jealousy at his wife, that she was only a mistress, after all. Quite losing control of himself, Keizō would fall into her arms." (IX, 11–13.)

It is a very warm summer, made more unpleasant still by a cholera epidemic; but Keizō does not mind. "The shop clerks would say that it was ninety yesterday, or that it was already eighty-three this morning. For Keizō, however, this year was an exception. The violent heat was more precious, more enjoyable, than the cool weather of spring and fall. He no longer saw O-chiyo done up in kimono and obi. She had even discarded her singlet, and lay sprawled out in a wraparound skirt that reached from her waist to her knees....

"The side streets of Kagurazaka all ran up the hill, and from the second floor of O-chiyo's quarters the geisha houses and places of assignation fell away in steps, like piled-up boxes, each with its back toward the rise. One did not notice during other seasons, but in the summer every aperture that could be made to admit air, every window and back door, was open, and in the evening, when the lights were on, there was more to be seen than merely the shadow of a high chignon on a paper door. Half-naked geisha making themselves up, roistering customers—they all were perfectly visible through hedges and fences and shrubbery.

"One hot night when there was not a breath of air, Keizō lay with O-chiyo under the mosquito net, the light out, and the doors along the veranda, and of course the back door, open. Suddenly the voices in the Ikuyo, a house of assignation next door, came up as clearly as if they were in the same room....

"Keizō thought he would have a look. He was curious to know what sort of geisha and customer they might be. As he leaned out of the window, the wooden blind of the house next door was right before his nose. The light was on, showing two holes in the shutter about the size of a finger. He pressed an eye to one as if to the window of a peep show, and brought a hand to his mouth to smother a startled cry....

"O-chiyo pressed her eye to the other hole.

"The conversation had died away, and it was as if the room were abandoned. As O-chiyo watched, her breathing became heavy....

"Presently—it was impossible to know which of the two had reached out first—their hands had met in the darkness, and a moment later they were in an almost lunatic embrace.

"And so, thanks to the woman and the neighborhood, Keizō was in a state of constant excitement such as he had never known before....

"One day he came earlier, in the worst heat of the day. Although he had been in the habit of calling daily, it had always been in the evening, never in broad daylight. He climbed Kagurazaka and turned up the familiar alley. It was a world of nocturnal life, and it lay as if deserted under the blazing sun, quiet save for the distant flute of a pipe-cleaning man.* The total absence of pedestrians was an aspect so new to Keizō that he felt as if he were turning up the alley for the very first time. Through lace curtains and reed blinds at open windows and back doors, the figures of the geisha in the dusky houses, struck down by the heat, their hair so unkempt that they might have

_____
* Persons of this now neglected calling specialized in cleaning nicotine from pipe stems.

been hospital patients, the skirts and breasts of their cotton kimonos pulled open, some of them without sashes to hold their kimonos together—to Keizō, strolling past and looking in upon them, the figures sprawled about in messy disarray were far more exciting than the same figures in the evening, carefully made up and properly bound in obis. Suddenly Keizō wondered about O-chiyo. She could get herself into the most appalling contortions when she was asleep. What would she be like having a nap in the heat of the day? The thought so excited him that it was all he could do to keep from breaking into a run." (IX, 14–19.)

But soon he discovers that O-chiyo is spending her afternoons in more than slumber, and so the story proceeds to its sly conclusion. Keizō stays away from Kagurazaka for three months. When he returns, he finds his erstwhile quarters closed, and, nostalgic, he sets out in search of the woman. This visit in chilly autumn to a place enjoyed on open summer nights seems very much in keeping with Kafū's own mood, for he was about to withdraw from the warm, bright center of the literary world; but the story is sensuous as few of his works are, and captures as well as anything he wrote the eroticism of summer nights in the great city. Hence the misgivings of the authorities.

It is perhaps worth adding that the principal piece of out-and-out pornography that can be definitely attributed to Kafū seems to have been written at about this time, or perhaps a little later. It is called "What I Found Under the Papering in the Little Room" (*Yojōhan no Shitabari*). An unauthorized edition after the Second World War almost landed him in jail, but the police, far more charitable than they had been forty years before, let him lie his way out. "What I Found" is a little tale of sexual prowess and endurance, told, with fine irony, in the elegant literary style of Edo.

In January 1916, Kafū moved from Tsukiji to Yanagibashi, another parish of the demimonde. It will be remembered that he had left the family house in Okubo after Yaeji's departure. In March, however, he was back in Okubo, his chronic gastric troubles somewhat worse. The same year he built a cottage in the garden of the Okubo house to which he gave the name Danchōtei, "Dyspepsia House." Danchōtei was thereafter to be one of his favorite noms de plume. The diary that he kept for more than forty years down to his death was published in part during his lifetime as *Danchōtei Nichijō*, "Dyspepsia House Days." The sobriquet also figures in a group of essays published individually between 1916 and 1918, and collected in 1918 under the title *Danchōtei Zakkō*, or *Miscellaneous Manuscripts from Dyspepsia House*.

The Dyspepsia House collection includes the "Cowpeas" essay already quoted, in which Kafū describes his relations with Yaeji. There is also a description of the house he occupied in Tsukiji. It was up a narrow alley not far from the Shintomiza, cathedral of the early Meiji Kabuki, and just around the corner from Kiyomoto Umekichi, one of the more famous classical musicians of the day. The house itself, two rooms upstairs and three rooms down, had been until recently a place of assignation. "There are houses of assignation and establishments of kept women all up and down the alley. As the third-quarter moon hangs over the bamboo poles on the laundry platforms, the alluring voices of geisha seeing drunken customers home startle dogs asleep in the gutters, and in the daytime the high, nasal voices of kept ladies sporting with their patrons come across the rooftops like the mewing of cats. Song to the accompaniment of finger-plucked samisen never ceases in the house next door, and every night the strolling Shinnai singers sweep down the street like showers." (xi, 15.)

The general tone of the collection is melancholy and autumnal. Besides telling the sad tale of Yaeji and how in his loneliness he started going off to Tsukiji for samisen lessons, Kafū hints that his writing career may be approaching an end. "Sometimes I am asked how long I mean to go on writing novels. I am told that it is remarkable, my persistence and my success in not running out of material. I do not know whether such remarks are meant as flattery or ridicule. A novel, whether it is lofty and obscure or simple and ordinary, must be a detailed description of the world and human emotions. . . . When, therefore, a writer tires of the world and seeks only the company of blue skies and green mountains, his work as a novelist ceases, whether he has talent or not. The life of the novel is plain, everyday life. The novel lives from contact with human beings, in the goings-on of the world. The West has placed emphasis upon the novel, and it is not difficult to see why the East has not." (xi, 69.)

Kafū makes himself sound like a truly burnt-out case: "No time is dearer to me than the midday hours when I lock the gate and go alone into the garden to rake leaves and fallen flowers. It has long been held that there is nothing like drink for driving away sorrows, but there are times when drink does not intoxicate, and one always has to face the gloom of sobering up. It is said, too, that poetry has the effect of alcohol in dispelling gloom; but when the pen becomes a way for making one's way in the world, the vulgar comes to predominate, and one has only a sense of shame at having fallen so low. With no particular anger and no particular sorrow, then, I have in the course of time turned my back on the world. I see nothing, hear nothing, and ask nothing. In boundless tedium, I vacantly pass the months and years raking the petals that have blown in from the neighbor's garden and the leaves that have fallen in mine....

"Among the changing scenes of the year, the fresh greenery of early summer and the yellow leaves of late autumn are the ones to choose. The evening light of both seasons is extremely beautiful. In the one the light coming through the thick leaves colors them like a printed Yūzen kimono; in the other it shines through yellow leaves like a brocade. The time of the new greenery, like the time of the cherry blossoms, is brief and fleeting. The soft green does not last, and when the light becomes stronger in the days after the early-summer rains have cleared, the leaves blacken and begin to gather the dust of midsummer. When at length there is a sharp chill in the morning and evening air, the leaves at the ends of the branches, rustling in the wind, begin to turn yellow around the edges. As the yellow advances on the shorter, shaded branches, the first leaves, their color by now quite changed, fall shimmering and dancing to the ground. For reasons I can scarcely describe, I find myself thinking deep thoughts, and morning by morning and evening by evening the melancholy grows deeper, and looking up at the fleeting changes, I am taken with emotions more intense than any brought on by cherry blossoms or new spring greenery." (xi, 85, 87.)

Most of the Dyspepsia House essays were originally printed in the monthly magazine *Bummei* (*Civilization*), which was founded in April 1916, just after Kafū's resignation from Keiō, and ceased publication the end of the following year. With the financial backing of the Momiyama Shoten, it was edited by Kafū and his boyhood friend Inoue Seiichi or Aa. The demise of the magazine was the occasion for

a spat between Kafū and Momiyama Teigo, whom he accused of
penuriousness. Inoue, it has already been pointed out, was perhaps the
nearest approximation to a friend Kafū ever had. He was a man, Kafū
was to say later in his diary, whose only desire was for drink. Offered
an important position on a daily newspaper, he chose instead a minor
post that left him more time to drink. Presently, in 1923, it killed
him. No doubt he appealed to Kafū as a person, for they had frequented the Yoshiwara together since adolescence; but his wasted
career, too, had its charms. Kafū did not approve of success in anyone
except himself, and his favorite hero, insofar as anyone can be called
a hero in his woman-centered novels, seems designed to prove that
failures and outcasts are nicer and more interesting people than the
famous and powerful of the world. Kafū's agreement to participate
in the *Bummei* project was an act of unusual selflessness for him. He
apparently hoped that it might do something for Inoue.

In the first issue of *Bummei,* Kafū announced that he had abandoned "the literature of affirmation" for "the literature of *shumi,*"
which we may take to be the literature of hedonism or dilettantism.
The announcement brought little change in his writing. It is to be
understood, rather, as a declaration that he was voluntarily leaving
the center of the literary stage, and that it was vacant for whoever
wanted it, notably the Shirakaba "idealists" whose writing so brimmed
with affirmation.

As he approached forty, he let it be known, too, that he sensed the approach of the end. "Flower Vase" (*Hanaike*), a rather badly constructed story written late in 1915 and published in *Mita Literature* early
the following year, is significant chiefly for its comments upon the
capriciousness of the artistic impulse. The two central figures, whose
histories are recorded in a manner suggesting less a short story than
a sketch for a novel, are friends approaching middle age, both married
to ex-geisha, one happily, the other unhappily. The happy one is a
recluse, a man who has resigned a post in a respectable company in
disgust at its hypocrisy. The unhappy one is a painter who has wandered from style to style, and who, when the story opens, thinks all of
his work embarrassingly bad. The flower vase of the title is an unim-
portant piece now gone, lost to a burglar, that has had sentimental
associations for the happily married pair. One morning, after a violent
quarrel with his headstrong wife and after her departure from the

house, the painter sits down to paint the vase, which he has never
seen, as he has heard his friend describe it; and at the end of the story
the picture, his one masterpiece, is ready for presentation to his friend.
Here is the artist's description of how he came to paint it:

"I know I will seem to be praising myself too highly, but I have
never before painted a picture that has satisfied me as this one does.
I dislike all the fashionable theories about art as much as you do. Art
is really a crippled, misshapen affair. I've managed this time to put
together a picture that satisfies me, and it's been entirely because of
family unpleasantness. I have a wife, and I find it impossible to be
fond of her. Sometimes I wonder where to turn. I can't forget my
troubles by playing with geisha and whores as I did in my younger
days, and these last three or four years I've somehow felt all the
warmth go out of life. And then one day I heard the story of that vase,
and I felt it all come back again. I thought I might be able to do
something about my loneliness by painting a picture of it. I don't
want to be boasting—but look at it. Look at the carmine and the
aquamarine. I wouldn't have thought myself up to producing colors
that please me as much as they do. I've worked and slaved, but I've
never done this before, come up with colors that express my feelings
as perfectly as these. And I had no trouble at all. It was as if I had
someone right here beside me, telling me how to put the paints together. Sometimes in the middle of the night the feeling was so strong
that it was almost frightening. Strange business, painting a picture."
(VIII, 166–67.)

. From April 1916 through 1917 and most of 1918, Kafū kept a chronicle of public and private events, which he called "Things Seen and
Heard Month by Month" (*Maigetsu Kembunki*), and which he
serialized in *Bummei* and its successor, *Kagetsu*. *Kagetsu* (*Flower and
Moon*) was a literary magazine that appeared during 1918, a venture
moved primarily by Inoue Seiichi after Momiyama withdrew his
support from *Bummei*. The "things seen and heard" have to do
largely with the theater, the literary world, and the demimonde, but
other events are recorded as well. Thus we are informed, in solemn,
old-fashioned cadences, that on August 31, 1916, there was a sparrow
war in a large tree by the Shinanomachi Barracks; that on July 28
of that year bathers on the beaches of Chiba Prefecture were cautioned
against swimming in loin cloths, lest they offend the sensibilities of

foreigners; that on October 17 a Keiō baseball team defeated a visiting foreign team, presumably American; and that late in February the following year, various animals and birds were already beginning to feel the spring. We are also informed, as if he were not the author, of events having to do with Nagai Kafū: of the building and naming of Dyspepsia House, for instance, and of various attacks of dyspepsia suffered within it.

The life such entries suggest is not one of complete seclusion, for there are dinners with other contributors to *Bummei,* and occasional meetings with people who are by no means failures and outcasts, such as the Kabuki actor Sadanji. Relations with the literary world seem uneasy, however. Charges of libel or something very near it are leveled at a large newspaper and an important magazine, and there is a tiff with two important playwrights, one of them a pupil of Kafū's at Keiō, over the publication, unauthorized, says Kafū, of an essay on the Edo drama. "Things Seen and Heard" also tells of a move to Asakusa, in September 1916, which is recorded in most chronologies of Kafū's life. No one seems to know when he moved back to Okubo, however, where the first entries in his diary find him early in 1917.

Chapter five Stragglers

Chronic dyspepsia, a growing contentiousness, a sense of no longer
being in the center of things, and the chilling approach of forty all
combined to make Kafū feel that the good years were over. Before
the gloomiest years came upon him, however, he had another brief
burst of activity. He had to take care of the stragglers, so to speak, the
last in his line of geisha; and when, after years of relative inactivity,
he was to settle down once more to the writing of fiction, a rather
different sort of woman was to occupy him, a sort that had little to
do with the Edo past.

From August 1916 until October 1917, he serialized a full-length
novel, *Rivalry* (*Udekurabe*) in *Bummei*. Between January and December 1918, *Dwarf Bamboo* (*Okamezasa*) came out in *Chūō Kōron*
and *Kagetsu*. Both works have had complicated textual histories.
Kagetsu ceased publication while *Dwarf Bamboo* was still being
serialized. As for *Rivalry,* the version published in *Bummei* was
thoroughly revised during 1917. Numerous deletions were made, and
three chapters were added. This second version was published pri-
vately late in 1917, and early the following year a commercial edition
appeared, a sadly expurgated version of the private or "secret" edition.
A somewhat bolder edition came out in 1949. Although it included
passages thought too strong in 1918, it still left out some of the bolder
ones, and it also left out a few passages that had been thought safe
enough in 1918. The publisher apparently feared that the occupying
powers might be ruffled by certain brief but uncomplimentary references to them. Finally in 1956 the complete 1917 text appeared in a
commercial edition.

The chief difference between the 1949 and 1956 editions is that the latter includes two long and racy passages which, in effect, display the advantages and disadvantages of a career as a geisha. In one of them a tired and unwilling geisha has forced upon her the attentions of a man of fearful sexual prowess. "When, at eleven o'clock, she finally escaped from his embrace, she was breathing great gasps, she could scarcely speak, and she had no will to get up. Entirely satisfied with this state of affairs, Yoshioka sped off into the darkness."* In the other a robust and energetic geisha is seen going about the carnal part of her business. It ends with an outrageous and altogether improper case of mistaken identity.

The two novels are frequently taken as a pair, contrasting studies of the demimonde, which, however, figures less importantly in *Dwarf Bamboo* than in *Rivalry*. Almost the whole of *Rivalry* takes place in the elegant "downtown" Shimbashi geisha quarter, for whose more conservative denizens Kafū does not conceal his admiration. *Dwarf Bamboo,* by contrast, is about a very unlovable bourgeois family in the more modern and fashionable "uptown" part of the city, and about the sleezy uptown geisha districts.

Komayo, the heroine of *Rivalry,* is a beautiful but—as people in her profession go—aging Shimbashi geisha. She loses a pair of contests to more crafty and unscrupulous rivals: the man who seems her likeliest source of financial support (the sexual virtuoso in the first long passage missing from the 1949 edition) is lured away by the fleshly accomplishments of another geisha (the robust one of the second such passage), and the actor with whom she is in love abandons her for a wealthy widow. In the end, however, she has her stroke of luck. The proprietress of her house dies suddenly, and the widower, unable to manage by himself, suggests that Komayo take over. As the action progresses, the seasons of the city pass in review, in the manner of *Tidings from Okubo,* from midsummer through autumn and on into the winter.

A great deal about the book recalls premodern Japanese fiction. The highly contrived plot, relying heavily on coincidence, could have been lifted bodily from a nineteenth-century erotic novel, perhaps by Tamenaga Shunsui, and the loving attention to the manners and appurtenances of the Shimbashi district takes one back to the *sharebon*

---

* *Gendai Nihon Bungaku Zenshū* (Tokyo: Chikuma Shobō, 1956), Vol. XVI, 209.

or "sophisticated books" of the eighteenth century. If too much attention is given to physical properties, too little goes to characterization—and so we seem to be back among those collections of caricatures, the *katagimono,* so popular in the seventeenth and eighteenth centuries.

The varieties of geisha and the varieties of hangers-on are summoned up, briefly surveyed, and dismissed, most of them to play little part in the main narrative. Among them are a scribbler of the new school, spokesman for the literary world from which Kafū was in process of withdrawing; a more conservative and therefore more likable writer who lives in a moldering house at the edge of town; a pushing sort of geishahouse keeper who has no respect for tradition; a more conservative and therefore more likable person in the same profession (he is the keeper of Komayo's house); his worthless son, a purveyor of pornography; a businessman who patronizes geisha for the prestige they bring (the man of prowess again); and other characters, too, all either callous or conservative, never both simultaneously.

Kafū's impatience with some of the male characters is such that they are not even good caricatures. Where geisha are concerned, matters are a little better. Some are likable enough if a trifle watery, among them being the heroine, Komayo, and the mistress of her house, an easygoing old person who refuses to become one of the powers of the quarter. Others are amusing and interesting—a giddy modern geisha, for instance, whose jargon suggests a postwar college boy; and, once again, the voluptuary whose practices are so fully described in the "secret" edition. Yet not even when the last lady is caught disporting wantonly in a communal bath does the reader feel that she has been revealed in the round. She remains a caricature from a *katagimono.*

Kafū's antique models would be acceptable, perhaps, if *Rivalry* did not occupy an uneasy middle ground. It is on the one hand nostalgic, lyrical, and reminiscent, and on the other a modern social novel, purporting to show how life for the geisha really is. And it is not all pleasure. Most of Komayo's customers — conservative writers approaching middle age seem to be the major exception—make life difficult for her. Sometimes, indeed, they leave her quite at the end of her resources. Here is her state of mind at the end of the long expurgated passage in which she figures so prominently: "She sighed, and chagrin and resentment came back with doubled intensity at the thought of the men who had imposed themselves on her in the course of the evening. She was battered to the very core. She wanted only to die."*

It might just be possible to accept the geisha and her quarter as simultaneously an escape from crass reality and the embodiment of crass reality. But the symbol is such a complex one that it needs to be more richly endowed with the illusion of life than it is here. One is not prepared to accept the unsupported word of the author in such complicated matters. Demonstration is required, not simple declaration; and it is very irksome to have the author himself on the scene, one of the pleasant caricatures, to throw darts at the unpleasant ones.

Yet, like most of Kafū's unsuccessful novels, *Rivalry* has some beautiful moments. The very fact that it does not really succeed as a novel— that it is not a unified exposition of conflicts and changes in the lives of believable characters—makes it an easy novel to quote from. As might be expected from the example of, say, *Sneers,* the good moments are quiet, lyrical ones when we see the life of the quarter and of the city accommodating themselves to the seasons.

"The fair in preparation for the midsummer festival was over, a fair that had kept the Ginza swarming with people all through the night. Up and down the little alleys the late evening twilight echoed with the calls of rickshawmen who had come for geisha. By the newspaper office on the main street there was a jangling of bells as boys set out to hawk extras. Here and there, before a latticed door, a geisha hurried away in her rickshaw, sent off by a clicking of flintstones; and overhead the evening star and the new moon cooled the noisy summer night." (IX, 77.)

"Toward the end of August the drought that had threatened a water shortage was ended by a sudden, pounding shower. It became a steady rain, which lasted through the night and well on into the next day, and when it cleared, the weather had changed, and there was autumn in the sky and on the leaves of the willow trees. There was autumn, too, deep in the night, in the bells of the rickshaws and the clacking of wooden pattens. The singing of crickets in the trash baskets was ever more insistent." (IX, 93.)

"As she came down, she passed old Gozan on his way up to water

* *Ibid.*

his morning glories. A watering can in his hand, he went straight to the roof. The samisens on which geisha had been practicing until but a few moments before had suddenly stopped. Evening in the pleasure quarter: it appeared to be bath time in all the houses, and the breeze, heavy with the smell of coal, turned the drying summer kimonos inside out. The busy hour for telephones had begun. Gozan looked up at the sky, one beautiful expanse of feather clouds. He forgot to count his morning-glory buds, and stood instead gazing at the ravens as they made their way home to the groves of the Beach Palace." (IX, 125–26.)

"It had become too chilly for an unlined kimono. The day had passed when the high fragrance of the first autumn mushrooms on the tables of the Kagetsu commanded respect, and now they were plentiful enough even in the bowls of the Matsumoto. The chrysanthemums that had brought people to Hibiya Park had vanished; the fallen leaves, mixed with dust and gravel, raced around with the students playing ball in the broad, empty sandlots. The Diet having opened, the teahouses had among the faces of their regular customers countrified faces and bristly, wizened faces. The companies in Marunouchi were all having their general meetings, and so, with parties of important executives night after night, rumors increased of impatient apprentice geisha who suddenly had businesses of their own. Although the yellowing willow leaves along the Ginza had not yet completely fallen, the shop decorations had changed, and all through the area red banners and green banners were more plentiful day by day. The blare of the brass band would make the passerby look back, and hurry his pace. The call of the boy hawking extras—from tomorrow the papers would be filled with the tribulations of *sumō* wrestlers. Geisha were beginning to plan for the New Year. Even in front of customers they would take memorandum books from their obis and, licking at the tips of old pencils that had never been sharpened, note down engagements for the New Year." (IX, 160.)

Such passages are in a deliberately antique style, marked by sudden transitions, and long, highly decorated, maze-like sentences. Many of them, when one has pushed through to the end, prove not to be sentences at all, but nouns heavily weighted with modifiers and unaccompanied by predicates. Although the grammatical forms are for the most part colloquial, it is a style that goes back to such Meiji writers as Higuchi Ichiyō, Izumi Kyōka, and Kōda Rohan, and through them to the fiction of the Edo Period. The Edo influence is most striking, perhaps, in the twelfth chapter, set in the house of the writer Kurayama Nansō, one of the conservative and therefore likable characters. All the paraphernalia of an Edo romance are present; natural backgrounds that tend to dim the characterization, a sweet melancholy, moldering houses admirably suited for assignations, and improbabilities in the plot—for who should turn up next door but Komayo and her actor friend!*

The twelfth chapter should serve to demonstrate the essentially undramatic nature of the book. Others tend to follow a similar form: a great deal of reminiscence and biography, much of it irrelevant to the story of Komayo and her rivalries; and a brief encounter between, usually, no more than two characters, few of whom, particularly if they are men, speak with individual voices. It is not because of the characters immediately present before the reader that the novel rises to moments of great beauty, but rather because of the background, because of the past and nature.

Despite its touches of realism, the world of *Rivalry* is a prettified one, with elegant surfaces and nostalgic mists covering or blurring the worst of reality. Nowhere in the book is there a suggestion that venereal disease might be one of the hazards of Komayo's profession. In *Dwarf Bamboo,* the companion novel, we are left in no doubt. Indeed the last sentence of the book informs us, for no compelling reason, of a death from complications brought on by venereal disease.

The world of *Dwarf Bamboo* is a very different one from that of Komayo, at least as the latter is reported in *Rivalry*. It is the world of the tawdry pleasure districts scattered among the bourgeois Tokyo "uplands," of tinselly, ill-smelling houses and harsh-voiced "geisha," who are usually found in unwashed kimonos or unaired bedding, and who frequently have suspicious skin ailments. It is also the world of bourgeois pretension and hypocrisy. Kafū's lofty contempt for it all can be a bit trying; but amused contempt for the tasteless world of the uptown geisha presently gives way to a certain sympathy for the unfortunate ladies. If loss of formal unity results, so does escape from self-righteousness.

* Most of Chapter 12 will be found translated in Part II (pp. 244–52), although an encounter between Nansō and the actor has been omitted.

The story has to do with the family of one Uchiyama Kaiseki, a very successful painter, and with his underlings, notably Uzaki Kyoseki, a very unsuccessful painter who, until an opportunity for blackmail falls his way, maintains himself by doing odd jobs for the master. Kaiseki's daughters have names ending with the aristocratic "ko"—the "O" prefix of plebeian Edo will no longer do. His worthless son, Kan, is married to the illegitimate daughter of a retired provincial governor. (She it is who is done in by venereal disease, acquired from the impure ladies via her husband.) The plot sees Kan and Kyoseki, the latter more a victim than an active pleasure seeker, in and out of various cheap geisha districts. In the end Kan is exiled to America, and Kyoseki, fortunate enough to catch the ex-governor's wife emerging from a house of assignation with a young student, uses the proceeds of the resulting blackmail to set up a house of his own, and so avoid the perils of free-lancing. The risks include police raids, one of which lands both Kan and Kyoseki briefly in jail.

If the hidden life of the bourgeois hills is of a most disreputable nature, so, Kafū tells us, is their public life. There is more than a hint that the master, Kaiseki, is a fraud, and the art dealers surrounding him are definitely frauds. Kyoseki, who is quite unable to get his pictures hung in any of the honored halls, finds one of them on sale for a fat price because his seal has been changed for Kaiseki's, perhaps by some art dealer, perhaps by the master himself. Kyoseki recognizes the painting immediately: it contains a rooster not originally meant to be there, hastily added to cover some slip of the brush. The ex-governor, Kan's father-in-law, turns out to be a real pirate. Known as a collector of antiques and thought to be incorruptible, he is asked from time to time to appraise the collections of noble houses, and uses his position to smuggle choice pieces into his own collection. Earlier he has lied to Kan and Kaiseki about the facts of his daughter's birth.

All in all, *Dwarf Bamboo* is inhabited by a race much less attractive to Kafū than the Shimbashi persons of *Rivalry*. Only one male character is not completely beneath contempt, Kyoseki himself, a ratty, ineffectual little man who has fewer opportunities than his fellows for behaving badly. Another difference is to be found in the absence of the lyrical passages that from time to time brighten *Rivalry*. Just occasionally there is a touch of something similar in *Dwarf Bamboo*, as when Kyoseki returns to a neighborhood he has once lived in and remembers how things were. More often, however, the description is merely a naturalistic catalogue, quite without the coloring that makes the review of the seasons in *Rivalry* more than simple description. In *Dwarf Bamboo,* one is seldom conscious what season it is.

Dwarf Bamboo, then, is wanting in precisely the qualities that make *Rivalry* occasionally memorable. But it is a better novel. It is stronger on plot than most Kafū novels. His plots tend to be either thumpingly ordinary or impossibly contrived, and one pushes ahead with them in the hopes that there will soon be another essay on another mood of the city. Although *Dwarf Bamboo* takes its time about getting started, it is sometimes genuinely exciting, as when Kan and poor Uzaki get picked up in that police raid.

Surprisingly, too, it has more character interest than most Kafū novels. A typical Kafū woman tends to be static. Kafū's attitude toward her may change, as it seems to change toward the unfortunate women of this novel, but the character herself seldom changes or grows before the reader's eyes. His men tend to be no more than sounding boards for Kafū's own prejudices. Kyoseki of *Dwarf Bamboo* is an exception. He is strangely alive in all his fecklessness, and he allows Kafū to demonstrate that when indignation and self-righteousness leave him, he is not without a sense of humor. Kyoseki recognizing his own painting with the master's seal on it and remembering why he painted the rooster is really quite charming, as is Kyoseki buying a newspaper for the first time in his life to see whether the story of his arrest is in print, and Kyoseki pulling himself up to attention, although he is quite alone, to read a letter from the distinguished ex-governor, Kan's father-in-law.

Here he is visiting the famous man: "The room was decorated with a two-panel screen and a monochrome landscape by Bunchō. The alcove contained a cloisonné bowl heaped with citrons, and a picture of an old man and a deer. Convinced by the venerable mounting that the artist must be someone very famous, Tanyū perhaps, Kyoseki, sitting in a deferential little bundle by the door, stretched his neck in an effort to read the seal.

"There was a low cough and the door opened. Kyoseki pulled his neck in like a small turtle. Then, almost backing into the door behind him, he kowtowed so profoundly that he was sprawled out like a spider. 'It was very good of you, sir, to send a messenger around this morning with that most remarkable gift. We wish you to accept our sincerest thanks and continued assurances of our highest esteem.'" (IX, 441–42.)

The aptness of plot and character is such as to make one feel, at the end of the book, that Kafū might be on the point of emerging as a true novelist. If the virtues of *Rivalry* are lyrical, those of *Dwarf Bamboo,* at least in its last stages, are dramatic. Yet the last chapters were written in 1920, when Kafū felt his powers to be failing, and when he stood on the edge of his least productive period. His best piece of writing during the 1920s, "Quiet Rain" (*Ame Shōshō*), can only be called a novel—it is often so called—if the term is used as imprecisely as the Japanese habitually use it. In fact "Quiet Rain" is a long essay lamenting the loss of youth and of old refinements, a subdued elegy. As a novelist, Kafū virtually gave up with the effort of finishing *Dwarf Bamboo.* One is reminded how, decades before, he produced *The Woman of the Dream* and so seemed by way of becoming Japan's first satisfactory realist, only to retreat as if in fright into the lyrical effusions of his French and American period.

Chapter six The Nineteen-Twenties

In the autumn of 1917 Kafū began keeping a diary that he was to keep until his death. It is in the nature of a long, discursive essay, an ancestor of which is to be found in such ruminations as *Tidings from Okubo*. Its value as a record of facts is questionable. Kafū is known to have gone over it from time to time, and it is not clear whether he limited himself to deletions or also made additions. It is just possible that certain antigovernment and antimilitarist sentiments, more popular when parts of the diary were published after the Second World War than when the entries were theoretically made, were added later. There is ample evidence, moreover, that, moved by spleen or self-pity, Kafū was capable of putting down an untruth now and then. Thus it seems clear that he was less concerned with truth than with persuasion when he set down his views on the disagreement with his brother.

Besides being open to a suspicion of inaccuracy, the diary is disappointing as a source of information about how Kafū worked. One does not go to it, as to the journals of Henry James, to find out how his books grew. The raw material is there sometimes, to be sure, as he wanders through the city and reads books, but the processing takes place elsewhere.

Yet it is an interesting and sometimes moving document, of considerable literary value in itself. The dominant moods are rancor and melancholy, broken by an occasional flutter of happiness, as when, on February 9, 1920, the sense of futility lifts for a time: "Indisposed and in bed, I started writing the last part of *Dwarf Bamboo*. I stopped work on it the year before last, when *Kagetsu* ceased publication, and have done nothing with it since. Then, bored and ill, I began scribbling in pencil, and found myself strangely interested. There is nothing as mysterious as creative writing. All through last year I kept trying to take up my pen, and failing, and now, in bed with a fever, I find myself writing on—a great delight." (xix, 95–96.)

Although it is in the Edo literary style, the diary has much in common with *Tidings from Okubo* (which is in an artificial style used chiefly for letters). It is for long passages a record of despondency, but it is also a record of tasteful pursuits, suggesting an Oriental hermit gone a bit European. There are French novels and Italian operas, there is much browsing in Tokugawa erotica, and there are innumerable samisen lessons and recitals of classical Japanese music. There is also a loving record of the seasons. Anyone who wishes to know what the weather was like in Tokyo on October 22, 1917, need not go long without an answer. It was clear and windy, and cold enough for a gas range to be lighted in Dyspepsia House.

On the first day of the diary a quiet rain calls for changing the Chinese poems over the door lintels, and in the days following we learn of the appearance in the Okubo garden of crickets, shrikes, bush warblers, caterpillars, and wagtails. On January 7, 1918, it is a dove: "A dove has flown in and is walking about the garden. Every day, in the coldest part of the year, a single dove comes into my garden. How long, I wonder, has this been the case? I remember how, in the winter after I came back from France, I heard my mother remark that it always snowed when that dove came into the garden. Every year, she said, there was snow on precisely the day the dove appeared. More than ten years have gone by since. The tree it roosts in is generally the same. In the days when the plot was much larger, before land was sold three years ago to Viscount Irie, it used to stay in the big elm and come down to look for food when no one was around. Since then it has hidden in the dark nettle tree by the fence that divides this land from Irie land, coming down into the garden occasionally to run about among the fallen leaves. I do not know where it is from, and whether it is the same dove as ten years ago, or perhaps another that looks the same. When the dove comes, in any event, I find myself feeling especially nostalgic for days when I was less lonely. Sometimes I slide the door open just a little and sit watching it, endlessly fascinated. Sometimes I go down into the cold garden in the evening and scatter rice and bread crumbs. It will not be tamed, however. When a human being appears it flies off with a sharp whirring of wings. It is apparently an eccentric that prefers to be away from the flock. How like me, and unlike other doves!" (xix, 15-16.)

Despite the hermitical claims for himself and the dove, Kafū was still seeing other writers, such as the Mita group and the members of the Thursday Club (the literary group mentioned on p. 62); and his friends included such successful and famous people as the actor Sadanji. His real companions, however, were malingerers like Inoue Seiichi and ladies either of or peripheral to the pleasure quarters. Some of these last seem to have been bedfellows (a Komagome geisha was for a time his "maid"), and some merely friends. His ex-wife, the Shimbashi geisha Yaeji, moves in and out of the diary, and Kafū is careful to record at precisely what date they ceased having sexual intercourse.

The diary also records his increasing isolation from his family. Late in 1918 Kafū sold the Okubo house, where he had been living alone, and moved to Tsukiji. The move was largely to spite his family, if the diary is to be trusted. The pertinent diary entry has it that he made his decision to sell when, going through the warehouse, he came upon some possessions of his father's that his mother had evidently tried to hide from him. This show of disregard for his feelings, he laments, has absolved him of his duty to watch over the family seat. He was later to regret selling the house, and despite the nearness of geisha and samisen, Tsukiji was to prove too dirty and noisy for his taste.

But Tsukiji, too, brought an occasional moment of happy awareness. Here is the entry for April 19, 1919: "I walked along Hatchō-bori Canal looking at the night stalls. There are many makers of blinds and doors and the like hereabouts, and as the night draws on, the sound of the blinds being woven in the back alleys makes you feel yet more intensely that spring is going and summer coming on. It is a mood that one does not come upon in the richer residential sections of the city. I walked along the dusky bank of the river and tried to compose a poem in the Tokugawa style, but finally had to give it up. There is nothing more difficult than trying to compose such a poem, or a Jōruri ballad." (xix, 62.)

And for May 24: "I have had a headache, perhaps because I am catching cold. In the evening I sat by the window and looked down over the lane. Sparrows were making a great din in the new greenery across the way, before the teahouses and the establishments of kept ladies and the like. The reed blinds in the windows, not yet out long enough to have gathered summer dust, give even this dark alley a feeling of freshness and newness. Somehow the contrast between the scene and my own ailing self made me feel all the sadder. In the evening I pulled myself together and worked at revising old manuscripts, for the fifth volume of my collected works." (xix, 66.)

The commoner tone, however, is one of querulous irritability. "It has become very hot. I went up on the laundry platform in search of a breeze, and had a complete view down over the alley. What a cluttered mess it is! Enough to make you feel again what you have felt all along, the lethargy and the squalor of Japanese life, wholly devoid of order. People are always ranting about the crisis in contemporary Japanese life, but when you thus inspect the state of affairs with us, you see that life is as it has always been, quite unlovely. Nothing has changed." (xix, 70–71.)

"I am able to live in the capital city and see myself safely through my declining years only with the help of the improper artistic products of Edo. Is it not something remarkable, something produced by no other people, this Edo culture of humorous and satirical poetry, of pornographic 'spring pictures,' of the samisen? If one wishes to live here in peace and well-being, one is forced to seek a modicum of consolation from the arts that went to make up Edo." (xix, 64.)

"Being ill, I have not been able to venture far afield, but today for the first time in three or four years I visited the suburbs. The manner in which the districts along the electric line are being built up is astonishing. A jumble of houses for rent and little factories, packed in quite without order—the unsightliness is even worse than in the worst parts of the city proper. It would seem that we Japanese are wholly lacking in the ability to build a city. The old pines and cedars in Ueno Park are dying at a faster rate than I had imagined." (xix, 80.)

The years of the First World War and after, down to the earthquake of 1923, were years when the whole world seemed to be rushing in upon Tokyo, and the city seemed on the verge of strangling itself. Class warfare had come to Japan, the flapper was about to come, and urbanization raced ahead. Edo was still near enough to make it possible for Chōkichi of *The River Sumida* to eschew the world of Meiji. In the world of Taishō the choice was no longer a very real one, and no number of samisen lessons lent much substance to the pretense that it was. It was this fact, perhaps, along with dyspepsia and middle age, that brought on Kafū's gloom and reduced him to near silence. Komayo of *Rivalry* was a last straggler from the tasteful, conservative demimonde of Meiji; and when Kafū presently began producing fiction of distinction again, it was in the sometimes dry, sometimes scowling, manner of *Dwarf Bamboo,* elegant remnants of Meiji being replaced by seedy representatives of late Taishō and early Shōwa. When finally, in his last years, the distasteful pre-earthquake years had mellowed sufficiently to serve as a stepping stone to Edo, his manner was once more to become reminiscent.

In 1918, the year in which the earlier part of *Dwarf Bamboo* was serialized, Kafū also published "A Chronicle I Might Better Not Have Written" (*Kakademo no Ki*), memoirs of his earlier career that have already been referred to. The same year, as if to signalize the end of his career, *The Complete Works of Nagai Kafū* (*Kafū Zenshū*) began to come out, the first of three such ostensibly complete canons to appear in his lifetime. It is to this first collection that the diary entry for May 24, 1919 (see p. 97), refers. It eventually came to six volumes, the last of them published in the summer of 1921.

The Tsukiji year, 1919, was a particularly barren one. Besides another pair of volumes in the collected works, there appeared under Kafū's name only an introduction to a miscellany by Tanizaki, and "Fireworks," the essay that has been seized upon by literary historians as evidence of the crucial importance for Kafū of the Kōtoku Shūsui incident (see pp. 45–47).

Kafū wrote a number of plays during these lean years. He had had tries at the theater in his earlier years, too, the earliest of them shortly after his return from France (it will be remembered that a play helped provide the occasion for the banning of *French Stories*). He was to write more plays later, as well as the libretto for a musical produced in Asakusa, and, after the Second World War, skits for the Asakusa burlesque theater, no more profound than such works ought to be. It might be well here to comment briefly on Kafū's dramatic writings and be done with them, for they show very clearly his shortcomings and the essentially nondramatic nature of his talent. The pieces in contemporary settings, when not downright frivolous, tend to be contentious, in the manner of *Sneers*. The historical works, on the other hand, offer opportunities for leading actors to strike impressive poses, but, as is the way with Kabuki texts, seem thin when the visual effects are cut away. All the plays are wanting in humanity. The characters speak with a single voice, too frequently querulous. If the characters in the novels, particularly the male characters, seem wanting in strong individuality, this fact is at least partly concealed by the bland, melancholy beauty of the background into which they merge. In the plays this saving element disappears, and the defect is out in the open. One sees why so much of Kafū's best writing is less fiction than lyric or essay.

In 1920 Kafū moved into a new house he had built for himself in Azabu, near the American Embassy. He had evidently had enough of life in the parts of the city where once the Edo townsman flourished. Azabu is a wealthy district. Kafū's near neighbors included foreigners, and not far away were the mansions of an imperial prince and of the heir to the Sumitomo title and fortune.

The new house was named the Henkikan, and Kafū lived there until the air raids of 1945. The name "Henkikan" might be translated "Eccentricity House," but there is more in it than that. *Henki* is an invented word, each of the two characters of which it is composed suggesting eccentric behavior; and the sound of the two in compound needs only a small diacritical mark to become *penki*, a borrowing from the Dutch that means "house paint." Hence Henkikan also means "Painted House" or "Western House"; and hence the eccentric of the Henkikan, its name tells us, has turned away from the repellent hodgepodge of modern Japan. The Henkikan no longer survives (it was a victim of the war); but pictures of it, plus a painting by Kafū himself, suggest that it must have been a rather gaunt, unfriendly, and undistinguished house, less than convincing testimony, perhaps, to statements one sometimes hears that Kafū had a unique understanding of the aesthetic principles of the West. (Although his picture of the Henkikan was not among his best, Kafū was a painter of modest talents, heir to the painting litterateurs of China and Edo.)

If not the handsomest house in the world, the Henkikan still had its advantages: "There are no Japanese sliding doors in the house, but only hinged doors, and no Japanese-style storm shutters on the windows but only window panes, and the unmatted floors have chairs upon them. One need not bother about raising the blinds in the morning or closing the shutters at night. When winter comes, there is no need to call anyone in to repaper the doors, and at spring-cleaning time there are no mats to take up. The Henkikan is most convenient for a person living alone.... The garden is small, but the house looks out over a cliff to the southeast, and so there is nothing to block the view. One can lie on the floor and look up at the white clouds. There is a bamboo thicket along the cliff. The rain sounds as if it were plucking the strings of some instrument, the wind is like a mountain brook. The houses below the cliff have gardens with flowers blooming in them. The grander houses above are ablaze with lights, and the human figures and the running horses are themselves like lights. Even when one sits alone by the window of the Henkikan, melancholy thoughts are few.... Because there is no one to sweep the stones, the moss is green and smooth even when there is no rain, and the voices of insects fail to distinguish day from night. The Henkikan is good for leisurely convalescing, and it is good for quiet reading. The only thing to complain about is the want of a maid skilled at brewing coffee." (xii, 303-4.)

The diary entries for the first months in Azabu are not free from complaints of the Tsukiji sort, but they tend to be brisker and more businesslike, and to be concerned with such happy matters as planting flowers.

In 1920, besides the rambling essay, sometimes lyrical in the manner of *Tidings from Okubo* and sometimes merely ill-tempered, from which this description of the Henkikan has been quoted, Kafū produced a theoretical treatise with the self-explanatory title *How to Write a Novel* (*Shōsetsu Sahō*). As an analytical work, it is garrulous and wanting in precision. Kafū's definition of the novel, or characterization of its nature, seems very near Wordsworth's description of poetry: emotion recollected in tranquillity. The emphasis is on tranquillity, and the lyrical effusion is frowned upon—novelists should write about themselves only when at sufficient remove to see themselves objectively. Werther and Fromentin's Dominique are offered as objects, not in every way admirable, for aspiring autobiographical novelists to study. Kafū rejects the Aristotelian notion that plot is of first importance, and argues that plot will follow along if characterization is effective. Next after character comes background, which can be used to construct character.

But having said this much, Kafū seems to change his mind. Perhaps with an eye on his own work, he decides that character is not *necessarily* the most important thing—there is another kind of novel, in no way inferior to the novel of characterization, that portrays a place or an institution. Both characterization and background must be given life from within; they must not merely be viewed from outside. The art of filling in background has more in common with music than with painting, he says, and Zola is an example of an inadequate artist who saw from without and merely sketched what he saw.

In the end the treatise leaves a suspicion that Kafū was not a clear thinker about his craft and not entirely certain what he was up to. He offers three models for the young novelist to emulate: Chinese literature, which is surely longer on plot than on character, and longest of all on mere verbal decoration; Gide, who would be a better model, one feels, for a frankly moralizing novelist like the Kafū of *Sneers* than for a novelist concerned primarily with the creation of character; and Claudel, who alone of the three seems really to the point. Claudel, however, cannot be thought to have had much influence on Kafū's own writing, and so the end result is something very near incoherence.

Perhaps the clearest thing that emerges from it all is that Kafū would like to be a sort of novelist he no longer thinks he can be. Early in 1921, as if to emphasize his feelings of futility, he published a little work that may be called one of his masterpieces: "Quiet Rain" (*Ame Shōshō*). It seems to turn its back on all the principles of excellence described in *How to Write a Novel*. Indeed, it is scarcely fiction at all. Kafū calls it such in his diary, but writers are not always the best judges of their own works. A revision of a manuscript first written in 1918, "Quiet Rain" is in a uniquely Japanese genre and one at which Kafū excelled: something halfway between essay and novel, frequently nearer the former than the latter, discursive, highly personal, wanting in sharp outlines, lacking in character and incident, and replete with vague, delicate, melancholy musings and perceptions.

When characters do appear in "Quiet Rain," they tend to discourse rather than converse. There are letters, reminiscences, poems in various languages. Everything is floating and misty, and uncertainly suspended in time. It is autumn and autumn—autumns are superimposed on one another in a piling up of reminiscences. And it is always raining, sadly and quietly. The sadness of the rain in the title persists to the end, except when someone is discoursing. It has a sort of murmuring, rustling quality, and ultimately it comes to seem like an anticipation of death. When the rain finally stops, so do the reminiscences. The narrator is left reading a French novel, thinking thoughts that he knows he will have forgotten in the morning, and listening to autumn insects. He turns the light out, and that is all. The work is an elegy and a nocturne, at times almost a threnody for departed vitality. It is saved from querulousness and self-pity by the fact that it has something like the strains of Sonohachi balladry running through it: life already seems to have withdrawn from it. Resignation is the strongest feeling that can be mustered up.*

In a way the work is misleading. It is clear that during the years after the First World War and before the earthquake, Kafū was not much disposed to write fiction. Yet the gloom and the impotence were not as complete as he would have them. He was still up to flights of humor in the sometimes flippant and sometimes sardonic manner of the Edo writers he professed to be following. Thus in *Ruminations from Eccentricity House* (*Henkikan Manroku*), serialized in 1920 and 1921, there are numbers of wry smiles, as in this list of rarities in the modern world: writers whose orthography can be trusted, newspaper reporters who know how to be polite, young men who have not had gonorrhea, waitresses who know what is on the menu, shopgirls who can add, streetcars that do not break down, and various other treasures. Here is another list: "Nothing is without its vermin. There are bugs in rice, maggots in sewage, worms in the body of the lion. There are worms in books, robbers roaming the land, newspaper reporters left at large, stagehands in the theater, cockroaches among one's guests, lice in the hair of geisha, all of them very difficult articles to be rid of.† Indeed, the more beautiful the parent object, the more loathsome its vermin. The greater the advantage, the greater the disadvantage." (XII, 306.)

Here is a comment on the popular arts: "Once I was asked by a cer-

---

* A complete translation of "Quiet Rain" will be found in Part II, pp. 253–77. The Yō-san of the piece, Kafū's companion through the rains, has been identified as Momiyama Teigo, for a time Kafū's publisher, and the man he was visiting the day Yaeji walked out on him.

† The expression "cockroaches" means something like "sponges."

tain person to suggest a plot for a movie. I was able to reply immediately. How about having some poor, impoverished old man run down by a rich man's automobile, I said. He dies and his son goes to work in a factory, but, involved in a strike, he is arrested, charged with a crime he did not commit. The poor old mother, left behind, is ill and has no money to buy food, much less medicine. The daughter, Miss Something-or-other, gives up the piecework she has been doing, pasting boxes together, and sells herself as a geisha. While she is thus caring for her mother, she acquires syphilis and loses the sight of both eyes, and so the whole family dies of starvation. How would that be? I asked. You would have them wailing in the aisles. He looked at me with wide eyes, said that I seemed to have dangerous thoughts he had not suspected me of, and did not come again." (XII, 334.)

There are of course complaints about the modern world, but there are also suggestions on accommodating the modern to the traditional: "People seem to think it an unsurpassed glory to ride in automobiles. There are ways, however, in which automobiles can be improved. They cannot yet be called perfect. In particular, there are ways in which automobiles are not wholly suited to Japanese roads and to Japanese feelings and customs. My plan is to use an automobile as a combined conveyance and teahouse. Stretching my automobile to the limit permitted by the authorities, I shall build it to hold four square yards of reed matting—quite enough space for eating, drinking, and sleeping. The seats will of course be removed to make room for the matting, and there must be a *kotatsu* foot warmer in the middle, and reed blinds at the windows. Will it not be a delight to speed along, nudging knees with a geisha and having a fine cup of sake? Surely this will be more pleasurable than riding in a roofed river boat of Edo." (XII, 329.)

Some of the descriptive passages seem almost parodies of such earlier works as *Tidings from Okubo*: "The willows along the streets have lost their leaves, the Chinese daffodils in front of the curio shop come into bloom, bêche-de-mer is cheaper, the yellowtail and other winter fish have just the right amount of oil, turnips and radishes are white in the vegetable shop, the notice pasted to the wall of the Western restaurant announces that fried oysters are available, and in truth winter has come. When rain falls, the muddy capital city shows to greater and greater advantage its special characteristics: the fenders of automobiles never have time to dry; the streetcar refuses to come and when it comes you cannot get on, you stand in a scrotum-tightening wind and watch it move past, and in truth winter has come. The time approaches for the Diet to open, and interesting encounters to take place between the police and rubberneckers in the gravel banks of the parks. The time approaches for streetcar conductors, taking advantage of the snowy weather, to stay away from work. The time is almost with us for hygienic masks to be lined up at the pharmacy door, awaiting influenza. The end of the year, the time for thieves and arsonists, has come. There is nothing unusual about the arrest of corrupt city councillors. Born in the muddied stream, we must have better, more enterprising, more startling incidents next year, incidents to outdo the movies. And so good-bye to 1920." (XII, 340.)

Ruminations from Eccentricity House can scarcely be called a good-humored work, but at least it is a humorous work, in the wry Edo tradition. The years that followed its completion were years of bereavement, bringing reason for gloom other than the unsatisfactory state of Kafū's work and his relations with the literary world. Here is the introduction to *Azabu Miscellany* (*Azabu Zakki*), a collection published in 1924 and including "Quiet Rain" and "Fireworks," the essay commonly taken to establish the importance of the Kōtoku incident in his career: "The various stories, occasional pieces, and essays collected in this *Azabu Miscellany* are no more than devices for putting off the repayment of my obligations to publishers. I have given the collection the title it has because most of the writing has been done in the five years since I moved to Azabu from Tsukiji. There have been many sorrows in these five years. My revered teacher, Mori Ogai, has betaken himself to fastnesses from which he will never return, and my friend in folly, the good Inoue, has, like him, gone back to the mountains from which he came. Since then I have had neither teacher to go to for instruction nor friend to talk pleasantly with. In illness and in loneliness, I have found the desire to write decreasing day by day. I have therefore not wished to publish any more of my inadequate works; but since the earthquake the master of the Shunyōdō has come repeatedly asking for new materials, and at length, unable to turn him away, I once more offer a collection of my unworthy manuscripts." (xii, unnumbered flyleaf.) Mori Ogai died in July 1922, and Inoue Seiichi or Aa almost exactly a year later.

It may be questioned how smooth the friendship between Kafū and Inoue really was. There is evidence in the diary that they were occasionally on chilly terms, as after the discontinuation of the magazine *Bummei,* and Kafū paid but a single sick call during June 1923, when Inoue lay dying. Perhaps it was with people as with cultures: they had to die to qualify for Kafū's affections. Kafū does seem to have shared with him, however, a genuine contempt for popular literature and a genuine concern for linguistic purity. Here, in an essay written shortly before Inoue's death, Kafū quotes his friend's views in the matter: "Foreign words are so popular these days because the city is full of rustics who don't know the perfectly good old words that could be made to do just as well. When it begins to rain, a young girl these days can't say that it looks like a storm, she has to say there seems to be a low-pressure area." (xii, 292.)

Yet one may doubt whether a concern for the good old speech of Edo was quite enough to make Inoue the companion and adviser Kafū represented him to be: "Whenever I finished a piece of writing, however slight, I always called in my old friend Inoue Aa, read it to him, and asked for his views. This was my practice even before I made my debut as a man of letters." (xii, 289.)

In upon these perhaps too fondly nurtured feelings of bereavement came the earthquake. Life seems to have been quiet enough in the months before it. There are complaints in the diary of illness and loneliness, but the latter does not seem to have been as complete, as, for instance, the introduction to the *Azabu Miscellany* makes it out to be. The Mokuyōkai or Thursday Club appears in the diary from time to time, as does the Nanagusakai, the "Seven Flowers Club," an organization chiefly of playwrights. If the city has its drawbacks, such as a water shortage in the course of which the tap drips "like urine from a gonorrhea patient," it also has its advantages: interesting walks among "the nests of unlicensed prostitutes" in Asakusa, rambles among cemeteries, encounters with women. Yaeji, his former wife, appears from time to time, and O-fusa, a public lady in whose behalf he bought a house of assignation, makes several appearances. Here such an encounter is described with more than usual clarity:

"Rain. In the valley called Tambatani there is a house with the name Nakamura Yoshigorō on the gate. I had heard that the business of the place was to arrange meetings for people who wanted mistresses or nonprofessional women. Showing a name card, not my own, I asked to see the proprietor, and was invited in by a refined woman perhaps forty years old, who took me upstairs and showed me pictures of girls. About an hour later the girl of my choice appeared. She was in her early twenties, rather small, with her hair in the foreign manner, the very image of the actress Otowa Kaneko. Because she was from Akita, her speech could not have been called elegant. I enjoyed her company until dark and gave her ten yen. She said that the woman who kept the house had once been a teacher in a girls' high school in Sendai, that she had no fixed husband today, and that she had a daughter in a women's university and a son in the Waseda Middle School." (xix, 216.)

Kafū's diary for August 31, 1923, finds him immersed in antiquarian researches, not notably despondent, though somewhat annoyed at a storm that disturbs his sleep. The entry for September 1 begins methodically with a report on the weather:

"Early in the morning the rain stopped, but a violent wind continued. From time to time the sky would cloud over darkly, and a delicate rain almost like smoke would fall. Then, at about noon, the earth began to rumble. I was sitting under the bookcase reading the posthumous writings of Hosoi Heishū, when, with some surprise, I found books falling on me.* I got up and opened a window. Outside there were great clouds of dust and smoke, reducing visibility to almost nil. Women and children were screaming, chickens were cackling, dogs were barking. The clouds of dust were from tiles falling outside the gate. As I set about making my preparations to flee, the earth once more began shaking. With a book still in my hand, I went out the front door and into the garden. In a few minutes there was another shock. I was swaying back and forth quite as if I were on a ship. Bracing myself against the gate, I looked fearfully back at my house. A few roof tiles had fallen, but the doors and windows were all in place. Feeling somewhat more at ease, I went out to the main street to have lunch at the Yamagata Hotel. The wall of the dining room having collapsed, there were tables on the street, where a few foreign

---

* Hosoi Heishū (1728–1802) was a Nagoya Confucian scholar.

guests were having lunch. After lunch I went home, but with the earth still quaking I could not go inside. I could only sit in the garden, in fear and trembling. The sky, blackly cloudy through the day, gradually cleared in the evening, and a half moon came out. After dinner at the hotel, I climbed Mt. Atago to have a look at the fires. At past ten, when I started up Edomi Hill on my way home, the fires in Akasaka and Tameike had already reached Aoi Bridge." (xix, 223–24.)

The immediate effect of the earthquake was to fill the Henkikan with people. Not even Kafū the misanthrope could turn refugees away. About one couple who stayed several weeks, there are bitter entries in the diary, the wife having been a liberated lady whose husband was under her thumb. Worse, she was most unattractive. Kafū, once a critic of male tyranny (in, for instance, *American Stories*), would have none of these new ways. With another pair of refugees matters were happier. They were a very pretty girl named Imamura and her grandmother. In the diary we soon find Miss Imamura and Kafū going off to the bath together, and when she and her grandmother leave, she is invited back again as a "housekeeper." Presently referred to in the diary as "Little Star," a Chinese sobriquet for "concubine," she seems to have had the faculty to make him happy. Thus we find him, on a rainy December day, reading a collection of Chinese poems while Little Star sits by the hearth and readies manuscript paper for him. Once a wife and twice a kept woman, Miss Imamura had had a life that could have come from a Kafū novel. She had an almond-shaped face and reminded him of an Edo print, particularly on nights when there was no electricity; and each time there was a new tremor—they went on for months—she would take his hand and run out into the garden with him.

The diary duly records the advent of autumn and the singing autumn insects, and gives little evidence of grief for the destroyed city. Indeed Kafū, like Tanizaki, seems to have felt at first that the old city deserved what it got, and that the world was better off without it. Here is the entry for October 3, 1923, a month and two days after the disaster: "Clear. Heard a shrike for the first time. In the afternoon I walked past Hibiya Park on the way to the Mitsubishi Bank. There are huts among the trees, and the stench from excrement is quite indescribable. Beyond the park the streets are blocked off because of operations to demolish the remains of the police building and others near it.

I walked to Sukiyabashi and along the canal to Kajibashi. The whole of the way, the stench was like that in a Chinese town. I came back by way of the Ginza, Karasumori, Mt. Atago, and Edomi Hill. Looking from the top of the hill, I saw only a vast, burned-over waste. The mountains of the Bōsō Peninsula across the bay seemed near enough to take in your hand, since there was nothing to block the view. The sight of the capital laid to waste is such that to call it sad would be a ridiculous understatement. Yet the city from the Meiji Period on into the Taishō Period has been a sham hallway, a grand façade with nothing behind it, a device for deceiving the foolish. There is no reason at all for regretting that it has been reduced to ashes. When one looks back on the general arrogance, the limitless greed, one cannot but think of the disaster as divine punishment. Why then should we grieve? The Japanese people had already lost their dwelling; their national treasurehouse was by way of becoming nothing. Concerned only about outward decorations, a country that has been unable to make long-range plans should expect to meet such a fate. It has reaped what it has sown; punishment has come swiftly." (xix, 230.)

But presently nostalgia begins to creep in, and a consciousness that divine retribution may have taken some rather nice things with it, too. "In the evening I went walking on the Ginza with my Little Star, and on to Tsukiji. The Tsukiji Theater is being put up on a corner of the land where Momiyama's house once stood. Next to it is a building that would seem to be a movie theater, although it was too dark for me to be really sure. Before the earthquake, Momiyama's house was deeply shaded by trees, but now there seem to be only rows of warehouses, and nothing is left to please the eye. In the days when the good Momiyama lived there, he would gaze out at his garden and compose such haiku as these:

'The cherry and the jujube, their branches intertwining:
autumn in my garden.'

'Good birds have come to my loquat tree: a day in winter.'

On long spring days, in this Tsukiji house, I wrote stories with such titles as 'The Warbler.'* Thoughts of the mutability of things, as of the blue sea become a green mulberry field, quite overcame me." (xix, 261–62.)

* "The Warbler" (*Uguisu*) is a shrill and unsatisfactory story written in 1916.

The earthquake was directly responsible for Kafū's most ambitious work during the decade of the 1920s, a chronicle first called *A Shitaya Story* (*Shitaya no Hanashi*) and later renamed *Shitaya Gleanings* (*Shitaya Sōwa*). The "Gleanings" were serialized in part in 1924, and published as a book in 1926. The opening sentences explain their origin:

"When I was four years old, my brother Teijirō was born. My mother therefore left me for a time to be reared by my grandmother in Shitaya. Grandmothers have long been prone to lose themselves in affection for their first grandchildren. It is not without reason that the popular saying makes the child reared by a grandmother 'three cents cheaper than most.' How delighted I was to leave my parents' house in Koishikawa and go to my grandmother's in Shitaya! I have already written of those times in a small essay called 'The House in Shitaya,' published in the first volume of *Mita Literature*; and fourteen or fifteen years have now passed.

"On the first of September last year, in the fire that came after the Kantō Earthquake and destroyed the better part of the city, the house was reduced to ashes. It is therefore to find consolation that I here undertake to tell of ancient happenings in the Shitaya house." (XIII, 5.)

The "Gleanings" concern the lives of two late Tokugawa Confucian scholars and writers of Chinese poetry: Kafū's maternal grandfather, Washizu Kidō, and Kidō's cousin, Onuma Chinzan. The narrative shows very clearly the influence of one of Kafū's recognized masters, Mori Ogai. In 1923, in an essay called "Mutterings of a Hermit" (*Inkyo no Kogoto*), Kafū had described the historical novels—as they are called, although "chronicles" might be an apter designation— of Ogai as unique in Japanese literature. Their terse economy he found remarkable. Perhaps it is; but they are not a taste easy to come by, having less the aspect of finished novels than that of notebooks for proposed novels.

The same may be said of *Shitaya Gleanings,* although the book does have a certain funereal beauty about it. Partly this is because so much of the gleaning was done from tombstones, Kafū's love for cemeteries never being more apparent; but partly, too, it is because he prefers Chinzan to Kidō, and Chinzan suffered that worst of fates for a Confucian, having his line die out. The book ends on a very touching note:

"Chinzan had a son, Shinkichi, born in 1864. Shinkichi learned Chinese poetry from his father and took the pen name Koun; but from before his father's death he was forbidden access to the family house, it is said. I once asked descendants of another branch of the Onuma family for information about Shinkichi, but they did not seem to want to talk about the matter, and I refrained from going too deeply into it. One day, however, when I went to copy the inscription on the tombstone of Chinzan's father, and talked to the resident priest of the temple, the Yakuōji in a back street of Mita, I was told that in the late summer of 1919, perhaps in August, a pale, sickly, and apparently impoverished lad of eleven or twelve appeared with two urns, which he said contained the ashes of Onuma Shinkichi and his wife and which he wished to have buried. Asked who he was, the boy replied that he was the son of Shinkichi. He never appeared at the temple again. . . .

"I have not been able to learn the fate of the orphan who brought the urns to the Yakuōji." (XIII, 224–25.)

If, out of deference to Kafū's apparent wishes, we are to call "Quiet Rain" a piece of fiction, it was the only such work of any importance that Kafū produced during the 1920s. There were short stories, to be sure, in a dry, laconic style, impersonal vignettes in contrast to the almost too personal tone of "Quiet Rain." One of them, "The Thaw" (*Yukidoke*), is not without merit, although the reader is likely to agree with the narrator that it is more like a *ninjōbon,* an amorous work of the late Tokugawa Period, than a modern short story. It is about a man who has deserted his family, and one day, just as in a *ninjōbon,* runs into his daughter in the doorway of a public bath. He is surprised to note that, unlike her mother, she is not repulsive, and the story closes with him drinking water from an icy teakettle, and reminiscing. Much of the naturalistic paraphernalia along the way, though perhaps unnecessary to the plot, effectively evokes the atmosphere of Tsukiji: geisha and kept women all over the landscape; a pair of newlyweds in the room beyond the laundry platform, whose conversation the hero, with the propensity for peeping and eavesdropping so common among Kafū characters, is fond of turning an ear on; his landlady, once a maid in a teahouse, whose gentleman friend, a person from the lower classes, comes calling when her husband is at work. The chief trouble with the story is the air of boredom and lassitude in the telling of it. A dreary subject does not justify a dreary manner, and Kafū's despondency gets in the way, perversely, as it does not in the more personal writing about despondency itself.

There are other little vignettes that have flickers of life from time to time, as when a geisha is heard exhorting her mother to work conscientiously at her new job, that of a kept woman. Most of the time, however, Kafū seems to be casting about for new material, and showing that he has little stomach for the work. In "Two Wives" (*Ninintsuma*), he attempts to write about proper married ladies, a subject of little interest to him since his very earliest work, and treated, when treated at all, with disdain. One would be quick to recommend divorce as a solution to the marital problems of the two, which are many, were it not for the fact that one scarcely cares what happens to them. Kafū would have done well to keep in mind an earlier attempt at a similar subject, described in a 1924 essay:

"When I was living beside the Honganji Temple in Tsukiji, I had myself all keyed up to write a long novel. It was to be called *Twilight,* and I got down perhaps ten thousand words of it. Then I shoved the manuscript into a drawer, and I never went on with it.... And why did I throw away so long a manuscript? Because I was just getting into the main part of the work and attempting to set down the character of the lady who was to be my heroine, and I saw that my powers of observation were not yet well enough developed. She was a lady who, after graduating from a college in America and returning to Japan, had associations with lady writers and was to give a literary lecture in the Kanda Youth Hall under the auspices of a ladies' magazine. At that point I gave up....

"On matters having to do with the character and feelings of what we refer to as the new woman, everything seemed shrouded in a fog." (XII, 288–89.)

The earthquake and its aftermath provided the background for a somewhat longer piece of fiction, *The Woman in the Rented Room* (*Kashima no Onna,* 1926). Kafū's visit to the Nakamura establishment (see p. 106) seems to have given him useful material, for the woman in the rented room, Kikuko by name, is a client of a similar establishment, known euphemistically as a "marriage brokerage." An attractive lady in her middle twenties with a striking resemblance to a certain movie actress, Kikuko is not above accepting one-night engagements, but she prefers the longer-range benefits of being kept. Partly because of her wanton ways, partly because she has rotten luck, and partly because of the beastly nature of the men with whom the marriage arranger arranges things, she moves from man to man, at length to get caught in a police raid; this final disaster occurs in the course of a one-night engagement in which she has been posing as the movie actress she resembles.

Behind the action, indeed overpowering it, is a sense of devastating change. The city is of course a shambles—dark, pitted streets, huts going up here and there among the wastes, pre-earthquake houses tottering precariously on the edge of them—and the physical disarray is accompanied by a sense of moral decay. This last is what is talked about, when, for instance, one of Kikuko's friends has a business lunch: "To discuss business matters, Nagashima took Takehara to an eel restaurant, the Owada, in Roppongi. As they talked of this and that, Takehara commented on how much cruder things had become since the earthquake, on how manners and morals had fallen into disorder. It was not only that so many people had lost their mates. One must consider also the fact that families of refugees had all been packed in together, men and women alike in one confusion of bodies, and that life in tents had continued for weeks on end. As an example Takehara mentioned a young relative of his, a youth who had come in from the country to attend Keiō University." (xv, 62.) It turns out, alas, by one of the coincidences that Kafū picked up from Tokugawa literature, that the lady with whom the student is behaving improperly is Kikuko, and so the poor girl loses another keeper.

When she is in form, Kikuko is a rather lively person. It is a pity both for her and for the novel that her world is otherwise inhabited only by pigs. There are passages, as her misfortunes build up to almost ludicrous extremes, that rival the best narrative sections of *Dwarf Bamboo*. They are not sustained, however. A general weariness and a distaste for his material seem to overcome Kafū, and presently he gives up.

The best of the story is in a series of three chapters laid on the first anniversary of the earthquake. The business of the city is at a standstill, for it is seized by a superstitious fear that the disaster will be repeated. (Confirmation that this was in fact the case is to be had in Kafū's diary.) Bored and not expecting her newest keeper to come calling, Kikuko goes to see her family, whom she hopes to devastate with the news that she now has not a rented room but a whole rented house, and a housekeeper to boot. She has no opportunity, because she finds them engrossed in preparations for moving to the provinces, a project they have not even bothered to tell her about. Chagrined, she goes home and quarrels with her housekeeper, who quits, and so she is alone in an empty house in a dead city. "Her eyes filling with tears in the intensity of her chagrin, Kikuko glared at the retreating figure. There was nothing more to be done. She heard a clattering outside the kitchen door. She was startled, but knew that it would be the neighbor's dog opening the lid of the garbage box, as it did every evening. She was much relieved; but then it came to her that there was no one in the house tonight except herself, and she began to feel uneasy. After hastily locking the chest, she went around closing the shutters from front to back. Last of all she went upstairs. As she tugged at a shutter she cut her finger. Crying out in pain, she brought the injured finger to her mouth, and her bridgework fell out." (xv, 112.)

Unfortunately it falls into the very narrow space between Kikuko's house and the house next door, an area that cannot be entered without consulting the neighbors, with whom Kikuko, a testy sort, is not on good terms. Knowing what a difference the absence of bridgework can make to a girl's appearance, and seized with the terror of growing old so common among women of her calling, she goes off to have a new bridge made, although it is the middle of the night. The man who deflowered her ten years ago happens to be a dentist. He makes her a temporary bridge for old time's sake, and she goes to bed with him, presumably for the same reason. When she returns home, just before dawn, she finds that her current keeper came calling after all and awaits her, certain suspicions in his mind. He thinks it unlikely that she has been to the dentist, and so he, too, joins her list of erstwhile keepers.

At this point, just when Kikuko has come nicely to life in all her vanity and petulance, Kafū quite gives up the fight. A brief synoptic chapter tells how she ends up in jail, and the book closes with a chapter in which a group of businessmen debate the cases for and against jailing prostitutes. They all sound very much the same, and the conclusion is rather like that of a typical Japanese newspaper editorial, that both sides of the matter must be carefully considered.

The story is marred by an adolescent prurience, and, more seriously, by a failure to give dramatic life to events that have received expository statement. This is true of the short, synoptic last chapter, of course, but it is true of earlier chapters as well. Thus we are given the following piece of information about Kikuko in the course of a scene in which she meets a new client:

"Even in the days before she had had fleshly knowledge of men, Kikuko had been quite unafraid of them, and had been in the habit of setting out to make fun of them. . . . Seeing that the man was rather taken with her, she could not let the occasion pass. She wanted to tease him as tease him she could." (xv, 73–74.) The reader has a right to feel cheated at having only this and nothing more. In the next sentence dinner is over, and at no time has he seen the little tease at work. Kafū is like a raconteur who tells all about a story but does not tell the story itself.

He had a number of other tries at fiction before the end of the decade, all of them shorter than *The Woman in the Rented Room,* and all of them even more dispirited. There is a certain amount of interesting material on changing manners: displays of nudity never before seen in the land, a taxi driver who touts for peep shows, another who carries a prostitute with him and runs a mobile operation. There is also interesting material on the changing language. One unpleasant character remarks to his unpleasant wife: "Ittai ano futari wa itsu rabu ni ochitan darō?" (xv, 15.) *Rabu* is a rendering into the Japanese syllabary of the English word "love," *rabu ni ochiru* is a direct translation of "fall in love," and the horrid patois can scarcely be described as Japanese at all. One seldom feels, however, that Kafū's heart is in his work.

His energies, such as were not taken up by women and visits to doctors and cemeteries, were spent upon polemics, discursive essays, and scholarship. The diary finds him passing whole days in the Nanki Bunko, the library of the Kii Tokugawa family, which is now housed, for the most part, in Tokyo University but was then independent. Besides Chinzan and Kidō, the two central figures of *Shitaya Gleanings,* and Ota Nampo or Shokusanjin, his interest was focused on Narushima Ryūhoku, a man with whom he found himself greatly in sympathy. Ryūhoku, who was born in 1837 and died in 1884, was one of the last true children of Edo, a man who saw his birthright destroyed by modernization and the country bumpkins. An official under the old regime and a journalist under the new, he devoted himself to lamenting the old and satirizing the new, for which activities he was put in jail and had part of his most important work banned.

The polemics were symptomatic of Kafū's growing isolation from the world of letters. In 1926 his principal adversary was Masamune Hakuchō, a critic, short-story writer, and leader of the naturalist movement. Hakuchō had accused Kafū of literary affectations, and likened his prose to an old woman's make-up. Kafū replied, in elegant Edo cadences, by calling Hakuchō an unlettered rustic: "Because your prose is of a sort utterly unrelated to that which I ordinarily see, there were not a few places in which I had to struggle to apprehend your meaning." (XIII, 423.)

In 1927 the adversary was the Shinchōsha Publishing Company, which he accused on very tenuous grounds of having slighted Mori Ogai. "I consider it my moral obligation to permit none of my works to be published by the house that made such unspeakably vile remarks about my teacher." (XIV, 110.) The unspeakable remarks had been made some five years before, at the time of Ogai's death. Against the advice of friends who thought that he owed it to himself to respect the declaration, Kafū let Shinchōsha reprint several of his novels after the Second World War; but by that time he had something of a reputation as a miser, and money was probably more important to him than consistency. When the controversy over Ogai boiled up again later in the year, Kafū suggested that his adversary, the critic Nakamura Murao, ought to have his head examined.

Simultaneously with his denunciation of Shinchōsha, Kafū announced a boycott on the newspapers: "I have only twice published novels in newspapers . . . and then only at the instance of masters I respected. To write for newspapers is to borrow their power for purposes of spreading one's works through the world, and means falling in debt to them. Having become aware of this fact, I have made it a policy to avoid writing for newspapers whenever possible." (XIV, 115.) Once again he was unfaithful to his resolve. Not many years were to elapse before *A Strange Tale from East of the River* (*Bokutō Kidan*) appeared in the *Asahi*.

In 1928 there was a tiff with Osanai Kaoru, a leader of the new theater, over publication rights, and in 1929 a quarrel with *Bungei Shunjū,* a powerful monthly magazine founded by one of Kafū's pet dislikes, Kikuchi Kan. An anonymous *Bungei Shunjū* article had taken Kafū to task for his willful and licentious ways. To this Kafū made telling reply: If a wish to be alone had anything to do with the matter, then Bashō and Saigyō, two of the great figures of Japanese poetry, must be bad writers; and if the same could be said of liking a drink now and then, Li Po must have been a bad poet. The rest of the article is more personal, accusing Kikuchi of having, among other things, dirty political ambitions.

Essays neither polemical nor scholarly tend to be about change and the changing city. "Mukōjima long ago lost its standing as a place for elegant pleasures. But since the death of my master, Ogai, in 1922, I have gone every year on the anniversary to visit his grave in the cemetery of the Kōfukuji, and so there is never a year when I do not at least once cross the Mukōjima embankment. I always look back at the pagoda of the Asakusa Temple, and see Mt. Tsukuba against the sky far upstream, and even now I am unable to deny the lyrical feelings that come over me. I yearn sadly for the culture of Edo, now so far away, and I think, too, of the days when I was young....

"Just across Azuma Bridge is the brewing company that has for some time owned the old Satake family garden. Even before the earthquake this famous garden was so neglected that there was scarcely a trace left of its former beauty. The garden of the Mito Tokugawa family, by Makura Bridge, completely ruined by the fire and earthquake, was at first a dump for building materials, and now it is evidently to become a park in the Occidental style. Soon we will see a new park of cement and chains, such as we already have in Hibiya and Aoyama....

"In the Meiji Period there were not a few people who loved Mukōjima and had their houses and gardens there.... After the flood of early August 1910, however, almost everyone departed.... In the changing times since, as the outskirts of the city have moved on, the cherry trees along the river embankment have died one by one, and at the beginning of the Taishō Period there were only two or three sick old trees left near the Mimeguri Shrine....

"In an inferior piece called 'The City in Summer' I described how, by the Honjo bank below Ryōgoku Bridge, there was still in the late 1890's a strand covered with reeds. When I came back from abroad a decade later, I sometimes went walking along the upper reaches of the river, from the Hashiba Ferry to the mouth of the Ayase River, where there was a profusion of rushes, and I would listen to the warblers in the early summer afternoon, and to the soft touch of the dew-wind against the rushes on nights when the moon was bright. The rushes and willows made me think of the Seine, and the lyrics of Henri de Régnier....

"But rushes and willows are day by day withdrawing from the city, and today you must go all the way to the Arakawa Drainage Canal or the Edo River to find them." (xiv, 33–34, 39, 43, 45.)

"There is a plaintive, sad note, something to move men's hearts, in the *charamela,* the little barbarian horns, sounding in the night, of sellers of Chinese noodles. There used to be the same sadness in the sound of the *charamela* which, in shabby, out-of-the-way parts of the city, candy venders would blow late in the afternoon; but this, in the course of the years, has disappeared. The flute of the masseuse, too, seems to have disappeared, save in the pleasure quarters. And so, in this Shōwa Period, only the seller of Nanking noodles has come forward to fill their place, to send forth his melancholy strain upon the night air of the city of Tokyo." (xiv, 180.)

"It was just before three, in the quietest part of the quiet afternoon, that the chirping of sparrows made me lay down my brush on a manuscript I had begun. It was the silent time of the day, and all noise had broken off in the lane before my gate and in the houses around mine. The middle-class wife, tired from the morning laundry, would have hurried through her lunch and be having her afternoon nap. The maid, having at length finished the morning dishes, would be absorbed in a newspaper serial. It would be some time before the troublesome beggars and questionable peddlers would have penetrated the lanes of this hilly district. The gadabout housewife would already have stepped out with her children, and even now they would be devouring their lunch in some department store, the Mitsukoshi or the Matsuya, perhaps. It was not unreasonable of the sparrows, therefore, not to have noticed me inside. Two or three of them, feeling quite secure, were picking insects from the pot of daisies at the window. The branches, trailing over like vines, waved gently in the wind, and the sparrows, trying to hold them still, were indulging in upside-down acrobatics, some with twisted necks, some with their tails half fanned out. Suddenly I thought of the sparrow dance created by the men of

Edo, and saw how cleverly it had captured the antics of a flock of sparrows and turned them into art. Some years ago people were rendered quite speechless by the Russian dancer Pavlova and a dance called 'Dying Swan' or something of the sort. More remarkable, it seems to me, is the fact that in our own Edo dances we have subjects ranging from a tiny bird like the sparrow to a ferocious beast like the lion. In the subtlety of their choreography our dances bear comparison with that swan dance, and it is a matter only of the fads of the day that the one is welcomed as new and fresh, and the other rejected as fusty and old-fashioned. The choice says nothing about the merits of the arts in question. It tells only how short on discernment the public has become." (XIV, 170–72.)

But though cemeteries and rush-covered strands and a disappearing past occupied much of his attention, Kafū was also concerned with more up-to-date phenomena. He first made the Ginza "cafés" and barmaids the matter for fiction in a very slight little piece published in 1928, but they had already appeared in essays, and they had for some years been competing rather successfully with tombstones for space in the diary. From 1926 on, the diary finds Kafū going almost every night to a café called the Tiger (cafés were actually bars whose barmaids were unlicensed prostitutes). "Apologia" (*Mōshiwake*), a bitter essay written in 1927, justifies the frequenting of such places. It is a very ill-tempered attack on the times, prompted by difficulties over copyrights, and difficulties with an aggressive little Tiger girl called O-tami in the essay and O-hisa in the diary. The former difficulties had to do with the insistence of the first publisher of *American Stories* that he still held rights, an insistence that Kafū characterizes as a manifestation of greedy capitalism. The latter had to do with nasty reports in the newspapers and magazines about him and the girl, as a result of which she came around demanding that he share his wealth with her; and so, says Kafū, she showed herself to be a disciple of greedy Communism.

Here is the justification for nights at the Tiger: "Our only desire is that we be able to see the truth, to learn that these sorts of lives are being lived in this sort of environment.... Greatly pleased with the literary theories of Turgenev and Flaubert in our younger days, we saw our respect for the great men of history and tradition move on to an interest in lowborn men and women, in inhabitants of dirty, narrow alleys. We thought it our life's work to set down in writing the subjects the Impressionists had favored in their paintings. Afterward it came to appear that this was altogether too narrow a view, but the influences upon one's younger days are not easily wiped away. And so it is that the interiors and exteriors of Ginza cafés take me back to the days when I was in Paris and remind Ikuta of old times in Berlin.* Thinking of long-forgotten naturalist writings and comparing them with the scene before us, comparing the Occidental past with the Japanese present, we would frequently forget how late in the night it was." (xiv, 133–34.) Elsewhere in the essay Kafū emphasizes the importance of "neutrality" and "sympathy" in relations between a writer and his character. It cannot be said, however, that in his own writings about the Ginza he was to be very true to his principles.

O-hisa or O-tami and journalists were not the only unpleasant denizens of the cafés. On more than one occasion, the diary says, someone came up and threatened to give him a cuffing, and the decor and manners of the cafés were not always able to take him back to Paris: "The cafés that are so popular throughout the city are to all appearances like Parisian cafés. The reality is much different. We try to imitate everything Western, and we always make a botch of it. The girls go to work every day and yet they do not receive salaries, and they must depend on gifts from customers for their livelihood. It is quite evident, therefore, that they actually live by prostitution. Fearing rumors and the threats of newspaper reporters, they must appear unwilling to surrender to the blandishments of drunken customers." (xix, 427.) There follows, in some detail, the table of organization of the Tiger, set down for use one day in a novel.

The diary records the departure of the Little Star, the lady who came to live with Kafū after the earthquake. It seems that she was left too frequently to spend the night in a lonely bed. Other women, with such designations as "the woman in Sakuragawamachi," come and go, probably unlicensed prostitutes on the model of the woman in the rented room; and there are suggestions that, though nice to have around, women are no longer as necessary as they once were: "There was a time, some years ago when I moved from Tsukiji, that the loneliness of the bachelor's life seemed quite intolerable; but since the

* Ikuta Kisan (1876–1945) was a minor novelist.

earthquake, possibly because I am at length growing old, I have come to find pleasure in the cleanliness of sleeping alone. It was for this reason that I let my Little Star go. . . . Yet I have not been wholly able to deny the temptations of the flesh. They are, after all, among the pleasures of this human existence. The melancholy pleasure of the solitary life is difficult to give up, and so, on the other hand, are the pleasures of keeping a mistress. Do I not have a surplus of pleasures, entranced with my studies and finding the life of dissipation yet more delightful?" (xix, 367–68.)

For a time in 1927 and 1928 it almost seemed that Kafū had made himself another marriage, though not a formal one. In September 1927, after a couple of visits to Karuizawa during the summer, the diary finds him out strolling with a Kōjimachi geisha named O-uta, a woman of many virtues:

"She says that her downfall came at the age of fourteen or fifteen, but for some reason the evil winds of the world do not seem to have left too much mark on her. She seldom reads a newspaper or a magazine, and she does not like the movies. Instead she loses herself in housework and sewing." (xix, 500.)

"She seems quite satisfied to serve me. Women are very strange. A girl just past twenty dependent on a man fifty, and a man in poor health at that, and she shows no sign of sadness, but goes on smiling pleasantly. A mistress of this sort was not uncommon in the old days, but it is very odd that such a one should still be found in our day of rebellion and individualism, and in the metropolis of human rights known as Tokyo. . . . Wanting from the start in the will to fight and grab, she has naturally learned the virtues of endurance. . . . I am at the border of old age and I have quite lost the ambition to create art, and as I lament the numbers of women in our country who are ruining themselves over literature and politics, I think it must be described as the luck of the aged that I should have come upon such an endearing girl. I am like someone who, exhausted at twilight, suddenly finds limitless consolation and sweet melancholy in the song of a woman pilgrim." (xix, 546–47.)

But presently it comes to seem that she is not so domestic after all. The diary tells us that her pretty little place in Azabu, paid for by Kafū after her release from indenture as a geisha, has become a refuge from reporters and literary persons. In March 1928, however, she declares her wish to go to work again, and so Kafū buys her a house of assignation in Kōjimachi. He gives it the same name as a similar establishment in "Summer Dress," the Ikuyo, which can be taken for a somewhat indecent double entendre. Kafū apparently meant it to be so taken.

The diary records pleasant, dreamy times in the Ikuyo: "Clear with a cool breeze. The music teacher came at about ten, it would seem, and samisen practice (the tenth act of *Taikōki*) began in the geisha house next door. The recital awakened me and I set off for a bath. When I got back, it was already noon. I went upstairs and, leaning on the sill where there was a good breeze, looked absently down at people passing back and forth in the lane. Then Kiyomoto practice began in the geisha house across the way. . . . The teacher was an old woman, and the style was extremely old-fashioned. It was the better for being so, quite without the contortions of Enjudayū and the people who rule Kiyomoto today. A girl of perhaps sixteen, an apprentice of some sort, was washing footgear and airing umbrellas in the house next door. Far off beyond the roofs there was a noonday moon, and hawks dipped and soared incessantly. Tomorrow will be clear again. The Kiyomoto practice was presently over, and when I saw the women pull their kimonos down over their shoulders and sit at their mirrors, the sun was slanting and evening was in the sky. I went to a dusky room downstairs and had a nap. O-uta, having made herself up, brought in tea and sweets. And so the summer day came to a close. After tea, at about eight, I set out for home." (XIX, 592–93.)

It has been averred that the Ikuyo contained yet another inviting feature, facilities for peeping in upon customers as they disported themselves.

The affair with O-uta went on into the next decade. In 1930 she began having fits of temper ("Never before have I seen a woman whose appearance and true nature were more completely in contrast," XX, 67), and in the diary Kafū's thoughts are likened to those of the aging Po Chü-i upon dismissing his mistress. In August of the following year, when O-uta came down with a nervous disorder, Kafū severed relations with her in a manner that seems to have hurt her and angered her family. The abandoned Ikuyo provided the setting for a few melancholy verses on "moon-viewing night," September 1931: "The moon in the rain, and an old woman, like a ghost, watching an abandoned house." "The second floor of a teahouse, its shutters closed; and the moon in the rain."(xx, 165.)

Meanwhile his relations with his own family continued to be eccentric. The diary records occasional visits to his mother and visits from her, Kafū's visits all, apparently, at times when he knew that his brother would be out of the house. Most of the pertinent diary entries contain unkind remarks about the brother's children—likening them to a pack of monkeys, or something of the sort. Kafū's other brother, a Christian minister adopted into the Washizu family, died of tuberculosis in December 1927. The diary contains a touching description of the funeral, and of the burial in a pale winter twilight while a sharp wind whistled through the Yanaka cemetery. There is no mention, however, through all the functions attendant upon the death, of the younger brother. Although Kafū's mother made a special point of telephoning him, Kafū refused to visit the grave, as custom required, on the sixth day after the death. In earlier entries the dead brother is almost never referred to by his own name, but rather, with stiff formality, as the Reverend Mr. Washizu. "How odd," remarks Kafū in the entry for the day of the death, "that this good, charitable man of religion should have had for a brother a profligate like me. I should have spent the night at his side like the others, I suppose, but I had a stomachache, and then it really was very cold on a Japanese floor in Western clothes, and so I left at a little past midnight." (xix, 526.)

As Kafū reached the end of his fifth decade and the century approached the end of its third, he was once more seized with a fear that the end was in sight. In August 1928, wishing to be rid of some manuscripts with which he did not want to be found dead, he tried burning them, but only succeeded in smoking out the neighbors and attracting the police. He then decided upon destruction by water, a process that proved almost as difficult. Upon his first attempt to throw the bundle into the river, someone courteously retrieved it for him. Eventually three such bundles did go in, including plays, juvenilia, and letters from as far back as his middle-school days. His reasons for wishing to destroy them are unclear. The list of manuscripts thrown into the river brings up a small puzzle, for two of the plays are to be found in his collected works, one of them complete and the other incomplete. Perhaps it was a preliminary version of the one and the final version of the other that went into the river.

Here, to give a suggestion of his mood at the end of the decade, is a part of the entry for the New Year's Eve leading into the year of his fiftieth birthday: "I have come to think that the happenings of the world have nothing to do with me and I do not concern myself with them. The pronouncements of scribblers are no different from the whining of mosquitoes, and the rumors that are noised about are but a nuisance to make me wish to cover my ears. All of my acquaintances tell me that there is no one more fortunate than I, and I am inclined to agree. The first piece of good fortune, I conclude as I look back over my life, is that I have had no fixed wife. Since I have no wife, I have no children or grandchildren, and I can die at any time with no regrets. Since I have no relations with the knights of the literary world, there is no danger that anyone will erect a wretched bronze statue to me when I am dead. The minute a writer dies these days, the people who have gathered about him put up a bronze statue extolling his name, for purposes of publicizing their own names. I myself consider the knights of the literary marketplace the dregs of humanity. I shall not, for the moment, speak of myself. The writers of the world know nothing about the world save the cafés and their own rented rooms. They cannot write a letter, they know nothing of courtesy or propriety, they are unable to distinguish what is in good taste from what is not. They are feeble, vacillating, loose, vain, really the most inferior of men. I once became a teacher at Keiō, but I had feelings of my own in the matter and quit shortly before I was forty, and I have since had nothing to do with literature. I have to this day numbered no writers among my friends, and this I must count as my greatest blessing. Because I have been in bad health and have had no surplus energy, I have fought with no one and I have injured no one. I have certain resources, though not large, and I have had to trouble no one for money. I have liked women, but I have never deflowered a virgin or led a woman into adultery. Looking back over my fifty years, I find that I have done nothing that need disturb my sleep. In this, too, I must count myself fortunate. The eastern windows are brightening and I hear the milkman at the gate; and so, cutting my New Year's ruminations short, I welcome the spring of the fifty-first year in which I have lived. Happy New Year." (XIX, 637–38.)

Chapter seven The Nineteen-Thirties

The dreary decade was out of the way, but it cannot be said that the next one began with a creative explosion. In 1930 Kafū produced a single story. It so displeased him that he did not allow it to be published. Only after the war was the text offered to a magazine, and then only because it had already appeared in a pirated edition.

The next year, however, was easily the best one he had had since the period of *Dwarf Bamboo* and *Rivalry*. Two short stories published in 1931 are generally numbered among his best, and the raw material stored away since the Tiger days at last took shape as a novel, *During the Rains* (*Tsuyu no Atosaki*), which appeared in *Chūō Kōron* toward the end of the year. One of the two stories, "A Tale of a Nettle Tree" (*Enoki Monogatari*) is a sport among Kafū's works in that the element of suspense is important. It consists almost entirely of a long letter, in the old epistolary style, which has been opened, upon the instructions of the writer, only when fifty years have passed since his death. He is a miscreant priest, and the letter is his confession. Having come upon a large amount of money by dishonest means, he has kept it hidden in a nettle tree, and draws upon it from time to time for nights of revelry. Presently, no longer able to climb the tree, he can but look up and wonder whether the money is still there. An acolyte has found it, however, and continued the work of spending it. In the process he is apprehended and put in jail, where he dies. The priest of course keeps silent about the true origins of the money, and only now, more than a half century later when it can do no good, does he get around to apologizing.

The story was warmly praised by two of Japan's literary elders, that Masamune Hakuchō with whom Kafū had exchanged sharp words some years before, and Tanizaki Junichirō. The latter admired the stark economy of the narrative, the former the fact that Kafū had managed in so small a space to work in a certain amount of characterization. It is true that Kafū's attitude toward his reprobate of a priest is ambiguous and somewhat ironic. He cannot merely be called a bad man, Kafū seems to be saying, for he is very Japanese. In a strange way, too—a way that runs against the general tone of Kafū's writing—the darkness of Edo comes across nicely, contrasting with the mood of the sunnier day when the letter is opened. Yet one feels that the praise of his colleagues has less to do with the story itself than with the spectacle of a brave old warrior making a comeback.

"Hydrangea" (*Ajisai*), the other story, marks the full emergence of what may be called Kafū's dry manner. As early as *American Stories* there had been traces of a spare, matter-of-fact narrative style, no doubt owing something to the French realists, and standing in marked contrast to the lyricism of *The River Sumida,* and, to a lesser extent, *The Woman of the Dream.* In *Dwarf Bamboo* the dry style was somewhat more in control, and it quite dominated the unsatisfactory stories of the years after the earthquake, notably *The Woman in the Rented Room.*

"Hydrangea" may not strike one as the masterpiece the Japanese frequently claim it to be, but it has considerably more assurance than its immediate predecessors in the same vein. The flower of the title is nowhere mentioned in the text. It is symbolic, having reference to fickleness, by virtue of the way hydrangeas have of changing color. We have the authority of the diary that an Ushigome geisha was the model for the wanton heroine as well as for the heroine of the slightly earlier story (see p. 124) that Kafū allowed to be published only after a pirated edition had come out. "I spent a lot of money on this girl," says the diary entry in question, "but because of her the urge to write, which had long left me, welled up again. . . . So it is with human affairs: you gain something and you lose something." (xx, 135.) She had jealous lovers, it seems, by whom Kafū was intimidated, and he did not long keep company with her.

A cheap little tramp of a geisha, the heroine has the ways of a hydrangea, and in the end gets stabbed and thrown in the river because of them. The narrator is a sort by now familiar to followers of Kafū, the useless man, in this case a mendicant musician, who lives off the earnings of the public ladies; and the excitement of the story, such as it is, comes from the fact that he has a butcher knife ready to do the job when a rival does it for him.

Actually he is a narrator within a narrative, the story having the frame in which Kafū seemed compelled to set so many of his stories, as if a little afraid of his material, or possibly as if hoping to use such formal devices to achieve an effect of distance and objectivity. Since the narrator of the "frame" meets the narrator of the story proper at the woman's grave, the device does here serve a certain melancholy purpose in setting the scene, but it has appeared so frequently in Kafū's writing as to seem mannered.

The taciturn ending will perhaps give some idea of the mood of the story. It mentions change but makes no attempt to evoke it, as a more lyrical Kafū would have done: "Honjo has changed completely. There is no trace now of that canal or of Mikura Bridge. I'd like to tell you how I married my present wife and moved to Yotsuya, sir, but I've talked too much already. You must be bored. Possibly I can save that story until I see you again." (xv, 229.)

If overuse of the narrative within the narrative can be irritating, it is undeniable that the stories in the dry style are better shaped than those in the lyrical. One can lift passages from *Rivalry* or *The River Sumida* and, with a moderate amount of explanation, let them stand on their own. With "Hydrangea" the choice is between giving the whole story and declining to give anything at all.

During the Rains is the work that really brought Kafū out of the doldrums. It has extravagant admirers in Japan, though again one may suspect that some of the admiration is less for the quality of the work itself than for the mettle of a flagging author who had finally come through. The novel demands comparison with *Rivalry*. Both are about the demimonde. In the one case, however, it is the conservative world of the geisha who preserves something of Edo. In the other it is the untidily up-to-date world of the Ginza café girls, the quest for Edo having been abandoned, at least for the time being. In both there is a wealth of sociological and biographical information, so that the effect is of a very cluttered closet, a book that should have been much larger if it was to encompass everything in it. The great difference between the two is that nothing in the second novel corresponds to the Negishi chapter of *Rivalry*. In the one novel the past is still present, inviting an elegiac ramble, as through a cemetery. In the other the present is everything, and it neither looks nor smells very good. To be sure, the seasons are a part of *During the Rains,* as the title demands that they be; but the seasons are not the seasons of the old city, where the keepers of doubtful houses also kept morning glories and lit festival fires. Here there are no morning glories. The view, rather, is of muddy expanses, dotted here and there by an unmade bed and an unwashed chemisette.

The story is of the vicissitudes of a Ginza café girl named Kimie. She is a very sloppy girl, and a very lascivious one, with remarkable bedroom accomplishments never quite openly described, and a belief that the more people in the bedroom the merrier. We are never allowed to be present at her orgies, however. We are merely told that she has exciting memories, and that other characters have peeped in upon her from time to time. The chief such character is a writer named Kiyooka, whom Kafū treats with all the scorn the diary and the polemical essays reserve for that literary satrap, Kikuchi Kan. "His concentration on profits was such that he might have been said to combine the functions of bazaar keeper and impresario.... When he and his friends gathered together, they immediately began drinking whisky and lolling about on the floor.... As for what they talked about, it was limited to horse racing, mahjong, slanderous talk of other friends, the rise and fall of publishing houses, and manuscript fees—and smutty talk about women." (xv, 307–8.) It may be asked how such passages are to be reconciled with the dictum that a novelist and his characters must be in sympathy.

Kimie has as foil a lady named Tsuruko, who is Kiyooka's common-law wife and whom he is apparently getting ready to abandon. She is one of the few relatively respectable female portraits Kafū ever attempted to draw; but, poor, sad, rejected woman, she is the merest sketch, an actress with a single scene. The emphasis is all on Kimie. Japanese critics have thought it Kafū's intention to contrast the two, one a nice, cultured lady of the old school, the other a sordid specimen of the new. Tsuruko, however, is much too shadowy a figure to set Kimie off in any real fashion, and Kimie, in her wanton way, is rather an appealing girl, as much a victim of the horrid literary person as is his wife.

Kimie's troubles are due to the fact that Kiyooka has come to think of her as his, but her amiable disposition and sturdy appetites make it impossible for her to be any one person's. Learning of her fickleness, he persecutes her in various strange ways: he seeks to arouse superstitious fears by having a disciple stealthily remove a sleeve from her kimono, by depositing a dead cat in her room, by releasing a story to the press about the strange behavior of the mole on her thigh. (Why the press should be interested in this last is not made clear.) He considers more dramatic steps, such as dumping her naked in Hibiya Park, the very center of Tokyo; and in the end he has her so filled with apprehension that she considers leaving the Ginza fleshmill and going home to the country. The conclusion is obscure, but the impression is that she is saved from this eventuality by being allowed to play savior to an old gentleman acquaintance just out of prison. Despite the critics, the evidence is that Kimie is basically a good sort.

But her surroundings are very unbeautiful. Just occasionally, as when the houses open up and everything is suddenly noisy, the advent of summer still has its old power to charm, and just occasionally, too, for fleeting moments, the city can seem beautiful again: "The embankment and the trees were dim, as if bathed in a green mist. The late-night breeze mixed the scent of the pale new leaves and the scent of grass, and from the opposite side of the moat, with its towering pines, there came the call of a night bird, a heron perhaps." (xv, 262–63.) But for the most part the rainy season is merely sticky. The one really pleasant scene has nothing to do with Kimie's world. It takes place on the western outskirts of the city, where Kiyooka's father is living in tasteful retirement.

Kimie's room looks out over toothpaste stains and laundry, and has an aspect of having been occupied but recently by someone who has not had time to unpack. At the main entrance to her place of employment, two naked Occidental ladies support the sign "Don Juan," in stucco and red lights. As for the side entrance, "the alley was so narrow that a person could barely pass, and yet it was lined with crates. Even in the coldest weather there were bluebottles buzzing in it. In the middle of the day old rats like weasels would come wandering out, and fly off, splashing the mud puddles with the tips of their tails, when someone approached.... At the kitchen door she was assailed by the stench of cheap oil, and cockroaches were scuttling about." (xv, 246.)

The only real break in the squalor is the old man's retreat, far out in the suburbs. Lacking associations with plebeian Edo, it cannot really bring in the lyrical note that the Negishi interlude provides so beautifully for *Rivalry*. If *During the Rains* does not have the virtues of the earlier novel, however, it unfortunately shares its vices. There are long, static passages in which the narrative is broken by a detailed account of the life and times of some minor character. This would be permissible, perhaps, in a long novel, but *During the Rains* would come to no more than about 30,000 words in English translation. Within this very restricted space, characters who appear but once are brought in with great portentousness. Thus Matsuzaki, an elderly person who once shared a lively bedroom with Kimie and another young lady, has but a single scene, in which he takes words out of Kafū's mouth: "He could only describe it as a dream, the comparison of the Ginza he had known as he had been driven to work each morning with the Ginza since the earthquake, changing every day of the year. It is not to be understood that he felt the profound emotions a citizen of modern Rome must feel in looking back upon its past. Rather, he observed his city with a light, easy admiration, as if watching a sleight-of-hand performance. A city that had gone so far in imitating the West gave cause for the greatest astonishment, and could even arouse in one a certain sweet sadness. The sadness was deepened not so much by the streets themselves as by the thought of the waitresses who lived on them. ... Although, like courtesans and geisha of old, Kimie was a woman whose charms were for sale, she was quite different from them. She was more like the unlicensed prostitutes so abundant in Occidental cities. The appearance of such women in the streets of Tokyo was a sign of the times—and there could be nothing more astonishing than its capacity for change. ... Well, praise and blame, fame and infamy, were alike without deep meaning. And so he must look back on his life as having been of the happiest. He was sixty and had never been ill, and he felt not the slightest shame at this open, leisurely sporting, as if he were still a young man, with twenty-year-old waitresses. This fact alone made his life a far happier one than those of kings and princes. Dr. Matsuzaki found himself laughing aloud." (xv, 337–39.)

There is something rather touching about this, suggesting that the bugs and artificial flowers of the cafés have brought Kafū out of his worst years; yet it does not seem right that a man with so remarkable a background—in addition to not being dyspeptic, Matsuzaki differs from Kafū in having served a prison sentence for malfeasance in office—should be brought in so ceremoniously for the single purpose of commenting on change. Other lapses are to be noted. The suburban scene has an air of floating unattached. In it Kiyooka's father makes his single appearance; Tsuruko appears in it, and very briefly in one other scene. The most conspicuous lapse comes when the novel is already two-thirds over. Kimie's landlady is introduced with heavy solemnity, and we learn about the account she gives the world of her past, and the less flattering account the world itself gives, and similar matters relating to her daughter; and this is a woman whose sole function is to boil water and make telephone calls, and now and again get out of the house so that Kimie and one or more friends can be alone.

In a curious way the novel seems to have too much in it and not enough. When a novelist or playwright has his characters right before our eyes, they must do and say things sufficient to account for an announced lapse of time. He cannot have them look at their watches, say that it is seven o'clock, talk of this and that for ten minutes, look at their watches again, and say that it is ten and they must be going. Yet Kafū is guilty of doing exactly this in, for instance, a scene in which Kiyooka bribes a pair of newspaper reporters with geisha.

In short, it is not a satisfying novel. Other works of Kafū's please even while they are failing to satisfy as novels, but here he has rejected the devices by which they please.

It may be, as he himself suggested, that the Ginza cafés took him back to French naturalism and made him give up the melancholy lyrics that were his true métier. Yet the diary indicates that French literature was much less with him than in the years following his return from abroad; and the most perceptive comment on *During the Rains,* by Tanizaki Junichirō, suggests native influences:

"The old-fashioned is fairly conspicuous in Kafū's recent *During the Rains.* Indeed in its style and the shifting of its scenes, it might be called the oldest of his novels yet. There are chance meetings scattered all through the book, which are used to further the plot, in a manner common enough in plays and novels of another era. The oldness of the form stands in subtle contrast to the modern colors of the material....

"Such things as psychological description or the expression of emotions and states of consciousness, the attempt to penetrate deep inside a character, have come into fashion only recently. Our old writers of fiction were more concerned with plot. All sorts of characters were brought on stage and made to go through all sorts of scenes in all sorts of postures, but they were for the most part no more than stage properties to make the plot more interesting. The element of inevitability in characterization was ignored if need be....

"I do not think these facts are to be explained entirely by immaturity of technique. We Orientals have a tendency to ignore humanity and to treat people like natural objects, like so many sticks and stones....

"Japanese writings have lacked the highly colored quality of Chinese. They show a sensitive feeling for nature, however, and one notes in them a certain warmth and gentleness; and yet in their depiction of human life it is the exterior and not the interior that is emphasized.... *During the Rains* is not, of course, a gigantic fantasy like such Chinese novels as *The Dream of the Red Chamber*.... But the nihilistic coldness of the writer is strong as it has not been in earlier Japanese literature.... Kafū's writing these last years seems to have dried up, to have lost its bloom.... His prose, so rich and sensuous twenty years ago, has undergone a profound change, and has become so cold and unfriendly as to recall that of Masamune Hakuchō. The fact that the styles of these two masters, who ought to be poles from each other, should thus have come together makes me feel keenly the passage of time."

Yet Tanizaki finds that the novel is after all rather French: "He quickly threw off the influence of Zola and stood in opposition to Japanese naturalism, and now his French training shows through, and there are elements in his writing to suggest Flaubert and Maupassant."*

Perhaps what the argument comes down to is that the Japanese have a way of seeming most Japanese when they think they are being most Western. If the Ginza cafés took Kafū back to the French naturalists, the telling of what he saw there derives as much from

* *The Complete Works of Tanizaki Junichirō* (*Tanizaki Junichirō Zenshū*, Chūō Kōron), XXII, 63–67, 72.

Shunsui's world of chance and coincidence as it does from the French world of inevitability. What is really missing is that other element in Shunsui, that elegant use of the passing seasons so admired by Kafū. It would be difficult to imagine Kimie with a plum blossom in her mouth.

The next years were once more quiet ones. In 1932 Kafū published a single essay, a reply to Tanizaki and Masamune Hakuchō. It shows an altogether mellower Kafū. He solemnly thanks both writers, and prays that no element of personal rancor be read into the essay in which he called Hakuchō a country bumpkin. In a fit of diffidence he says that he became the champion of Edo literature only because he lacked the talent to be anything else; and he is willing to accept being designated a latter-day successor to Saikaku, for he thinks Saikaku a writer of much less stature than the playwright Chikamatsu.

The same essay contains a suggestion that the material of *During the Rains* might not be quite so up-to-date as Tanizaki thinks it: "When I stopped teaching I felt under considerably fewer restraints, and so I naturally turned to the writing of such stories as *Rivalry,* about geisha and the pleasure quarters. Looking back on that period now, I can see that the taste of the world was moving from the geisha to the stage actress. I sought to describe the cult of the geisha as a survival from the Meiji Period.

"The waitresses in the cafés were then still known as 'girl-boys,' and were considered about the equivalent of girls in poultry restaurants.* Suddenly, from about the early twenties, they came into vogue and held sway over the world, and along with movie actresses, took away the popularity of stage actresses. Today, however, a decade after the earthquake, the vogue of the café girls would seem to be passing. And their passing is the reason for my *During the Rains*." (XIV, 199.)

One may wonder why, in his pursuit of vanishing worlds, Kafū did nothing for the stage actress. Something went wrong in the 1920s, it would seem, which left him without energy for that melancholy task. Perhaps, just as in his youth he seemed to be reproving his father and family for having at once too much and too little authority, so in his middle years he preached a philosophy of individualism even while

---

* The English word "boy" designated a waiter. Hence in mixed Japanese-English a waitress became a "girl-boy."

his real grievance at the state and the times was that they did not keep people sufficiently in line. Perhaps the return of authority in the 1930s had something to do with his revival.

His next work of significance appeared in 1934, after two unproductive years. In 1932 there was the single article already quoted, and in 1933 a book of essays, most of them from earlier years. The kernel of the 1934 story, *Flowers in the Shade* (*Hikage no Hana*), is to be found in the diary entry for February 10, 1930, in which the keeper of a geisha house near the Ikuyo stops by for dinner and tells Kafū his life history. "He said that if he but knew how to write as I did, he would set down the events of his life, somewhat startling even to him, for the entertainment of others. I asked him how so, and he replied that he was now approaching fifty, that he had known his first woman at the age of fifteen, and that in the more than three decades since, he had not tried even once to make his own way in the world. He had lived on the earnings of women—it embarassed him to speak of his own uselessness." Yet speak he does, in great detail, beginning with his seduction at the hands of his uncle's mistress, and ending with his decision to team up with a geisha and open an establishment of his own. "How about it, sir? A man's life comes to something like fifty years, and how better to spend it than being taken care of by young women, and having a place to lie in the quiet winter sun at the end of it all? But no—when you find yourself talking like this, everything is finished. I have taken too much of your time." (xx, 72–74.)

The title of *Flowers in the Shade* refers to a Japanese word for "outcast," *hikagemono,* literally "a person in the shade." The hero, Jūkichi, has made a career similar to that of the old man in the 1930 diary entry, and the heroine, O-chiyo, has been through the whole repertoire, serving girl and unmarried mother and wife and divorcée and serving woman and café woman and prostitute and finally kept woman. In many ways the manner of the narrative is like that of *During the Rains,* but in at least one important respect it is different: it contains no successful or respectable people of any importance, and so no objects for Kafū's spleen. Everyone is a "flower in the shade," a prostitute or a procuress or a parasite dependent on a prostitute.

Kept by a wealthy woman in his student days, Jūkichi finds after her death, like the old man in the diary, that the habit of being kept is strong. A go at the real estate business after the earthquake lasts only until the banking crisis of 1927, after which he follows his natural inclinations and lets O-chiyo, a prostitute when the story opens, support him. The more degrading this way of life becomes, the happier he is, although it may be said to his credit that he earns a little money from time to time, by copying dirty books. There is a subplot straight out of an old romance, as Kafū himself remarks, about O-chiyo's illegitimate daughter. She was put out for adoption as an infant and she of course turns up again, as a fellow prostitute. When at length mother and daughter meet, the girl's first remark might be translated "How's business?" (xvi, 108.)

As with *During the Rains,* the narrative is dry and matter-of-fact, even more achromatic than that of the earlier work. The sticky rains of the title are very much present in the one book, the other is altogether more sere and hibernal. If Tanizaki thought Kimie and her companions to be puppets, he might well have had that feeling even more strongly in the case of O-chiyo and hers. Once again the use of coincidence is quite unabashed, most strikingly so in the circumstances that bring O-chiyo and her daughter together. Once again the chief interest is in the plot, with the fear of police raids and middle age hanging over it. Once again the world is a harsh one, the declining world of the cafés, by now virtually undisguised houses of prostitution —the rule in a cafe where O-chiyo works briefly is that "waitresses" are not to wear underclothes. It is a world on the brink of disaster, a carry-over from the 1920s into a sterner decade.

If, however, the principal interest is in the plot, it must be added that, as with the story of the rains, the management of the plot does not seem altogether satisfactory. The story begins late in 1931 and ends in 1932, but seven of the thirteen chapters are reminiscent. They tell of the hero's life from his days as a kept student—he is in his early forties in 1932—to his meeting with O-chiyo; in another flashback, of her life from her period of domestic service up to the same point; and of their life together, with particular attention to the period when the effects of the banking crisis force her to seek the services of a procuress (who later, in an unnecessary and disconcerting scene for so short a work, dies of a toothache). This is a very large chunk of life for a very small book—*Flowers in the Shade* is shorter even than

During the Rains—and much of it is necessarily a compendious recital of tribulations long over. The reader may be forgiven for being
a little impatient to move on to tribulations nearer at hand. In the
very last chapter the daughter appears, traveling an Evangelinesque
path at one point along which she and her mother take clients to the
same inn without knowing it; and so we must learn of all her old
tribulations, which are very complicated, including her deflowering
by an aged pawnbroker who helps her after the earthquake, and
including also a few days in jail. The story closes with a long letter
from the girl to a childhood benefactor, describing her first meeting
with her mother. It is a maladroit device, this bringing in a new character to have the very last word, and it reminds one of the forensic
note on which *The Woman in the Rented Room* ends.

Yet the letter itself is both amusing and touching, and closes the
harsh narrative with a note of pathos. "I wanted to ask my mother
if she still knew the man who was my father, but somehow the conversation did not give me an opening, and besides, I grew up not
knowing that there was such a thing as a father, and I do not feel any
very great desire to see him now. The person I would most like to see
is not my father but my grandmother, who took care of me in Funa-
bori. She died when I was no more than two or three years old, and
I do not remember her face. But when I am alone in the dark, staring
off into space, worn out but unable to sleep, and finally do doze off,
I sometimes think I can see her, and a country scene with a river in it.
I wonder if it is only my imagination that there is such a scene somewhere. And as I told you in my last letter, the happiest time of my
life was when I was in your house in Shinsakaimachi. Your wife
would take me by the hand, and we would walk along the Sumida
by Akashichō and catch crabs. I will never forget it. And so there is
water flowing through my two happiest memories, and the two people
I would most like to see are both dead.

"We have decided that I will live with my mother for a while. I
will let you know if there are any changes." (XVI, 110–12.)

The retrospective nature of much of the book makes the careers
under discussion seem remote and chilly and somewhat lifeless, the
sort of record a memorial stone might carry if memorial stones were
erected to people like O-chiyo and Jūkichi. Yet there are moments of

confrontation when one sees that chilliness is in fact the essence of these lives. Thus there is the moment when Jūkichi is left alone after the death of the middle-aged widow who has been supporting him. The funeral is over, the quarreling relatives have departed, and he is in the dead woman's house and the late-autumn chill, with nowhere to go:

"Left behind, all by himself, he felt that the long, long dream was over. He had no notion what he should do next.

" 'Dinner is ready, sir,' said a woman's voice. Startled, he looked around. It was drawing on toward evening. The room was dusky, and a lonely wind rustled through the trees in the garden. A woman brought a tray to him as he stood up to turn on the light. It was not the maid who usually did the housework, but rather the woman sent around by an agency to help with the funeral.

"She seemed to be in her mid-twenties. She was not especially good-looking, but the fair skin of her round face and the wide eyes with their rich, long lashes gave her a sort of liveliness. The voice was the clean, unspoiled one of a sixteen-year-old. Jūkichi was aware of it for the first time.

" 'Thank you. Maybe I will have something.' He held out his rice bowl.

"The woman did not seem in the least uncomfortable. She apologized for not having brought a tray on which to serve rice properly. 'And I don't suppose you'll find it very appetizing. I didn't know what to get.'

"Outside he could hear the maid closing the shutters.

" 'Oh, it's fine.' Jūkichi finished half of the soup in one breath.

"There had scarcely been time for eating before and during the funeral, and the hunger of several days seemed to come upon him all at once. The fact was that he did not know whether the food was good or not.

"But his words of praise seemed to please the woman. 'You have yourself a good meal, now,' she said. 'Now that it's over, you'll find everything will catch up with you all at once.'

" 'Your name was O-chiyo, I believe. Have you had any funerals in your own family, O-chiyo?' " (XVI, 26–28.)

And so, with no great reluctance and no great enthusiasm, she keeps him company through the night after the funeral. A want of

Kafū in Chinese dress. Shanghai, 1897.

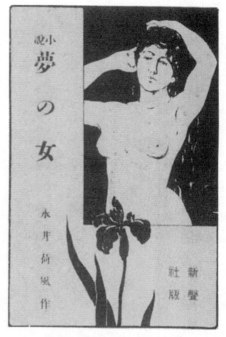

Cover, unauthorized edition of *The Woman of the Dream*, resembling that for the first edition, 1903.

Kafū during his years abroad, probably 1907.

Cover, first edition of *American Tales*, 1908.

Kafū (right) immediately after his return from
France, with his friend Aa (Inoue Seiichi).

Wedding picture, 1912.
The bride is Kafū's first. See p. 47.

Illustration for *The River Sumida*, 1909.
See p. 193.

Family picture, Okubo, Tokyo, 1902. Kafū is between his parents at the left.
The middle of the three brothers, Teijirō, second from the right, was adopted into the
Washizu family. It was with the youngest, Isaburō, at the far right, that Kafū feuded.

The family house in Okubo, sold by Kafū in 1918.

Painting and poem presented by Kafū to O-uta
(Sekine Uta), who was born in the Year of the Ram.
See pp. 120–22 and 142.

Painting by Kafū of the Henkikan,
in Azabu, in which he lived from
1920 to its destruction in 1945.

Self-portrait, painted on fan, 1922

Painting by Kafū, calligraphy by the Kabuki actor Sadanji. Probably early 1920s.

Drawing of a Ginza café and coffee house. From the diary entry for August 27, 1932.
See p. 137.

Kafū, 1932, with his friend Kōjiro Sōyō (see p. 298) and O-uta.

Illustration by Kimura Shōhachi for *A Strange Tale from East of the River*.
See pp. 288–89.

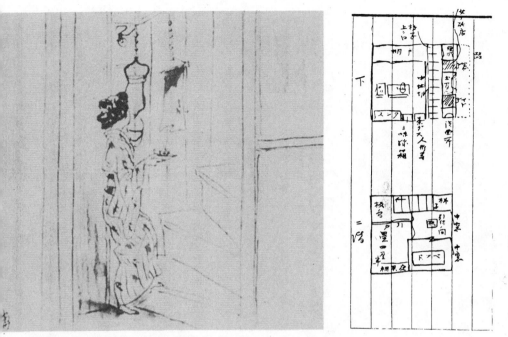

Another Kimura illustration for *A Strange Tale*. On the right is the floor plan for Kafū's favorite house in Tamanoi, from the diary entry for September 7, 1936.

Cover by Kafū for *Sinking and Swimming*.
Limited edition, 1947.

Women observed on a streetcar.
From the diary entry for August 7, 1944.

Kafū (center) on the stage of the Rokkuza, Asakusa,
in a burlesque skit of his making, 1950. See p. 174.

Beside a poster advertising the movie
version of the same skit, 1950.

After receiving the Imperial Cultural
Decoration, 1952. See p. 171.

A late photograph, 1955.

deep attachments has always characterized Kafū's men and women, but nowhere is it more apparent than in the novels of this period. Listlessly people come together and listlessly they stay together. Jū-kichi is helped along by economic necessity and by the vicarious thrill of watching O-chiyo at work, and O-chiyo, we are led to believe, is happy to have a man who will so degrade himself; but essentially they are an unloving pair, as dry and rustling as the narrative style and the autumn garden.

The diary for the early 1930s, the period of *During the Rains,* is full of complaints about the Ginza and its environs. "Clear. The sunlight as if to burn things quite up. The crepe myrtle outside my window is not blooming this year. Read in the afternoon. Dinner on the Ginza, after which I immediately came home. The men and women on the Ginza have gotten steadily worse this last year, and the waitresses are even worse than they used to be." (xx, 163.)

But there is also a good deal of lively information: descriptions of jerry-built cafés whose young ladies will, for a few yen, go upstairs, disrobe, and "do whatever the customer wants them to do" (xx, 236); of houses with exotic names like the Rheingold, their young ladies, though Japanese, going by equally exotic names, Paula and the like. A "salon" called Haru (Spring) had a set of admonitions for its young ladies so pleasing to Kafū that he copied it out in the diary: "Let us show warm affection in each detail of our everyday life. Let us be fair and selfless in our work. Let us be modest and unassuming with everyone. Let us pass our days clean and upright in mind and spirit. Let us save money, for one another, for our house, for our nation." (xx, 310.)

He was still spending a great deal of time on the Ginza, but other sections of the city interested him too. The diary for 1930 records an anonymous letter from a resident of the Tamanoi pleasure district, east of the Sumida, inviting him over to explore the attractions of the area: low prices, outdoor side shows, seven hundred bawdy houses with sixteen hundred women in them. And all this for a four-sen bus ticket from Asakusa. Over the years the diary records a number of long walks through the districts east of the Sumida, and frequent satisfaction with scenes and manners observed there: "Most of the newly built areas of Tokyo...have a sameness about them, a want of distinguishing features. In the districts east of the river, there are

no grand mansions. There are only the sad little houses of the poor—
and this state of affairs makes the eastern part of the city a better place
in which to live a secluded life." (xx, 197.)

"Awoke at eight to find that it was snowing heavily, and the
branches of the beech tree near the window seemed ready to break
under the weight of the snow.... Toward noon it began to clear....
The sky being blue and high in the afternoon, I went by bus to Asakusa, made an offering at the temple, took a second bus on to Senjū,
and stood leaning against the railing of Senjū Bridge, looking at the
river. The sun had already set, and clouds trailed across the sky like
a range of mountains. The last of the twilight colored the snow on
the roofs of the houses, turning it a deep purple. There were lights on
the bridge and in the windows, but because of the light in the sky and
on the water, the houses lining the bank seemed dark, and even the
snow on their roofs seemed to be turning black. The pattern of the
evening clouds changed from moment to moment, and then, suddenly, through a break in the clouds, I saw Fuji. There is a print of
Senjū in Hokusai's 'Thirty-Six Views of Fuji,' but I had never before
seen the mountain from Senjū Bridge. Much taken with it, I made a
sketch in my notebook by the light from the bridge." (xx, 393.)

His first trip to the Tamanoi district of the anonymous letter came
early in 1932: "Wishing to have a look at the rushes, I walked along
the embankment of the Arakawa Drainage Canal. Soon it was nightfall, and the moon came out in the evening sky. It would be the
fifteenth day of the twelfth lunar month, and so a full moon. Out
upon the river where the withered rushes were less thick, the moon
floated like a tray, the effect somehow one that could not be captured
in a painting. I descended from the embankment as Yotsuki Bridge
came near, and found myself in the alleys of Terajima. A sign said
'Shortcut to Tamanoi,' and a half hour's walk brought me out on
a broad avenue, off which, in both directions, were the alleys where
live the bawdy ladies.... Stopping to question them, I learned that
there are five districts, and that in the first district there are many
high-spirited women, whereas in the second district they tend to be
more reposed, affecting the manner of actresses. The gift expected is
one or two yen everywhere." (xx, 198–99.)

Explorations in the districts beyond Asakusa meant turning away
from the Ginza to less up-to-date places, and so to the past, and were

before too many years to bring back the lyrical, reminiscent mood of an earlier Kafū. This time the inspiration was to be not Edo but Meiji, so noisome while it was still present. An insistent awareness of how rapidly the present becomes the past hangs over the diary for the early and middle 1930s, the years when Tamanoi and other plebeian districts were asserting themselves in Kafū's affections. Here are some samples.

"A dark, cloudy day. Looking out the window, I chanced to see white flowers among the trees at the back gate. The loquat is in bloom. When I moved here in the summer of 1920 I saw that a loquat was sprouting from a seed someone had dropped in a corner of the garden, and in the autumn I transplanted it to where it is now. So the stars and the frosts of thirteen years have passed. It is not strange that my loquat should be seven feet high and bearing blossoms. How swiftly the months go by. Times change, I grow old." (xx, 289.)

"A still, cloudy day, of the quiet sort that is called 'the overcast for the new greenery.' Toward evening I heard a temple bell. Since it came from the southeast, I knew it must be from the Mountain of the Three Bonds, the Zōjōji in Shiba Park. What a great delight it is to hear a temple bell in this day of airplanes and automobiles and radios and phonographs. Sometimes at night, too, when I cannot sleep, I hear a bell. Sometimes I hear it toward dawn of the short nights. Perhaps because the wind makes so much noise, I seldom hear it in autumn or winter. Sometimes, when the cherry blossoms have fallen and the new leaves come out and we are going into the rains, I hear it as if it were at my ear. Since there is no one in the house except me, I am taken back to Edo. To get through the world as we know it, one must cultivate the enlightenment and resignation of the man of Edo. When I hear the bell from the Mountain of the Three Bonds, this is the lesson it teaches me." (xxi, 31.)*

"Visited the unlicensed prostitute Odai Fumiko in her room at the corner of the Shintomichō market.... I heard a sound of wooden clogs in the hall, and saw a woman in a Western-style nightgown, her arms and legs bare, her hair bobbed, going out shopping. Before the earthquake Shintomichō still preserved the special manners of the Edo Shitamachi, but now, when occasionally I look into a room there-

---

* This entry and the preceding one about the loquat were expanded into essays.

abouts, I find a way of life in which nothing remains to appeal to my sense of beauty." (XXI, 45.)

"After visiting my father's grave and those of Narushima Ryūhoku, Lafcadio Hearn, and Iwase Osho,* I went for a walk in the direction of Mejiro and on to Otowa.... There are still considerable numbers of wells in the lanes below the hill, most of them boarded over, but the little stream I remember from the old days has quite disappeared. ... The Edogawa Canal is a dirty ditch now, with nothing to arouse one's interest save the sound of the water after nightfall. This last quite took me back to my childhood." (XXI, 91–92.)

"To the Nakasu hospital in the afternoon. I then crossed the river, thinking I would like to count the bridges on the Rokkembori Canal in Fukagawa.... In an alley behind the Chōkeiji Temple there used to be a tenement where, in about 1909 or 1910, my late friend Inoue Aa had his lodgings. I thought I would at least like to find the site, but though I wandered here and there, things had so changed that I was quite unable to make it out.... Returning home after dinner on the Ginza, I thought of my old friend, and took out the magazine *Bummei,* which carried his writings about Fukagawa, and read far into the night." (XX, 224–25.)

Alongside sadness for the past, there is of course irritation at the present.

"Had dinner on the Ginza. The toy stalls are selling dolls dressed up in military uniforms, and planes and tanks and torpedo boats, and every evening this last year the phonograph shops have been playing military songs.... I think back over the past, and see that since the Sino-Japanese War, we have had a war about once every decade.... Efforts to arouse enthusiasm for our current war seem even more frantic than those for the Russo-Japanese War.... It is said that our troops mean to go on from Manchuria to take Mongolia, thence to threaten Russia. We will be lucky if we do not suffer the fate of the German Empire." (XX, 223–24.)

"They seem to have a new radio next door. Every morning it quite precludes sleep with its calisthenics and military music. I sometimes turn an ear to the weather reports, and hear of a 'northeast wind' or a 'southeast wind.'... This is very strange, for ... in Japanese we are

---

* Iwase Osho, or Tadanari (1818–61), was a Tokugawa official, one of the negotiators of the 1858 commercial treaty with England.

accustomed rather to 'east-north' and 'east-south.' . . . It is all very vulgar and distasteful." (xx, 268.)

In one rancorous entry, Kafū records the laudatory preface with which he obliged an unidentified lady writer: "I do not know what sort of person the author of this book is. She came to see me with a letter of introduction from a respected friend. Showing me this book, already in the process of being printed, she asked me to write a preface. I do not know why my friend introduced this writer to me. I do not know why this writer wants a preface from me. I replied that I must refuse, seeing that there was no way to write a preface to an unknown work by an unknown author. She would not let me off so easily, however. And so I have strung together these useless words. I do not know whether or not this writer will find them a suitable introduction to her book. I wish to record, by way of excusing myself, that this has been a great trial." (xx, 448.)

Although lady writers are not among them, ladies, along with memories and the pursuit of the past, are the principal pleasures of the diary. A maid who disappeared leaving behind a trail of unpaid bills became the occasion for a review of the ladies in Kafū's life since his return from France. There are sixteen names on the list, beginning with a Yanagibashi geisha whom he knew briefly before she was set up in Mukōjima by a "patron," and ending with a Miss Watanabe "whose real name is unknown." Uchida Yae, the Shimbashi geisha who was Kafū's second wife, is fourth on the list. For a time in 1920, says Kafū, their affair "began to burn again," but from 1922 they were strangers. Kafū's first wife is not on the list at all. The other items are: Fujita Yoshi, a Hamachō prostitute, whom he knew from January to November of 1909; Yoshida Kō, the Shimbashi geisha Tomimatsu, December 1909 to autumn 1910; Yoneda Miyo, a Shimbashi geisha whom he redeemed for five hundred yen in 1915, kept as a mistress through part of 1916, and thereafter set up in Kagurazaka, and who after the earthquake was active in Tamanoi; Nakamura Fusa, a Kagurazaka geisha whom he redeemed for three hundred yen late in 1916, employed as a maid in Okubo and Tsukiji, and set up in a Yotsuya geisha house in 1920, and who died in an insane asylum; Imamura Ei, the Little Star of the postearthquake days; Nonaka Nao, a prostitute whom he kept in Akasaka for a time in 1925; Otake Tomi, a prostitute whom he kept in 1925 and 1926; a pair of Ginza café maids, one of them the O-hisa of the troubles (see p. 118); a teacher of Kiyomoto; Sekine Uta, the O-uta of the Ikuyo; Yamaji Sanko, real name unknown, a Kagurazaka geisha who was redeemed in August 1930 for a thousand yen, and left in a Yotsuya geisha house late the same year, and with whom he parted company the following year; a Miss Kurosawa whose real name turned out to be Nakayama, and to whom he paid fifty yen per month from late 1933 through 1934; and, finally, Miss Watanabe, who also received fifty yen per month. Miss Watanabe brought a gentleman friend with her on assignations, and Kafū watched and took pictures of their dalliance. "There were other emergency affairs that I have not time to record," the entry concludes. (XXI, 104–5.)

On February 23, 1936, there is a melancholy entry indicating apprehensions lest the roster of names be complete forever, Miss Watanabe its last name. Miss Watanabe, performing with her gentleman friend, interested him for a time, says the entry, but she does so no more, and the one lady he has kept company with since has interested him only because of the sad story of her life. Seeing that with the end of passion the end of life itself may be in sight, Kafū writes down instructions for the disposal of his affairs upon his demise: there is to be no funeral, and no hearse or tombstone, and the bones are to be left in the crematory; the estate is to go to the Académie Goncourt; there is to be no commercial edition of his writings, nor any "stupid advertisements"; instead his savings are to be used for printing a private edition.

The essays of the period, like much of the diary, are elegiac, in sharp contrast to the rancor and contentiousness of the 1920s. Collected under the title *A Housefly in the Winter* (*Fuyu no Hae,* 1935; expanded edition, 1945), they have to do largely with the Tokyo of Kafū's youth. The title is from a haiku by Kikaku, and suggests a person who has outlived his time.

The reminiscences go back to Kafū's childhood, with particular emphasis on his adolescence and early youth, the years of his great illness, his first visits to the pleasure quarters, and his stay in China. When something is found to be unchanged from Meiji, it is usually something unpleasant, like rows of shacks in Fukagawa with tin roofs and drying rags. It is the good things that have gone. Here is a touch of Fukagawa as it was back in the days when Inoue Aa was living there, in illicit union with a woman disapproved of by his family: "In those days you never saw artisans reading newspapers on streetcars, and Socialist propaganda had not yet reached the back streets of Fukagawa. There were pots of morning glories at all the bamboo-latticed windows, and little wind-bells tinkling under the eaves. All of one's neighbors had been born in this run-down part of Tokyo, and all of them lived secure in a world of superstition and ancient customs. A person who wore Western clothes and whiskers had to be, for the inhabitants of these back streets, a policeman or perhaps a Salvation Army man, a person, in either case, from a wholly different class, whose speech and manners were wholly foreign.

"Here it was that my friend Aa, 'The Night Crow of Fukagawa,' went calmly ahead down the road he had chosen, the pursuit of haiku, with no desire for membership in the literary club or companionship with literary people. I thought him wholly admirable, true heir to that unique tradition, the poetry of Edo. . . .

"As I amble down the new concrete highways and observe the Fukagawa of the new age, I see, late though I have been in coming to the decision, that I must shed my old notions of beauty as a cicada sheds its shell." (XIV, 252–53, 257–58.)

With the Yoshiwara, matters are just as bad, despite an occasional glimpse of the past: "Back in the days when the old plays and romances were giving us our first enthusiasm for literature, the loneliness of the streets and farmlands outside this Yoshiwara had a powerful fascination for us. . . .

"Wild flowers bloomed along the embankment and there were pussy willows, and there was a series of decaying wooden bridges, Hairwashing Bridge and the rest. . . .

"In the autumn of 1908, when I came back from several years abroad, I felt like an old devotee for whom the rules had been turned upside down. There were beer halls on the central street of the Yoshiwara, and the harmony of 'the two rows of lanterns, that first sign of autumn,' had already been destroyed. The rows of ladies waiting in the houses had disappeared. The Five Streets were dark, the rickshaws along the embankment were conspicuously fewer in number. The flood of August 1910 and the great fire the following April quite changed the Yoshiwara and its environs, and so began the process whereby it turned into the drab, featureless place we have today. . . .

"Tokyo three or four decades ago offered a delicate balance between the moods of the writer and the facts of his life such as is quite unimaginable today. . . .

"There was a sad, plaintive harmony in the life and scenes of the Yoshiwara, like that of Edo plays and ballads. It was not the creation of novelists who put their skills to the uses of their tastes. And it was not limited to the Yoshiwara. In the Tokyo of past days there was a sad harmony in the crowded lowland flats and in the quiet hilly sections, too. . . . But time passed, and the noise and glare of the frantic modern city destroyed the old harmony. The pace of life changed. I believe that the Edo mood still remained in the Tokyo of thirty years ago. Its last, lingering notes were to be caught in the Yoshiwara.

"I do not wish to urge the revival of the quarters; I do not ask new prosperity for its inmates. Who among admirers of Greece would wish to revive its classical arts?" (xiv, 270–71, 280–83.)

The year 1936, which brought Kafū's specifications for his own funeral, also brought new life. It began with unusual incidents public and private: the military uprising of February 26, a day Kafū spent at home observing the snow and listening to the horn of a bean-curd vender; and a funeral, at which he met his younger brother, the first meeting, says the diary, since 1914. It was not these, however, nor nostalgic thoughts about the Yoshiwara, that were to be important for his writing. It was rather a return to Tamanoi.

One of the cheaper of the quarters, Tamanoi had a brief history. It did not survive the Second World War, and its origins went back only to about the time of the First. Kafū's own writings on the subject indicate that Terajima, a district beyond the river to the north and east of Asakusa, was marshy land at about the beginning of the Taishō Period, or just before the First World War, at which time, however, the name Tamanoi did not exist. The pleasure district came into being when, with the replanning of the city after the earthquake, the dubious houses around the temple and park of Asakusa were transplanted east of the river.

It has been noted that Kafū's first visit to Tamanoi occurred early in 1932, but then he did not really know his way around. In 1936 the diary finds him with a map, exploring the quarter more thoroughly, and finding the houses cleaner than he would have imagined. Most of them, he finds further, have baths. At a rate of five yen per hour, young ladies will join the bathing, though some demand as much as thirty yen per hour or five yen for shorter plunges. Kafū recommends the proprietors of street stalls for information on where the most interesting girls are to be found. He himself has learned much: Mariko at No. 48 is by nature so bawdy that she sometimes sends an inexperienced client fleeing in shocked surprise; Yukari at No. 73 and Chieko at No. 57 have remarkable if eccentric talents, and Taeko at No. 54 will, for a special fee, allow use to be made of an interesting arrangement of mirrors. There is also information about health tests, the native provinces of the ladies, and the economics of getting into and staying in the business. (xxi, 137–39.) Kafū's first serious visit to Tamanoi is also described in an essay entitled "A Chronicle of Terajima" (*Terajima no Ki,* 1936):

"At the sound of steps the women in the windows would call out 'Hello Mister, Hello Mister.' And then: 'Hello there, you with the glasses.' The voices had a strange lilt, exactly of the sort I knew when I was twenty or so, in Rashōmon Alley of the Yoshiwara, or Kekoro in Suzaki, or the alleys behind Asakusa Park. I suddenly felt that I had been taken back thirty or forty years. Even the water in the ditch, quiet and stagnant, took me back to the Yoshiwara of the days when the Moat of the Black-Toothed Beauties had not yet been filled in.*

"I fell into a strange, reminiscent mood. The voices along the alley became more insistent with each step. 'You, there. Come on over,' one would say, and another would invite me in for a cup of tea. Some only smiled, and others watched in silent composure, as if to say that there was no point in bothering with someone who would not cooperate in any case." (xiv, 340.)

Kafū did go into one of the houses for a cup of tea and a chat, if his account is to be believed. He carefully noted down what he saw inside, and what he learned of the past and the possible future of the lady who offered him tea, and how the quarter felt, when, later in the evening, the tea consumed, he started for home. It was alive with hecklers and amusement seekers and wandering musicians and street venders and delivery boys, and, always more insistent, the alluring calls from the windows. "Aren't you the fickle one, though. I know what you've been up to, you over there, the one that went by a few minutes ago." (xiv, 345–46.)

* Courtesans traditionally blackened their teeth.

Visits to Tamanoi were frequent through the summer of 1936. Early in the autumn Kafū decided that he would write a novel about Asakusa, but it was Tamanoi, on beyond the river and Asakusa, that continued to occupy his attention and the space in his diary:

"September 7. Already in the morning the temperature was above ninety. In the evening I went walking in Sumida Park. Everywhere, on the benches, on the grass, along the shore of the pond, unkempt men lay sprawled about almost naked. They did not seem to be strollers or vagrants, but rather young persons who lived in the neighborhood. Considerable numbers had women with them. No doubt it is the same in all the parks of the city: men in dirty undershirts lie sleeping among the litter of waste paper and banana peels. I crossed Kototoi Bridge and took a bus to Tamanoi. I have been coming, since March or April, on repeated trips to investigate the quarter, and I have found by chance a house that is most convenient for resting. It contains but one lady, and her keeper never puts in an appearance. There was a maid when I first started visiting the place, and one or two have since followed her, but now there is none. The woman says that she was once a courtesan in Suzaki. She would appear to be approaching her mid-twenties. Although she has a north-country accent, her face is round, her eyes are large, and her mouth is firm, and one feels that she could find a better place to work. The fact that she does not haggle over payment and is generally liberal and easygoing makes it seem possible that she may indeed have been in one of the great houses. Knowing how to please women in her calling, I always bring a small present from Asakusa.

"This evening while I was having a smoke over the brazier in the backroom downstairs, she sat at the small front window, talking to me through the bead curtain that separates front from rear. Then, suddenly, she stopped a man in the street and went upstairs with him. (The light being out in the backroom, he could not see me as he came in.)* She came down shortly, and said that she had 'an engagement.' 'If you have nothing else to do, would you mind watching the place for a while?' She threw off the kimono she was wearing and, opening a drawer, took out a summer one, a very clever imitation of Akashi

---

* The remark in parentheses, small type in the original, was evidently added at the time of publication.

crepe. 'Where are you going?' I asked. 'I don't really know. Maybe Mukōjima. He's giving me fifteen yen for an hour. You never know about a customer. Well, next time you come out with me. I'll make it ten yen for you.' She was in such a hurry that she scarcely had the breath to say even this much. Tying herself into a narrow obi, she went upstairs and came down again with her customer. In white trousers and a black coat, he was of a sort common among shopkeepers and bill collectors. As she took out a pair of sandals wrapped in newspaper, she asked him to go out ahead of her. She would meet him at the letter box on the corner to the left, she said, and signaled to me with her eyes that I was in charge.

"And so I was left to guard the place, theoretically for an hour, though I feared that the one hour might grow into two or more. Not easily ruffled, I was still a trifle uneasy. But it was just past nine by the clock on the wall. I settled down, feeling a little better. To while away the time I went through her cupboards and chests. Contrary to my expectations, she was back at shortly after ten. I asked her where she had gone and how it had been. To an inn in Mukōjima, she said. Something had evidently been arranged in advance, and she gathered that she had been used as a performer in a peep show. It was possible, indeed, that someone had taken pictures. She had thought all along that the conditions were too good, fifteen yen from a passerby she had never seen before. Taking the money from her obi, she held it to the light to see whether or not it was good, then shoved it into a box attached to the brazier. It was approaching eleven. I started out, saying that I would come again. In her absence I drew a chart of the house, here appended." (xxi, 161–63.)

"September 13.... Crossing Kototoi Bridge, I walked to Tamanoi, through the pleasure quarters behind the Akiba Shrine, and passed the time of the evening at the usual house. The woman, suffering from an attack of tonsillitis, was resting downstairs in the dark, under an old mosquito net. We talked until about eleven, when I left. There was a special charm about the humming of the mosquitoes, taking one back to the past." (xxi, 163–64.)

"September 15.... To Tamanoi in the evening. On the way I looked at the festival decorations for the Ushijima Shrine. At the usual house I had an ice with the woman, at thirty sen, really an astonishingly high price.... The autumn mosquitoes came in swarms, and as she drove them away with a broken fan, the sound brought back thoughts of olden times." (xxi, 164.)

Most of this, and considerably more—for instance, a diary entry of October 25, 1935, about an old bookseller north of Asakusa—was very shortly to find its way into a piece of fiction, or semifiction. On September 20 it was decided that not Asakusa but Tamanoi would be the setting for the piece. Kafū began work on *A Strange Tale from East of the River* (*Bokutō Kidan*) toward the end of the month, when the evenings were cooler, and the neighbors' radio was no longer troublesome enough to make him seek refuge in Tamanoi (indeed, he was beginning to feel that he had paid his last visit to the lady there). It was finished the following month and published in a limited private edition in the spring of 1937. Despite his apparently strong views about people who descend to newspaper writing, it was serialized in the *Asahi* between April and June 1937—the first of his works in the almost four decades since *Sneers* to be subjected to that indignity.

Coming after *Flowers in the Shade,* the *Strange Tale* is something of a surprise. It is a highly personal lyric, rather in the vein of "Quiet Rain," and, like that work, in many ways scarcely a novel at all. It is less about Tamanoi than about Kafū in Tamanoi. He found himself briefly at home there, and he wrote an evening elegy to tell us how it was.

The story is of an aging writer who spends the hot evenings of a summer with a Tamanoi prostitute and who ceases doing so when the cold weather comes. Necessarily made personal and subjective by the nature of its slight little plot, the "novel" becomes yet more personal because of digressions on such subjects as the police, the writings of Tamenaga Shunsui, and the writings of Nagai Kafū, and it trails off into a poem after the hero has paid his last visit. It belongs to the uniquely Japanese genre to which "Quiet Rain" also belongs, the leisurely, discursive "essay-novel," its forebears the discursive essay and "poem story" (*utamonogatari*) of the Heian Period, and the linked verse of the Muromachi Period and after. The structure is still further loosened by quotations from and comments upon the novel the hero is in process of writing. The device was probably borrowed from Gide, but here it works to a much different effect. *The Counterfeiters* is a book about writing. *A Strange Tale from East of the*

River is rather a novel, or essay-novel, about the moods of a man who happens to be writing a novel. The feeling that there is a certain want of inevitability in the relationship between the novel and the novel-within-the-novel is intensified by the fact that the latter, about a retired schoolteacher who abandons his family, is not very interesting. The two passages quoted from it are largely dialogue, and dialogue, as has been seen, was not Kafū's strongest point. The second of the two comes to a listless close ·with a long row of dots.

Yet *A Strange Tale from East of the River* is justly included among Kafū's masterpieces. It must be taken on its own terms, as a lyric and not a novel of conflict and resolution. If it is about the moods of an aging author, it is wonderfully successful in evoking the occasions for those moods. The heavy, still summer night is an almost tactile presence, less a cause for discomfort than an invitation to join in, to become one with the season. The natural elements and the artificial appurtenances are of such a oneness that modern additions like the flit gun would quite ruin them. Even the most uninviting manifestations of summer, the humming of mosquitoes, for instance, do their bit toward taking the hero back to old summers. Indeed the mosquitoes are almost as important as the woman O-yuki herself. It is they that bring memories. In one of the most touching passages it is memories of nights in Inoue Aa's Fukagawa rooms. In the 1935 Yoshiwara essay quoted above (see pp. 143–44), Kafū wrote admiringly and wistfully of Higuchi Ichiyō's "Growing Up" (*Takekurabe*), and lamented the passing of the Yoshiwara as an inspiration for such writing. Yet, in spirit, the conclusion to the *Strange Tale* is not altogether unlike the conclusion to "Growing Up." Although Ichiyō's is much the more carefully shaped work, the poignant sense of a summer that will not come back hovers over both.

It is very subtle and elusive, this milieu in which one can feel affection for buzzing mosquitoes, but perhaps the discursive and loosely articulated nature of the story increases the possibility that something can be brought across in translation.*

While the *Strange Tale* was being written and published, Kafū's relations with his family went their usual eccentric way. A few days

* A complete translation will be found in Part II, pp. 278–328.

after the visit to Tamanoi described above, Kafū's brother called to say that an uncle had died, and to tell him about the funeral plans. "And so Isaburō seems prepared to let the emotions of twenty years simply evaporate away." (xxi, 186.) The uncle in question had slightly earlier been the subject of a bitter piece of invective, in which he was described as the very model of the bureaucratic hypocrite, lecturing the public on morality even while he was busy producing an illegitimate child. (The illegitimate child, the novelist Takami Jun, who was thus Kafū's first cousin, had during the summer published a volume of short stories making this state of affairs clear.) Kafū's diary entry on the uncle concludes with practical advice about how to avoid the misfortune of having illegitimate children: "But I suppose my good uncle was so busy preaching to the public that he had no time to learn of such devices as the condom." (xxi, 161.)

On March 18, 1937, came the news, through a nephew, that his mother was seriously ill. "Because Isaburō's family is living with my mother," Kafū says in the diary, "I do not wish to pay a sick call. I am determined not to put in an appearance even if the worst comes. This is not a decision I have made upon the spur of the moment. When I gave up the house in Okubo in 1918 and moved to an alley in Tsukiji, I was already reconciled to what must happen. I said that I took the day of my departure from Okubo to be equivalent to the day of my mother's death. I did not answer my nephew's letter because I knew that it would be useless to write of things that happened twenty years ago." (xxi, 212–13.)

Kafū's behavior during the months of his mother's last illness was extraordinary. On April 3 the brother himself came calling, to say that the illness was serious. Kafū apparently refused to see him, and the diary entry describing the incident closes with a lament not for the mother but for the state of civilization, because Kafū in the course of the day has detected a misprint in an advertisement. On April 7 another letter came from the nephew, and Kafū's response was to summon the geisha Yaeji, his second wife, for consultation. On April 30 there was a report that his mother's condition was worse. Kafū went for a walk in Asakusa, in the course of which he evidently fumed, for he came home to record in the diary his bill of indictment against his brother: that Isaburō had been out of sympathy with Kafū's writing; that he had forced a split in the family at the time of

Kafū's marriage to Yaeji; that he had removed himself from Kafū's family register and set himself up as the head of an independent family; and that he had encouraged his children to taunt Kafū.

The diary contains no further mention of the mother until her death in September. Kafū paid no sick call and did not attend the funeral. Instead he seemed intent upon bringing about a repetition of the circumstances of his father's death, when engrossment in the demimonde had so interfered with his filial duty. Much of the time went in the usual pursuits, long walks through the city and evenings on the Ginza, where his favorite haunt was no longer a café (the Tiger had closed its doors in 1935) but a restaurant and coffeehouse called the Fuji Ice. Somewhat more remarkable were his visits to Tamanoi with "young W.," partner of that Miss Watanabe to whom Kafū for a time gave fifty yen a month (see p. 142). The diary contains brief and fleeting hints that some of Kafū's adventures may have been homosexual.

The most striking thing about these months, however, is the revival of interest in the Yoshiwara. Unlike the visits to Tamanoi, visits to the Yoshiwara sometimes kept him away for days on end. "It is strange, but houses of the courtesans have come to seem like my abode, and my house itself like little more than a library." (xxi, 238.) The ostensible reason for the visits was to collect material for a novel. He found that almost everything about the place had changed save the tendency of the ladies to behave in bed like wooden dummies. Yet occasionally something pleased him: "The girl Kozuchi is clean and fresh in her appearance and quiet in her behavior, a reminder of famous courtesans of the Meiji Period." (xxi, 252.)

But he tended to be more stirred by dead courtesans than by live ones: "Asking directions to the Jōkanji Temple from the old woman in the tea stall, I started out along the road under the elevated tracks, and immediately came upon the temple, surrounded by a stone fence. Under the eaves of the gate, where it is protected from wind and rain, there are still traces of vermilion paint, to call back memories of thirty years ago. In the old days, when you walked along the brook below the embankment, there was just such a red gate.... To the left of the main hall is the grave of a Kadoebi courtesan. Here is the inscription:

" 'The Story of Wakamurasaki. She was an Osaka girl whose real name was Katsuta Nobuko. Wakamurasaki was her name as a courtesan. She first gave herself to the Kadoebi house in the Yoshiwara in 1898, and became its leading courtesan, her manner and her appearance delicate beyond all others. Her great day would not return, for she was in her prime; and alas, on August 24 of this year, she was stabbed by a deranged guest, and so her life of twenty-one years came to an untimely end, a pity and a shame. Her bones lie buried here.... Certain comrades have gathered together and, thinking to console her spirit, have erected this stone in her memory. This spot is hereby named Wakamurasaki's Mound. October 11, 1903.'... I went to the door of the priest's quarters and there bought incense and asked directions to the graves of the courtesan Moriito and her lover. The priest pointed to the left of the gate, between the well and the hedge, and so I started off with incense sticks and myrtle in my hand. A girl who seemed to be about eleven or twelve, playing alone, showed me the two tombstones, remarking as if to herself: 'There they are, friendly as can be.' Probably she shows visitors to the graves and knows their story, but I stared at her in astonishment for a time, wondering how a child that age could understand a love suicide....

"At home by a few minutes after ten, I took out an English book about the Nightless City, and saw that it has the graves not side by side as today, but some slight distance apart. No doubt the present stones were put up later. Since June I have been going to the Yoshiwara in the evening and leaving in the morning, and I have not regretted the time spent on my way home exploring the streets nearby; but nothing has given me such pleasure as seeing the Jōkanji again this morning, for the first time in thirty years. The city has changed completely, but what a delight to know that the gate and the hall survived the earthquake! If anyone considers erecting a monument to me when I die, let him choose a spot here among the leaning, crumbling stones of the courtesans, and let him put up a stone no more than five feet high, and inscribe on it only the words 'The Grave of Kafū the Scribbler.' " (xxi, 245-46.)

On September 8 the cousin who had been with him in America came to say that his mother was dying, and pleaded with him to visit her. Kafū replied that he would do so after he had changed clothes. Having thus disposed of the cousin, he set off for Asakusa. On the following day an old family retainer came with news of her death. "Knowing of my relations with Isaburō, Sakai came but to report the facts. He said that the funeral would be conducted by Isaburō's family, and that I need not be present. We went out together and had dinner on the Ginza. . . .

"My mother was born to the Washizu family, and her name was Tsune. She was born in Okachimachi, Shitaya, Edo, on the fourth day of the ninth month, 1861, the second daughter of the Confucian scholar Washizu Kidō.* She was married on July 10, 1877, to Nagai Hisaichirō, a pupil of Kidō's. She had one daughter and three sons.† She died on September 8, 1937, in her home in Okubo, Tokyo, aged 76, and is to be buried in the Nagai plot in the Zōshigaya Cemetery. "In memoriam:

'Autumn rains, and a night of tears has come.' Kafū. 'The autumn wind this year has taken my mother away.' Kafū."
(XXI, 270-71.)

Kafū continued to visit Tamanoi for some time after the completion of *A Strange Tale from East of the River*. On October 13, 1938, the diary records a chance encounter with the Tamanoi lady who was so kind to him. She has left for the Western suburbs, there to seek employment as a waitress.

From late 1937 the diary finds him with a new interest: "The singing at the Asakusa theaters is not much better than that in the Imperial Theater back in the days when it had a musical troupe, but I feel none of the distaste I used to feel in Marunouchi. There is a pleasant sadness, rather, in sitting among the unlettered masses and watching a performance in Asakusa." (XXI, 289.)

In the November 30 entry he learns to understand "something of the situation" in the Asakusa theaters, from a long talk with an actress named Mariko. On December 12 he chances upon a pair from the Opera House, his favorite theater, and follows them west from the park. "They went into one of the rented houses behind the Honganji Temple. The woman hurried out again to buy pickles, and then hurried back inside. They were finally having dinner, after three afternoon and evening performances. Somehow I felt the poignant sadness in their lives." (XXI, 295.)

---

* The date of the mother's birth follows the old lunar calendar.
† The daughter, who has not been mentioned before, died in infancy.

By early 1938 he and the dancing girls were such close friends that he frequented their dressing room, and so aroused the suspicions of male members of the troupe. Presently the functionary in charge of the dressing room admonished him for his behavior and urged a measure of restraint, but by that time Kafū had already begun work on the lyrics for a musical called "A Katsushika Love Story" (*Katsushika Jōwa*), produced at the Opera House in May. Despite a certain ugliness in his relations with the young gentlemen of the troupe (a rumor reached him in April that one of them meant to beat him up), the young ladies, the diary makes clear, were a source of much comfort: "The performances and the dancing practice being finished, I went with the dancers Fumiko, Michiko, Tomiko, and Chieko to the Himpōrō restaurant beside the Shōchiku Theater. It was already past one in the morning. As we saw Michiko home, we passed along the main street of the Yoshiwara. Under a profusion of cherry blossoms, three or four strolling musicians were singing popular songs to the accompaniment of guitar and accordion.... Stopping the cab, we walked to the Sumire, in an alley in Kadochō, and had something to eat. A strolling Shinnai singer came by, and the dancers laid down their chopsticks, so intent were they upon the old love story he sang of. The contrast between the music and their up-to-date garb was complete, and most amusing. All around twenty years old, they take a lively interest in everything.... I am quite unable to describe how moved I was. Home at four o'clock." (xxi, 326.)

Meanwhile the Chinese war dragged to the end of its first year. The diary records the effects on the city. There are reports, for instance, that the theaters are to be closed. Strange persons, these militarists, Kafū says wryly: while closing down theaters at home, they recruit platoons of prostitutes to serve the boys overseas. But not everything militaristic is bad: "To the Opera House in the evening.... There being no neons, the moon lit the tall buildings, cold and clear, and cast tree shadows upon the street. A most compelling scene. The prohibition against neon signs must be described as an enlightened act by our unenlightened military government." (xxi, 353.)

"It was cloudy in the evening but later it cleared, and the moon was bright. Tonight was the last of the air-raid drills. The city has been very quiet these last few nights. There have been no radios and no automobiles, and only the shriek of a warning siren and an occasional gun have broken the silence. I am taken back some thirty or forty years." (XXI, 460.)

Visits to the Opera House continued, but the pinch was beginning to be felt: "Because there have been so few cabs since this spring, I have spent fewer of my nights watching the practice at the Opera House. I was much moved, however, to see the district again this morning while it was still sleeping." (XXI, 431.)

"It has become quite impossible to look at the shows around the park. The manners of the audiences and of the people in the streets have quite changed this past year, to make one feel most intensely the passage of time. There is no longer anything appealing or distinctive in the moods of the Shitamachi." (XXI, 446.)

A new decade was at hand, and it added disasters to the annoyances: "I read only dispatches from England and France about the European War, and ignore everything from Germany.... Day and night I pray for a French victory. It is at such times that a Joan of Arc should appear." (XXII, 29.)

"The fall of Paris is imminent. I find myself inconsolable, and dinner this evening was a tasteless affair." (XXII, 30.)

New disasters were in sight, and it was necessary to look for haven: "All sorts of requests and invitations come these days from right-wing organizations and bureaucrats, and there is a danger that I may one day find myself on the same platform with a performer of Osaka ballads. I have given thought to ways of avoiding this fate. One such way might be to sink myself into disreputable surroundings. Going to Tamanoi a number of times this last month, therefore, and having the good fortune from some years ago to be on friendly terms with two or three establishments there, I have asked how the chances would be of buying a bawdy house and making it my refuge. Day before yesterday I chanced upon a certain house, and this evening after dinner went again to see it. In each of the three second-floor rooms there is a large mirror by the pillow, and from the closet of one room it is possible to look into the next. The owners wish to sell for cash, if they can find a good buyer, and retire to the country. They have a son who graduated from the university last year and is in the Formosan Service." (XXII, 39–40.)

Others, too, were seeking shelter. Along toward the middle of 1940, certain ladies began coming to him with their problem: "The census was taken on the first of the month, and everyone, man and woman alike, has had to fill out forms making clear his or her occupation.... And so the world has become a most inconvenient place for people who walk in the shade. Several women with whom I was once friendly but of whom I had quite lost track have called to say that, in such-and-such a rented room, they yet pursue the old business. Now they are having trouble with the census. Might they, as a formality only, say that they are being kept by me? I have had to refuse. What would the tax office say if it found me with all these mistresses?" (XXII, 41.)

The disaster of the 1940s was to destroy both Tamanoi and Kafū's Henkikan. The only difference, had he bought that bawdy house, might have been that when the fire raids came, the crowded flatlands would have been more difficult to flee from than hilly Azabu.

Chapter eight The Nineteen-Forties and After

The years of the confrontation came. Numbers of writers who were swept up in the hysteria have said since the war that they had no alternative but to participate. Kafū's example shows that there was in fact an alternative: to lapse into silence, and think what thoughts one wished. Japanese authoritarianism never went to the extreme of forcing people to speak when they did not wish to.

Few writers of the period managed to preserve the sad calm that is to be found in the diary of choleric old Kafū:

"It has been four years since I commenced this life of solitude, living in the maid's room and cooking for myself. At first there was a certain novelty in the arrangement. Then, toward the end of last year, the ways of the military government began to grow more arbitrary, and there came a change in the world; and somehow the drab and inconvenient life of the bachelor has come to seem so appropriate to the moods of the days that I would not now find it easy to change. Indeed my feelings and thoughts are quite beyond description when, on an evening of a sudden autumn rain, I drag my sandals along the cliff, taking care that the frayed thong does not break, and buy onions and radishes in Tanimachi. I am quite drunk with the melancholy poetry of it all. However malicious and arbitrary may be the ways of the government, it cannot keep one's fancies from running free. There will be freedom while there is life." (XXII, 107.)

"On my way back from shopping in the afternoon, I looked in on the cemetery of the Kōmyōji, this side of the Iigura Hachiman Shrine. ... At the top of the hill beyond a fence is the Dutch Legation. There were windows open, and there still seemed to be occupants. The home country has been destroyed by wolves, and now its lands in the Indian

Ocean are threatened.* And are the emissaries of the lost country still living here? How very touching." (XXII, 124–25.)

"Rumor has it that teachers of Shinnai, banned last year, have now been forbidden to put out their signs. Both branches of Utazawa are also banned. . . . Some lament the destruction of Edo music, but there is nothing to be done. It would have died, government order or none, for the elegant music of plebeian Edo is not something to please the popular tastes of our day. The same may be said of my writings." (XXII, 126.)

It should not be thought, however, that all was sweet resignation. In 1940 Kafū refused to go to a nephew's funeral because he feared he might meet his brother. The same year Iwanami and Fuzambō joined the list of publishing houses he wished to have nothing to do with. The former was unacceptable because of its closeness to the Mita group of writers. Though the Mita people had once been his friends and disciples, Kafū thought that they were trying to make unscrupulous use of him. Fuzambō's offense was to claim certain rights to Shitaya Gleanings. Kafū thought the claims fraudulent, though they were evidently supported by contract. Equally unfriendly was his behavior when, again in 1940, an old friend, the actor Sadanji, died: he refused to compose an inscription for the memorial stone. Sadanji in his last years, Kafū notes in his diary, was not true to the spirit of Edo. Kafū did, however, compose a number of valedictory verses, one of them suggesting that the Tsukiji Canal, running past the Kabuki Theater, would be warmed with tears. For all his lyrical talents, Kafū was not very good at formal verse.

Pearl Harbor came. Kafū's reaction was to start writing again. He had written no fiction since 1938, but on December 8, Pearl Harbor Day in Japan, he began work on a novel. Finished early the following year and published after the war as Sinking and Swimming (Ukishizumi), it is the least satisfying of his wartime writings. It has an air of weary determination. Although one can see why Kafū felt compelled to see it through, one cannot help feeling that he would have done better to keep it to himself.

The general scheme of the book is like that of an earlier and better book, The Woman of the Dream. It describes the life of a woman who

* The word translated "wolves" is hitora, literally "thick-necked tiger," but phonetically "Hitler."

is constantly on the verge of going under. Her plight fails to compel attention, however, both because she soon comes to seem like one of those comic-strip characters who walk around with perpetual rain clouds over their heads, and because the reader soon comes to realize that each time she is about to go under some remarkable coincidence will save her.

There is, to be sure, a certain amount of commendable enough reporting on the customs and manners of the immediate prewar years, evidently gleaned from the diary, as when the heroine accepts a position in a "café" catering to foreigners and is required to call herself Theresa so that they may feel at home. But in the end, as if hurrying to be done with these people, Kafū deserts both them and the techniques of dramatic presentation. The last pages, reminiscent of the last pages of *Flowers in the Shade,* are in the form of a diary. It is the diary of a man in whose company the heroine finds brief haven before going out to battle the waters once more, and she comes upon it by coincidence. The man is a typical Kafū outcast and failure, and if his diary does not do a great deal for the novel, it perhaps does tell something of Kafū's despondency in the first months of the war: "I have given up thoughts of family and descendants and status. I no longer think about the future.... Autumn is passing and winter is coming. Are the cultures of the countries that lie in the range of fire to disappear? Are Gothic cathedrals to go the way of the pyramids? Looking at the late-autumn sun upon autumn grasses already dropping their seeds, I have been sunk in the deepest emotions." (xvII, 193, 198.) The last of the entries is dated October 1941.

Kafū's other wartime writings include a number of essays, one of them a scholarly study of Tamenaga Shunsui that is much admired by specialists; two short novels, *Dancing Girl* (*Odoriko*) and *A Tale No One Asked For* (*Towazugatari*); and two pieces that are generally described as short stories, though there is not a great deal of fiction in them. None of the fiction or semifiction was published during the war. Of the two "short stories," one is a somewhat strident airing of a personal grudge against two young literary persons who were introduced to Kafū by the novelist Satō Haruo, and who then proceeded to make a business of faking Kafū manuscripts. It is not on the whole in very good taste, and perhaps rises to the level of literature only at one point, a sweetly sad passage in which Kafū describes what led him to take the two men into his confidence. They seemed to be without ambitions in the bright literary world, and so they took him back to his youth, and, yet further, to Edo, when novelists were frequently outcasts.

"In a day when the whole world seemed to be mad for profits, I happened to come upon two young men who somehow did not fit into the mood of the times. In my delight at finding them, I had no time to think about the reasons, the personal histories, that lay behind this refusal to be caught up in the dominant currents. Just as there are sudden sports in trees and grasses, so every age has its freaks. There was no need for particular surprise that two young men like Shirai and Kiba should exist in the age of Shōwa." (XVII, 213–14.)

The other wartime story, "The Decoration" (*Kunshō*), is a nostalgic vignette about the dead world of the Asakusa dancing girls.* Or, more precisely, it is a joining of two things, a detailed description of the girls' dressing room in the Opera House, and the pathetic story of an inconspicuous death, almost unnoticed in the Asakusa swirl. The germ of the latter incident, which is the heart of the story, is to be found in the diary entry for October 24, 1938, in which Kafū describes photographing an ancient Opera House personage who proudly displays a medal from the Russo-Japanese War. The two elements of the story may seem badly joined, and the clutter of the dressing room may seem to clutter up the story itself; but it is very touching all the same, this story of a death gone unnoticed in the great stew of Asakusa.

"The Decoration" might be considered a sort of prelude to a longer, equally sad story about the dead world of the Asakusa theaters: the novel *Dancing Girl* (*Odoriko*), written in 1944. Both are about lives wasted in the dirt and noise of Asakusa, and about its power at once to fascinate and repel. The wasted life in this case is that of a musician of onetime promise (by his own admission, for he is the narrator) who has played in a cheap Asakusa theater for upwards of a decade, and who, on the eve of war and middle age, gives it up to play the piano for a nursery school in the western suburbs. The main action covers a year, from spring 1936 to spring 1937, and is concerned principally with an affair between him and the sister of his mistress. The mistress is a dancer, and the sister variously a dancer, a low-class geisha, and

---

* It is translated in Part II, pp. 329–35.

a kept woman. The sister has a baby in the course of the year. Everyone suspects though no one, including the girl herself, can be sure that it is by him. The story of how the three live in a single room verges on the smutty, and invites pornographic retelling. There are in fact several pornographic editions, none of which, however, seems to be by Kafū himself.

In addition to the near-smuttiness, the plot is marred by false leads. Thus we are given rather elaborate preparation for future encounters between the hero and the illegitimate child, similar, it would seem, to those between mother and daughter in *Flowers in the Shade*; and then, suddenly, the child comes down with pneumonia and dies. Two synoptic chapters take the three principal characters into the war years, and the book comes to a weary close.

Yet it is far more successful than *Sinking and Swimming*. In both cases one soon loses interest in the plot, but in *Dancing Girl* there is something to take its place: the seasons of Asakusa, and the sleaziness and warmth of the dancing girls' lives. The sadness comes not from the hero's personal defeat, for he is not a very real person, but from the love and hate that Asakusa life, apparently dead when Kafū was writing, seemed to inspire in those who had to live it. The hero does not really seem sad, a fit subject for so much complaining, until, in the last chapter, he has deserted Asakusa and settled down in his nursery school.

In recording the passage of the seasons, Kafū appears to have made good use of his diary. Variations from normal weather, such as a late snowfall in the spring of 1936, actually occurred. When events can be pinned down to specific days, the weather is just as described in the diary. Thus New Year's Eve of 1936 was warm, with a bright moon late in the night.

That the effect of the book depends little on characterization and dramatic action is apparent from the fact that in some of the most effective sections almost no one appears and very little happens. A good example is the tenth of the thirteen chapters, perhaps the best concentration of Asakusa mood and chorus-girl humanity. Only one remark is quoted directly, and that by an anonymous dancing girl.*

The last chapter is such a mixture of what is good and what is bad

---

* A complete translation of this chapter will be found in Part II, pp. 336–38.

about the book that one hardly knows whether to call it a bad ending to a novel that is insufficiently dramatic, or a last, fading lyrical note to bring back in total recall the song that has gone before. Moved by the pastoral calm of the suburb in which he was born, and worn out by the dirt of Asakusa, the hero abruptly departs; and in the waste that it has caused, the world of the Asakusa dancer comes to life again. Perhaps, after all, this little love poem to Asakusa, written with no hope of publication, has the best ending it could have.

The last of Kafū's war writings actually straddled the surrender. The first half of *A Tale No One Asked For* was written late in 1944, the last half late in 1945. It is the only one of these writings that really says anything about the war. *Sinking and Swimming* stops short of the war, and *Dancing Girl* is brought into the war only by the last chapters, in which we learn very little save that the hero managed to escape conscription. *A Tale No One Asked For* goes straight through the war years, and in the end the hero, an aging and unsuccessful painter, is driven back to his birthplace (the province, in fact, to which Kafū himself was driven by the bombings of 1945), there to face a lonely old age, growing vegetables but painting no pictures.

The "tale" is the story of the painter's life, from his youthful studies in Tokyo and France down to this bleak conclusion. It is a story of lost friends and lovers, and changes in a city where once there were both. Two friends of his youth, with whom he lived as a student in the Koishikawa of Kafū's boyhood, early leave him, one to die, the other to become an expatriate in Europe. When, years later, he comes back to Koishikawa to bury the ashes of his mistress, he finds that a great firebreak has been cut through the district in preparation for air raids, and that only a loquat tree still stands as a memento of youthful revelry. In the end he must also give up the daughter of the mistress, with whom he has had quasi-incestuous relations, for she has gone to work for the American Occupation, and, as was then the case with ambitious Japanese ladies, disdains the company of Japanese.

The book has a serious formal defect, and might better have ended with the part written in 1944. The second half, seeing the hero back to the provinces after the war, violates one of those conventions of the novel of which the reader is scarcely conscious until they are violated. An author, writing in the past tense, is assumed at the outset to stand at a point in time from which he can survey the completed action.

He cannot, without seriously upsetting the reader, write of things taking place later than the point in time he has initially chosen. At the beginning of *A Tale No One Asked For,* Kafū clearly stands in relation to his material at some point prior to the surrender. From it he can survey the completed action of the first part of the novel—but not the second. The reader feels that something has gone wrong when he starts writing of things he cannot have known of at the time first selected. There is no sign that Kafū ever saw fit to apologize, however; nor is there much sign that the defect bothers the Japanese.

A chilly, lonely, autumnal book, *A Tale No One Asked For* contains some good reporting on the years after the surrender, and it has moments of high, austere sadness, the sadness of one left alone to bear the burden of too much change. Here is a bit of reporting:

"Young people did not seem to mind having to eat food so coarse as to be quite intolerable to us of an earlier generation, and in the Ginza and Marunouchi there would be groups of three and four, laughing and talking, arm in arm, quite as if the life they were leading were a perfectly ordinary one, nothing to be displeased or discontented about. They had no interest in society or politics, and their minds and eyes seemed ceaselessly at work to seek out an hour, a half hour, of idle pleasure, free from the gaze of their supervisors. Although there were reports that delinquents would assault women who happened to be loitering in dark streets and parks, no one seemed in the least afraid. People would visit friends or be visited by them, and even when they had nothing to eat, spend an evening in the theaters. Everything was a puzzle to me, from great matters of state to small matters in the everyday life of women and girls." (xvii, 337.)

And here a touch of sadness, the occasion being the burial of the mistress:

"As I took the body to the crematory, I wondered where to bury the ashes. My own home was in Okayama, and there was no temple in Tokyo with which I had a bond. At length I remembered that behind the Koishikawa shrine of all the memories, there were two temples. Nowhere could there be a place with which I had firmer bonds, I decided; and so I chose one of them for her resting place.

"The house in which we had lived as students and the house next door, in which she and her sister had lived, were both gone, replaced by new houses for rent; but the loquat tree at which I had gazed, vaguely restless, on that day twenty-four years before, when the others had gone out and left me to watch the house, was still standing, exactly as then, in a corner of the cemetery.

"I asked the resident priest to have the stone put under the tree. And I took care of another chore—an odd way to put the matter. I had the posthumous name of the sister carved on it beside Tatsuko's. Not knowing what their family crest was, I made a sketch of some loquats and asked to have it carved over the names. It was but an idea that came to me as I stood there.…

"On one of those summer evenings when the heat only seems to grow more oppressive as the hours go by, I crawled from the mosquito net and went over to sit in the window sill. There was no moon, but in the light of the stars, under the clear sky, the garden and the vegetable patch beyond lay quiet, as in a dream.

"I thought of the meadows around a Provençal village I had once stayed in. And I thought of how Tatsuko and I had sat in the windows of our room in Ningyōchō and looked out over the city, deep in the quiet of night." (xvii, 335–38.)

The major events in Kafū's private life during the war years were the adoption of a son and the loss of his Henkikan. The foster son was the son of a cousin, the samisen musician Kineya Gosō. Kafū was soon to regret the adoption, from which he was not allowed to escape, and he and the boy never lived together.

The entries in Kafū's diary for the first months of the war are for the most part brief, no more than terse notes about the weather. Now and then something proves interesting enough for a longer note: the strange sight, observed at a shrine near Tamanoi on February 18, 1942, of the ladies mustered to give thanks for the fall of Singapore; a pair of lovers observed at Ueno on March 1, offering evidence that romance survives; the first American raid on April 18, greeted with official silence and a wild rash of rumors. (Out of deference to American sensibilities, such expressions as "enemy planes" were changed to "American planes" when the diary was published after the war.) For the rest, the chief evidence of the war is the presence of bureaucrats. They warn Kafū that the fire-prevention facilities at the Henkikan are not adequate, and so set him to looking, not very wholeheartedly, for accommodations elsewhere. They also inspire him to dump certain gold trinkets into the river rather than contribute them to the defense effort.

As the war moves into its second year, the diary still finds Kafū seeking comfort among his chorus girls in Asakusa: "I cashed the bonds I was forced to buy last year by the neighborhood association. ...Went from Dosubashi to Asakusa. In the dressing room of the Opera House were several girls who moved this month from the Tokiwaza. They greeted me happily. In this world apart, there are no ashes of war. I left in the evening, and saw long lines queued up before all the tobacco shops." (xxii, 238–39.)

"By the time I had cleaned the kitchen and had something to eat, it was noon. In midafternoon I went from the Dosubashi Hospital to Asakusa. It is as it has always been. I watch people passing up and down the lane before the temple, and I forget my usual irritation and feel an indescribable repose." (xxii, 267.)

And the bureaucracy continues to annoy: "Since last month there has been an order out from the neighborhood association to dig a hole under the veranda or in the garden. This is to be a refuge in case of air raids. Do they not know that holes fill with water in the summer to breed mosquitoes, and in the winter produce frost needles to crack the earth? Last year we were told to hide in closets, this year we must dig holes. What will it be next year?" (xxii, 277.)

With the third year, the pinch really begins to be felt: "From tomorrow restaurants and teahouses are banned. It is said, too, that the Kabuki Theater and the other large theaters will presently close. There are reports that the shows in Asakusa are growing fewer by the day, and that there are but three or four left. Geisha have not yet been banned, but they appear to be moving into other trades for want of engagements. Without theaters and geisha, the music of Edo, based upon the samisen, will perish. A clear day, with a cold wind." (xxii, 317.)

"Clear. Tanizaki came in the afternoon, on the way to arrange for moving his daughter to his lodgings in Atami. The house into which she has married, in Shibuya, is in danger, it is said, from air raids. It has been said, too, since the beginning of the month, that the air raids are not far away." (xxii, 318.)

"Ogawa of the Opera House came yesterday to tell me that the last performance was to be today, and that I must be present. And so, barely finishing dinner, I set off by subway at five, and made my way from Tawaramachi in the evening light. Upstairs, all the mirrors were gone from the dancers' dressing room, and several old women, apparently mothers of the dancers, were carrying off personal effects, bundles in kerchiefs, umbrellas. At a few minutes past eight, when the last curtain went down and the audience was about to leave, the manager, Tashiro, brought all the actors and actresses on stage and said a few valedictory words, and the director, Nagasawa, was so moved when he answered that he cried aloud. At that, all the forty or fifty members of the troupe burst into tears. Some of the dancers were still sniffling when they got back to the dressing room. They began writing down their names and addresses and passing them around to others. I was moved to tears myself—the air was completely different from when I came a few days ago upon learning that the theater was to be closed. . . . Of all the theaters in Asakusa, the Opera House has had the most Asakusa-like abandon. Now it is closing. Nowhere will we catch again this flavor of the past. By chance, I came upon a world apart when I was already sixty, and there were years when I went there almost every day; and those years are a dream that will not return.

"When, forlornly, I left the theater alone, there was a half moon in the cold, windy sky, to light the streets. As I passed the lane of shops before the temple, all of them closed, on my way to the subway, I found myself weeping again, tears wetting my collar, and I looked back toward the park. I have been witness to all of it, Tokyo going to ruin; but until this last year I have not been particularly moved. Since the sudden closing of the Kabuki Theater, however, every new incident has affected me deeply. I have felt that if the flavor of the city must go, I would like to go with it. The people of the Opera House are perhaps stupid and uneducated, perhaps profligate and frivolous; but they are without the cunning, avarice, and arrogance of those who have come to the fore in the world, and the more one sees of them the more one loves them. When I have been angry and irritated, I have always found peace backstage in the Opera House, talking with the girls. And now my place of refuge is gone, destroyed. How shall I bear the sorrow?" (XXII, 322–23.)

"It is time for airing books; but, not knowing when the war fires will claim them, I have no heart for the work and have taken care of only those I use most. Indeed I have no heart for anything. I know that the death of Meiji culture is in sight. Japanese culture has moved forward only when it has been under the influence of foreign cultures: Nara, when Buddhism flourished; Edo, when Confucianism was at its strongest; and Meiji, when the culture of the West came in." (xxii, 346–47.)

"Having business in Nihombashi, I went on to Asakusa to look at the remains of the theaters. There is no trace at all of the Opera House, the Sanyūkan, the Gidayūza, the Shōchiku, the Park Theater, or the Shōwa. Only the shooting range behind the Opera House remains. A drizzling rain in the evening. The street was lighted but feebly from the doors of movie houses. With the Kokusai Theater as my landmark, I wandered among the wastes, and at length made my way to the Iriya streetcar stop." (xxii, 362.)

"Drizzling rain. Finished transcribing Ryūhoku's travel diary, which I first read in 1897 in Ryūhoku's collected works. As I copied it out, I felt afresh the gentle sadness that flows from its pages. I felt, too, how admirable, how lovable are the meanest of people who appear in it. Sir Rutherford Alcock has written similarly of the warm affections he found in old Japan. Remembering now, in the midst of war, how it was in early Meiji, one can only be astonished at the violence of the changes that have overtaken us. That we have since Meiji become sly and petty is due, perhaps, to the rule of the southwestern clans, so given to intrigue." (xxii, 369.)

"The year 1944 ends, and we face a forlorn New Year. We have not faced such another since the founding of the country, and for this fact we may thank the militarists. Let their crimes be recorded for eternity." (xxii, 375–76.)

And so into the year of the air raids. In the diary the sense of impending disaster grows. "When I arose at eleven-thirty, a powdery snow was falling, just like three days ago. A neighbor came through the snow while I was getting something to eat and said that numbers of American planes were expected at one-thirty in the afternoon. On edge, I brewed some of the coffee that is among my treasures and was quite unstinting with sugar. Then I filled my pipe with Occidental tobacco, another treasure, and had a leisurely smoke. I wished my last moments to be happy. After the neighbor's radio, there came a booming of guns to rattle the windows. I could not go into the hole outside because of the snow, and so I crawled into the closet where I kept my bedding. I lay there thinking of one thing and another, until presently it was quiet, and someone called out that the alarm was lifted. It was four o'clock and already growing dark. Low clouds closed off the sky. There was something different, something terrible, about the falling snow. In times of peace snow calls up poetic thoughts and memories of old pleasures, but today I felt that my end and the end of the world were coming." (xxii, 388.)

In March came the largest of the raids, and the end of the Henkikan. "Clear and pleasant. In the night there was a raid. At four in the morning my Henkikan was burned down. The fire broke out halfway up Nagatare Hill, and, fanned by a northwest wind, soon spread to the main Ichibeichō street. I was startled by the light at the window and the shouting next door, no ordinary sort of shouting, and I took up the briefcase that contained my diary and manuscripts and went out into the garden. . . . Whipped by the wind, sparks were landing in the garden. I saw that disaster was inevitable, and started out toward the main street through the clouds of smoke that already hung over the neighborhood. Thinking to go to Kido's house in Mita,* I asked at the police box whether the Iigura street was passable, and was told that since the district from Senzoku Hill to Kamiya was in flames, it was unlikely that I could get through. . . . An old woman who was leading a little girl by the hand had apparently lost her way, and so I took them down to Tanimachi from beside the Sumitomo house, and on to Tameike. I then went back up Reinan Hill and rested in the vacant lot beside the Spanish Legation. A thin crescent of a moon rose horribly over Mt. Atago. . . . I knew where the fires were and the direction of the wind, and was fairly sure of my escape route; and so I turned back to the gate of the Tanaka house, thinking that before I left this Azabu, I would see what I could of the burning of the Henkikan, in which I had lived for twenty-six years. Since there were policemen and soldiers keeping people away from the prince's gate, I hid in the shelter of trees and posts. I was standing at the end of the lane, looking toward my house, when Mr. Freudelsberger from the house next door came running by, hatless and in slippers and a padded

* Kido was a restaurant owner with whom Kafū was on friendly terms.

kimono.* His house had been caught in a flood of sparks from below the cliff, he said, and seemed even then to be going up in flames.... I went a few steps up a side alley, and saw that the oaks by the foreign house next door and the big tree in my own garden were masses of flame. The wind blew great vortices of black smoke at me. I could not get near enough to see the house itself go. I could only watch the flames mount higher into the sky. And in that moment I knew that my Henkikan and my ten thousand volumes were gone." (xxii, 392–93.)

By foot and streetcar, Kafū made his way in the early morning to the house of his cousin, Kineya Gosō. The next diary entry indicates mixed feelings about the Henkikan. It has been a great deal of trouble, "and so perhaps the fact that I lost everything last night will work for peace of mind in my old age. And yet the novels and poems I bought in Europe and America forty years ago—it is intolerable to think that I shall never hold them in my hand again." (xxii, 395.)

There is also a report on the state of the city: "The fires last night virtually reduced it to ashes, from Senjū in the north to Shiba in the south. The Asakusa Kannon and its pagoda, the Yoshiwara, the temples and mortuary shrines in Shiba Park, were all laid waste. The people who took refuge in the Meiji Theater died in the flames, every last one of them. The districts beyond the river, Honjo and Fukagawa, the Kameido Shrine, the Tamanoi quarter, Mukōjima, all went too. I was in bed at two in the morning. When I turned out the light and closed my eyes, I could only see columns of sparks and hear the shriek of the wind; but presently these hallucinations passed, and I fell into a deep sleep." (xxii, 395.)

On March 11, Kafū and Gosō's two sons went to dig in the ruins of the Henkikan. They came back with a few relics: a seal given to Kafū by Tanizaki Junichirō, a tea bowl that had belonged to Kafū's father, a pipe that had belonged to his maternal grandmother. "What better mementos of the disaster—and how strange that these three objects should have come through undamaged!" (xxii, 396.) Passing the Henkikan a month later, Kafū saw that his hyacinths were sending out shoots.

Kafū presently moved from Gosō's establishment to a room in the

---

* "Freudelsberger" is a reconstruction of the Japanese phonetic syllabary.

western reaches of the city. There, on a pleasant day in May, when the young sparrows were leaving their nests, he was once more burned out, and forced to flee with his manuscripts. This time he took shelter with an acquaintance in Shibuya, in the southwestern part of the city. Early in June he was persuaded to move again. With Sugawara Meirō, the man who had composed the music for his Opera House musical, he departed on June 2 for a small town west of Kobe. "At four-thirty the train pulled away from the platform. There was no whistle, there was not a sound, and the sorrow of leaving the city was the more intense for the silence." (xxii, 411–12.)

After a few quiet, pastoral days, the two moved on to Okayama, there to stay in an inn. Their planning could scarcely have been worse. By then the raids were directed chiefly at medium-sized cities, and in Tokyo the worst was over. On June 28 the diary records a sinister bit of information: the young swallows have left their nests and not returned. That night Kafū was burned out yet a third time. Still with a firm grip on his manuscripts, he moved yet a third time, to a rented room that he shared with Sugawara. On August 13 he went to visit Tanizaki Junichirō, who had taken refuge not far inland from Okayama. At noon on August 15 he was aboard a train, returning to Okayama. He did not learn of the surrender until later in the afternoon. "Very good," says his diary. (xxii, 436.)

On August 31 he was back in Tokyo, but, unable to find lodgings, he retreated to Atami, there to join Kineya Gosō once more, in the villa of Kido, his friend the restaurant owner. Atami brought happy associations: "Ever since my very early youth I have been unceasing in my admiration for Ryūhoku the man and the writer. How boundless is my joy at now being where he was!" (xxii, 443.)

By the end of 1945 Kafū was in print again. Late in the year a collection of essays appeared, largely prewar, but including some short pieces done during the war. The next year his wartime writings began to flood forth, and he was as near being a literary lion as at any time since his Keiō days. His complete postwar writings fill only three slender volumes, but the total count of his postwar publications is in the hundreds. He had a bewildering variety of publishers, including Shinchōsha, a house that at one time he had vowed to have no truck with; and besides making him once more a very famous man, with an antimilitarist reputation of the sort fashionable in the years after the war, they made him a rather wealthy man. He was not, as he complained to friends, as wealthy as he had been in the days after his father's death; but he was prosperous enough all the same.

The movie companies contributed to this development, for in the postwar years there was a rash of movies based on Kafū's novels. Although he himself probably did not profit directly, a bullish book market was another manifestation of his new popularity. A newspaper reported in 1949 that a copy of the banned edition of *French Stories* was bought by a secondhand book dealer for ¥38,000, or upwards of a hundred dollars at the legal exchange rate, and sold a few days later for ¥60,000. This was in the impoverished days before the Korean War.

Kafū amused the newspaper-reading public in the spring of 1954 by misplacing a Boston bag that contained his bank books and various negotiable instruments. It was found and returned by an American soldier. Reports varied considerably on how wealthy a man the misplaced documents showed Kafū to be, but the authoritative version now seems to be that they gave evidence of over ten million yen in time deposits, and over five million in regular deposits. There were also certain lesser instruments, and ten yen in cash. When Kafū died in 1959, there was again much speculation and a rich variety of rumors, and, happily, we are once more in possesion of an authoritative report: his liquid assets totaled ¥23,021,470, including ¥491,619 in "stamps and postal savings," a curious item for a man who prided himself on not opening and answering letters.

Kafū received honors as well as money in the postwar years. In 1952 he was given the Bunka Kunshō, the Imperial Cultural Decoration, the highest mark of official recognition for Japanese writers and artists, and the next year he was made a member of Japanese Academy of the Arts (Geijutsuin). His citation for the Cultural Decoration said: "His many works replete with a warmly elegant poetic spirit, with an elevated form of social criticism, and with a penetrating appreciation of reality; his pioneering researches in Edo literature; his many achievements in bringing foreign literature to Japan: in all these respects he has left behind mammoth footprints."

A bit florid, but as accurate as most citations. Had someone with less of a penchant for rhetoric written it, it might have gone something like this: "A querulous, self-righteous man, whose social criticism rarely rose above the level of personal complaining, and whose grasp of the complex reality that is the human spirit was less than adequate; but a man, withal, whose love for his city and its traditions never wavered, and who expressed that love in prose worthy of the great classical Japanese essayists."

Kafū's style of living did not reflect his means or his fame. It was such, indeed, as to make the public think him a miser. Early in 1946 he moved to Ichikawa in Chiba Prefecture, just across the river from Tokyo. Ichikawa was to be his home, if it could be called that, for the rest of his life. He first lived with Kineya Gosō. The relationship between the cousins was a complicated one, however, and a year later Kafū moved to a rented room elsewhere in Ichikawa. His diary is full of complaints about the household radio and about Gosō's samisen. He was also a victim of petty thievery, and the culprit turned out to be Gosō's daughter. And, most complicated of all, there was the matter of Gosō's son and Kafū's adopted son. It has been noted that Kafū adopted the boy during the war. It was not long, though, before he came to suspect that the cousin was after his money. Gosō's refusal to take the boy's name back into his own family register even after strenuous petitions from Kafū lends credence to the suspicion. Since the postwar civil code puts most of the weapons in the hands of an adopted child, Kafū was in the end unable to dislodge the boy. In 1959 he inherited the whole of Kafū's estate.

For these reasons and possibly others, Kafū moved, early in 1947, to the house of a scholar and translator of French literature. The second venture as a roomer was not much more successful than the first. In early December 1948 he was suddenly asked to move. There are many theories on why matters should have come to this pass. Some say that Kafū had a way of purloining rationed food even while being very niggardly with his own supply. Others say that his slipshod housekeeping and his habit of leaving his room open in times when robbers were about was at the root of the trouble. A more bizarre theory is that Kafū's proclivities as a Peeping Tom got the best of him, and that he made the landlord's wife uncomfortable. The landlord himself passed up various opportunities to come into print with his version of the affair. He feared Kafū's vindictiveness, he explained, but would have things to say when Kafū was dead. He died first, and so we shall never have the things.

In any case Kafū moved, to a shabby three-room house for which he paid, by the standards of the times, a very stiff price, and in which he was to live for nearly ten years. His last move, in 1957, was to a house, also three rooms, that he built for himself when the leaky roof of the earlier house became intolerable. The real-estate agent responsible for his buying the earlier house evidently felt guilty, for he was present to the end ministering to Kafū's domestic needs.

The scenery around Ichikawa pleased Kafū, reminding him of the Yoshiwara a half-century before: "In the afternoon I walked among the paddies, and saw bits of colored paper put out to frighten away birds. The rice seems to have been planted already. Here and there from among the reeds in a reservoir, white herons would fly up into the sky in twos and threes. It was nearly fifty years ago, at our summer house in Zushi, that I first saw cranes in the paddies and king-fishers starting up from the streams, and I saw them, too, early in the morning almost half a century ago, when I walked among the paddies of the Yoshiwara. And now I chance upon them once more as I approach seventy, and I am taken back to the brave days when I was young. It will not be easy to forget the poetry of my temporary lodgings in Ichikawa."*

Companions in his last years included a businessman whose villa he used as a refuge from radio and samisen, and who is the compiler of the most authoritative chronology of his life; a *Mainichi* reporter to whom, despite his famous dislike for journalists, he apparently told everything, and who, since Kafū's death, has won a literary prize for his probings into obscure corners of Kafū's career; and various functionaries associated with Chūō Kōron, which published most of his postwar writings, as well as the twenty-four-volume third version of his "collected works." (The second, which has not been mentioned, came out after plates for the first had been lost in the earthquake.)

There were also unpleasant relationships. The two forgers who figured so prominently in one of Kafū's wartime stories (see pp. 159–60) continued to operate in the background, and one of them seems to have been responsible for a development that threatened to bring in the police: the publication, in a rich variety of pirated editions, of the little piece of pornography composed at about the time of *Rivalry* (see p. 79). Although the text thus released to the public does seem

* *Nagai Kafū's Diary* (*Nagai Kafū Nikki,* Tokyo: Tōto Shobō, 1959), VII, 120.

to be substantially what came from the master's hand all those years before, the police were satisfied with the explanation that the published version was unauthorized and inaccurate.

And there were women. Kafū frequented the Asakusa burlesque houses, writing plays for the strip queens who were the successors to the Opera House girls, and making a personal appearance in at least one of them. He also frequented the Ginza. Upon his death the newspapers and weekly magazines devoted a great deal of space to the last women in his life, and there were numbers of women, more concerned with fame than with chastity, who stepped forward to claim the honor of having been the very last. Those who assert, however, that he was in his last years much too concerned with his bank account to risk expensive liaisons have a credible case.

Kafū's diary for the postwar years is full of tart remarks about the new order of things, notably the alacrity with which democracy succeeded militarism. A number of remarks about the Americans were deleted for immediate postwar publication, but an amount of tartness remains, as in this entry on censorship: "There were a number of dead and wounded, it is said, but because of American censorship, there was nothing about the incident in the papers. The Americans talk about freedom, but they conceal what is to their disadvantage. How very laughable."*

The diary contains much information about postwar manners. We learn, for instance, that the girls of Tamanoi, now scattered all along the line to Ichikawa, charge foreign guests ¥130, Japanese guests only ¥100. Assiduous as ever in these matters, Kafū went out inspecting the new pleasure quarters, notably Tokyo Palace, a group of factories and barracks on the Chiba highway. It had been occupied by girls from the Kameido quarter and turned into the most spectacular of postwar bawdy complexes. All the details, including prices, are carefully noted down in the diary entry for February 25, 1947, together with a summation (February 27): "This nest of whores would seem to combine the sort of life more usual in that calling with the life of factory girls and students."†

Kafū did not visit the central part of Tokyo until 1948. Early in the same year he made the rounds of the districts he had once visited so many times. In some of them he found familiar landmarks, but not in Tamanoi: "In the afternoon I walked through the ruins of Tama-

* *Ibid.*, p. 112.   † *Ibid.*, p. 156.

noi. Those streets of painted faces, so prosperous for two decades after the earthquake, are now a weed-choked waste. The days when I was writing *A Strange Tale from East of the River* are like a dream."*

Some aspects of the city pleased him: "To the Ginza in the afternoon.... Yamazaki, the secondhand book dealer, has his stall in front of the Matsuzakaya as always. We stood talking for a time, and congratulated each other on having come through."†

And some did not: "In the evening I went off to Asakusa with Mr. Kodaki, but the review houses were already closed.... We went by subway to Ueno to look at the streetwalkers. In the darkness by the stairway into the park and at the entrance to the Keisei station, there were swarms of them and swarms of vagrants. It was an extremely dark and depressing sight, and I found myself scowling. Exactly like the 'nighthawks' of Yoshidachō in the Edo Period."‡

"On the way home from Marunouchi I stopped by the Mannendō on the Ginza. I was introduced to the manager, who took us around to several Ginza cafés. There was neither interest nor profit in the excursion. The cafés are noisy and dull, just as before the war. I was seen home by automobile at about ten. Unable to sleep. Have a headache, am exhausted."§

His favorite ground was still Asakusa, where he was by the end of his life a legendary figure. In his last years he would follow an unbending routine when he was not at home with dyspepsia or otherwise indisposed: he would appear in the same Asakusa restaurant daily and sit in the same seat. When it was occupied, he would mutter something about the crowds and stalk out.

From 1946 until almost the end of his life he continued to turn out a trickle of short stories and essays, plus the Asakusa plays already mentioned. The trickle was progressively more feeble, and the last short stories are very slight indeed, tiresome set pieces making it quite evident that one prostitute's bedroom is much like another's. They also tend to have trick endings, irritating for their irrelevance and their failure to pick up loose threads. The reader puts down such stories feeling that he has been had, and that he can hear old Kafū cackling away at his discomfiture.

Among the stories down to 1950, however, there are several of a

---

* *Ibid.*, p. 201. † *Ibid.*, p. 204.
‡ *Ibid.*, p. 208. Mr. Kodaki worked for Chūō Kōron.
§ *Ibid.*, p. 212.

much higher order. In the best of them Kafū returns to the naturalism of his youth, and produces telling reports on the unsettled postwar years. The material is rather different from what one has grown used to in his writing. To be sure, bar girls and dancers, far more scantily dressed than before the war, hover about in little clusters and groups, but the best subjects are ordinary people inconvenienced by the bombings and the economic collapse, people who would not have figured in Kafū's world had disaster not come to them and him.

"The Scavengers" (*Kaidashi*), the best of them, has to do with people who, lacking generous publishers, were turned into foraging animals by the defeat and the collapse. It is one of the tersest accounts we have of what it was like to be a Japanese in those harsh years.*

Kafū's last short story, a slight little affair about boredom, was published in the summer of 1958. In March 1959 he injured a foot, and thereafter he scarcely left his house, save to take an occasional meal at a cheap restaurant near Ichikawa station.

On the morning of April 30, 1959, his body was found, fully clothed, by the woman who came in to do his housework. He had died during the night of an internal hemorrhage. These are the last words in his diary: "April 29. Holiday. Cloudy."† The funeral took place on May 2. His brother, with whom there had been something of a reconciliation after the war, was in attendance. There had been speculation that his wish to be buried among the Yoshiwara courtesans might be honored (see p. 152), but the brother, whose sterner view of family responsibilities may have been partly responsible for the old quarrel, had other ideas, and the ashes were buried in the Zōshigaya Cemetery with those of his parents. Kafū's own wishes were revised once more when the time came to put up a tombstone. The inscription says, as he had asked for it to say, "The Grave of Kafū the Scribbler." The statement is slightly more prolix than he would have wished it to be, however, for it uses six Chinese characters and not the five he had specified.

The newspapers and weekly magazines wrote their own sort of epitaphs, much lengthier. Bits of Kafū's past kept floating up, as when a tattoo mark was found on his arm commemorating an early love, the Shimbashi geisha Tomimatsu. A television program went into the smaller details of his untidy death, and O-uta, the lady of the happy

---

* The story is translated in Part II, pp. 339–44.
† The quotation is from newspaper accounts. At the time of writing, the last years of the diary had not yet been published.

Ikuyo interlude, was brought in to weep. Fujikage Shizue, the dancer who was his second wife, told the magazines all about the unsteadfast nature that had made him a bad husband. The contents of his desk were hauled out, including, most touchingly, a map of the Koishikawa house and grounds of his boyhood.

The story is not yet over. There has been public unpleasantness about his estate, the property now of his adopted son, and particularly about the status of his copyrights. Miffed by some of the polemics, the young man refused to let the diary go to the Keiō library, where everyone assumed it would go, and refused to let Chūō Kōron attempt the definitive edition of Kafū's works, as everyone assumed it would. Instead Iwanami, not a favorite publisher of Kafū's, was entrusted with the task. The first volume came out late in 1961. On the assumption that the final edition would be its to do, Chūō Kōron had gathered certain esoteric materials that are not likely to be in the Iwanami edition. Perhaps, then, we will have to wait until 1989, when the copyrights expire, for a really definitive edition, and so for an end to his troubles, real and imagined, with the organizers of the literary world.

Part two The Writings

The River Sumida

The River Sumida was first published in 1909 in the magazine *Shinshōsetsu*. It appeared in book form two years later. For a discussion, see pp. 41–44.

Shōfūan Ragetsu, teacher of poetry, had missed his midsummer visit to his sister, who gave samisen lessons across the river at Imado.* Every day he told himself that he must go. He could not bring himself to venture out in the heat of the day, however, and so he would wait for evening. In the evening he would go out in back, where morning glories climbed the bamboo fence, and splash water over himself. Then, still half naked, he would have a drink of sake, and presently get around to his dinner, and when he had finished that, the summer twilight would be giving way to night, and smoke would be rising from the incense put out in each window to keep away mosquitoes. Beyond the reed blind and the row of dwarfed plants beneath it, the street would be coming to life, with the nasal songs of artisans, the clatter of their wooden sandals, bits of conversation. Given a prod or two by his wife, O-taki, he would start out for Imado. And then someone along the street, out taking the cool of evening, would greet him, and so he would sit down again. Always ready for a good talk when he had had his drink, Ragetsu would talk away the evening.

Presently the mornings and evenings were cooler, the sun was quick to go down, and the morning glories were smaller by the day. As the western sun poured into the small room like a flame, the shrilling of the cicadas would strike the ear with a new urgency. And so August, he saw, was half over. Sometimes in the night, the wind rustling the corn behind the house would make him think it was raining. He had enjoyed himself in his youth, and one memento of his profligacy was the aching in the joints that greeted the change of seasons. He was al-

* Above Asakusa, on the right bank of the Sumida.

ways the first to know that autumn had come, and when he felt autumn he would feel with it an indefinable restlessness.

Suddenly wanting to be on his way, he left the house in Koume
when the quarter moon was still a pure white in the evening sky, and
walked briskly toward Imado.*

Following the canal, he turned left from Hikifune and made his
way through twisting lanes that only a resident of the area would
know, and so past the Inari Shrine and out upon the Sumida embankment. In reclaimed paddy land along the lanes, there were newly built
rows of cheap houses waiting for renters. Then there were houses with
garden stones for sale, spread out in a wide array before them, and occasionally the new rows would give way to a succession of thatched
cottages as if the city were far away. Sometimes, through a bamboo
fence, he would see a woman bathing in the evening moonlight. Even
at his age the ways of his youth had not left him. He would stop for
a casual peep. Usually, though, it would prove to be a housewife no
longer able to startle, and, disappointed, Ragetsu would quicken his
pace. Passing a sign that offered a house for rent or land for sale, he
would pause to calculate the profits, and tell himself that he should
look for a chance to make some quick money. As the lane turned
through open fields again, there would be a pond with lotuses blooming in rank profusion, and in the evening wind riffling the green
blades of rice beyond, he would be a master of verse once again. For-
getting the calculations that had occupied him, he would think how
wonderfully appropriate they were, the old verses that passed through
his mind.

It was already dark in the shadow of the cherries along the embankment, and there were lights in the houses beyond the river. In the river
breeze, yellowing leaves fluttered to the ground. He stopped to catch
his breath, and, pulling the front of his kimono open, fanned at his
chest. It had been a long walk, and a warm one. He saw a teahouse
that was still open and hurried up to it.

"A glass of sake," he said, sitting down. "Cold sake."

Directly across the river was Matchi Hill with its temple.† Little
boats scurried back and forth, their sails filled with the evening wind.

* Koume is in Honjo, on the left bank.
† Above Asakusa.

As the light faded, the white of the seagulls became whiter still. It was a sight to make a poet want a drink.

"What good are they, these cherries of mine, without a drink to go with them?" he murmured to himself, although the old epigram was scarcely in keeping with the season.

The lady of the house poured for him, into a glass that was not as large as it looked. Ragetsu drank down and climbed aboard the ferry. Toward midstream the boat began to rock and the sake to take effect. How cool was the moonlight bathing the cherry trees! And the smooth waters of the flood tide—how happily they seemed to glide beneath the flowing breeze, even as in the popular song! Ragetsu closed his eyes and began to hum it.

Remembering an oversight, he looked for a confectionery on the opposite bank, and, having purchased his gift, proceeded on across Imado Bridge. No one was quite his equal, he thought, when it came to walking a clean straight line. In fact he was staggering a bit.

A few shops selling Imado bowls gave the place its one distinctive feature. The low houses could have lined any back street in the farther reaches of the city. Under the eaves and up the alleys, evening strollers were here and there having talks, their cotton kimonos a gleaming white in the dim lights. There was a hush over the neighborhood, save for the barking of a dog or the crying of a baby. As he came to the Imado Hachiman Shrine, its trees high against the Milky Way, Ragetsu picked out the lamp he was looking for, tucked in under the eaves. "Mojitoyo, Teacher of Tokiwazu," said the letters in an old-style script. It was his sister's professional name. Two or three strollers were standing by the door, listening to the music lesson inside.

From time to time a mouse would scamper noisily across the hollow ceiling. The hanging lamp, its wick but an inch or so long and its chimney clouded, caught the corners of the room in its forlorn, wavering light: the paper doors patched here and there with patent-medicine advertisements and pictures of beauties that had come as a New Year's supplement to the *Miyako Shimbun*; the brownish old chests; the walls stained from leaking rains. Beyond the veranda, along which there were shabby reed doors to admit the breezes, a wind bell was tinkling sadly, and there was a quiet hum of insects from a darkness so intense that one would have been hard put to know whether or not there was a garden. O-toyo, the music teacher, her back to the alcove in which were ranged potted plants bought at some shrine fair and in which hung a painting of Fudō,* knelt somewhat limply with a samisen on her knee, now and again running the oaken plectrum through her hair, and punctuating the samisen accompaniment with calls to mark time. Before her, a score open on the low paulownia table between them, her pupil, a man of perhaps thirty whom one would take for a shopkeeper, was rendering the ballad of Koina and Hambei in a moderately low voice.† It was nearing a conclusion, for the two were already in flight: "What are you saying? Surely we are beyond the stage of calling ourselves brother and sister."

Ragetsu sat fanning himself by the veranda until the practice was over. Not quite sober yet, he would from time to time hum a strain of the ballad to himself. Then, his eyes closed, he would let out an unrestrained belch, and, swaying from side to side, glance over at his sister. She was in her forties, and the sad light of the lamp made the emaciated little figure look yet older. And she had once been the pretty, pampered daughter of a successful pawnbroker—the thought did not fill Ragetsu with nostalgia or sorrow or any other mood akin to reality. No, it took him beyond such feelings, and made him think only how very strange it all was. He had been young and handsome in those days himself. He had been popular with the ladies, and he had had his good times, and finally he had been disinherited for all of the seven lives to come. Now he could scarcely think that any of it had actually happened. His father, who had once hit him over the head with an abacus, the faithful old clerk who had wept as he pleaded with Ragetsu to mend his ways, O-toyo's husband, who had been set up in a branch establishment—they had raged and they had laughed, they had had their sorrows and their joys, they had sweated and gone on working, and now they were all dead, and it made no difference that they had lived. They would stay in his memory and O-toyo's as long as the two of them lived, and then one day he and his sister would be gone as well, and so the others would vanish like smoke.

"As a matter of fact," said O-toyo, "I had been thinking I ought to go see you one of these days."

* Attendant upon Vairocana or Dainichi, "Buddha of Great Light."
† A story of violent but steadfast love between a geisha and a man of the merchant class. It is to be found in several schools of Edo balladry, including Tokiwazu.

Having finished "Koina and Hambei," her pupil had several times gone over the beginning of a similar ballad, the one about O-sai and Hachirōbei, and taken his leave. Ragetsu brought himself to attention and lightly tapped his knee with his fan.

"As a matter of fact," said O-toyo again, "they're widening the streets, and the cemetery in Komagome is to be cleared away. And so we'll have to move Father to Yanaka or Somei or somewhere. I had word the other day, and I was thinking I ought to go see what you thought we should do."

"I see." Ragetsu nodded. "We'll have to do something, I suppose. How long has it been since Father died?"

He cocked his head as if trying to answer his own question, but O-toyo pushed ahead with the details of her problem: how much it would cost to rent a lot in Somei, and how much the temple would expect besides, and so on. She indicated that it would be far better for Ragetsu to make all the arrangements. She was only a woman.

Ragetsu had been the heir to the Sagamiya, a pawnshop in Koishikawa, and upon his disinheritance he had become a young man of leisure. After the death of his stern old father, his brother-in-law, O-toyo's husband, who had been the chief clerk, took over the business with vigor and determination. With the changes after the Meiji Restoration, however, things began to go badly, and just at the worst possible time there was a fire, and so the Sagamiya went out of business. The young man of taste, for want of a better alternative, had to make his way as a teacher of poetry. To add to her misfortunes, O-toyo was widowed; but being a licensed musician in the Tokiwazu school, she was able to earn a living as a music teacher. She had one child, a boy now seventeen years old. The single pleasure the unfortunate woman had in life was contemplating her Chōkichi's prospects. She knew how precarious were the affairs of merchants, not sure from one day to the next that they would not face bankruptcy; and she was determined, even if she had to go without her three meals a day, to see him through the university and established as an office worker.

"And how is Chōkichi?" asked Ragetsu, draining the last of his cold tea.

A touch of pride came into his sister's manner. "He's having summer vacation. But I didn't think it would do to have him wasting his time, and I'm sending him to night school in Hongō."

"I suppose he's late getting home."

"Generally around ten. There are streetcars, but he has to take a long way round."

"Young people these days are different from us. I have great admiration for them." The teacher Ragetsu paused. "It's middle school, isn't it? I wouldn't know, not having any of them myself. And how long will it be before he's ready for the university?"

"He graduates next year, and then he takes his examinations. But before he can get into the university he has to go through another big school." O-toyo would have liked to explain everything in clear, simple terms, but she was after all a woman not completely in the current of the times.

"It must be setting you back a good amount."

"Oh, more than you can imagine. Why, just the tuition alone amounts to a yen a month, and when it comes to books and examinations, two and three yen don't get you very far, and then he has to wear foreign clothes the whole year through. He uses up two pairs of shoes a year."

Warming to her subject, O-toyo put emphasis into her words such as to make her trials seem twice what they were; but it always struck Ragetsu that if things were really as bad as all that, it should be possible to find for Chōkichi a path more in keeping with his resources. Not thinking the matter one to argue about, however, he looked for another subject, and his mind turned to Chōkichi's childhood companion, O-ito, the girl in the pastry shop. In the old days, when he had come to see his sister, he had always set out for Asakusa with Chōkichi and O-ito, there to look at the stalls behind the temple.

"She must be a fine young lady by now, what with Chōkichi already seventeen and all. Does she come for lessons?"

"Not here. She goes to Kineya's up the street every day. Before long she'll be coming out in Yoshichō. As a geisha, you know." O-toyo fell silent, sunk in thought.

"Yoshichō? Well. That's very splendid indeed. She always was a pretty girl, a little grown-up for her age. Wouldn't it be nice if she were to come by this evening."

Ragetsu was suddenly lively, but O-toyo tapped her pipe sharply against the ashtray. "Things aren't what they used to be," she said. "Chōkichi has his studies."

Ragetsu laughed. "We wouldn't want them to make any mistakes, I suppose. You're right. In that business you can't be too careful."

"Absolutely." O-toyo leaned toward him. "I may be imagining things, but there's something very funny about Chōkichi these days. He has me worried."

"That's what I'm saying." Ragetsu tapped his knee lightly with his fist.

Scarcely stopping for breath, O-toyo poured forth her worries. She really did not know why, but O-ito and Chōkichi had her almost beside herself with worry. Every morning, even though she had no particular business, O-ito would stop by on her way from her Nagauta practice, and Chōkichi would be waiting for her, not budging an inch from the window until she came. Not long before, O-ito had been sick in bed for a few days, and Chōkichi had been so dreamy and absentminded that it had almost been ridiculous.

As the clock in the next room struck nine, the door was flung open. O-toyo knew by the sound of it that Chōkichi was back. She halted her discourse and looked around.

"You're early."

"The teacher wasn't feeling well and let us out an hour early."

"Your uncle from Koume is here."

They did not catch the answer. A bundle was thrown down in the next room, and the door slid back to show Chōkichi's pale, shy, gentle face.

II

The sun these last hot days had been more intense than in midsummer, burning up from the broad surface of the river and yet more brightly from the white walls of the university boathouse; and then, as suddenly as if a lantern had been put out, all was a dusky brown, and the sails of the cargo boats gliding on the flood tide were whiter and whiter. Like a curtain falling, the twilight of early autumn gave way to night. Against the dizzying glare of the waters, the ferry passengers rose up like black figures in an ink wash. The long line of cherry trees on the opposite bank was an almost frightening black. The barges that had seemed to be having such a good time but a little while before had all disappeared up the river. Only a few small boats were left behind, bobbing like leaves, fishing boats on their way home, apparently. The surface of the River Sumida was broad and empty again, still and even sad. Over the upper reaches hung a bank of clouds, a last relic of summer, and thin lines of lightning flashed into the gathering night.

Chōkichi wandered absently about, now leaning against the railing of Imado Bridge, now stepping down from the stone embankment to the ferry wharf, gazing at the aspects of the river from afternoon into evening, from evening into night. O-ito had promised to meet him on Imado Bridge, when it was dark enough that they would not be recognized. Since it was Sunday he could not claim night school as his excuse, and scarcely finishing his dinner, he had slipped out of the house before sunset. The stream of people hurrying to the ferry had dwindled and almost disappeared, and the lights of the barges moored under the bridge floated upon the waters of the Sanya Canal, which also carried the reverse image of the tall Keiyoji grove. From a new two-story house with willows at its gate came the sound of a samisen, and the masters of the low houses along the canal were beginning to emerge half naked from latticed doors to enjoy the evening cool. Chōkichi gazed intently across the bridge. It would be time for her to come.

The first figure to cross the bridge was a priest in a dark hempen robe. Then, in tights, a hitched-up kimono, and rubber shoes, came a man who might have been the head of a building gang, and after him, some minutes later, a rather shabby housewife carrying an umbrella and a small cloth bundle, inelegantly kicking up gravel with her high clogs as she walked along in great strides. There was no one else. He turned his tired eyes toward the river. The surface was brighter than before, and the threatening bank of clouds had quite disappeared. Then he saw, rising over the embankment and the grove of the Chōmeiji Temple across the river, a red moon, probably the seventh full moon of the lunar calendar. The sky shone like a mirror, and the embankment and the trees against the moon were ever blacker. Only the evening star was in the sky, all the others having been blotted out in the too-bright moonlight. The wisps of cloud stretching along the horizon were silver, and as the moon rose above the trees everything took on its white glow—the tiled roofs in the evening dew along the river bank, the wet stakes in the water, the bits of seaweed coming under the bridge on the flood tide, the hulls of boats, the bamboo poles.

His own shadow was clearer on the bridge. A pair of strolling singers paused for a moment to admire the moon, and hurried down the canal, to sing coaxingly before the houses that fronted on it:

> The young man waits at the railing of the bridge.

But seeing that their efforts were not likely to bring money, they hurried off again, scarcely finishing their song, in the direction of the Yoshiwara.

Quite beyond the frettings that are the usual experience of waiting lovers, Chōkichi was taken with a very special kind of sadness. What would their future be, his and O-ito's? No, not their future—what would the very next day, after their meeting tonight, have for them? O-ito was going for consultations with the Yoshichō geisha house of which she had spoken earlier, and she had promised that they would walk there together, and talk things over. Once she had become a geisha, their daily meetings would end, and it was possible that tonight might be their very last. It was as if she were going off to a strange, remote country from which she could never return. He would not forget the moon tonight. It was a moon, he said to himself, such as he would never see again. Memories, countless numbers of them, came back to him like flashing lights. How O-ito and he had fought, almost every day, when they were grammar-school students in Jikatamachi. How there had been mischievous scribblings about them on the walls and warehouses of the neighborhood. How his uncle had taken them to Asakusa to see the sights behind the temple, and how they had fed the fish in the pond.

One year, at the Sanja festival, O-ito had appeared on a float, and she had danced *Dōjōji*. And she had danced more than once on the boat when the people of the neighborhood had gone on their annual clam-digging excursions. Almost every day on the way home from school she had waited for him on Matchi Hill, and they had gone walking through back alleys of Sanya such as almost no one knew of, and on to the paddies of the Yoshiwara. Why did she have to become a geisha? He wanted to stop her, to tell her it would not do. He had to stop her, whatever her own views in the matter—but then he knew that he would be no match for her. He felt utterly forlorn, and resigned. She was only fifteen, two years younger than he, but every day she seemed to be getting farther and farther ahead, becoming his older sister. No, she had always been stronger than he. She had had about her far less of the coward. When there had been those scribblings on walls, she had not been bothered in the least. Yes, of course he was her husband, she had shouted back at them, not blinking an eye. She had been the first one to suggest, the year before, that they meet by the Matchi Hill temple, and that they go buy standing-room tickets at the Miyatoza Theater. She had always been the less worried of the two when they were late getting home at night. Let's just go on this way, she would say, delighted, when they had wandered up some strange alley. They could always ask a policeman, she would add.

She came clattering across the bridge, quite unconcerned about the noise she was making.

"I'm late: I can't stand my hair the way Mother does it." She pushed it back in place. The running had so knocked it down that it seemed ready to fall about her shoulders. "I'm sure it looks funny."

Chōkichi could only stare at her with wide eyes. She was in her usual bubbling spirits, but on this occasion of all occasions he thought them out of place. He wanted to ask if it did not make her a little sad, going far down into the city and becoming a geisha. But the emotions were too much for him, and he could not bring the words out. She seemed quite indifferent to the jeweled light of the moon, shining upon the water.

"Let's go. Quick." She hurried off. "I'm rich. I'm going to buy presents in Asakusa on the way."

"You'll be back tomorrow?" Chōkichi stammered. "You're sure?"

"If not tomorrow then the next day. In the morning. I promise. There are clothes and all sorts of things I'll have to pick up."

They took a narrow alley skirting Matchi Hill.

"Why are you so quiet? What's the matter?"

"If you come back the day after tomorrow, you'll go away again. You won't be one of us any more. You'll be one of them. I won't be able to see you any more."

"Oh, come on. I'll be coming back all the time. But then I *will* have to work hard. I'll have all sorts of practicing to do."

Her voice faltered slightly, but not enough to satisfy Chōkichi.

Silent for a moment, he blurted out: "But why do you have to be a geisha?"

"Aren't you funny. Asking the same thing over and over again."

Once again she told the whole long story that he already knew quite well enough. He knew that everything had been decided two or three years before—no, even longer. It had all begun while her father, a carpenter, was still living. Her mother, who took in sewing, had among her customers a certain kept lady at Hashiba, by the river, who, when she saw O-ito, promptly announced that she wanted to take the girl in and see her launched on a splendid career as a geisha. The lady was from a Yoshichō family, proprietors of a large and influential geisha house. O-ito's parents were not in particularly straitened circumstances, however, and, reluctant to let a beloved daughter go—she was then at her most winsome—they undertook to give her music lessons and the like at home. Then, at a loss for a livelihood after she lost her hubsand, O-ito's mother had opened her pastry shop through the good offices of the Hashiba lady; and so, although no one pressed the point, it had come about, partly because of the financial obligations but more because of goodwill on both sides, that O-ito should go to Yoshichō. It was not that Chōkichi wanted to hear what he knew well enough already. It was rather that, since she must go, he wanted her to show a little more sorrow at parting. He saw that his feelings and hers were no longer in harmony. They no longer communicated with each other. He felt even gloomier.

The gloom was scarcely bearable by the time they turned through the Asakusa temple gate toward the lane of shops. O-ito stopped short amid the bustle of evening strollers and tugged at his sleeve.

"Look. That's the sort of thing I'll be wearing one of these days. Silk net, I'm sure that's what she has on."

Chōkichi looked around and saw a geisha with a high chignon. Beside her was a fine gentleman in a summer cloak of black gauze. And when O-ito became a geisha, it would be just such a gentleman who would be walking with her, taking her by the hand. How many years would it be before he could cut such a figure himself? His narrow obi, his student's dress—they seemed indescribably wretched. No, it was not only a matter of the future; even now he felt that he was incapable of easy companionship with O-ito.

Presently they were at the mouth of the Yoshichō lane, with its rows of votive lights. Chōkichi was beyond even thinking himself forlorn. He gazed up the dark lane as if in mute surprise. It seemed to wind back endlessly.

"Let's see. One, two, three—there it is, the one with the gas light, the fourth one. See? The one that says Matsubaya. See?" O-ito pointed at the light, by now familiar from visits with the Hashiba lady, and from various errands she had had to run.

"Well, I'll be going, then." But still Chōkichi stood beside her.

O-ito tugged gently at his sleeve, and her voice took on a cajoling tone. "I'll see you when I come home. Tomorrow, or maybe the day after. All right? Promise, now. Come over and see me. All right?"

Chōkichi nodded.

Apparently satisfied, O-ito started off, her sandals clattering over the gutter boards. She did not look back. To Chōkichi, the sound was as of someone fleeing. An instant later he heard a door open. He started forward; and just then there was a voice and the first door up the alley slid open. A man came out with a long, bamboo-handled lantern. Somehow ashamed to be seen standing there, Chōkichi fled out into the main street. The round moon seemed smaller and its light was whiter. It had risen into a star-filled sky, high above the roofs of the warehouses ranged quietly along the back streets.

III

As the moon rose later each day, its light was clearer. The dampness of the river wind was more and more apparent, and the air was too chilly for a single kimono. Presently the moon was no longer up before people went to bed. The sky was cloudier in the morning, at noon, and on into the evening. Clouds piled upon clouds and milled about incessantly, covering the sky but sometimes separating as if deliberately leaving a particularly blue trace of sky. The air would at such times be muggy, and perspiration sticky on the skin; and then, at such times again, a wind of uncertain strength and direction would blow up, and rain would begin to fall, and stop, and fall again. There was a special sort of strength concealed in the wind and rain, to pass with a sound never heard in the spring and summer, through the temple groves and the reeds along the river bank, and over the board roofs of the poor little houses stretching into the far reaches of the city. The days were a terror of brevity, and immediately the long nights would begin, lonely and hushed. A temple bell at eight or nine, which in the summer would have been drowned out by a clattering of sandals in the evening cool, sounded through a hush as of midnight. The crickets sang busily, and the lamplight was really too bright. Autumn. It was autumn. For the first time Chōkichi knew about autumn, the loneliness that sank into one's bones.

Yesterday school had begun. Early in the morning he had set out with the lunch his mother had prepared, wrapped up with his books; but on the second and third mornings the will to walk all the way to Kanda quite left him. Always before he had somehow felt nostalgic for the beginning of classes as the long summer vacation drew toward a close. This year the fresh briskness of old quite deserted him. What a bore it was—could he really bear it, all this learning? School was not the place to give him the happiness he wished for. Learning was quite unrelated to happiness—it came to Chōkichi for the first time.

On the fourth morning he left home as usual, before seven in the morning. When he reached the precincts of the Asakusa Temple, however, he sat down heavily on a bench beside the main hall, like an exhausted traveler resting on a wayside stone. The gravel, wet with the morning dew, had already been swept, it would seem, for there was no litter. Free from the usual bustle, the temple grounds seemed vast, and quietly worshipful. Several sinister-looking men, who had evidently passed the night there, were sitting on the veranda of the hall, and some of the more brazen ones were calmly untying the short sashes of their dirty kimonos and redoing their loincloths. The sky was low and leaden as it had been for several days, and worm-eaten leaves, still green, fell one after another from the trees. The calls of crows and roosters and the beating of pigeons' wings sounded up clear and strong. The stones of the purification font, wet with overflow, were somehow chilling in the shadows of the flapping towels. Even so, each of the morning pilgrims, man or woman, would wet his hands before proceeding up the temple stairs. Among them Chōkichi chanced to see a young geisha, a pink handkerchief clutched between her teeth, her hands stretched out and her white arms visible to the elbows, so careful was she not to wet the sleeves of her unlined cloak.

"Look, look," said one of the students on the next bench. "Look. A *singer*." The last word was in German. "Not bad."

The slight, round-shouldered figure with the high, swept-up coiffure, the round face and the firm little mouth, even the age of the girl, perhaps fifteen or sixteen—everything about her made Chōkichi think of O-ito, and with such urgent immediacy that he almost started from the bench. O-ito had, as she had promised on that moonlit night, come home two days later to gather the baggage she would need for a long stay in Yoshichō, but Chōkichi had been taken aback at the change. She was a different person. The young girl with her plain red muslin obi had, in the course of a single day, been changed to a figure exactly like the geisha whom Chōkichi now saw before him. O-ito had even had a ring on her fourth finger. Much more frequently than seemed necessary she would take a mirror case from her obi, and retouch her powder or straighten her hair. She left the rickshaw waiting outside, and was off again in one short hour or perhaps even less, with the air of a person who has very urgent and important duties to perform. The last words with which she left him were a request that he give her regards to "the teacher," by which expression she meant his mother. She had, it was true, said what he wanted to hear, that she did not know when she would be making her debut, and that she would therefore be around to see him again soon; but it was no longer the innocent promise it would once have been. To Chōkichi it sounded like an offhand remark from one schooled in the ways of the world. The O-ito who had been a girl, the O-ito who had been his childhood sweetheart, no longer existed. The smell of cosmetics, indescribable, lingering on after the rickshaw had started briskly off and awakened the dog by the gutter—how it had stabbed at him, how utterly forlorn it had left him!

The young geisha, who had gone inside the hall, came lightly down the stairs again and went out the gate, the bare toes in her sandals pointed slightly inward. As he looked after her, all the resentment of that moment of seeing the rickshaw off came back to Chōkichi. He got up from the bench as if it had become intolerable. Then, almost involuntarily, he started after her, down the lane of shops. When he came to the end of it, however, he had lost her; she had apparently turned up one of the side streets. The shopkeepers on both sides were dusting and putting out wares, getting ready for the day's business. Quite beside himself, Chōkichi strode out toward Kaminarimon, at the lower end of the lane. He was no longer pursuing the young geisha. Rather he was pursuing the image of O-ito, so vivid in his mind and his alone. He forgot about school, he forgot about everything, as he made his way down the river, from Komagata to Kuramae, Kuramae to Asakusa Bridge—and on to Yoshichō. When he came to the main Bakurochō streetcar track, he was a little confused, not sure which side street to turn up. But he knew the general direction, and, with the pride of one born in Tokyo, he was reluctant to seek assistance. And somehow it seemed wrong to ask a passerby about the place where his love was staying. It was as if his innermost secrets might thus be exposed to strangers. At random he turned left and then left again, and came out twice on what appeared to be the same canal, lined by wholesale establishments, in the solidly built style of warehouses. Seeing the high roof of the Meiji Theater far beyond, he at length came out on a fairly wide street, and the whistles of river steamers down at the end of it told him for the first time where he was. A wave of exhaustion came over him. Sweat poured out, around the band of his school cap and even around his obi. He could not rest, though, not even for an instant. It was after yet further trials that he found the lane to which he had been brought on that moonlight night.

With the morning sun pouring into it, the lane was bright to its deepest recesses. It was lined by more than little houses with latticed fronts: now, in the daylight, he saw that there were also high-roofed warehouses. There were board fences topped by spikes, and above the spikes the branches of pine trees. There were lime-sprinkled bathroom doors, lines of garbage boxes, cats slinking about. And there were remarkable numbers of people, turning sideways as they passed one another on the narrow walks. The strains of samisen practice mixed with the sound of voices, and laundry water was splashing busily. Girls with hitched-up kimonos and red underskirts were sweeping the boards, and others were polishing away at the latticework, strip by strip. Chōkichi felt a bit shy that there should be so many eyes to see him, and it came to him for the first time that, having arrived, he did not know what to do next. He had thought that he might slip past the Matsubaya and perhaps catch a glimpse of O-ito, but the street was altogether too bright. Should he then stand at the entrance to the lane and wait for her to come out on some errand or other? But it seemed to him that all the eyes up and down the street were fixed on him alone, and he could not bring himself to stand there for even five minutes. He would have to reconsider. He started off into the alley opposite, where an old candy vender had come up clapping a pair of sticks to attract children.

The alley led him gradually toward the river. He now saw that it would be useless to expect her out in the daytime. He was already late for school, however, and if he was to take a holiday, he was faced with the problem of how to kill time until three o'clock. His mother knew well enough what his school hours were; it upset her if he came home an hour early or an hour late, and she would nag at him for an explanation. Chōkichi would have been capable of putting her off with devious answers, it was true; but he disliked the trouble his conscience gave after so much lying. He came out on the river. Several men sat in the shadows of the willows, where the bathhouses had been torn down. Passersby stood watching on the bank. Chōkichi thought that it would be a good idea to join them and pretend to be watching, too. He no longer had the strength even to stand. He squatted down, his back against a stake that supported a tree.

Large parts of the sky had for some time been blue, and although there was a steady wind, the autumn sun, damp and yet burning, sent up a dazzling radiance from the river before him. The thick branches reaching out over the earthen walls on the far side of the street were most inviting. An old seller of sweet sake had put his red utensils down in the shade. Because the sunlight was so strong, the tiled roofs and the rest of the scene across the river looked battered and dingy, and the clouds driven off by the wind formed an unmoving layer, considerably lower than the smoke from the factory chimneys. From a shop that sold angling equipment a clock sounded eleven. Counting the strokes, Chōkichi was startled at how long he had been walking, and at the same time comforted with the thought that it would not be so difficult after all to kill the hours until three. Seeing one of the anglers take out his lunch, Chōkichi unwrapped his own lunch. Suddenly shy, however, he looked around to see whether anyone might be watching. Fortunately, with noon at hand, there were few people in the street. He gulped down his lunch, rice and vegetables and all. The anglers were as still as wooden statues, and the old sake man was dozing. As afternoon came on, the river front was yet quieter, with not even a dog passing by; and Chōkichi began to feel ashamed of his own shyness.

After doing a turn between Ryōgoku Bridge and New Bridge, he made up his mind to start back for Asakusa; but then a thought came to him, and he went once again toward the entrance to the Yoshichō lane. Relieved to see that there were not as many people as there had been in the morning, he crept timorously past the Matsubaya. From the street the house seemed pitch dark, and there was not even the sound of a samisen, not even a human voice. To have passed by the house where she lived, however, and to have had no one to reprove him for it—Chōkichi felt as if he had been on the wildest sort of adventure, and the thought gave him some satisfaction. He had no regrets for his long walk.

IV

Chōkichi somehow managed to get to school for the rest of the week; but the following Monday he took his streetcar as far as Ueno and abruptly got off. He had done none of the algebra he was supposed to turn in that day. Nor had he prepared his lessons in English and Chinese. And it had come to him that today he faced what he hated and feared most of anything in the world, gymnastics. To dangle head-first from an iron bar, to jump from a platform higher than a man could reach—however much the instructor, an old army sergeant, might try to force him on, however much the other students might laugh at him, every last one of them, this was not the sort of thing that Chōkichi was up to. In matters having to do with physical exercise he could not go the distance with the other students, and he found himself isolated, in a chorus of contempt. The next stage would be open persecution. And so school had become a harsh and uninviting place. Whatever the views of his mother, Chōkichi had not the slightest wish to go on to high school. It was the rule, he had heard, that if admitted he would have to spend his first year in the turbulence of dormitory life. He had long been horrified at stories he had heard of happenings in the high-school dormitories. Always at the head of his class in art and calligraphy (indeed no one could rival him), he found his inclinations taking him in quite another direction from iron bars and judo and the other appurtenances of "the Japanese spirit." More than anything else he loved listening to the samisen with which his mother made her way in the world. Without having had a lesson, he had picked up the repertoire of her school, and he would only have to listen once to a popular song that went the rounds to have that by memory, too. His uncle in Koume, Ragetsu, teacher of poetry, had

early seen that he had the makings of a master, and had urged O-toyo
to have him apprenticed to a teacher of the first rank, any such teacher
would do. O-toyo was adamant in her refusal, however, and thereafter
she forbade Chōkichi even to take a samisen in his hands.

Ragetsu had been right: had Chōkichi started taking lessons early,
he would by now be an accomplished artist. And so, Chōkichi said
to himself, he would not have had this misery in store for him, even
if O-ito did have to become a geisha. Well, there was no repairing the
damage now. The arrangements for his career had been in error from
the outset. Resentment at his mother came welling up. And with it
came a wave of affection for his uncle. He wanted to throw himself
upon his uncle. Experiencing for the first time the pains of love, he
began to put a new significance on a story that he had heard more
than once, from his mother and from his uncle too, but that had not
particularly interested him: the story of Ragetsu's sybaritic past. He
remembered how his "aunt from Koume" had been a courtesan in one
of the great Yoshiwara houses, and had come to his uncle for help
when, after the Meiji Restoration, the Yoshiwara had been liberated.
His aunt had been extremely kind to him in his childhood. It seemed
nonetheless that his mother did not think well of the other woman,
and her manner made it clear that she acquitted herself of the calls
expected in the summer and at the New Year only as a matter of duty.
Once again, displeasure and resentment at his mother came over Chōkichi. The very intensity of the affection with which she kept watch
over him, scarcely letting him out of her sight even at night, was most
burdensome, and made him think how, if his mother were but a person like his aunt in Koume—his aunt, seeing them play together, Chōkichi and O-ito, had once said in the warmest tones that the two of
them must *always* be friends—if his mother had been such a person,
then surely she would have understood the sufferings he was going
through, and sympathized with him. She would not have tried to
force upon him a state of well-being for which he had not the slightest
wish himself. He compared the ways of the two women, the respectable one who was his mother, and the other, the woman with the past.
And he compared the sort of person he had teaching him in school
with the sort of person his uncle was.

Until about noon, Chōkichi lay on a rock among the trees behind
the Tōshōgū Shrine, and thought such thoughts as these. Then he

took out a novel hidden among his books and lost himself in it. And he deliberated plans for borrowing his mother's seal without her knowing, and affixing it to the written excuse he would have to have with him the next day.

v

There was rain for days and nights on end, and for several days not a cloud in the sky. And then the sky would suddenly cloud over, and a wind come up to blow at the dry gravel in the streets. The weather was each day colder. Doors and windows, now tightly closed, rattled sadly and without pause. To be at school by seven, Chōkichi had to get up by six. Each morning at six it was a little darker than it had been the day before, and presently it was as dark as night, and he had to have a light to dress by. That dull, yellow light every year at the beginning of winter would bring the most intense gloom and revulsion. To encourage him on his way, his mother would always be up before him, shivering in her nightgown, to have a hot breakfast ready. Grateful enough for these ministrations, Chōkichi, scarcely awake, would want to spend a little more time warming himself. But his mother would have an eye only for the clock, and presently she would send him out into the cold wind from the river. Once, annoyed at these excesses of attention, he had purposely taken off the scarf he had been ordered to wear, and so caught cold. And another time, long ago, in a day that would not come back, his uncle Ragetsu had taken him and O-ito to the Otori Fair;* and every year, when he remembered, he would find that cold December was upon him again.

It was clear to Chōkichi, as he thought of winter this year and last year, last year and the year before, as he went back through the years —it was clear to him how much happiness a person loses as he grows up. In the days before he started to go to school, he had been able to sleep as long as he wanted on cold mornings—and the cold had not bothered him then as it did now. On days when there was rain and a cold wind, he had in fact particularly enjoyed going out to play. How different it was now—how hard to tramp through the frost on Imado Bridge early in the morning, and in the afternoon to hear the cold wind in the old trees of the Matchi grove, and to see the evening

* Held twice or three times in November at various Otori shrines, the largest of them, the one referred to here, being just outside the Yoshiwara.

light so early! And what new trials would each coming year bring to him? Never quite so vividly as this December had Chōkichi known the sorrow of the passing days. The New Year's market was already laid out in the precincts of the Asakusa Temple. New Year's gifts from his mother's pupils, sugar sacks and dried fish, were beginning to take their places in the alcove. Yesterday the term examinations had ended, and his mother had received a warning in the mail about his remarkably bad grades.

Knowing that it would be on its way, Chōkichi but stood with hanging head as his mother gave him her pitiful story. It always began with "a widow and child alone in the world." The little girls who came for lessons in the morning had gone home, and the girls who had lessons after school would not be coming until three, and it was the idlest time of the day for O-toyo. The day was quiet and windless, and the winter sun flooded the windows at the street.

Suddenly, almost before the sound of the opening door, there came a lively, girlish voice.

"Is anyone at home?"

O-toyo got up in surprise, and a moment later the voice from outside went on.

"It's me. How are you? I haven't been very good about keeping in touch, and I've come to apologize."

Chōkichi was trembling. It was O-ito. She came in, slipping off a splendid cloak as she did so.

"Well, what do you know! Here's Chōkichi. Are you having vacation?" She added a little giggle, as if as an afterthought, and knelt down to make her formal greetings. "And how have you been?" she asked O-toyo. "I've really been very bad about keeping in touch—but it's all I can do to get out of the house."

She took a box of sweets from a crepe kerchief. Quite struck dumb by the sight of her, Chōkichi could but watch in silence.

Herself somewhat taken aback, O-toyo made her thanks. "And aren't you looking nice," she said. "I would hardly have known you."

"I've put on years overnight. Everyone says so." Smiling a pretty smile, O-ito redid the cord of her purple silk cloak, and while she was about it, took a red velvet tobacco pouch from her obi. "See? I'm smoking." This time she gave a high, clear laugh. "I'll bet you think I'm awful."

"Why don't you sit over here? You must be cold." O-toyo took the kettle from the brazier and began to make tea. "And when did you have your coming-out?"

"Oh, not yet. Not till on toward the end of the year."

"Oh? Well, I'm sure you'll be very popular. You're so pretty, and all, and they can't hide real quality. It shows through."

"Well, I owe it all to you." O-ito fell silent for a moment. "As a matter of fact the lady at the house has been very pleased with me. She says there are older ones that don't do half as well."

"That's how it would be these days, I'm sure." O-toyo remembered herself, and took a jar of sweets from the shelf. "I really don't have anything in the house. But you might not find these too bad. They're from the Dōryō Temple." She fished one out for O-ito.

There were two shrill voices at the door, and two little girls had come for their lessons.

"Please don't worry about me," said O-ito.

"Oh, it's all right. They can wait." But after a moment O-toyo went into the next room.

Overcome with shyness, Chōkichi sat looking at the floor.

O-ito did not seem in the least disturbed. "Did you get my letter?" she said softly.

The childish voices came in unison from the next room: " 'The cherries are in bloom, at Omuro in Saga.' "

Chōkichi sat fidgeting, his head still bowed. It had been some time before the first of the Otori Fairs that he had had a note from O-ito. It had merely said that she was unable to get out of her house. He had immediately sent back telling her in great detail of everything that had happened to him since their parting. But the prompt answer he had hoped for had somehow not come.

"The New Year's fair is on at Asakusa. Shall we go this evening? I can stay out tonight."

Afraid that his mother might hear, Chōkichi did not answer.

O-ito felt no such reticence. "Come for me as soon as you've finished dinner." A moment later she added: "And I suppose your mother will be coming too."

Chōkichi nodded weakly.

O-ito seemed to remember. "Your uncle from Koume—how is he? He got drunk and had a fight with one of the stall keepers. Remember? When was it? I was really scared. Wouldn't it be nice if he were to come by this evening."

Finding a break in the lesson, O-ito took her leave of O-toyo and hurried off. "I'll see you this evening, then," she said.

VI

Chōkichi came down with a cold. Because he overtaxed himself and tried to go to school the day after vacation ended, it turned to influenza, and he was in bed for the rest of the month.

In the precincts of the Imado Hachiman Shrine there had been drums from early morning, for it was the Day of the Horse, the first such day in the New Year. Across the papered window, warm with the soft sun of the winter afternoon, the shadows of the birds under the eaves flitted back and forth. The sunlight filled even the dusky recesses of the Buddha shelf, far back in the breakfast room. The plum in the alcove was beginning to shed its petals. And so the brightness of spring had come into even this tightly closed house.

Up several days now, Chōkichi had taken advantage of the warm weather for a walk. Now that he had quite recovered he could look upon the three weeks of illness as an unexpected blessing. He had thought all along that he had not the least chance of passing the final examinations, which were coming up the next month, and now that he had had to be out of school, he had the perfect excuse with which to face his mother.

He found himself at the rear entrance to Asakusa Park. One side of the narrow street fronted on a deep moat, and among the tall, bare trees beyond the moat and the iron railing on the far side of it, the archery ranges in the park presented their shabby rears. The low houses lining the street on the other side were as if pressed down on the moat from behind, and perhaps it was for this reason that the street, not really so crowded, always had a rushed and urgent look about it. Evil-eyed rickshawmen loitered about, pestering the relatively more prosperous-looking pedestrians for business. Chōkichi had come as far as the crossing from which, past the stone bridge on the left where a policeman was always standing guard, the way was clear as far as the Awashima Shrine. He joined the cluster of people inspecting the theater posters at the corner of the Miyatoza.

In the middle were listed the names of the principal actors, in stylized characters packed so closely together that they were far from easy to read; and on either side the actors themselves were portrayed in various contorted postures, their faces tiny, their eyes enormous, their fingers thick, their garments like so many quilts and mattresses. Along the eaves protecting the posters were lines of artificial flowers, pretty as on festival floats.

Warm though the day might be, it was still very early spring. Chō-kichi had been looking for a spot where he might be out of the wind for a time, and, seeing the posters, he started for the narrow standing-room entrance. Inside there was a precipitous stairway. The light from the door penetrated no farther than the landing. The warm, sour smell of the theater crowds pressed down from the yet darker regions above. He could hear shouts of encouragement for favorite actors. They brought on a pleasant anticipation, the excitement peculiar to the theater of the great city. Running up two and three steps at a time, Chō-kichi pushed his way into the throng at the rear of the balconies. The floors and ceiling sloped together, as in the hold of a large ship. It was almost pitch dark, the naked gaslights in the rear corners being blocked by the heads of standing spectators. Beyond the iron railing to which some of them clung like monkeys, the ceiling was vast and open. By contrast the stage itself seemed tiny and remote in the clouded air. To a sound of wooden clappers the revolving stage had just come to a stop. Below a stone embankment, remarkably straight, a dirty azure cloth had been spread, and on the backdrop was painted, small in the distance, the wall of a daimyo's estate. The sky above it was an unbroken black, exaggerating, if exaggeration were needed, the effect of night. Night and the river bank: Chōkichi knew that it would be a murder scene. In youthful eagerness he stood on tiptoes and stretched his neck. Sure enough—to an accompaniment of muffled drums there was a clattering across the stage boards, and a manservant and a woman with a bundle under her arm appeared, arguing loudly, from behind the watchhouse on the left. The audience laughed. The two on the stage assumed postures as of looking for something. One of them picked it up, and immediately their attitude changed.

"*An Evening Moon Among the Plums and Willows,*" read one of them in the clearest tones. "The story of Izayoi and Seishin. And the actors are. . . ."

It was the signal for shouts of anticipation from the audience. Upon a modest signal from the wooden clappers, a stage attendant in black swept away a curtain on the right, revealing three singers and two samisen players, all in formal dress, crowded together on one small stand. The samisens began, and shortly the singers took up in unison. Chōkichi had long loved this sort of music, and despite the crying of a baby somewhere off in the theater and the shouts of spectators reproving it, he had no trouble catching the melody and words:

"In the misty night, two stars, now three. And four, and five, the sound of a bell. Will there be someone pursuing me?"

Again there was a light clattering of footsteps, and there were frantic cries from the balconies. The audience was brought to electrified attention. And for good reason: a courtesan in festive dress, a broad band of purple satin at her throat and a red singlet showing beneath it, came running out, bent forward from the effort, along the passageway that led through the pits to the stage. Her face was half hidden in the scarf around her head.

"Sit down!"

"We can't see!"

"Sit down, damn it!"

The actor impersonating the courtesan stopped to look back as he approached the stage, and spoke a few words:

"I have run away, they will not know where—as fearful of pursuing eyes as small fishes of nets and flares."

The singers took up again:

"She stops. From upstream comes a song. A boat has returned from the plum groves. 'If you are to come, my love, let the night not be a dark one. The moon awaited so fretfully, the moon of the sixteenth night. The night shall be without clouds, my love.' Was it a portent? The tempest passes, and suddenly, in the moonlight, face to face!"

Another murmur ran through the audience. Even from where Chōkichi stood, it was easy to see the strings pulling away clouds to reveal a light, a large round hole in the black screen. It was a moon so large and bright that the wall of the daimyo's estate seemed to recede in the distance. Neither for Chōkichi, however, nor for the rest of the audience was the effect such as to spoil the illusion. Indeed as he thought of the round, round moon, the enormous moon he had seen with O-ito from Imado Bridge that late-summer night, the stage was no longer a stage.

His hair disheveled, no cloak over his kimono, a man came staggering onstage. He gave every indication of being at the end of his resources. He passed the woman.

"Izayoi?"

"Seishin?" The woman fell upon him. "How I wanted to see you!"

Again there were shouts from the audience.

"What a handsome couple!"

"You're making me jealous."

There was laughter, and the true devotees called for silence.

As the lovers plunged into the river, seeking to drown themselves, the stage revolved once more, to show the woman's rescue in a fishing net. Then it turned back to the earlier scene. The man, equally unsuccessful at drowning himself, climbed the embankment. A roistering song in the distance. A longing for riches, the joy of being alive. Despair, opportunity, fate. Seduction, murder. Complication piled upon dramatic complication, the act at length came to a close. At Chōkichi's ear a shrill voice called out: "Buy your tickets for the next act, please." The standing-room audience flooded toward the door.

Chōkichi walked briskly off once he was outside. It was still daylight, but the street was in shadows. A confusion of curtains and flags on the main Senzoku street flapped busily in the wind. He crouched down to see if there might be a clock inside one of the low-eaved shops. The interiors seemed pitch dark, however. Walking yet faster, afraid of the effect the wind might have on him after such a long illness, he came out on the Sanya Canal. There he had to stop for a time, to look at the River Sumida, beyond Imado Bridge. The surface of the river was ashen, and the mists rising from it clouded the far embankment, hurrying the winter sun on its way. Seagulls dipped and crossed among the sails of the barges. The flowing waters seemed lonely to Chōkichi. One and two lights were already showing on the far shore. The wintry trees, the dry stones, the shabby tiled roofs—everything he saw seemed faded and chilly. The lively faces of Izayoi and Seishin, still with him from the moment of leaving the theater, floated up all the more vividly, like faces on a New Year's battledore. He found himself so drawn to them as to be almost resentful. He could not be one of them however much he wished to. It would be better to die than to go on as he was—if only there were someone to die with him.

As he crossed Imado Bridge, the cold wind struck him square in the face, like a blow from a clenched fist. He shivered, and suddenly from the depths of his throat came a fragment of a Jōruri ballad. He scarcely

knew where he had learned it. "What more can one say? And yet...."
It was a fragment of Kiyomoto, a turn of phrase such as no other
school could imitate. Chōkichi did not, of course, render it with the
straining of the body, the fullness of voice, that one would have expected from a real master. The phrase came from his throat and was
lost in his mouth; but it brought a lessening of the scarcely tolerable
pain. "What more can one say? And yet... it is true, it is true... the
willows below the cliff...."

Still humming over the fragments as they came to him, he slid back
the latticed door of his house.

VII

The next afternoon found Chōkichi again standing in the Miyatoza.
He wished once more to make himself drunk with the sad beauty he
had known for the first time the day before, the beauty of the stage
lovers, taking each other by the hand and together lamenting their
fate. That was not all: however gloomy it might be there between
blackened walls and ceiling, he was drawn with a strength he could
not deny to the myriads of lights, the swarms of people. He was inde-
finably sad, and the sadness now went beyond the fact that he had lost
O-ito. He did not himself understand it. He was merely sad, and
lonely. He yearned for something to ease the pain. He wished to appeal, in the vague, indefinable torment within him, to a beautiful
woman who would answer him in a soft voice. It need not be O-ito
herself. He dreamed of making his appeal to some woman whom he
passed in the street, to someone with the high chignon of an unmarried girl, to a geisha, to a lady with the modest coiffure of a housewife,
it did not matter whom.

For Chōkichi the play, which he was seeing for the second time, was
as exciting as if he had not seen it before. This time he had an eye, too,
for the lively balconies to the left and right of the theater. All these
women in the world—and why could he not come upon one among
them who would comfort him? Anyone would do. If a single one had
a single soft word for him, then he might be able to forget about O-ito,
even a little. The more he thought about her the more he wanted some
drug to lessen the pain, and so take him away from thoughts about
school and his hopeless future.

He looked up startled. Someone there in the pack of standing spectators had tapped him on the shoulder. From a slightly higher spot to

the rear, a young man with dark glasses and a visor cap pulled low over the eyes was leaning toward him.

"Kichi!" But Kichi had changed almost beyond recognition. Chōkichi was at a loss for words. A friend from their days in the Jikatamachi Primary School, Kichi was the son of a barber on the main Sanya street, and it had been he who had cut Chōkichi's hair. He had a silk scarf around his neck and a cloak of fine weave showed beneath his cape, and he smelled a bit too powerfully of cologne.

"I'm an actor, Chō." Kichi bent lower to murmur the words in Chōkichi's ear.

In the press there at the back of the theater, Chōkichi could but wait in astonished silence. As yesterday, the action progressed to the scuffling on the dark river bank, and the hero, the stolen money stuffed inside his kimono, started up the passage toward the rear of the pits. Then he struck a defiant pose, and wooden clappers signaled the end of the act. The curtain slid closed. Again came the shrill voice requiring that tickets be bought for the next scene. As the curtain came all the way shut, the flood poured toward the narrow exit. Backstage the curtain drum boomed.

"Are you leaving already?" Kichi tugged at his sleeve. "Why don't you stay for another act?"

A coarse-looking person in theater dress came around with an oiled-paper basket to take money for the next act. Though somewhat uneasy about the time, Chōkichi stayed on.

"We can sit down over there. It looks clean enough," Kichi went back to a space by a window and motioned for Chōkichi to sit beside him on the sill. "I'm an actor," he said again. "Have I changed?" He pulled out the printed sleeve of his crepe singlet and polished purposefully at his gold-rimmed glasses.

"I hardly recognized you."

"Were you surprised?" Kichi laughed in open pleasure. "Do me a favor, Chō. I really am an actor, whatever you might think. A new face in Ii's troupe.* We're at the Shintomiza again from the day after tomorrow. So here's what I want you to do. Come around and see the show when everything's in shape, and then come to the stage door and ask for Tamamizu. Will you do that?"

"Tamamizu?"

---

* Ii Yōhō (1871–1932), an actor in the modern, Westernized theater.

"Yes. Tamamizu Saburō." Kichi groped for a small case and showed his name card. "See? Tamamizu Saburō. I'm not the old Kichi any more. I'm right there on the program, Tamamizu Saburō."

"It must be fun to be an actor."

"Oh, it has its ups and downs. But there's no shortage of women, that's one good thing you have to admit." He glanced at Chōkichi. "How are you with women?"

Chōkichi did not answer. To tell of his inexperience would have been an affront to his masculine pride.

"Do you know the Kajita Tower? The best house in all Edo? Well, come along with me tonight. There's nothing to be afraid of. I don't like to brag, but there's a special reason why there's nothing to be afraid of." He laughed, somewhat self-consciously. "We're more than just acquaintances, you might say. See what I mean?"

"I imagine geisha cost a lot of money," said Chōkichi abruptly.

"What? You like geisha? A waste of money." The young actor looked curiously at Chōkichi. "Oh, they don't cost as much as all that, really. But it's silly to pay money for women. I know several houses in Asakusa. Let me show you around. You can get away with anything—it's just a question of nerve."

Spectators trickled in, and the stands were becoming crowded again. Those who had stayed for a second act were restless. At widely spaced intervals wooden clappers sounded backstage. Gradually they came nearer. Chōkichi got up from the uncomfortable window sill.

"It'll be a long time yet," said Kichi, half to himself. "That's just to let the actors know that the stage is ready. It'll be a long time yet." He took a leisurely puff on a cigarette.

"I see," said Chōkichi admiringly. He did not sit down again, however. He looked through the iron grillwork toward the stage.

The pits were in confusion, for those who were not as well informed as Kichi on what the clappers meant were hurrying back to their seats, under the impression that the curtain was about to open. The late-afternoon sun, somehow wan and sad, came in on the curtain from the side balconies, picking up the dust and smoke in the air. Occasionally a gust of wind sent a high wave across the curtain, which was inscribed to an actor, Ichikawa Something-or-other. Below his name were those of the donors, a group of Asakusa geisha.

"Do you know any of them?" asked Chōkichi.

"Oh, come on. Asakusa is my home ground." Somewhat miffed, Kichi rolled off the careers of the geisha in question, together with limitless information about their looks and dispositions. Chōkichi could not be sure how much was fact and how much fiction.

There were two sharp blows of the wooden clappers. Then came samisen and singers; and, slowly at first and gradually faster, to the timing of the clappers, the curtain was drawn back. Already the standing-room audience was calling out the names of favorite actors. The desultory talk stopped, and a brightness as of the break of day came over the theater.

VIII

O-toyo had gone as far as Imado Bridge before she realized that it was high April—and spring. The sky was blue and the sun poured through the window, and the willow by the door of the shop across the street put out its threads of green, to make even O-toyo, a woman alone and sorely pressed, notice the change of seasons. But now, from the low ground in the outer reaches of the city, with the view blocked off by shabby tiled roofs on either side, she came out on the bridge, and an uninterrupted view of the Sumida in April. She left her own street no more than two or three times a year, and she wondered whether her aging eyes might not be deceiving her. The shining flow of water, the green grass on the embankment, the line above it of cherries in bloom, the university boathouse with its banners flying, the shouts of people and the roar of guns, all of these under a cloud-less sky. And the confusion of blossom viewers, getting on and off the ferries. This sudden flood of color was too much for the weary O-toyo. She started down toward the ferry landing, and then, as if in fright, she turned back and hurried south, in the shade of Matchi Hill. There she picked out the dirtiest rickshaw she could find, and the most timid-looking runner.

"To Koume, please," she said in a small, frightened voice. "What is your lowest rate?"

She was in no mood for looking at cherry blossoms. She did not know where to turn. Not only had the son upon whom she had pinned all her hopes failed his examinations, but he said he no longer wanted to go to school. He was finished with lessons and learning. O-toyo had no recourse other than to go consult with her brother Ragetsu.

The third rickshawman with whom she tried bargaining agreed to take her to Koume for a price she was willing to pay. Azuma Bridge was swarming with people, bathed in sun and dust. The old rickshawman made his tottering, uncertain way among the brave vehicles of gaily dressed young people, all of them out viewing the blossoms. Once across the bridge he turned up a street toward Narihira Bridge, and the blossom-viewing crowds were behind them. Only the warm sun on the dirty shingled roofs told of the spring. The sky reflected blue from the stagnant water of Hikifune Canal.

In the street before her latticed door, where passersby were few and the quiet was broken only by children playing with their tops and marbles, Ragetsu's much-loved wife O-taki, who was said to have been a courtesan in one of the great Yoshiwara houses, was stretching a laundered kimono out on drying boards. The sun was full against her wrinkled face, which showed the effects of cosmetics too generously applied. She had a towel around the neck of her quilted kimono.

"Well, this is a surprise!" she said as the rickshaw came up and O-toyo dismounted. "The teacher from Imado is here," she called through the open door.

Ragetsu, master of poetry, was seated at a low desk by the veranda, along which were ranged pots of lilies. He was busy judging contributions to a poetry contest.

He took off his spectacles and came to the middle of the room. Greetings went on and on between the elderly women, the two of them about the same age. O-taki had let down the sleeves of her kimono.

"And is Chō well?" she asked as the bowing went on.

"Yes, he's well enough. But he has me worried."

And so the purpose of the visit was laid before Ragetsu with remarkable speed. Quietly he knocked the ashes from his pipe. Everyone, he said, had his little ways while he was young. He had had them himself. And at such times a parent was an adversary. Might it not be well to avoid interfering, to let the boy do as he pleased?

But the constricted breast of the mother, filled with terror at the hidden future, had no room for the laissez-faire of the worldly person before her. She talked on in hushed tones, as of the blackest omens, telling how, long before, Chōkichi had stayed away from his special course in mathematics and stolen her seal to counterfeit an excuse.

"And so I ask him what he means to do if he doesn't want to go to school. And can you imagine what he tells me? He's going to be an actor. An actor! Can you imagine it? It's all I can do to control myself when I see how far he's gone."

"An actor?" Even Ragetsu was surprised for a brief moment; but then he remembered how Chōkichi had played with samisens when he was scarcely more than an infant. "Well, if that's what he wants, that's what he wants. I don't suppose there's much we can do. I see what you mean, though."

She herself had become a teacher of vulgar music, said O-toyo, because of family misfortunes; but to have her son fall to a similar level —how could she face the ancestral tablets with the news? Ragetsu, who had himself been so dissolute as to require eviction from the family, was considerably discommoded by this mention of family misfortunes. He wanted to scratch his bald head in embarrassment. Long drawn to the world of music and the theater, he was half inclined to attack O-toyo's narrow prejudices; but he feared that anything he said would but bring on another lecture about the ancestral tablets. He set about tidying up the conversation in such a fashion as to leave O-toyo somewhat more at ease.

"Well, let me have a talk with him. It's best to get your troubles over while you're young. Tell him to come and see me tonight, tomorrow, I don't care when. You needn't be so upset. I'm sure I'll be able to talk him out of it. Things are never as bad as they look."

Asking him to do his best, O-toyo withdrew despite O-taki's urgings to stay longer. The red sun was low over Azuma Bridge. It set off the confusion of cherry-blossom viewers, now starting for home, even more brightly than before. Students in their brass-buttoned uniforms strode vigorously past. O-toyo could not be sure whether they were university students or not—but if only she had been able to turn her Chōkichi into such a fine figure of a lad! The tragedy of it, struggling alone all these years, and now having hope itself desert her—it was altogether too much. She knew that she could expect little from Ragetsu. And not just because of his profligate youth. The point was rather that to make Chōkichi see where his duty lay was beyond the powers of an ordinary human being. She could but lay her case before the gods. At Asakusa she hastily descended from her rickshaw. No longer shy about the crowds, she hurried to the main temple gate. She prayed in silence for a moment, then chose one of the yellowing bits of paper on which omens for the future had been printed from wood blocks.

"Number 62: Great Good Luck.

"Disaster ebbs: your troubles will gradually recede, even as fortune approaches.

"Fame rides the tide: your fame will spread to the ends of the earth, hiding itself from no one.

"Old things are renewed, blessings increase: the old is made over, and brings new bounties with it.

"With new heights to be mounted, well-being will grow of its own accord. The way to success being open, wealth and esteem will accrue.

"Prayers will be answered, the ailing will recover, what has been lost will be found, the awaited one will come. A good time for building, for travel, for marriages, for coming-out ceremonies."

O-toyo felt better. But then she remembered that "great good luck" was particularly prone to turn into disaster, and once again she started going over the list of her worries. She was exhausted when she reached home.

IX

There was to be a poetry meet that afternoon in the precincts of the Ryūganji Temple, at Kameido, some distance beyond Koume. After lunch with Chōkichi, who had come in the morning, Ragetsu suggested that they walk toward the Ryūganji along the Oshiage Canal. In the low noonday tide, the muddy bottom of the canal lay bare to the April sun, and gave off a considerable odor. Industrial soot floated down from somewhere, and from somewhere came the noise of industrial machinery. The houses along the way were on a lower level than the road. Housewives in the dark interiors, busy at piece-work of various sorts to round out family budgets, and indifferent to the warmth of the spring day, were quite exposed to the passing eye. On dirty boards at the corners of houses were pasted advertisements for medicine and fortune-tellers, and scattered among them were notices that factory girls were needed. The twisting lane began to climb a little; and the scene abruptly changed. The reddish fence of the Myōkenji Temple lay along one side, and on the other the pleasantly scrubbed board fence of the Hashimoto restaurant. Uncle and nephew had come to the edge of the depressed Honjo quarter, and beyond the grassy embankment of the canal, crossed by a wooden bridge, a spring-time vista spread before them, the fields and groves of Kameido.

Ragetsu stopped. "See the roof by the pines? On up the canal there? That's where I'm going."

"I'll say good-bye, then." Chōkichi snatched off his cap and made as if to leave.

"Don't rush off. I'm a little thirsty. Let's sit down somewhere."

Ragetsu led the way along the board fence of the Myōkenji and into a tea stall at the gate, shaded by a reed awning. Here, too, the straight line of the canal showed its dirty ebb-tide bottom, but the breeze from the distant fields was fresh, and on the far embankment, where the gate of the Tenjin Shrine was to be seen, the trailing lines of spring willows waved and tossed invitingly. Sparrows and swallows chirped on the temple gate just behind him, and despite the fact that there was a chimney here and there, one could enjoy the sweet languor of a spring afternoon as if far from the city streets. After gazing at the scene for some time, Ragetsu glanced at Chōkichi.

"You understand, then?"

About to have a sip of tea, Chōkichi nodded. He did not otherwise answer.

"Just try to stand it for another year. Once you've graduated—your mother is getting old, and won't go on being stubborn forever."

Chōkichi nodded again, his eyes on a point in the distance. From a boat moored in the canal, two or three coolies were hauling earth to a factory beyond the embankment. On the near bank, until then deserted, two rickshaws appeared from the direction of Tenjin Bridge and stopped at the temple gate. Someone had come to visit a grave, it would seem. A woman with a wifely chignon took the hand of a little girl and led her through the gate.

Chōkichi left his uncle at the bridge. Ragetsu seemed troubled. "Well, then." He was silent for a time. "Well, I know it won't be much fun, but try to stand it a little longer. The best policy is to do right by your parents. It always pays in the end."

Chōkichi took off his cap and bowed slightly. Then, turning on his heels, he as good as ran off in the direction from which they had come. Ragetsu's figure meanwhile disappeared among the spring grasses on the far embankment.

In all his near-sixty years he had never been assigned a task more

difficult, thought Ragetsu. O-toyo's request had not been unreasonable, and yet he could see nothing wrong with Chōkichi's wish to go
into the theater. Every worm will turn, every person has his way. For
better or for worse, thought Ragetsu, no one should be forced to do
what he does not want to do; and so, caught between, he could agree
unconditionally neither with the mother nor with the son. Given his
own past, Ragetsu could see to the bottom of the boy's heart. How un-
bearably dreary it had seemed in his youth, sitting in the dark pawnshop, the family enterprise, and having to work as if the warm spring
sun were not outside! How much pleasanter than sitting with a ledger
under a smoky lamp it had been to lounge in a bright upstairs room
looking out over the river, and to read some gay novel about the life
of the pleasure quarters! Chōkichi said that he did not want to be a
stiff, bewhiskered office worker, he wanted rather to live with the
theater he so loved. The one was a career, and the other was too. But
so long as Ragetsu was forced to function as an adviser, he had to
keep his views to himself. He could only do what he had already done
in the case of the mother, offer some fugitive remarks to put the patient at rest.

Chōkichi walked up one shabby Honjo street and down another,
indistinguishable from it. He did not wish to go straight back to
Imado. Nor was he taking a circuitous route for purposes of amusing
himself. He was in despair. If he was to have his way and become an
actor, then he would need the help of his reasonable uncle. He had
been sure that his uncle would help him, and his wishful thinking
had deceived him. His uncle had not lashed back as savagely as his
mother, it was true; and yet, prefacing his remarks with the truism
that advance reports tended to suggest heaven when the actuality was
hell, Ragetsu had proceeded to tell him numerous other things he was
perfectly aware of already: that the route to success was difficult, that
theater life was hard, that professional relationships could be fussy
and troublesome; and finally—again something that Chōkichi knew
well enough already—that he must think of his mother. Old people,
mused Chōkichi, were most conveniently arranged. They could forget the things that had worried and upset them when they were
young, and the only task that remained was to preach to those whose
day was coming next. Between the old and the young there was an
unbridgeable chasm.

The earth was dark and damp, the streets were narrow, and so

twisted that he expected to find himself up a blind alley. Mossy
shingled roofs, rotting foundations, leaning pillars, dirty planks, drying rags and diapers, pots and cheap sweets for sale—the dreary little
houses went on in endless disorder, and when on occasion he would
be surprised by an imposing gate, it would always be a factory. A
soaring tiled roof would be a temple, more than likely in bad repair,
the cemetery plainly visible through gaps in the earthen walls. Clusters of wooden grave-markers and moss-flecked tombstones lay falling over into marshes that had once been garden lakes but had so
decayed that it was difficult to know where bank gave way to water.
There were no fresh flowers at any of the graves. Frogs were croak-
ing, already at noon. Last year's grass lay rotting in the water.

Chōkichi chanced to look at a number on a gate. The address was
familiar—he remembered a book he had just read, Shunsui's *Calendar
of Plum Blossoms.* So it was in this damp, unpleasant neighborhood
that the unfortunate lovers had lived! His interest aroused, he saw
that there were indeed bamboo fences like those in the illustrations.
The bamboo was dry and eaten away at the edges, and looked as
though a push might topple it over. A scraggy willow sent a few precarious shoots out over the low wooden roof of a gate. To just such a
melancholy dwelling, perhaps, the geisha Yonehachi had gone in
secret to visit the ailing Tanjirō. And it would have been in such a
house that Hanjirō, telling ghost stories one rainy night, first took
O-ito's hand in his. An intense longing and sadness came over Chōkichi. Visions and dreams swept through his mind. How he wished
that he could have lived just such a life, made sport of by just such a
fate, sweet and soft, then suddenly cold and hostile! The dreams
spread their wings, the blue sky was bluer and higher. From the distance came the sound of a confectioner's flute. The weird, low strain,
unexpected in these back streets, added a touch of sadness, mysterious
and quite beyond description.

For a time Chōkichi forgot his dissatisfaction with his uncle. For a
time he forgot the anguish of reality.

x

Just as when summer gives way to autumn, so it is when spring
gives way to summer: there are likely to be heavy rains. No one was
surprised, for it happened every year, that the district from Senzoku
toward the Yoshiwara should be under water. Having heard that

there had been floods in Honjo, too, Ragetsu thought it might be well to see how his sister had fared. One evening several days after the floods, on his way home from an errand somewhere, he made his visit to Imado. There had been no flood; but he was startled with news of a wholly different sort of disaster. He arrived in the midst of the excitement: his nephew Chōkichi was being carried away on a stretcher to the Honjo Isolation Hospital. O-toyo told him what the doctor had told her, that Chōkichi's cold had turned into typhoid fever. He had caught cold because he had gone out without a coat, and then splashed through mud and water from evening on into the night, watching the excitement in the flooded parts of Senzoku. In tears as she spoke, O-toyo followed the stretcher. Ragetsu found himself left behind to watch the house.

The ward office had disinfected it with sulphur and carbolic acid. The silence, added to a disorder like that of spring-cleaning or a moving day, made him think of a house after the funeral is over and the coffin has gone. Outside, beyond shutters that had been closed from before dark as a sign of deference and withdrawal, a sharp wind seemed to have come up. All through the house shutters and doors were rattling. There was an unpleasant chill in the air. Occasionally, as a gust of wind came through the battered kitchen door, the dim light of the ceiling lamp would threaten to go out, a cloud of oily smoke would darken its chimney, and the shadows of the disordered furniture would move across the scarred floor and up the peeling walls. In a nearby house a voice was chanting a Buddhist invocation, the sound of it dark and oppressive. Time passed slowly for Ragetsu, left all alone. He was bored, and he was dejected. At times like these, he said to himself, a man needed a drink. He went for a look around the kitchen, but of course it was a household run by a woman, and he could not find even a wine glass. Going back to the window, he pulled a shutter partly open and looked out. He did not see, among the lights on the other side of the street, the mark of a single wine merchant. Although it was still early, most of the shutters were already closed in this unflourishing neighborhood. The chanting voice, dark and gloomy, sounded out the more clearly. A violent wind from the river set the electric wires above the house to singing, and the stars seemed to have been swept cleaner; and the windy night, as windy nights will, brought a feeling that winter had suddenly returned.

Closing the shutter again, Ragetsu sat down absently under the lamp. He had a smoke, and looked at the clock on the wall. From time to time a mouse would scuttle noisily across the hollow ceiling. Ragetsu thought he might perhaps find something to read. He looked through closets and desks, but all he came upon were Tokiwazu scores and an old almanac. Taking the lamp in his hand, he went upstairs to Chōkichi's room.

There were several books on the desk, and with them a book box of cedar. Ragetsu took out his spectacle case and looked curiously over the textbooks, bound in the Occidental manner. Something dropped to the floor. It was a picture of O-ito, in the festive spring dress of a geisha. Ragetsu put it carefully back into the book from which it had fallen, and went on with his inspection. This time he came upon a letter. It seemed to be unfinished, the last sentence being interrupted where the paper had been torn off. There was enough all the same to make clear what the finished letter would have contained. Chōkichi and O-ito had said good-bye, and day by day, as their worlds moved farther and farther apart, their hearts must also grow apart. They had been friends as children, but they would one day be strangers. Chōkichi told in great detail how it grieved him, the knowledge that even if they were to meet from time to time they would no longer share the same feelings. He had therefore decided to be either an actor or a musician, but these wishes, too, had been denied him, and now, helplessly envying the good fortune of Kichi the barber's son, he passed useless, aimless hours. He did not have the courage to kill himself. His one hope was to fall ill and die.

It came to Ragetsu with a sudden, intolerable conviction that Chōkichi had purposely walked through the flood that night hoping to fall ill, and that there was no chance of his recovering. And why had he, Ragetsu, sought to block the boy's wishes with arguments that were not in his heart? The memory came to him again of how it had been when he was young himself, led astray by women and driven from his father's house. He would be Chōkichi's ally. Otherwise there would have been no point in it all, bringing ruin upon the house of his ancestors and making his way through the trials of this gloomy world—there would have been no point to it unless he helped Chōkichi become an actor, and brought him and O-ito together. The name of Shōfūan Ragetsu, master of poetry, man of the world, had been shamed.

Again a mouse scampered across the ceiling. Still the wind blew on.

The flame in the lamp wavered and wavered. Ragetsu thought of the beautiful young couple, Chōkichi with his thin, pale face and his large eyes, and the round-faced O-ito, her mouth winsome and her eyes turning up at the corners. He drew the picture over and over again in his heart, like an artist working out a frontispiece for an old romance. Rest easy, Chōkichi, he said. No matter how ill you may be, you are not to die. I am with you.

The Peony Garden

"The Peony Garden" was first published in 1909, in the magazine *Chūō Kōron,* and later included in the 1912 collection *Night Tales from Shimbashi.* For a discussion, see pp. 49–50.

Once, on the impulse of the moment, the geisha Koren and I decided to have a look at the peonies in Honjo, and took a fast boat from under Ryōgoku Bridge.

It was late in May. Perhaps the peonies would already have fallen. We had run into each other at a play the evening before, and spent the night at a Yanagibashi inn, and rain had kept us from going home, as we had planned, early in the morning. It had not stopped until after noon. Because we had been shut up in a cramped little room all day, the street gave us a feeling of release, and the breeze that blew down the rows of houses from the river was indescribably fresh against faces recovering from overindulgence. We found ourselves leaning against the railing of Yanagibashi Bridge.

It may have been because the rain had stopped that the day seemed far longer than the days before had been. Wisps of cloud from the storm trailed across the sky, like stylized Kanō-school clouds on a temple ceiling. The deep, glowing blue of the sky was especially beautiful, and the fading colors of evening. The rich green of the Kanda Canal in the rising tide shone like a freshly polished sheet of glass, catching the sun as it sank into the grove of the Kanda Shrine. At the mouth of the canal where barges and little boats were collecting, the waters of the Sumida spread before us, the more radiant for the depth of the scene. Along the measured lines of the stone embankments, straggly willows waved in the breeze, quiet and languorous beyond description. Samisen practice in the geisha houses near the river had died away. The moving clouds grew brighter by the minute, despite the advance of evening. The faces of passersby and the stripes of their kimonos floated up in the evening light. The whole city, washed of dust by the rain, seemed clean, relaxed, pleasant. Women on the way back from the bath, towels and cosmetics in hand, would strike up conversations as they passed one another, their throats astonishingly white. Bats were already out, and children were already chasing them. Near at hand there was a clanging of streetcars, while in the distance the horns of boats would give forth long blasts and fade away, to be followed by samisens in unison from the second floor of the Kamesei, its great roof thrusting out toward the mouth of the canal. Two newly lacquered rickshaws with red leather steps waited beside the wooden fence of the Ryūkōtei, not yet dry from the rain. A geisha in a long, sweeping kimono a solid color but for the pattern at the skirt, and her apprentice, in a dazzlingly bright printed kimono, hurried through a gate over which trailed a willow. People in the street turned to look.

"Let's go," said Koren.

I started down the main street toward Ryōgoku Bridge. "Are you going home right away? Shall I get the rickshaw?"

She shook her head and walked on.

I arched my back as I looked up into the sky, opening from the street to the Sumida. At the approach to the bridge, in the smell of little restaurant kitchens, there was a confusion of streetcars, of people waiting to board them, of carts crossing the bridge. It suddenly seemed to me that, coming from an inn with this woman, I had nothing to do with a world that had gone on moving without me. The world and I were controlled by separate destinies, taking us in separate directions. A sort of quiet always came over me at evening, but this time the quiet was as of a complete loss of strength, and it brought with it a vague, indefinable sadness. I was not especially sorry to say good-bye to the woman. Nor did I regret a day spent in dissipation. Nor was it that the flowing of the waters somehow moved me. I had exhausted the man-made pleasures that a city has only for those born in it, and now, in the wake of the dream, it was as though I were looking back over the whole long series of dreams.

"Be careful." I took Koren's arm as we crossed the streetcar tracks. She read the sign by the river.

"Express boats to the Fourth Bridge peonies. Four sen."

"Shall we go?"

"Let's." Her voice was unusually young and gay. "I've never been."

We crossed to an old barge by the plank laid from the embankment, and from the barge to a lighter with thin rush matting on its floor.

The young boatman, perhaps twenty-one or twenty-two, an old-style bib over his frayed undershirt, had been talking to the captain of the empty boat moored to his. Suddenly coming to life as we climbed aboard, he rose to greet us. "Anyone else for the Honjo peonies?" he called, waving a freshly lighted pipe. "We're off for the Honjo peonies."

We could only see legs and feet on the embankment high above us. Fearing that if we had to wait for other passengers we would reach the garden only after dark, I told the man I would rent the whole boat. He took up his oar, and, in fine spirits, threw down a tinder set on the deck, in case we wanted to smoke.

The little boat moved off, swaying in the flood tide of evening, as the sturdy young arms pushed and pulled at the oar. With the swaying came distant, gentle memories, somehow cut off from the present, of how my nurse had rocked me in her arms:

> Rock-a-bye baby, let the boat rock.
> And where will it rock us off to?

By the railing of Ryōgoku Bridge, people were watching the ferries as they put in at little boxlike landings by the bridge pilings, and the passengers in the confusion of embarking and disembarking. As the right bank receded into the distance, childish pictures on the signs lining the Mukōjima roofs came up sharply. A dark cloud was just then blotting out the evening sun, and beyond the low, crawling form of New Bridge, where the sky descended to cap the mouth of the river, the smoke from the factories spiraled upward. In the middle of the river we brushed prows with the ferry to First Bridge. There were two men on deck. One, apparently a merchant, had a large, square bundle tied to his back in a pale-blue kerchief. The other was a younger man, very handsome, perhaps a gambler, hatless, and with his lined kimono pulled so wide at the chest that his belly band was showing. Our little boat rocked in the wake of a passing steamer, and the flat-bottomed ferry rocked yet more violently. The waves slipped across the water to Hamachō on the right bank, where wonderfully luxuriant spring foliage rose over earthen walls. The spray, threatening to break over the embankment into the street, was clear from across the river. In the wake of the steamer, our sharp-prowed boat moved ahead of the ferry toward the mouth of the Tatekawa Canal. On land jutting out into the river was a line of new two-story houses, perhaps little restaurants. Two young women with chignons were looking down at the water from veranda railings where quilts were airing.

The boatman called up to them: "Nice weather we're having, ladies."

They fled in some consternation.

"What are they up to?" I asked.

He smiled contemptuously. "Whorehouses. Good place for them to set up businesses."

Koren frowned in distaste and tapped me on the knee. "Let me have some tobacco."

With a strong thrust of the oar the boat passed the embankment and headed up the canal. Just beyond the mouth was a bridge with a wooden marker: "First Bridge." The canal was a fairly wide one, but wherever there was water, there were barges piled with every imaginable sort of cargo. Work seemed to be over, for a boatman squatted in the prow of each and looked up at the sky as he smoked. Some were washing away sweat with canal water. In the cabins, women with babies strapped to their backs were lighting fires and washing out pots. Their fuel seemed to be coal scrap, which sent up very smelly fumes. Here and there a red cloud of smoke reflected from the canal.

Koren looked curiously at the jumble of barges. "Do they sleep on them?"

"Of course."

"How nice." She looked back at me. "Away from the world."

"Don't think about it. It's impossible, and that's that." So I said, but I, too, was strangely sad. Once we had had a house together in Tsukiji. After about six months, however, we had agreed that she would again become a geisha.

"You wouldn't think of trying to live with me again? You wouldn't like that?"

"Well, I wouldn't exactly dislike it. But it just wouldn't do. Remember how soon you get tired?"

"Yes. But it's no fun being a geisha."

"It's no fun being anything else either. You wouldn't like being someone's wife and having to do the housework. I said it would be better for us to have our fun while we were young. I'll be thirty-five in a few years, and you'll be thirty. And you agreed, didn't you, when you went back to work?"

"That's so. But I'm more trouble to you now than when we were living together. So I think I'd like to struggle along and be your wife."

"The idea is all right, maybe. But it's one thing to enjoy yourself and not worry about the teahouse bills, and another thing to get down to work. You're sure to pay plenty of attention to who's giving a party and who's having a coming-out and all that sort of thing. But I don't remember that you were much interested in the water bill."

"So we'll never get married?"

"That's not the point. You'll just have to wait a little while. Till you aren't so worried about falling in love and being fallen in love with, and you don't have any regrets for what you're leaving behind. The days when you worry about whether you're being cheated—those are the days to enjoy. We'll just sort of come together if we don't worry too much about whether we're going to get married or not."

"What a stupid world it is, though."

"Very stupid."

We passed under Second Bridge with its streetcar track, and the canal stretched on ahead, a series of low wooden bridges crossing it, all very much alike. One bridge would pass and another appear. Children swarmed over them like insects. And not only the bridges. Every open space, a landing perhaps, had its crowds of mischievous children. Among them were girls not to be outdone by boys, shouting from both banks:

> Look at the runt on the other bank.
> His head is three inches long.

The shrill voices crossed the canal, and, following the bank, seemed to come down on us from behind, pushing us faster on our way. The breeze stopped and the evening air was suddenly quiet. The white walls of the warehouses reflected clear and fresh from the water, and the fires on the barges were yet redder. The shadows of the kindling wood, in beautiful gabled stacks, were already dark. Sheaves of bamboo standing on end at the approaches to the bridges were sharp, black towers against the evening sky. But the scenery was unchanging, however far we went, and the charm of the boat was vanishing, leaving only the discomfort of the thin rush mats.

"How far do you suppose the canal goes?"

"To Kameido."

"Is it much farther to the peonies?"

"Not much. That's Third Bridge." We both bit back yawns. "Why don't you go find yourself a good-looking actor to keep you amused?"

"You couldn't pay me to. It used to be very exciting when someone would make fun of me, but now it's all such a bore. It isn't even fun when someone starts talking about *you*."

"No, it's no fun, all this gossip. But it'd be no more fun if we tried living together again."

"Maybe we should think about committing suicide together."

"Maybe we should."

"What would people say, do you suppose?"

"All sorts of things. And we'd be forgotten in three days."

"That wouldn't be fun."

"No fun at all."

We yawned again.

"Maybe you should decide to get along without love and men. That might be cleverer."

"I'll bet you could get by without women if you decided to. You've had them all."

"And you? You say you're even tired of actors."

"Just actors. Actors and husbands are different."

"Let's say men in general."

"They've all given me up. I suppose I can get by well enough if no one comes along. But it's no fun, watching other people laugh, and cry. Look—let's go out and live in the country somewhere. Back in the mountains somewhere, away from everyone."

"It wouldn't last long. You know you can't stand it for even a week. Not in the liveliest mountain resort."

"So there's nothing for me. Very tiresome."

The boatman signaled to me as he came up beside a lighter among the barges. There was a landing of sorts between warehouses, and beyond it a rickshaw stand. We climbed ashore. Across the lane, over a gate flanked by a bamboo fence, was the sign of the peony garden.

The low-lying outskirts of town are humid at best, and the lane that day was muddy. Picking our way through the puddles, we went in the gate, and on along flagstones among old dwarfed trees. The evening light was shut off by a low reed awning, shelter against the rain, and the inner garden was dark. Some serving women were setting out lamps. Rows of tree peonies floated up vaguely in the dim, yellow light and what of the evening light came in. The peonies were already falling. Even the blossoms that had not lost all of their petals were faded badly, their hearts black and gaping. Had they been exposed to bright sunlight and fresh breezes, they would have fallen by now. The weariness and boredom of having been made to bloom too long seemed to flow from each blossom. These peonies had something in common with us, I thought. Although there was no wind and not the sound of a footstep as we stood watching, a heavy petal would fall here and a heavy petal would fall there, as if upon some unheard signal. One would fall on dark leaves, another would trail off into the darkness among the leaves, where the light of the lamps did not reach. There were no visitors besides us, for the hour was late and the season past. From time to time the clamor of the children along the canal would increase, as if with a swelling of their ranks.

She turned to me. "Are these the Honjo peonies? Are these all?"

"Famous places are always disappointments."

"Let's go back."

"Yes, let's go back."

Coming Down with a Cold

"Coming Down with a Cold" appeared
in the magazine *Chūō Kōron* in 1912, and in
the same year in the collection *Night Tales from
Shimbashi*. For a discussion, see p. 52.

"Plum blossoms one by one. Just enough warmth for plum blossoms, one by one. In the snow, so ready to melt in the sunlight of early spring, the dreariness of a rented room. Even that he owed to Yonehachi, the winsome one with the samisen, who, in the warmth of her womanly heart, sent him enough to keep up certain appearances, and see his way through the days."

They sat facing each other across the *kotatsu*.* The man was softly reading a chapter from *A Calendar of Plum Blossoms*. He was interrupted by the jangling of the telephone at the foot of the stairs.

The woman, who had felt a cold coming on since morning, raised her chin from the quilted kimono with which she sought to keep off the chill, and frowned. They heard a noisy banging of the kitchen door and the hurried steps of the maid, who called from halfway up the stairs.

"It's from the house. They want to know if you're ready to have someone come over."

"Is it already that late?" Startled, the woman looked at the clock on the dresser.

"It's five," said the man, his voice the matter-of-fact one of a person who knows how short a winter day can be when you sleep late in the morning. He reached under the quilt for his pipe. "How do you feel? You ought to be able to take at least one night off."

The woman was silent for a moment, thinking. Then she saw that the maid had come to the head of the stairs and was standing with a hand on the bannister. "Tell them I'll call back right away."

---

* A quilted arrangement for warming the hands and feet.

The heavy steps went downstairs again.

"I promised three days ago, and Haruwaka says she has to have me play the samisen for her."

"She's going to dance? That's very brave of her."

"She says if she has me to play for her, she can get by without rehearsing. She called yesterday and especially asked me to. What should I do?"

"But are you feeling any better?" He reached a hand to her forehead.

"Do I still have a fever?"

"A little one, I'd say."

"Enough to hurt me?"

"Of course. You have to remember that you aren't strong, you know."

"That's true. I've lost even more weight this last year. How many more years do you think I have?"

Her composure was almost frightening. The man did not answer. As if avoiding her eyes, he leafed through the book before him, looking at the illustrations. These soft silences came to them once or twice every day as they sat thus facing each other, and no longer troubled them. At first there had been times when the pain of it all would bring tears to their eyes, and then there had been times when they would do their best to avoid inauspicious subjects. Finally they had come to the point of letting matters take their course, and refusing to allow new sadness. If something sad came up, indeed, there was a certain comfort to be drawn from talking about it and so resisting it.

In the autumn, two years before, not yet an independent geisha, she had had a sharing arrangement with the house called the Jeweled Fan, and she had come down with acute pleurisy, and presently been informed that she was suffering from an incurable lung ailment. This misfortune, however, was a source of much happiness for Masukichi. The gentleman who had for some years been seeing to her needs had not thought it proper to cut her off simply because her lungs were bad, and, paying her hospital bills and giving her a modest solatium, he had promised that if she meant to go on in business, he would continue to be one of her steady customers. Moreover, the four or five geisha of the Jeweled Fan and the others, too, the ones who would one day be geisha, had all been sleeping together in a confined Tsukiji upstairs, and although it hardly seemed tactful to come right out and state the obvious fact that there was a danger of infection, the keeper of the place said that if Masukichi was so inclined he would set her up in her own business, her accumulated debt to be repaid as seemed appropriate from her earnings. Masukichi saw that the two of them, the old patron and the proprietor of the Jeweled Fan, wished to keep their distance; but that fact only made her happier.

Her reason was simple. She had come to the point at which, because of relations with the other girls in the house that only a geisha would understand, it had become quite imperative for her to have her own business. Her senior colleague at the Jeweled Fan was a lady named Kokane. The others were all about twenty and had made their debuts two or three years later. Kokane was a rather spiteful person who had come out five years before, some three months later than Masukichi. And now she had found herself a splendid patron, and had already had her own business for some months. She was a grande dame, in fact, with two junior geisha to work for her. Masukichi naturally thought of her as a rival, and even considered moving to another quarter, so great was her chagrin. It was at this point that she fell ill.

There was another reason for her happiness. If she were independent, she could live as if married to the man because of whom her name had from time to time been in the papers, and because of whom she had been in danger of losing her patron. The man she was so fond of had said—and she had wept tears of joy the whole night long at the words—that he would not complain if for the sake of love he, too, were to come down with tuberculosis. Still pale from her stay in the hospital, she went walking with him through all the back streets in search of a house to rent, and just a year ago she had put out her own signboard: "Masukichi's Jeweled Fan."

"Soon it will be two years. Well, if we can be together I really don't care when I die."

She leaned forward to gaze into his face, then languidly got up. He was silent. Long abandoned to the ways of this special world, he knew well enough the feelings of a geisha with an engagement ahead of her.

"Don't stay too long," he said as if to himself, his eyes still on the book.

"But it'll be a nuisance if I make myself sick again."

"And so I tell you not to overdo it. Remember that you're not a strong person. When you have a cold, you should be satisfied with a little less money, and not make so many promises every night."

"I'm such a reckless sort." She shook her head in mock irritation, and called down from the head of the stairs: "Masa. Tell them I'm waiting." Turning back to the dresser for cosmetics paper, she tightened her obi and at length went downstairs.

Soon she was back again. Pulling the light to the far side of the room, she sat down at the dresser by the window. The maid brought warm water for retouching her hair.

The woman seemed to forget that she was complaining of a cold, and that, troubled by a headache, she had not even gone to the bath. As if pouring the whole of herself into the mirror, she slipped her kimono down over her shoulders, there in an unheated back room, in the gathering darkness of the February cold. Deftly taking the combs and bodkins from her hair, she wrung out the washcloth, and as if she meant to pull it out by the roots, began rubbing at the side of her chignon.

As the maid, who had finished her telephone call, came up and spread an underkimono on the warmer before him, the man leaned back against the wall. His eyes filled half with admiration and half with pity, he looked at the figure before the mirror, at the fragile, round shoulders and the shoulder blades that stood out so sharply. Man and woman had nothing to say to each other. The woman knew that, had she spoken, the man, absorbed in contemplation of her hair, would not have been able to give a proper answer. Outside there were evening sounds: wooden sandals hurrying through the dusk, the bells of rickshaws, the whistle of the pipe-cleaner's cart, the drum of the sandal mender. And within the room: the opening of a drawer, accompanied by an impatient click of the tongue, and a rummaging about for combs to suit the day's fancy; and presently the chignon, disordered from a day of forestalling a cold, was as it had been the afternoon before, done by an expert hairdresser of the quarter. The back hair arched gracefully down, like the tail of a golden pheasant, modishly soft and yet with a touch of the aristocratic, as if floating over the fresh line of the neck and the almost too-white shoulders. Above the combs holding the sidelocks to the left and right, she added fresh, wavy lines with comb and water, so that the locks seemed to rest in soft repose, while the front lock rose abruptly from her fore-

head, bold and vigorous. The twin rings of the chignon shone in the
electric light as if lacquered.

But Masukichi looked at her handiwork like a dissatisfied artist,
dissatisfied and yet forced to be satisfied. Retouching could, after all,
go on forever. She took one last glance at the mirror, reflecting the
back of her head from another mirror. Without a second's pause, she
moved on to the next task. Pouring her palm full of lotion, she spread
it thickly over her face, her throat, her breast, her shoulders, her back
as far as she could reach. Then she daubed on white paste until her
face was a solid mask, without eyes and without nose. She blinked
furiously as she wiped her eyes and lashes clean, and added powder
with a great, soft puff until the spots of paste had quite disappeared
from her face, her nose, her throat and neck and ears.

There was someone at the door—the attendant who would help her
dress and who would carry her samisen. The maid came running back
upstairs.

"And which kimono shall I get out?"

Masukichi touched her cheeks with red, and drew long, black
lashes, such as an actor might affect.

"Let's see." She turned to the man. "Would you look in the notebook there in the drawer?"

"The twenty-fifth." He could read her writing only with difficulty.
"Shimaya. Five."

"Good evening. Very chilly this evening." The newcomer was in his
forties. His kimono and cloak were of heavy homespun, his head was
shaven smooth, and his attitude, practiced and deferential as he took
his place against the wall at the head of the stairs, was such as to suggest a male performer in the geisha quarters, or perhaps a storyteller
on the variety stage.

"It doesn't seem to be anything special, does it, Tame?" she asked
him.

"No, ma'am. Nothing special was mentioned."

"Well, let's make it that one, the one with the snow crystals at the
foot."

As she gave the order, Masukichi pushed the dresser drawer shut,
and, slapping the powder from her knee, stood up. Tame stood behind her. As soon as she had changed her socks, he took up the singlet
the maid had handed him from the *kotatsu* and laid it over Masukichi's shoulders. Her heel on the skirt to keep the neckline in order,

Masukichi brought the singlet and the embroidered neckband together at her throat, and pulled a narrow sash so tight that it cut into her waist. Tame promptly took up the lined kimono she had chosen and spread it over her shoulders, and while she was bringing it together at the throat, knelt down to arrange the trailing skirt with one hand, and with the other to take from the matting the end of a silk under-obi that must have been a good twenty or thirty feet long. Both the woman being dressed and the man helping her had the practiced assurance of professionals. Without a hint of confusion things moved lightly forward.

Over the months and years the man had become as familiar with the process as one can be. He would lie back with his head in his hands and gaze on and on, and this was not the first time it had come to him that the geisha, at the sound of the word "party," braving illness, careful about the latest, newest detail of her dress, was like a young warrior at the sound of the battle drum, heedless of love and of tears, putting on his grandest scarlet armor.

The samisen case in his hand, Tame withdrew bowing ceremoniously, as he had come in. Masukichi knelt beside the man, taking out the tobacco pouch she had only just slipped into her obi. "I feel much better now that I'm dressed up. Well, I'll be off then. I'll make them let me come home early. Don't have dinner before I get back. I hate eating alone."

"The rickshaw is here," the maid called from below.

The man sat up and nodded, and the woman took his hand lightly in hers. "If you get hungry you can have my bottle of milk. All right?" She smiled, and lifting her train, swept down the stairs.

He heard a clicking of flint stone against steel, to wish her good luck for the evening. He laid his head again on the *kotatsu,* and with a great yawn looked at the clock. It struck six. The chimes, as languid as dripping rain, played *Miyasama, Miyasama.**

II

It was dark, and the cold from outside seemed to come through the badly fitting sash-windows in jets. As if there were no remedy for his boredom, the man sat up and once more opened the *Calendar of Plum Blossoms.* He was no longer interested in the illustrations, however.

* The song called "March of the Mikado's Troops" by W. S. Gilbert in the second act of *The Mikado.*

He looked vacantly around him, rather, at the cluttered upstairs room. The electric light seemed to grow stronger as the light outside faded, and the room to take on a new aspect.

It was the upstairs of what might have been called a third-rate brick tenement, a sort of relic, very shabby, of early Meiji. It was put together with remarkable clumsiness. There was a ceiling so low that one's head brushed against it, papered in a manner most unsightly—it had become a dirty accumulation of rain spots and rat spots and patches. If the grooves that could accommodate sliding doors were taken for partitions, the place could be counted as three rooms, but both of the small ones, that at the head of the stairs and the one next to it, were cut into inconvenient shapes by a brick arrangement resembling an Occidental chimney. The third room was fairly spacious, though it, too, was cut by a closet that had been added after the rest of the house. At exactly the spot where their presence was most difficult to understand—on the grooves where there should have been sliding doors to wall off the next room—there was a pair of slender pillars. When the man and woman had first seen the place, they had laughed and said that the pillars must be there for the cat to sharpen its claws on.

From that autumn two years before he had spent his nights as he was spending this one, looking aimlessly about him at the three rooms made into one, Masukichi having gone out on her evening's engagement. And each night his question had been the same: what would become of him? Today the women of the quarter all addressed him as an equal, but his was an old and proper family name, and he himself had once been proper enough to commute from his father's house to an office in Marunouchi. It all came to seem intolerably foolish, however. The fetters of work, not allowing a day's or a half-day's respite, became unbearable; and, rather like a snowman beginning to lose its base in the heat of the sun, he began to spend his days in the second floor of this geisha house, quite as if he were its master. Sometimes, in his boredom, he would try to think of the brisk vitality of the well-ordered life he had thrown away, as of an old dream that would not return; but he knew that, having come this far, he could never go back to the discipline he had not had much patience with in the first place. Jumping out of bed and putting on Western clothes at the sound of the alarm clock on a winter morning; waiting for a streetcar in the rain by the moat; pushing through the crowd when one finally came; and pushing and pushing in the office, too, climbing from rank to rank and calling oneself a conscientious worker; and, as must be the way in places where men gather, playing by turns the enemy, the rival, the obsequious underling, the malevolent detractor, in the process of what was known as gathering for friendly social intercourse—as such memories of the old life came back to him, he knew how incomparably better it was to loll about in the upstairs of a geisha house. He looked about him once more.

Against the wall opposite the closet, there were two new chests of drawers and one so old that it would scarcely have been possible to guess its age. On top of them were smaller chests, and dolls in cases, and a decorated battledore, and a music rack, and all sorts of toys and accessories, and, up against a corner of the ceiling, a rake bought at the Otori Fair for purposes of raking in good luck, and a lantern in the shape of a blowfish, bought at the Anamori Shrine;* the clutter somehow melted into a seductive harmony not to be found in a more proper establishment. By the far window there were large and small dressers with mirrors, and at the wall by the near window hung an everyday kimono with a frayed singlet over it. On the worn straw matting by the gaily quilted *kotatsu,* clothing was scattered in complete disorder: a padded kimono with a lining of figured silk, a night-gown with a cotton kimono over it, the narrow sash that had bound these two garments. They lay as she had thrown them, on a flowered mat, like a discarded shell, the shape of her body still there at the neck and shoulders. The dirty old walls and floor and ceiling stood out in contrast, quite out of keeping with the softness of the furnishings and the voluptuousness of the discarded clothes. The incongruity somehow put the man in mind of his own fate, as if he were watching a bird with clipped wings, and at the same time it brought the supremely soft consolation of knowing that he was at home. Even when the woman was out, a sort of warmth seemed to radiate from the clothes she had left behind, to spread softly over the man's heart. The sweetness and sadness of the battered old house always fused together to dull the very roots of the man's conscience and the urge to face life that every man has in some measure. On his way to and from

* The Anamori Inari at Haneda, in Tokyo. For the Otori Fair, see the note on p. 199.

the bath in the morning, with a made-over woman's kimono for his cloak, he would sometimes look from the alley at the bustle of the main Ginza street, and feeling a harshness in the air that he could not endure, he would hurry back to the soft silk and powder of his retreat. He had said to Masukichi that he had no fear of infection. Matters might as well be put in order for one who had no escape. Indeed there was something he feared more than death: that Masukichi might die first and leave him to go on alone.

III

An automobile passed, rattling the drawer handles. As some guests in the little restaurant to the rear began singing a folk song, the hoarse voice of an almanac peddler approached along the near side of the street. With a wide yawn that smelled of pickled radish, the maid laid Masukichi's nightgown on the *kotatsu*.

He looked around. "I'm starved. Isn't there anything to eat?"

The maid, who was about thirty and had been in this sort of work for years, answered with practiced coolness. "I'll only get scolded if I feed you first."

"But I have to have something. Are the sardines all gone?"

"It won't be much longer. Don't forget that she's hungry, too, and looking forward to dinner." Her manner was that of a geisha's assistant reproving some forward young customer. After putting away the clothes, she went downstairs again.

The telephone rang. It was still a little early, but he listened hopefully, thinking that Masukichi might be asking for a rickshaw to bring her home. It was from another teahouse, however, about an engagement for the next evening.

The maid called up the stairs. "Shall I send word to her?"

"Did you accept?"

"I said she was out at a party."

"Then I suppose you should let her know."

He replied with a frown—he would prefer not to be consulted in these professional matters by such people as the maid. Although he was quite alone, he looked away as if afraid someone might see him. For some time the maid had been in the habit of consulting him in Masukichi's absence when even slightly complicated matters came up about the house and her work. It was true that his curiosity had led him, in the old days, to check Masukichi's account books and see what her earnings might be, but now that he had become almost completely indigent and had nothing to do but kill time, such matters seemed most humiliating.

The maid cranked away at the telephone, and once more came to the stairs. "I can't get through. The line keeps being busy."

He did not answer. He was beginning to sweat—the *kotatsu* had just been refueled. Tired of lying down and tired of sitting up, he tightened his obi and started for the toilet. Then, as if he had had a change of heart, he leaned against one of the slender pillars between the rooms and glanced downstairs. The first floor had once been as large as the second, but now it was cut in two by a wall so thin that a fist would probably go through it with little trouble, and an aging baker and his wife occupied the other half. What remained was so constricted that there was barely room for the maid to sleep among the kitchen utensils. She was alone, but when his eye fell on the brazier in the middle of the room, he thought of Masukichi's father, a plasterer who would sometimes come to drink and always quarreled with Masukichi when he did, and of Masukichi's secret, how at the sacrifice of her health she had accepted customers who did not please her, simply so that she could send twenty yen to her father every month. And there was something that bothered him even more: the incessant coughing of the woman beyond the thin wall. It made him think of his mother bewailing the downfall of her son.

The calls of the noodle and bean peddlers and the bell of the dumpling man told him that night in the back street was drawing on. He sat down again. Then, just as he had picked up the *Calendar of Plum Blossoms* and was trying to interest himself in the lovers' banter, he heard the rickshawman's voice at the front door. Masukichi was back, remarkably early.

"Let's have dinner right away, Masa," she shrilled, and her footstep was on the stairs.

The man did as the Utazawa ballad tells us is the practice of men kept waiting: he pretended to be asleep, but in a fashion somehow insinuating. Masukichi came to the head of the stairs and took off her shawl.

"See how early I am," she said in a small voice, falling against his shoulder.

He shivered as the ice-cold kimono touched his cheek, and took her hand.

"Now you really do have a fever."

"I couldn't stay any longer. I had chills all up and down my back." She looked weakly into the man's face. "I'm afraid I've overdone it."

"And didn't I tell you not to go?"

"Don't scold me. I'm sorry." There was something very winning about the apology. She went on softly, in a cajoling tone: "And I didn't have a sip to drink. I knew I shouldn't. I always get around them, that's how careful I am. I have a little and then go off to the toilet and paint myself a little redder and come back and pretend to be drunk."

"I've never said, have I, that you drink when you don't have to? Well, get out of those clothes, and we'll have something warm to eat and off you go to bed."

"What time is it? You must be starved." She glanced up at the clock. Still leaning against him she slipped off her cloak and started to loosen her obi. "Just past nine. I'm fairly early."

"If you want to see a doctor, maybe you ought to send Masa out right away."

She thought for a minute. "It's just a tiny little cold, and I still have some of the medicine from last time." The smell of a fish chowder drifted up from below. "Isn't that nice of Masa—my favorite dish."

"Come on, now. Off with it. You can't stand there freezing."

"It's hot. You'll scorch yourself." He had taken the nightgown from the *kotatsu* and thrown it over her shoulders. She wriggled out of her underclothes, her body white and seductive.

The front door opened, and Tame called in to ask if she was back.

"Thank you very much," said Masa. To judge from the sound of knife against trencher, she would be dicing vegetables.

They looked at each other in silence, and smiled.

Tidings from Okubo: Excerpts

Tidings from Okubo was serialized in the
magazine *Mita Bungaku* in 1913 and 1914.
The first complete publication in book form
was in 1916, in a collection entitled *After Tea*.
For a discussion and more excerpts, see pp. 61–67.

July 20: "Since the end of the rains it has suddenly become warmer, and the summer trees, here in the hilly Yamanote district of Tokyo, are alive with the shrilling of new cicadas. In the evening, insects swarm around the light, but outside in the garden it is still too early for crickets. The pomegranate is in full bloom. The crepe myrtle, the silk tree, and the oleander are beginning to come out."

July 28: "There has been no rain for some days, and the heat continues. In the middle of the day I went upstairs to read, leaning against the balustrade and waiting for the evening cool. I was calm and at rest, all desire having left me. Amid the languid singing of the cicadas the sound of a koto came sleepily from the house next door. There is nothing as quiet as the middle of a hot day. At the roots of the pine trees, seven or eight sparrows dug the soft earth and scattered it over themselves.... Here in the hills the melting frosts of winter can be troublesome, but in summer the leaves and the flowers and the birds are most conducive to the quiet life."

August 21: "There were showers in the evening, and the night, even cooler than last night, already feels like autumn, like the end of September. There is nothing more difficult to describe than the feel of the change of the seasons, one moving unpredictably into another. This evening as I sat alone with my elbows on the desk, my summer kimono pulled tight, and looked out at the soft rain and the darkness settling over the garden, I was somehow sad. Shall I say that it was like the sadness of an old sorrow remembered, or like suddenly touching the cold hair of a sleeping woman?... In New York and Chicago ... there is no time to savor the mood of late spring and early summer, the wistful thoughts of late summer and early autumn. For us Japanese the feelings stimulated by the change of seasons are nothing superficial. They have had a profound influence on our thoughts and our spirit. Because of the moods of the seasons, whatever violent emotions we may feel become softened to thirty-one syllables left behind by an ink brush."

September 2: "After three days of rain, autumn suddenly deepens. Not waiting for the night, the crickets sing their loudest under the verandas. Their singing somehow brings to mind a Japanese wife of old, sad and yet alluring, at work on her husband's clothes in the dim light of a paper lantern.... Under the old lunar calendar the festival of the dead came at the beginning of autumn. Every unfilial son, however profligate and however forgetful of home he might have been on ordinary occasions, must have thought of his dead mother and father in the sadness of the autumn dews. But now we have imitated the West and adopted the solar calendar, and the festival comes just after the June rains or toward the middle of the summer. The sadness with which the dead ought to be remembered is wholly lacking. The morals of a country are in danger when they are cut loose from the beauty of its soil and its seasons. The makers of our new age have been careless in many ways."

September 3: "The wind this morning was enough to chill the bones of a weakling like me, but the clear autumn weather brings a new freshness. The autumn cicadas are singing in the tall trees by the gate."

September 24: "We almost always have rain at the equinox, but this year the weather was fine. Yesterday there was no sign of the red dragonflies that come in autumn, today there are swarms of them, shimmering in the sunlight."

September 25: "There has been a mistlike rain. The sky is still, it is a heavy, gray day. The bush clover bows under the weight of the collected drops, and the autumn flowers are past their prime. As the days have gone by, the floods of shrilling cicadas have quite disappeared, and only the crickets hum on, even in the daytime.... I took out the samisen in the alcove and, muting the strings, played two or three pieces I have been practicing lately. My greatest pleasures are sitting quietly alone and looking at old colored prints and reading historical romances and playing the samisen. Although I am neither old nor bent, I seem to have cut myself off from the world. The lady-like way of plucking the samisen does not please me, and on the other hand it seems a bit ostentatious to bring a male musician into the house; and the problem of getting along with such a person can be troublesome. Having to rely on others is a source of irritation—you do better to fend for yourself. And so, late in life, I have taken to playing the samisen again. Drink alone, live alone, sing alone—be as self-contained as a spinning top. If you are disturbed at the thought of having your line die out, then follow the dictates of the ancients and 'borrow a belly'—a concubine will quite suffice. Once you have children, you must impose numerous restraints upon them in their early years, lest they become novelists.... The day when a child could be relied upon to console a parent in his old age is past in any case. Today a parent is respected only if he has money. If he has none, then children and house are of no use whatsoever. Growing old is a melancholy business with or without children, and the best you can do is get it over with, trying not to think about it too much."

September 26: "Yesterday's rains have quite cleared, and the weather is that of 'little spring.' Perhaps because it was especially chilly in the rain and so seems especially warm today, the cicadas are once again singing happily in the *shii* tree by the gate. Suddenly, in half-withered morning-glory leaves, the face of the summer morning appears again. So it is with this weather—one realizes how aptly the season was named 'little spring.' To understand the beauty of the seasons and the natural moods of Japan, one can do no better than study the poetry of Edo."

October 6: "I had thought that Japanese silverleaf bloomed only in the cold of winter, but here, unseasonally, are its yellow flowers, by the stone lantern in under the spur of the fence. The loquat is finally coming into bud, and every day there are more figs than we can eat. The other day a man brought some grapes from Yamanashi, and with them some jujubes. You get only Western fruits in the groceries, and the jujubes took me back to old times. That clean, cool taste, sweet with a touch of astringency, lingers on and on in your mouth. The jujube is a food for a saintly mountain recluse."

October 9: "A quiet, cloudy, windless day. It is good, in these last days of autumn, when the clear weather of 'little spring' has continued for some time, to have an occasional cloudy day. Such a day is for looking at knotgrass in bloom around the pond of an abandoned garden, or willows shedding their leaves in the palace moat, or the reflection from the waters of a canal somewhere in the old part of the city. Because blue shows now and then through a break in the clouds, you can go walking with no fear of rain, and on such a day, out walking, you remember a faraway friend whom you have not seen for a long time, and so go to spend an afternoon in pleasant conversation. A man feels a poignant sadness as he puts on a mended autumn kimono. How much more, in the chill of morning and evening, must a woman be drawn back to the gay kimonos of her youth! In the late evening hours the shops on the main street are shuttered tight, but there is a light in the kimono shop up the side street, and crowds of needleworkers remind one that winter is near."

October 23: "The season for pike has come. As noon approaches, there is the smell of it roasting all up and down the alleys. In poor back streets where tenement children play in front of the confectioner's, the shop curtain of the marriage broker flutters, and in its shadow is the face of an alluring woman; and you hear the concertina of the medicine seller as the smell of roasting pike floats through the air— it is a scene and a mood such as you encounter only in the back streets of Tokyo. Pike is of course not a very elegant fish, but it comes as something new every year to make you think of the high, clear autumn skies over the beach at Kujūkuri."

November 12: "All yesterday and last night there was a biting wind, and today it is bright and clear and the red of the maple leaves deepens. The warm 'little-spring' days of October are very good in their way, but the blue of the Tokyo sky is more beautiful when early winter is passing and the last of the chrysanthemums are in bloom. As December approaches, the color deepens, and seems to drip from the sky. Possibly because the cold weather has come earlier than usual this year, the sky already has the December color."

December 5: "Because of the freakish weather, the winter myrtle in the garden had buds in November and is now in full bloom. My dead father brought it back from Hangchow. It usually blooms the end of December. When the garden is its most lonely, this flower from another land sends out a compelling fragrance."

December 22: "We have had a series of warm, still days. The evening sun at the end of the year is even more beautiful than the evening sun of late autumn, and the street scenes seem to take on a new liveliness. The pale blue of the evening mist as the warm sun sinks in the sky is indescribably fine. As you look down upon the flats from such a rise as Kudan, the houses and trees are sunk in an indigo mist, and from among them a red light blazes up. It is a scene such as one does not find even in the prints of Hiroshige."

December 28: "Two or three blossoms open every day on the plum in the alcove. As I read alone at night, warming myself at the *kotatsu,* and look at the alcove, they are so white that they seem to float up from the tree. Casting faint shadows on the painting in the alcove (it is of a courtesan), they are sweet and sad, and tell of a quiet study late at night in the dead of winter."

January 7: "The plum in the alcove is in full bloom, and two or three of the Chinese narcissuses on the bookshelves begin to open, filling my study with perfume. When I come home late at night and open the door, a wave of clean fragrance strikes me full in the face, pleasing beyond description. I fear that in so characterizing it I will seem to have the spurious good taste of some teacher of polite maidenly arts, but I cannot help myself. Shall we say that the fault is one I have inherited from my ancestors? I have been more and more struck this last year or two with the fact that, however much we may imitate foreign countries, we still remain Japanese. Just as our ancestors welcomed them before us, it is our greatest pleasure to welcome the flowers and birds of the land that produced us. Why need we impress people with a love of the strange and exotic? Literary fads change aimlessly—yesterday it was Ibsen, today it is Shaw—but we may take comfort in the pictures of nature unchanged for a thousand years, the warbler with the plum, the martin with the willow, the butterfly with the peony."

February 15: "Spared the cold winds that sweep down from Mt. Tsukuba on the eastern flats of the city, the plums of these western hills bloom early. In the perfume of the plums, sandals are hung to dry beside a few strips of fish, at the broken-down fence of some rented cottage. It is a plain enough scene, and yet it makes one see that in the poverty of Japanese life there is nothing more ennobling than the plebeian poetry of Edo, with its careful attention to the beauty in the simple and the plain."

March 20: "In the warm spring evening, the wind having stopped, the willows shimmered as they caught the lights of the Ginza. There I went walking, and looking at antiques in the shop windows."

April 1: "Thinking to look out into the long spring twilight, I went upstairs and, leaning against the balustrade, saw that the warmth of these last few days has already brought pillars of mosquitoes, in under the eaves. They were fascinating as they banded and scattered and wavered in the wind. The cobwebs at those same eaves have long been a pattern for kimonos, but I did not remember having often seen kimonos patterned after mosquito pillars. And so I lost myself in the usual senseless musings: how would it be to use them on the cover of the magazine?"

April 8: "It is clear, but the wind is as cold as in the winter, and at night the moon is wonderfully bright. The sound of wooden sandals and the barking of dogs give a melancholy suggestion of the Yoshiwara, back in the days when it had night-blooming cherries.... Avoiding people, I spend my days quietly though somewhat tediously at home."

April 12: "It is bright and clear, and for the first time really like spring. The sun warms the ground where the cut stems of daisies and autumn flowers and the rest are sending out shoots, and the trees cast deep shadows, making you feel that summer is near. And is the spring over already? Spring this year, with snow and sleet fading the cherry blossoms even while they were still in bud, was somehow like a sickly maiden, lonely and aging, languishing at home, unable to marry."

April 21: "The wind brings a blizzard of petals from the double cherries next door, and the young leaves of the plum and maple are every day more beautiful. To sit under deep eaves out by the veranda of a small room made still duskier by young leaves, and to have a meditative smoke, not really thinking of anything, and listen to the birds— it is, I think, a mood that goes only with a Japanese house. Apparently the fashion with the rich is to avoid darkness by having shallow eaves, whatever they may look like, and by removing the shrubbery to a distance from the house, thus giving a clear, uninterrupted view; but it seems to me that too much brightness is out of harmony with the coloring, the manners, the dress of the Japanese, and with the hangings in the alcove of a Japanese house and the ornaments on the shelves."

April 24: "The wisteria, the azaleas, and the peonies are all coming into bloom. As I look out at this polychrome array, rich as nothing in other countries, I am reminded afresh of the art of Kōrin, that powerful piling up of blues and greens on a gold or silver ground."

May 3: "The pale green of the new maple leaves is at its most lovely.... The greenish yellow of the pine cones against the dark green of the needles puts one nostalgically in mind of that color combination, green and yellow, used so often by Kiyonaga and Utamaro. I believe it to be a peculiarly Japanese combination, not found elsewhere."

May 5: "All of the dear things in Japanese life—reciting from memory an appropriate old poem while enjoying the special foods and drinks of the four seasons in unexceptionable dishes, walking along a river bank to visit an old friend while the snow of winter or the rain of spring falls on a Japanese umbrella, watching tree shadows on a reed blind at the window of a tree cottage—all of these are to be approached in a free, light, uncomplicated mood."

May 6: "My study was really too tight with the shutters closed from early evening, and so, opening a shutter over a little window, I looked out. The moon found its way dimly through the clouds. It was a windless night, and the midnight trees were indescribably still. On just such a night, I said to myself, the poet of old listened for the cuckoo. The scene was so compelling that I stood for a time with my elbows on the sill, looking up at the tips of the new-leafed branches."

May 20: "The rain of last night has cleared, and today the wind is fragrant with early summer. The green leaves, washed free of dust, seem to turn gold in the sun. Potted saffron, peony, and iris are a riot of bloom, to make one feel that all the clean well-being of the world is concentrated in this one garden. From just before sunset there was a great expanse of mackerel sky to the east, and the mist in the western sky promised good weather for tomorrow too. As I looked out from the upstairs window and saw the crows heading home for their shrine grove, my mind moved to the ink paintings of Kawanabe Gyōsai.* Whenever I look at the sky or at the grasses and trees, I think how nature about us is perpetually and continuously telling us the secret of Japanese and Chinese painting. Is it that I am sickly and aging, and so am the victim of a certain slackening of the spirit? Or is it that with the passing of the years I have at length shaken off foreign influences, and so become able to grasp the mood and spirit of what we have from our ancestors?"

* 1828–89.

Rivalry: From Chapter 12

Rivalry was serialized in the magazine *Bummei* from August 1916 to October 1917. The private or "secret" edition appeared in 1917, and the first commercial edition in 1918. For a discussion of the book and its complicated textual history, see pp. 85–90.

A secluded house in Negishi: there were still swarms of mosquitoes in striped trousers even when the wagtail and the bush warbler had come; and by way of compensation it was no trick at all to have an elegant little stream run right under the study window. In the summer, when the water oats were in bloom, the shower of fireflies beyond the reed blind, and in autumn the wind in the rushes coming to one seated meditatively at a desk—even here in the city, as the mornings and evenings went by, they gave one a feeling as of the loneliness of the Toné Marshes. The master of the house, Kurayama Nansō, now entering middle age, could only watch aghast at the speed with which the seasons moved over the trees and grasses of his garden.

The lotus pads on which an evening shower sprinkled jewels were suddenly broken and withered, and a high wind riffling through the rushes caught the ear. The autumn of the amaranth gave way to the autumn of the chrysanthemum, sudden rains brought down the leaves of the maple, and it was winter and the end of the year, and time to begin counting the plum blossoms. In winter there was the strangling smell of fertilizer to see the old trees through the cold weather, but there were also bright red berries of holly and nandina, more beautiful in the snow than any flower. Cosily shut in against the winter, over a pot of tea late at night, he would note that the daffodils and the crocuses on the bookshelves had bloomed and faded, and soon the equinox would have come, time to separate the roots of chrysanthemums and to plant flowers and grasses, time for so many things that the garden lover would find the day gone before he was ready for night. The hundred flowers would bloom and fade, come and go, allowing scarcely time to turn one's busy eyes to the new green shoots

before the summer rains had come to the garden, the plums ripened
and begun to fall; and then the mimosa leaves, folding themselves in
sleep, the blossoms of the pomegranate blazing vermilion, trumpet
honeysuckles falling to the ground, and the hot days; and in the deep
of the night, while dew formed on the water plants, an insect voice
and then another would already be heard in their shadow, two threads
in the darkness.

The passing seasons were like a survey of the occasions for poetry.
Last year's bush warbler was back again, singing its winter song far
back in the shrubbery, and the familiar wagtail was once more strut-
ting at the edge of the pond, lashing away with its tail. There was the
pleasure of an old scene revisited in these little birds that came in their
proper seasons, far more reliable than human emotions. Moved at the
sound even of pruning shears, Nansō would find himself at the fence
separating his garden from the next. Through breaks in the bamboo
fence, from which long, snakelike gourds were hanging, he had a
clear view of the neighboring yard in the bright sunlight, all the way
to the main house, its veranda hanging over the garden pond.

Always, looking through the fence and the shrubbery at the house
next door, he would stand entranced, brought to his senses only by
the stinging of the mosquitoes, at how much the scene before him
was like an illustration for an old love story: the gate of woven twigs,
the pine branches trailing down over the pond, the house itself. Now
long unoccupied, it had once been a sort of villa or resthouse for one
of the Yoshiwara establishments. Nansō's family had been living in
his own house for some three generations now, and in his childhood
he had heard old people talk about how it had been in the neighborhood long ago. He remembered how, when he was still a child on his
mother's knee, he had heard and felt very sad to hear that one snowy
night a courtesan, long in ill health, had died in the villa next door,
which had served the Yoshiwara women since before the Restoration.
At the sight of that old pine, trailing its branches from beside the
lake almost to the veranda, Nansō could not believe, however old he
grew, that the songs of sad Yoshiwara beauties, Urasato and Michitose and the rest,* were so many idle fancies, so many yarns dreamed
up by the composers. Manners and ways of feeling might become

* Fictional courtesans in Edo drama and balladry.

Westernized, but as long as the sound of the temple bell in the short summer night remained, and the Milky Way in the clear autumn sky, and the trees and grasses peculiar to the land—as long as these remained, he thought, then somewhere, deep in emotions and ethical codes, there must even today be something of the ancient sadness one catches in narrative ballads.

His nature and training had made Nansō seem destined to become a man of letters. His great-grandfather had been a physician and at the same time a scholar of the Japanese language and Japanese literature, and his grandfather, also a physician, had made a name for himself as a writer of humorous colloquial poetry. By the time his father, Shūan, succeeded as head of the family, its position was well established, and had the world been a more settled place, Nansō would naturally have become the fourth physician in the line. But then came the Restoration, and Chinese medicine went out of fashion, and Shūan was no longer a doctor. Changing his professional name to Shūsai, which did not have such medical connotations, he turned to carving the seals that had earlier been a hobby. Since he was also adept at Chinese poetry and calligraphy, he presently came to associate with the illustrious gentlemen of the world, and for a time he was rather well known in literary and artistic circles of the Eastern Capital. Rather to his surprise, he found himself with more income than he had had as a doctor. At length he departed happily from the world, leaving behind an estate sufficient that his children and grandchildren need not know the harsher trials of life.

Nansō was then in his middle twenties, and had already written newspaper novels in the antique style of Bakin. After his father's death he had a number of newspaper owners and editors among his acquaintances, and so he turned to letters. He had nothing to do with the fashionable Kenyūsha group, however, and knew nothing of the new and radical literature of Tōkoku and his fellow romantics, and he had no opportunity to meet Shōyō and the early Waseda group. He spent his time in solitary pleasures, over Japanese and Chinese classics and the essays and miscellanies of the Edo Period that he found in the warehouse of this Negishi house. For twenty years he spun out romances, earnestly and tirelessly, always in the low, frivolous Edo style, sometimes in imitation of Chikamatsu, sometimes of Saikaku, sometimes of Kyōden and Samba. But times change, and even Nansō, who took little more interest in the customs and manners of his day than he did in literary and artistic developments or trends in the theater and music, found as Meiji gave way to Taishō that a great many things made him angry. For the first time he saw that his way of life would not do, that he could not end his days as the producer of salable commodities to please women and children. As Kyōden and Tanehiko had done in their last years, he turned to the study of the manners and artifacts of an earlier day. As for his fiction, he gave it only enough attention to satisfy obligations to newspapers and publishers.

The old house and garden in Negishi were therefore treasures he could not part with. New building overtook the district, and Negishi of the bamboo thickets seemed on the way to extinction. He would think how on this veranda, now eaten by worms, his great-grand-father, well over a century before, had looked at the plums by the lake and recited a poem in praise of the Japanese seasons, and how under this deep-eaved roof, already leaning precariously, his grand-father had looked at the autumn moon and composed one of his poems. However expensive maintenance might be, and however un-comfortable the old house might have become, thought Nansō, he must leave it and its garden exactly as they had always been. Each time a carpenter came to repair a leaky roof, he would say that it would be better in the long run to pull the place down and start all over; but Nansō would only laugh, and when, three years before, the foundations had had to be repaired, he had almost become a carpen-ter himself, so closely had he supervised the project. He looked upon every tree and every plant in the garden as a relic, something that had inspired poetry in his ancestors, and all the books and utensils and household furnishings in the warehouse were similarly prized treasures. Fearing the careless ways gardeners had with their shears, he would faithfully take care of the spring and autumn pruning him-self.

His affection was not limited to his own house but went past the fence to the garden and house next door. After the failure of the Yoshiwara enterprise, the house had for some time been vacant, with no one wishing to buy it. Then, presently—it was impossible to know where they might have come from—stories began to spread, of how that dead courtesan appeared as a snow-white maiden, and badgers and foxes and other sinister animals were up to malevolent antics; and so it became yet more unlikely that the place would find a buyer. But no one in Nansō's own house, not even the women and children, saw anything strange or unsettling about it. On moonlight nights, old Shūsai, Nansō's father, having exhausted the possibilities of his own garden, would go through a hole in the fence into the empty garden next door, and, strolling along the bank of the pond, recite Chinese poetry in sonorous tones.

Sometimes, pressed to deliver a seal and troubled for an answer, he would go hide in the garden next door, and his wife and the maids, not knowing what to say to the visitor, would search through the house, and finally go next door themselves. His father, thinking it a pity, whoever might buy the house one day, that the branches of that pine tree, so beautifully trained over the years, should be left untended, would send his own gardener to shake off the dead needles; and when a storm would blow over the gate of plaited twigs, he would tell himself that it was a piece of work no artisan could reproduce today, however much you paid him, and quietly have it repaired. Finally he forced open the shutters and had a look at the front room, and he found something mysteriously compelling about it, perhaps because he knew that here courtesans of old had lain ill, and written their diaries, and burned their perfumes. He would bring wine over and enjoy a solitary drink, and so the old Yoshiwara villa became a sort of villa for Shūsai himself. Despite rumors that the place was haunted, the master of the Kurayama house would invite visitors over for a look at it. In the course of time they grew used to it, and one of them even insisted that he must have it for his own. This was the Kabuki actor Segawa Kikujo, foster father of Segawa Isshi. A man with such acquaintances as the forceful calligrapher and sealmaker Shūsai, Kikujo had literary inclinations unusual for an actor. He thought to spend his last years quietly in the old Yoshiwara villa, finding rest from his work in such elegant occupations as poetry and tea-making. Then he died, and his widow—she was his second wife, much younger than he—said that she preferred to live in a livelier part of the city. After the year of mourning she moved back to Tsukiji. So the villa was empty again. Yet the Segawa family had no reason to sell it, and, installing a caretaker, kept it as a country house, to be visited on certain occasions in the spring and the autumn.

Nansō's father had died some years before Kikujo, but the intimacy between the two houses continued into Nansō's generation. Nansō having long been rather famous as a drama critic, Isshi came calling almost every day in the weeks after his father's death. Nansō, who had ambitions in the theater, was delighted.

The two gradually drifted apart, however, with the removal of Isshi's stepmother to Tsukiji. Since the distance was great, Isshi seldom came to visit the place, and Nansō, his interest in literature and the theater diminishing year by year, would look through the fence morning and evening and think upon the old days; but he did not especially want to see the young actor. The deserted house seemed to sink deeper into the quiet as the years went by, and the dead leaves piled up, and there was no sound of shears to be heard at pruning time in the spring and fall. In the spring there were raucous cries of shrikes, and in the winter there were noisy sparrows; and for the rest there was silence. The house was again what it had been when the child Nansō had timorously followed his father through the fence. Looking through that fence as he tended his own garden day by day, he concluded that the widow of Kikujo and the present head of the Segawa family had no interest in the old Yoshiwara villa, and, leaving it to rot, would gladly sell it the moment a prospective buyer appeared.

Although he had lost his literary ambitions, Nansō sometimes had to write drama criticism for the newspapers. After a play in which Isshi had appeared, he would go to the dressing room for a talk, and feel that he would like to hear about plans for the old house. He thought he would like to recommend in a friendly way that if the house must be sold, it be sold to someone with an eye for such places; after all, the pine and the gate were good enough that his own father had quietly kept them in trim. But then he would reconsider and decide that his advice was not wanted and would do no good. The times were such that it was fashionable for noble families like the Daté, lords of Sendai, to sell off treasures handed down from their ancestors, despite the fact that they did not need money. And so he kept his silence, and looked through the fence in dread each day, wondering if today a buyer would appear, if tomorrow the pine by the lake would be removed.

One night as rain rustled the dead lotus pads outside the window,

Nansō, having arranged the books and papers on his desk, was lighting a long silver pipe for a bedtime smoke. Suddenly he heard a new sound behind the sound of rain. He sat up and listened more carefully, certain that it was a samisen. Samisens were not uncommon in the neighborhood, to be sure. What surprised Nansō, rather, was the melody it was playing. A sensuous woman's voice was singing in what appeared to be the Sonohachi style. Nansō, who had a taste for vocal music, opened the round window of his study, and his astonishment grew. There was a light in the house next door, which he had thought to be deserted. Beyond the rain in the garden the voice was singing, in the thin, plaintive Sonohachi style, of the love suicide on Mt. Toribe, to a yet softer, sadder accompaniment.*

Nansō wondered for a moment if the house next door might not indeed be haunted. Had the song been in the Nagauta or Kiyomoto style, the thought would not have come to him, however melancholy the rainy autumn night. But Sonohachi, the saddest, darkest, most plaintive style of all, concerned entirely with love suicides, and telling of them in a voice such that a person wondered whether it could actually be living? Perhaps the ghost of a courtesan who had died in that house deep on a rainy autumn night had returned, to complain of the wrongs done her while she lived.

"I've brought you a cup of tea." His wife quietly slid open the door.

"So it's true after all."

"What's true?"

"The ghost has finally come out."

"You mustn't try to frighten me."

"But listen. There's Sonohachi in the house next door."

His wife was relieved. "Oh, I see. You almost did have me frightened. But I know more about it than you seem to."

Nansō was puzzled that O-chiyo, usually so timid, should be quite undisturbed. "You know the ghost, do you?"

"Of course. Haven't you seen it?"

"No."

"Twenty-three or twenty-four, I'd say, or maybe she's older than she looks. A round face, a darkish complexion—just the sort you would like. Very stylish, a little past her prime." O-chiyo listened for

* The story is treated also by Chikamatsu, in whose version the characters have different names. For more about Sonohachi, see "Quiet Rain," pp. 253–77.

a moment. "A very good voice, too. Just the right touch of roughness. Do you suppose she's playing her own accompaniment?"

Though an amateur, O-chiyo was better versed in the old narrative styles, Sonohachi, Katō, Itchū, Ogie, and the rest, than an ordinary geisha would be. The daughter of a wealthy gentleman-artist, she had been used to the company of artists and actors and men of letters from her childhood. Now thirty-five, she had been married for ten years, and she was the mother of two children; but when she did her hair up in a youthful fashion and went out shopping, she was still sometimes mistaken for a geisha. Her youthful, brisk, easygoing manner was in contrast to Nansō's own morose introspectiveness, with the result that they complemented each other and got on remarkably well.

"How do you know so much about it? Did you go have a look?"

"No. But I have my methods. My secret methods." She laughed. At length she revealed that on her way back from certain errands toward evening, she had thought it strange to see two rickshaws come running up behind her and stop at the neighboring house; and, looking back, she had seen Segawa Isshi get out, and then a trim lady, rather like a geisha, slightly along in years. She laughed again. "Take her in secret to your country villa and no one will suspect a thing."

Nansō joined in the laughter. "They say he's very popular these days."

"Do you suppose she's a geisha? Or maybe his mistress?"

"The rain seems to be letting up. Light a lantern and I'll go have a look."

"Oh, don't overdo it," said O-chiyo. She promptly went out to the veranda, however, and lit a white paper lantern that she took from a closet.

"Are the children asleep?"

"Long ago."

"Then you can come along. Go first and be the lantern bearer."

"It's stopped raining." O-chiyo stepped down into the garden sandals, and held the lantern to the ground. "I feel like an attendant in a play."

"It has its points, walking in the garden at night with a lantern. I'll be the young master in 'The Genji Dozen.'"* He laughed. "And so

---

* *Genji Jūnidan* or *Jūnidan-zōshi,* the prototype of Jōruri balladry.

here we are, husband and wife, going out to peek jealously through a fence together."

"They'll hear you."

"Poor crickets, still singing, so late in the year. You can't go that way, O-chiyo. There's always a puddle of water under the pomegranate. Go over by the myrtle."

Picking their way along the stepping stones, the two were at length in the far shrubbery. O-chiyo shielded the lantern with her sleeve and held her breath, but the Sonohachi had stopped, and there was only a faint shadow on the paper door. The old villa was silent.

Quiet Rain

"Quiet Rain" was written in 1918, and in 1921 was
revised for publication in the magazine *Shinshōsetsu*.
In 1924 it was included in the collection
Azabu Miscellany. For a discussion, see pp. 101-2.

That year, if I remember correctly, there was a moon and the weather
was cool on the evening of the two-hundred-tenth day.* On the two-
hundred-twentieth, the day was so much like all the days in the last
of the summer heat that one scarcely took notice of the danger. Only
a shrilling of locusts disturbed the afternoon. As if by way of reminder,
there was rain in the night, but the wind was not enough to split the
leaves of the banana or to knock over the amaranth or the asters. I do
not need to consult my diary to remember how it was that year. The
weather changed abruptly after the night's rain. From the next day
it was suddenly too cool for a summer kimono. I had to add a second
kimono, and if I was up even moderately late into the night, slip a
cloak over my shoulders. Sickly though I was, I could not remember
that I had ever before had to take out a cloak until after the equinox;
and always now, when autumn comes and brings a sudden chill into
the night air, it is those days that I think of.

"Those days," I say, but I do not mean to imply that there was any
change in the monotony of my life. The point is that for some years
I had been reasonably content with my solitude; but now, for no very
good reason, I began to fear that solitude would be the way with me
until the end of my life. There would be no more pleasures, nor would
there be great sorrows. My life would draw to a close like a leaden
autumn day, without wind and without rain. I would not live again
in the richly decorated manner. I would not again take a wife, I would

* Counting from the day in early February when spring is held to begin. Both the
two-hundred-tenth day and the two-hundred-twentieth, falling in the typhoon season
and at about the time of the harvest, are looked forward to with apprehension.

keep neither mistress nor maid nor pet. I would have no flowers in my garden and no birds in my window and no fish by my veranda. Because of a certain incident, I had come to see that times had changed. In a day when lads and maidens of good families were busying themselves in the movement to outlaw smoking and drinking, it was nonsense to think of a clean, quiet pipe in the morning, of the pleasant bitterness of well-brewed tea, of properly heated sake. One could do no better than to sew one's own clothes in the manner of the old Zen monk, or to take a lesson from a hermit's book, and rake leaves for warming one's own sake.

Ten years before, I had left my wife, unable to bear her stupidity, and seven years before I had parted with my mistress, appalled at her jealousy. Since then I had lived alone. When the spirit moved me I would jump into a rickshaw and go off to quarters of doubtful repute, but around me I kept only bellflowers and songbirds and books. There were times, after I fell victim to an intestinal ailment and on cold nights would have to light a fire to warm my medicine, when I wished some kind lady were around to take care of me; but I did not then, as I do now, look upon my solitude as a trial. Indeed its quiet, melancholy music was an inexhaustible spring of poetry. I pursued the melancholy and sought the quiet. I cannot forget one year—then, too, it was on about the two-hundred-twentieth day. Aroused by a torrent that beat on the roof like a waterfall, and unable to go back to sleep because I thought I heard dripping somewhere, I lit a candle and went to hunt for the leak. I kept but one old woman, whose room was off the kitchen, at the other end of the house. Through the empty rooms, as in some old temple, the mustiness of the sliding doors assailed me with peculiar intensity. As the flame wavered in the draft, my shadow crept like a monster across the centipedes on the matting, and on up over the wall and its lizards. Shielding the candle with my kimono sleeve, I went from room to room, looking into the farthest corners and into all the closets. I did not find the leak. What I had heard was presumably water spilling over the drains. At length I opened the wooden door to the detached wing that had been my late father's study. On the sandalwood Chinese table were a crystal paperweight, a bronze vase, and a bookstand of teak. A rather spacious room, it was just as it had been when my father was pursuing his studies of Chinese poetry there. Horn-rimmed glasses lay on an open volume of poetry, one thick bow pointed upward, as if waiting for the dead man to return. The camphor to keep off bookworms was almost enough to make my eyes sting, and seemed to reprove me for having stayed away so long. I sat on a stand of flecked bamboo, and, holding up the light, read the Chinese poems at the pillars and above the lintels.

> The trees, a mist of green, above the waves of evening.
> Clean autumn not yet over, the traveler passes again.
> His village is to him like the mist of evening trees.
> No migrant birds to tell of it. Only wind and rain.

This is but one of the poems, one that remains with me today. I sat in reverie until the candle had gone out, and with daybreak the wind and rain at length subsided.

The second of January is the anniversary of my father's death. Late one New Year's Eve I went out into the cold, moonlit garden to cut some winter myrtle, which I meant to put on my father's grave the next day. In those days I still had the energy to set such matters down on paper.

It must have been about then that the old woman who had served me so long died of a respiratory ailment called Spanish influenza or something of the sort. I have not been able to find another domestic so faithful, and I have had to perform small services for myself—cut my bread, boil my coffee, uncork a bottle of wine. This in-between way of life did not trouble me in the days when I still felt the urgings of poetry. If I was in the neighborhood of the Ginza, I would stop by the Seiyōken and buy bread and canned goods. One piercingly cold night when snow was threatening, I bought a loaf of bread. It seemed to have been freshly baked, and all the way home it warmed my hand and arm. The Seiyōken being in a district where geisha frequently pass, I was put in mind of a Chinese poem I had long been fond of, by Mori Shuntō:*

> The ruby panes, all six, now closed and shuttered,
> I warm my hands inside the dear girl's bosom.

I smiled to myself. When it came to keeping warm, a loaf of bread did quite as well as a singing girl! So it was in those days.

* 1818–88.

As long as there is poetry, the life of solitude need not be a life of loneliness. In poverty and illness, too, one has a modicum of consolation when one remembers the poems by Lang Shih-yüan:*

> Though horse and coach may shun my far retreat,
> Thrush and flower still come the pauper's way.

And Po Chü-i:

> Trial but strengthens the soul of the man of honor.
> Illness but deepens the heart of the cultured man.

But the poetic urge is a strange, mysterious affair. It does not come when you beckon or answer when you call. In your solitude you seek the promptings of poetry and they fail to come, and for the first time solitude moves from melancholy to sheer wretchedness. And the solitary pleasure in which the poet so prides himself, the pleasure of reminiscence and reverie, becomes a source of regrets and descends to womanish complaining. Walking down a street, I have had to avert my eyes from the shimmering colors in the windows of a kimono dealer, for I have not wished to remember the pleasures of a youth that would not return. As the smell of cooking in the house next door has come drifting to mine, I have angrily closed the window. For I have been unable to endure the memory of family gatherings of which I was once a part. Going down to plant flowers in my garden, or waiting in the street for a cab, or simply feeling a touch of wind at my sleeve as I have raised the window blind, I have been like a traveler in the gathering darkness, thinking of home. For one who lives alone the worst thing, worse than the wind or the moon or the singing of autumn insects, is rain. I once wrote in my diary: "The long rains continue, and the chill causes stomach cramps. In the night there is a wind to blow at the light, but it brings no dreams. I think thoughts I would prefer to be without. 'Alone in bed on a night of sad, still rain'— this is from a popular ballad of Edo. And this from a poem by the famous Little Tu:†

> A sleepless night. To the ear of the lonely traveler
> Comes a rustling of leaves from without, from another's garden.

* 727–?80.   † Or Tu Mu, 803–52.

And this from one by Tu Hsün-ho:*

> Midnight before the lamp. The things of a decade—
> In an instant, at the sound of rain, they all come back.

The rain beating against the window, flowing from the eaves, dripping from the trees, pouring over the bamboo thicket, is a stronger agent to move men's hearts than is the wind moaning in the trees or water roaring down a mountain valley. The voice of the wind is an angry one, and the voice of the water a wail. The voice of the rain does not rage and does not complain. It but speaks, pleads. Human emotions are forever unchanging; and who, alone in bed listening to the rain, is not moved to sadness? Who, in particular, when he is ill? If it rains for three days the stomach cramps invariably come back, and I find myself sunk in truly dyspeptic thoughts.† There is a poem in *Almost Rain,* by Wang Tz'ŭ-hui:‡

> A sick man's bones are the surest prophets of rain.
> He turns from the lamp. Insects echo his moans.
> No wife to sweep the dust, the fallen leaves.
> Disordered books, cold censer, lonely bed.
> Worries, insistent, swell like a monstrous gourd.
> Health is good—but shall herbs wrack the wasted bowels?
> No, better to hear again the words of the sage:
> 'Gaze into the well, see the worm that you are, and be cured.'

Because this poem speaks for me, I here set it down. Such is the life of the ailing and lonely."

That year. From the evening of the two-hundred-twentieth day, rain washed the blossoms from the bush clover and knocked its branches to the ground, but the tall asters and the heavy-headed amaranth did not fall. It rained steadily for two days and two nights. On the third day it had not yet cleared, and the gloom brought nocturnal flowers, cereus and evening primrose, into cautious bloom while it was still daylight. The dampness was even worse than in the worst of the rain. My desk seemed to ooze dampness, to emit dew. The handle

---

* Active in late T'ang.
† *Dancho no omoi,* a reference (see pp. 79–80) to Kafū's Danchōtei.
‡ Active in late Ming. His *I Yü Chi,* here translated *Almost Rain,* appeared in 1618.

of my writing brush and the stem of my pipe were sticky. The paper
on the doors had so slackened that I feared it might rip away in the
wind coming through the cracks. It seemed certain that if the dampness went on for another day or two, a person who had had to take
out a cloak and lined kimono even before the equinox would have to
call a doctor. Ailing bones were indeed a prophet of rain. But then I
noticed that the skin of the samisen I had left in the alcove had for
mysterious reasons failed to break, and I knew that I would be spared
the worst of the usual pains. I went to the Ginza to do some shopping, and to clear away the gloom of three days in prison.

I had been to the Kyūkyodō to buy fifty of the writing brushes I
like best, those known as "A Thousand Words from the Heart," and
two packets of joss sticks, and to the Kameya to buy two bottles of
white wine, and had started for the streetcar line around the palace
moat. It was then that I met O-han and learned what had happened
to her. The mistress of a gentleman one of whose elegant literary
sobriquets was "Master of the Saisendō," she had once more become
a geisha.

A cloudy autumn day is quick to end. When I opened my gate,
there was already a light at the eaves. I uncorked a bottle of white
wine and had dinner, and when I had finished, without even pausing
for a smoke, I took up paper and writing brush.

"I have been so remiss in my duties toward you that I scarcely know
how I can face you when next we meet. Please put down my failure
to observe the proprieties as a mark of the boorishness of us scribblers,
and be magnanimous about it. The truth is that I passed a very difficult winter, and feeling the ravages of the years, I have been quite
unable to set myself to work at anything. I have not even begun the
new Sonohachi lyrics you asked of me last year—it was at the time,
I believe, of the completion of your Saisendō mansion. That I should
respond to your kindness with such a display of incompetence seems
wholly beyond excusing. As for my main work, the writing of novels,
I have quite abandoned it. Unable to avoid the urgings of publishers,
I ask the ridiculous price of a yen for each character. Apprehensive
about my old age, however, I sometimes tell myself that my present
ways will not do, and sit down at my desk with a frown; but I have
written no more than a word or two when my brush stops and irrita-

tion overtakes me. I am reconciled to the fact that I must give up writing for the time being and concentrate on regaining my health; and so I get what consolation I can from senselessly rereading the books I read when I was young. It is an almost unbearable trial even to get through the days, rising in the morning, and eating, and going to bed again. My samisen is put aside because it is too much of a nuisance to change the broken strings, and my songbird has been returned to the bird shop. I of course no longer attend Yūrakuza concerts or any others, or the theater, or other elegant places of entertainment. My one real regret in all this is that I have had no occasion to inquire into your affairs. I had thought that your efforts to revive Sonohachi continued apace, and it was therefore with the greatest consternation that I chanced to meet O-han this evening, and to learn that she was no longer at the Saisendō. Since we were on a busy street and the sky was threatening, I learned only that her geisha permit was likely to come in a few days, and I was quite unable to guess what this news signified. In my bewilderment I therefore write to apologize for my remissness, and to ask that my wish to pry into the affairs of other people be forgiven as one of those quirks of the novel-scribbler. I shall hope to call upon you one day soon.

"To the Master of the Saisendō,
"From Kimpū the Scribbler."

As I was stamping the envelope, the maid came in to clear the table. The chill of my study seemed easier to bear than in the daytime, perhaps because I had eaten, perhaps because there was a light on, perhaps because the shutters were closed. It had once more begun to rain, however. I could not hear the drops, but the heavy sound of the umbrella opening as the maid started through the side gate to mail my letter came back, sad and lonely, through the singing of insects. It was a silent rain, a mist of a rain. Since the dampness of such a rain on an autumn night can be even more penetrating than during the rainy season, I lighted a fire and burned powdered flies to repel bookworms, and, taking a pawlonia box from the closet, put away my samisen. While I was about it, I took out the wicker box in which I kept letters from friends, and hunted for the packet from the Master of the Saisendō. There is little else for a bachelor to do on a rainy night.

"Master of the Saisendō" is the sobriquet of a gentleman who directs an important company. I am reluctant to give his real name, and shall therefore favor him with the sort of diminutive that a geisha might use, and call him Yō-san. I first met him some twenty years ago in an American university. When he was a student in Japan, he had something of a reputation among devotees of the genre as a composer of haiku. Even now he comes out with a good verse now and then, and if I were to mention the name he uses as a haiku poet I have no doubt that he would be recognized. I suspect, however, that I am the only one who knows that other sobriquet, "Master of the Saisendō." The house known as the Saisendō may survive, but there is no one living in it, and Yō-san will not again have occasion to use the name. Its origins are explained in the following letter:

"I have been reading your new work on my way to the office. Although I have only been able to make my way in some haste through the first half, my admiration for the rich tapestry of your prose makes me forget from time to time that I am riding in an automobile, and indeed I suspect that the fact of my being so busy makes me better able to savor the poetry. In this season of new foliage and late warblers, I greatly envy you your surroundings. The hut by the Toyokawa Fox,* about which I so troubled you for suggestions last year, has at length been finished, down to the drying of the walls, and O-han moved in yesterday. I wonder, therefore, if I might ask for the honor of your presence, along with that of the usual assortment of people, at a mere token of a housewarming, the day after tomorrow, in the evening. Since Miyasono Sensai, Uji Shisen, and Miyako Gochū will be present, you must be resigned to the fact that it will be no more than a family gathering.† I should be most grateful if you could call me some time tomorrow, by which time the telephone should be connected.

"To the Honorable Mr. Kimpū,

"From the Master of the Saisendō.

"P.S. As planned, I have covered the doors of the six-mat room—the one under the deep eaves—with the papers I bought last year from the gentleman at the Edoza. You will remember them, the little notes

* Or Toyokawa Inari Shrine.
† All classical musicians. Miyasono Sensai seems to have been the "maestro at Yakembori," who appears again on p. 262.

from Yoshiwara ladies, written I believe in the early nineteenth century. They have proved to be remarkably appropriate for the house of, shall we say, a patronized lady, and I have therefore given the place the somewhat eccentric name Saisendō, 'House of the Bright Billets-doux.' The name is a stupid one, however, dreamed up by a person with no knowledge of literature, and I shall be hoping for better suggestions when we meet."

Yō-san is a rich man, but not newly rich. He is a man of erudition and breeding, and his hobbies are varied. In his letters he would use pseudonyms appropriate to the business at hand. Once when I had written inquiring about the notebooks of the calligrapher Tōkō,* he signed his reply "From the Stupid Occupant of the Apple Hermitage." This little flourish came to him, I take it, because Tōkō also called himself "Occupant of the Hall that Welcomes the Birds."† Another time I wrote inquiring after him when he had had an automobile accident, and, with that easy knack for word play so characteristic of frivolous Edo literature, he signed his reply Tonda Sainan.‡ The signature to the following letter would appear to be a double reference to the hero of "Omi Woes,"§ which he was then practicing with the maestro, and to his relationship with O-han:

"You must forgive me for having kept you on against your will last night. My outrageous behavior left quite exposed the unseemly figure of a man approaching fifty who must always have a mere girl at his side; and even though the place was more appropriate for such happenings than most, I was very red-faced indeed when I recovered from my intoxication. But then, thinking that the revelations of the profligate might in the future be of some use in the writings of his revered companion, I made my confessions quite without reservation in response to your inquiries. The day after tomorrow there is unfortu-

---

* Sawada Tōkō, 1732–96.

† The "flourish" has to do with a rearrangement of the characters with which the two names are written. Its full significance, of course, disappears in translation.

‡ Which, with the characters written here, could conceivably be a name, but which, written differently, becomes "dreadful accident."

§ *Kuzetsu Hakkei,* a Sonohachi ballad. Hambei, the complaining hero, is an Osaka merchant who has fallen upon hard days because of dissipation, and been forced to move to the province of Omi.

nately an emergency company meeting, and I must forego my lesson at Half-Moon House. I want definitely to finish 'Omi Woes' this month, however, and I trust that you for your part are working hard. I look forward to doing 'O-hana and Hanshichi' with you.*

"To the Honorable Mr. Kimpū,

"From Hambei."

In those days, despite everything, I still had traces of youth in me. I see now that the way in which, hearing the voice of forty, I took up my brush to complain in my journal and in miscellaneous jottings of the advent of old age was itself evidence that old age had not yet completely overtaken me. A person need not despair while he still has the spirit to grumble. The fact of being able to proclaim shamelessly before the world that the samisen of the geisha these days was not worth listening to was evidence that desire had not left, and that there was still an impulse to partake of pleasures. And with that there remained, too, an impulse to study, and to write. Hearing someone sing Sonohachi the whole night through and wanting myself to sample that antique flavor, I went for a time to the maestro in Yakembori. In the course of a conversation I chanced to learn that my old friend Yō-san, too, after having played with Nagauta and Kiyomoto and the other styles, had at length turned to Sonohachi, which he was pursuing most earnestly, and that for some years he had been going to Half-Moon House in Tsukiji for lessons from the same maestro. We clapped with delight at the coincidence. Urged on by Yō-san, I gave up my morning lessons and went with him instead to Half-Moon House in the evening.

On lesson days, Yō-san would arrive in his automobile at four-thirty, and when we had finished, he would keep me for dinner and call in certain favored geisha. Regularly at ten-thirty he would begin his preparations to depart. On rainy nights he saw me home in his automobile. I am told that among the geisha he had been in the habit of calling, there had been adepts of Nagauta and Kiyomoto and the like, but now he had turned rather to Katō and Itchū and Sonohachi, and the very youngest geisha in these schools were in their mid-twenties. Among them were elderly ladies who seemed less like geisha than

---

* Another Sonohachi, about love suicide. The story is the same as that of Chikamatsu's *Nagamachi Onna Harakiri* ("The Suicide of the Woman at Nagamachi").

like teachers. And then there appeared Ko-han (or, familiarly, O-han), still in her teens, the one spot of crimson in all the foliage, so conspicuous that one almost felt sorry for her. And one knew immediately that she was being helped by Yō-san.

Ko-han was a big, healthy girl. She had bright eyes and thick eyebrows, her hairline was good, and her features were well-defined; on the other hand, her defects, her too-large mouth and her jutting jaw, were most conspicuous. It was a face wanting in winsomeness and quite incapable of expressing melancholy. Yet if voluptuous women are the up-to-date ones in any age, Ko-han fitted the mold. I cannot deny that I thought it a bit strange to find Yō-san patronizing an up-to-date girl. My surprise was quite erased, however, by the discovery that Ko-han, despite her appearance and years, had gone a considerable distance toward mastering the Sonohachi samisen.

One evening we had finished our lessons and moved into another room as usual, and I was exchanging cups with Yō-san. Ko-han and the other geisha who were our usual companions were all at the Kabukiza for some sort of geisha recital, and did not appear until almost nine, and the maestro, too, had excused himself just after our lessons, saying that he feared he was coming down with a cold. Having only a maid to pour for us, Yō-san and I somehow felt less constraint than usual, and the talk moved from the value of plebeian Edo forms as music and the possibilities in the modern world to the prospects the future might hold for them. Samisen music, I said, was a delicate and plaintive art that had reached perfection more than two centuries before, nurtured by the pleasure quarters. It would probably survive as long as the pleasure quarters continued to hand down their legacy from an earlier day. The samisen, with the Kabuki and the Ukiyoe, had little to do with our society and our standards. It was not a living voice. A murmur from the past, it was an art whose sweet-sad melancholy could produce limitless emotions and poetic impulses—it was like "the woman of Shang, unaware that her country was lost, who went on singing, beyond the river, of the flower in the inner garden."* Such, I said, was the worth today of plebeian Edo music. I was repeating a favorite theory of mine.

Yō-san replied that, seeking consolation every day after work, he found music far easier to listen to than pictures to look at. Hideyoshi was a tea fancier, but Edo balladry was far more appealing than tea.

* From a poem by Tu Mu.

And among the Edo styles none was better than Sonohachi, the quietest, saddest of them all. The classically elegant yet coldly voluptuous notes of Sonohachi, he said, were like listening to the soliloquy of an Edo beauty in a dream.

In sum, we were toying with Edo music as with antiques.

Biting back a yawn, the maid left us. She would bring more sake, she said. Yō-san sat up and addressed me as if there were something very special on his mind. "I have been wanting to speak to you for a long time. About Ko-han. What do you think? Will she ever amount to anything? I want her to learn Sonohachi, really learn it, and take over as head of the school some day. What do you think?"

Unlike other schools, Sonohachi had few students, and it was in danger of disappearing unless something was done very soon. Yō-san had the inclination to do something, and the money, and no one could find fault with his plans for looking after the faltering Edo classics. I had long recognized, moreover, that Ko-han's accomplishments, far beyond her years, showed great promise. I nodded. Taking a sip of sake, Yō-san told me of his plans.

"When you get to be my age, you don't call in geisha just for the fun of sleeping with them. You have to enjoy teaching them something. I wouldn't be as frank with most people, but because it's you I'll tell everything. The truth of the matter is that I'm a moralist at heart, whatever I may look like. I have no use for the gentlemen and the rich people of today. Not that I have any more use for the Socialists. If I tried to be serious, no one would pay any attention to me, and so this is the way I spend my evenings. Well, that's neither here nor there. I have my reasons for wanting to give music lessons to a geisha, even though I might not seem the best person in the world for the job. It's a form of dissipation, I suppose, spending a fortune on tea bowls and pictures, and it's dissipation to start training a geisha.

"I've tried to help a great many people. I've been quite serious about it, but all I've succeeded in doing is making myself see what the times are like. I have three students in my house right now, and next year my oldest boy will be ready for the university. I don't ask that they keep bowing to me and flattering me, and I don't much care whether they amount to anything or not. All I want is that they turn into people I can talk to. Everyone I've helped has been a success, but I can't say I've been very pleased with the form their success has taken.

"I won't mention any names, but it was seven or eight years ago. I helped a young artist because I was asked to, and because I myself thought he had promise. I thought he might some day turn into an unpretentious sort of painter like Buson or Kazan. But I couldn't have been more mistaken. The critics praised him in an exhibition or two, and he started to get famous, and so he became a master and took all sorts of disciples and formed his faction and used the newspapers and magazines to advertise himself, and generally behaved like a politician. I must say that it worked out very well for him. It's less than ten years now, and that student is already the master of a house as grand as Tani Bunchō's.

"Another of my students did very nicely, too, and managed to upset me. When he was in school, he asked me to teach him haiku, and I lent him some of my books—I rather like haiku myself. Sometimes I would ask him how he was doing, and revise his poems for him. But afterward I saw that he wasn't really interested in haiku at all. He thought he would play up to me by asking me to read a poem from time to time. And so, being a clever sort of person, he graduated and went off to teach in a girls' school in the provinces somewhere, and promptly got himself adopted into a rich family, and now he runs a private kindergarten and elementary school, and they say he's very well thought of. If that were all there was to the story, it would be very fine indeed. What I don't like is the way he goes about his work, as if education were like running a shop or a company. Every year he comes to Tokyo and meets all sorts of influential people, and one year he went off for half a year to America—called it a study trip—and came back and made speeches all over the place. Well, there's nothing wrong with that, I suppose, but what really annoyed me was what happened last year. He's just forty years old, maybe not even that, and he had a bronze statue of himself put up in a local park to commemorate his achievements. We can't do much about it when the descendants of the great Itohei put up a stone in his memory,* no matter how gigantic it may be, and there is nothing wrong, I suppose, in putting up a bronze statue of yourself in your own garden if that's the way your taste runs. But what he did was quietly set out collecting

* Tanaka Heihachi, owner of a silk-spinning enterprise in the early Meiji Period, was known as "Tenka no Itohei," or something like "the thread merchant who rules the world."

contributions from the parents of his pupils and organizing the press and stirring up public opinion, and then he pretended he had had nothing at all to do with the matter.

"I do not like the ways people choose to get ahead in the world. I'm happy to lend money to someone who's come a cropper if his intentions are good; on the other hand, I don't care how well a man does if he's not a decent person. And so I've come to dislike trying to help people. All of these things are not my immediate reasons, of course; but while I was having Ko-han take lessons in Sonohachi, it came to me that I'd like to make her over to my own tastes—although as I've said I may not be the best person in the world to do it. The more usual ways of giving out money had all gone wrong, somehow, and so I asked myself how it would be to produce a real artist. You know well enough that not one of them, man or woman, is worth a thing these days, and it's not likely that any first-rate performers will come out in the future. And Sonohachi is not like Nagauta or Kiyomoto. Once the maestro is gone there will be no one to take his place, and so if Ko-han will only go ahead and work as hard as I want her to, my dissipation will become something more serious. It will—if I may state the matter with excessive solemnity—turn into the preservation of old Edo music."

It was some months later that arrangements were made for Yō-san to support Ko-han, and he set about building her a house. Here is a letter I had from him:

"I am much concerned about your cold. Given the season and the delicate state of your health at best, I must ask that you take most particularly good care of yourself.

"There is something about which I would like to ask your advice. I had thought that I would see you in the usual place yesterday, and was much disappointed that we were unable to meet because of your illness; and so I take up brush despite the drunken disorderliness of my writing. You will remember that I have been asking about for a suitable house for Ko-han. Hearing from an agent about two houses that seemed appropriately priced and situated, I went to look at them on my way home from work. One is in Yanagibashi by the river; the other is in Akasaka, behind the Toyokawa Inari Shrine. I had thought that Tsukiji would be convenient, and put in my order accordingly;

but since nothing appropriate has thus far turned up, and since a person has a way of losing interest when these matters are too long protracted, I had hoped to ask your advice and then decide on one or the other, Yanagibashi or Akasaka. Ko-han herself says the river place would be a little more convenient as a situation, but that there would be all sorts of troublesome rumors; and so, despite its inconvenience, she prefers Akasaka. The Akasaka place has an old garden with some fine trees, though the house itself will be good only for tearing down. The river place will be livable enough if the doors are re-papered, but the district being what it is, the houses are crowded close together and there is little sunlight, and the river itself is not visible even from the second floor. The price does not include the land, which is rented. Although the owner says he cannot come down, I think that the price he quotes, ¥10,000 for a house perhaps a hundred square yards in area, is more than he expects to get. If one chooses to live in the Edo style, one must be prepared to do without a garden, but it seems a pity that the place does not front on the river.

"The agent says that since Akasaka is a district where the newly rich keep their mistresses, I will be able to sell again for a good price if I do not like the house. The price is ¥15,000 for the house and nearly three hundred square yards of land. Since it is sloping land, the natural aspect is pleasant, with the grove of the Toyokawa Shrine just beyond the fence. It therefore seems a most appropriate situation for living in retirement or keeping a mistress. When I went to look at it yesterday, I was much pleased with the clapping of the pilgrims and the faint singing of birds through the greenery. The shade of the Toyo-kawa grove being to the northeast, the house faces generally south-west. If something can be done when the house is rebuilt to keep off the afternoon sun, there should be a cool breeze, and I need not be afraid of finding myself in the plight of Dempuku:* 'How hot it is, in a house so badly built!' And then there is a verse you will remember by Tōrin:† 'A cold wind down from Fuji, to strip off the leaves in the very heart of the city.' Tōrin was nearer the heart of the city, but in the Yamanote, too, the things to be feared are the afternoon sun of autumn and the western wind of winter. I do not know the directions as precisely as I have stated them, since I did not bring a compass; but

* Kawada Dempuku, 1721–93.   † Amano Tōrin, 1639–1719.

I mean to have another look, and I hope that when you have quite recovered, you might, in the course of a stroll, go survey it for yourself. This will be a great inconvenience, I know; but it has long been said that in youth a man plays with women, in middle age with the arts, and in old age with house and garden, and that if he but shows restraint in these matters he will prosper. It seems to me most amusing that even my impulses toward extravagance should so fit the advice of the ancients. As my final gesture, I wish to build a house correct to the last detail, and so, when you find the time, I should like suggestions on the design. Given the various possible Edo styles, I think that for doing Sonohachi and Itchū, something older than the illustrations to *A Calendar of Plum Blossoms* might be in order, perhaps a Harunobu setting. His was the best time of all for Edo, the best time of all. 'Oh for winter to come, when you cover your head as you will.' Each day will be like the passage of a thousand autumns as I await your recovery.

> "To the Honorable Mr. Kimpū,
> "From Hambei."

We were all wonderfully prosperous in those years because of the European War. Since new companies were springing up three and four a day, there can be no doubt that an old, established company like Yō-san's was making vast profits. The more expensive the article, the better it sold. Rice was high, and even farmers were in the stock market, and it was a most appropriate time for housing a mistress. Since noble families were accepting closed bids for their treasures, it was a good time, too, for furnishing the sort of house Yō-san wanted to build. He would take me with him to survey the articles for sale each time such an occasion arose, and this even before he had chosen his land. His taste running to haiku, he did not bid on huge screens and other grand appurtenances of daimyo mansions; but regardless of the price he bought up everything that might be of use in his mistress's house—metal lanterns, trays and bowls, braziers, stepping tiles, bits of old chintz or striped Canton silk. At the urging of the master and the artists invited to the housewarming when at last the Saisendō was finished, I could not refuse to write something to commemorate the occasion, and I was also urged to write lyrics for a new Sonohachi work.

The next day I started looking through books that might be of use, all the old chronicles and fugitive essays and the like reproduced by the Society for the Publication of National Writings, *The Ten Varieties of Jade* and the rest.* Thinking that I would begin writing as soon as I had come upon the material I wanted, I would pore over works touching upon Edo customs, *Pine Needles* and other collections of ballads, by the light of my bed lamp. I thought that going over such works, even as the frivolous writers of Edo had done, was not only amusing but important. Without the slightest qualms, I stopped work on a novel I had begun. I thought that the vernacular style that had become virtually orthodox for novels since Futabatei Shimei was doing great harm to the lyrical impulses of Edo. The fact is that after I have been reading old books, I find it most unpleasant, the monotonous modern style in which each sentence must uniformly tell us that "the fact is that." The fact is that, seeking somehow to escape from this wretched "the fact is that," and in the end failing, I have only been able to lament the fact that I do not have the literary genius of an Ichiyō or a Kōyō. I wanted to write something as boldly voluptuous as Chikufujin's elegy for Tamagiku, with its "clouds in rags and tatters," or his elegy to Ranshū, "three drops, now four drops, nothing, indeed, calling for an umbrella."† When, a year before, I had been told by a doctor that my illness was incurable, I had felt that I wanted to leave behind a piece or two in something like the discursive prose of Yayū,‡ something in the elegant narrative style of Saikaku.

Since Shokusanjin was quite unstinting in his praise of the works gathered in the *Quail's Cloak* of Yayū, there is no need for us latter-day persons to add our poor praise; but each time I read it afresh, I find myself pounding the desk and saying that as long as Japanese culture endures, as long as it has any need for Chinese characters, a thousand years from now, even, this will continue to be a model for Japanese prose. There are few writings that can compare with the thoughtful passages of the *Quail's Cloak* in complexity and in the

* *Enseki Jisshu,* a reference work of the late Tokugawa Period.

† Chikufujin's dates are 1678–1759; his family name is unknown. Tamagiku was a courtesan, Ranshū a musician of the Katōbushi school. Both were active in the early eighteenth century.

‡ Yokoi Yayū, 1702–83. The expression "quail's cloak" (see the next paragraph) indicates a badly tattered garment.

breadth of the learning it draws upon. There are few things old or new that can compare with the clean, smooth flow of that prose. The warp from which the cloak is woven is the whole of classical Chinese and Japanese literature, and the woof is the plebeian literature of the seventeenth century and since, and the color comes from Yayū's own particular style, his very special genius. Here, for the first time, one may be permitted to use words like "completeness" and "perfection." It was almost too great a fondness for the *Quail's Cloak* that made me want to write a chronicle of the Saisendō for Yō-san. The chronicle was presently finished and provided with a splendid frame and mounting, but I did not succeed in producing the Sonohachi lyric. There are still fragments of it somewhere in a desk drawer.

I had thought to use in my new Sonohachi the story of the suicide of the courtesan Uneme, recorded in *Illustrated Guide to the Famous Places of Edo,* in the entry for Uneme's Mound, at Hashiba, on the river north of Asakusa. I thought that once I had Yō-san's agreement I would begin work; and then, at about the time of the midsummer Bon Festival, our music lessons were discontinued as usual because of the heat. Yō-san left for his Oiso villa with his family. Overcome by the heat, I took to my bed for ten days, hoping to return to my desk when, with the cool weather, the Saisendō lessons began once more; but then the maestro fell ill. In October, when he was once more able to come out, Yō-san unfortunately had to go to Korea and Manchuria on company business. The New Year came shortly after his return, and it is the custom of musicians not to give lessons in January.

And so I presently lost interest in Uneme's suicide. In February came the invitation from the Saisendō to begin lessons again; but during the cold months, from January on to the equinox, I make it a practice to stay at home except for walks on warm, windless afternoons. Pleading a heavy writing schedule, I waited for the season when once more a single kimono would do. The life of the bachelor is twice as free as that of other people, but the inconvenience is twice as great when he falls ill. The matter is of little concern when the illness is severe enough to put him to bed; but when it is a light one that does not call for a nurse, the bachelor himself must wrap up the money for the doctor's rickshawman, and be sure that the maid has put out a basin of water and a towel for the doctor. Indeed convalescence keeps him busier than does his work when he is well. Knowing that it is better to avoid colds from the outset, therefore, I am as sensitive to the cold as are hothouse plants.

It was a bad year. Despite my usual precautions, I fell ill with an epidemic infection when already the birds were singing and the cherry blossoms were falling; and then, perhaps because there was a great deal of rain, I had to warm my stomach with a hot-water bottle every day until the new bamboo was springing up and the loquats were ripening. I had to take potions and powders six times a day, before and after meals. When I tried to read in bed, the hand holding the book soon fell, and when I tried to sit up and take brush in hand, the urge to write would desert me. I was barely able, on orders from publishers, to revise and correct old manuscripts that might better have gone into the wastebasket. I spent my days thinking of times that had been happier, and sometimes, laying aside my brush and the red ink for revising manuscripts, I would think of another poem from *Almost Rain,* and so dispel the sadness to some slight extent:

> I shall tie up my books. There are not many left.
> Oh, the tracks I left behind me, those years and years ago!
> Long hair flowing in laughter, cups among the flowers.
> In a moonlit boat the giddy one composed her velvet brows.
> The old man smiled in anger.
> The maiden charmed with scowls.
> They all are gone, those joys from long ago.
> And what remains is a wisp of smoke from a censer.

I felt no desire to take up my samisen and sing a ballad, and the summer went by as if I had quite forgotten that I owed an answer to the Saisendō. Autumn was half over, and then came that evening. Suddenly, on the Ginza, I learned that Ko-han had left the Saisendō. I was startled from my lethargy, and wrote to learn what had happened.

I could hear water running into a basin from the eaves. It was no longer a quiet, misty rain. I could also hear leaves falling on the roof in the wind. Seeing that the room was a little close, what with tobacco and the vermicide I had been burning, I reached to slide open a door. Just then the maid, back from mailing my letter to the Master of the Saisendō, brought in the mail she had picked up at the side gate on her way in. Everything was sodden. There were three postcards, two of them brokers' advertisements, the third one of those rude affairs that come from magazines: "Please tell us the name of your favorite geisha and restaurant. Our deadline is...." There were two letters, one of them, I could tell by the writing, from the Master of the Saisendō. I was sure it would have news of Ko-han.

"Not having had word of you in some time, I have been wondering how you are. It has occurred to me that with the chill and the long autumn rains following upon the heat you might be indisposed. If it does not clear in the next few days, we will have floods, the railroads will be out, and the price of rice will climb yet higher.

"I am writing to tell you of O-han. There were certain displeasing things that forced me to send her back to her old nest. It is the height of folly to discuss these matters, for, as was said long ago, the flower that blooms in quiet should be observed in quiet—to pluck a single spray is to destroy the freshness. I must for a time bear the shame of having people learn of my folly. With your usual perceptiveness, you will have guessed the nature of what has happened. Actors and geisha being in a sort of symbiotic relationship, I was quite ready, had the man been an actor, to pretend that nothing was amiss. I was, moreover, aware of the danger when I set her to practicing Sonohachi, unlike the other styles in its preoccupation with tragic love. 'A man a woman had to fall in love with. The sweet words of evening were for the evening only. With lusterless hair in the morning....' And so on —things particularly calculated to stir one's passions. Though I would not wish to sound like the complaining Hambei in 'Omi Woes,' I may say for myself that I am no rustic unaware of what to expect from the pleasure quarters. I found the situation impossible to tolerate, however, when I learned that the object of her affections was not an actor but— a narrator for the movies! Though I would have found him distasteful, I would have tolerated, I think, even an actor in the new style, or an Osaka comedian; but however much one may wish to conduct an affair in the grand Edo manner, however much one may hope to see it through with verve and flair, revealing nothing, like a cleanly striped kimono that hides a complex lining, one is not likely to succeed when a chauffeur or a movie narrator thrusts himself upon the scene. Perhaps I may take the liberty of assuming that my aesthetic theories accord with your own, and that I may count upon your sympathy.

"I do not know whether O-han chose to become a geisha once more, or whether she married the movie yawper. In any case, the Saisendō is now without a master. Well drained on the slope where they were planted, the begonias that you so kindly gave me from your own garden bloom in a watermelon-colored profusion, objects of more regret than three hundred pieces of lost silver. To be quite safe, let us say thirteen hundred.

"These trivialities I pass on for your amusement.

"To the illustrious Mr. Kimpū,

"From the former Master of the Saisendō."

Finally the rains stopped. If it is clear, the most memorable weather of the year comes at the time of the autumn equinox. The skirt of one's lined kimono is fresh, the sleeves of the gauze cloak over it do not annoy. There is something very poignant about the wind that whips at the blinds, and the sky is astonishingly blue; and boundless thoughts come to one who, no prince merely enjoying his retirement, watches the clouds trail across the sky. On windless, overcast days, the flowers and the wings of butterflies float up in fresher colors, the images of the castle-city are reflected from its canals, motionless, and ponds and ditches and even rain puddles become mirrors, reflecting those same images.

> Last night, through all the rain, I was shut inside.
> Now, in the new, clean coolness, I hang out reed-grass blinds.
> Chrysanthemums bud at the hedge, olive flowers are fallen.
> An autumn of amaranth. Red claims all the garden.

Murmuring this Chinese poem by my late father, I went out. My feet took me to the gate of the Saisendō. On a pillar of untrimmed nettle the signboard bearing the name of the house was still in place, and the door to the side gate, the knotted boards of which were joined by strips of flecked bamboo, was closed tight, as is the way with houses of kept women, so that the grounds were not to be seen. Not having visited the place for a long time, and being fond of the architecture, I of course wanted to have a look inside. I told myself that there would by now be a certain mellowness in the wood of the veranda. The garden would have taken on a settled look, and since there had been so much rain, the garden stones would be mossy. I thought of the letter telling me that the begonias transplanted from my garden were blooming in watermelon-colored profusion, and unable to hold myself back, I tried the side gate. It opened readily. From inside, beyond the hedge, came, if I was not mistaken, the sound of a samisen. The middle string had been sharpened, to produce a plaintive minor key. There was a preliminary pluck or two, not a woman's touch. It would be the maestro. I listened, wondering what work might have required the special key; and then came the low-pitched voice of the Master of the Saisendō. "We shall weep no more. What must be must be." Ukihashi and Nuinosuke would have "gazed into each other's eyes and burst into tears," and so the ballad of the love suicides on Mt. Toribe would be drawing to a conclusion.* It would be impertinent of me to open the door and push in upon the lesson. Gazing at an autumn spider spinning a web under the eaves, I listened on.

"No, it was a piece of damned foolishness," said the Master of the Saisendō when at length I went in. "Imagine anyone who could have the bad taste to get worked up over a movie narrator. I misjudged her from the start. And even if he hadn't come along, she would have been hopeless, I'm afraid. I thought she had talent when she was a geisha, but that was because she happened to be aggressive by nature. She hated to lose in any sort of contest, and her competitive ways showed in her music. But once she was no longer a geisha, there was no more competition to keep her going. After a month or two she was playing the samisen only out of a sense of duty. At first I scolded her a great deal. I told her that she had talent, and that she had to get to work while she was young; but she had no idea of her own talents, and I gather that she had no real interest in music. Even when time was heavy on her hands, she never thought of picking up a samisen and brushing up on an old score. As a matter of fact there didn't seem to be much of anything that she really did like to do. She didn't sew and she didn't read or write. She would just go off to see a play and wander around the lobbies with her cronies, or go to the Mitsukoshi or the Shirokiya and have something to eat, or go to a movie in Asakusa. She finally began to talk back when I scolded her—always as if she were asking what the point was in becoming a stupid old samisen teacher.

* See the note on p. 250.

And so I decided that the prospect was hopeless and let her go. She's
not the only one, though. All of them are alike these days, whether
they're in business or whether they're proper young ladies. The girls
at the office are all good talkers, but not one of them has the spirit to
knuckle down to hard study. It was my mistake, thinking I could get
a young geisha to learn Sonohachi. I should have known from my own
daughter, the one who's in high school. Girls can't read anything in
cursive styles anymore. Everything has to be in block letters. They can
read newspaper serials but not old novels. The wood-block edition of
the Sonohachi texts was printed toward the middle of the last century,
and O-han wasn't born till the end of the century. It's no fault of hers
that she can't read them. A girl born in the city today knows nothing
of wells, and she has no idea what it is like to see a moon at dawn over
a well pole. She can talk about 'subtle thoughts grown quite beyond
the well frame,' but it doesn't interest her, and as for 'a litter that has
come for one who is all too lovely'—she has no notion what the expression even means. And so she gets bored. Why, after all, should she be
interested in something she doesn't understand? You or I would be
willing to pay any price for an old text of *Poems from the Five Peri-
ods,** because the blocks were made from the handwriting of Kikaku
himself, but that is because we're haiku fanciers of the old school. The
new school can only read eight-point print, and has no need for wood-
block editions. It's only from habit that the geisha goes on playing the
samisen. And so it is with 'haiku poets.' All they have managed to preserve is the word 'haiku' itself. I'm not talking about right and wrong.
I'm only wondering how much longer we can carry on with these old
tastes of ours. Last night it finally happened. We finally got around to
having a strike in my company. It should be in the evening papers.
The place has as good as closed down, and so I took advantage of the
unexpected luck to call in the maestro and go over two or three pieces."

Yō-san telephoned to a wine merchant in Tameike and kept me for
dinner. As I boarded the streetcar for home, I somehow joined his
words to a story by Henri de Régnier, *Marceline, ou La Punition fan-
tastique,* which I had been reading three or four days before. It is about
a man angry and sad at his inability to understand his wife's tastes. He
loves Italy and especially Venice, and he chooses it for their honey-

* A collection of poetry by Kikaku, one of Bashō's disciples.

moon; but his wife is not interested. He pays a high price for some delicate old glass puppets, which he finds in a curio shop, and takes them back to the old family home in France. The two gradually drift apart. A certain doctor, scorned by his fellows but with a strange fascination for women, tells her that her husband is suffering from a mental illness, and she thereafter treats him like a lunatic. One day the husband returns to find the old house, in the family for generations, so changed that it might have been torn down and built over. All of the old furniture to which he is so attached has been changed for the gaudy modern things to be seen in Paris furniture stores. In his rage, he flails about him and falls into a trance.

Home from my talk with Yō-san, I crawled inside a mosquito net and read the last half of the story. The puppets bought in Venice have in his absence been tossed into a storeroom, but they come out in the moonlight and begin talking to him. Uncertain whether he is awake or asleep, the excited hero begins to feel that he may indeed be mad, as people have been telling him he is. And so ends the story.

As I reached through the net to turn out the light, I heard a bell in the distance. It signaled two in the morning. I lay sleepless, thinking of many things, and outside in the garden, as in the small hours of all the nights through the deepening autumn, and especially on nights after rains, the crickets sang and sang. I wanted only to get to sleep, but I drifted deeper into my thoughts. They were endless, rambling thoughts, and in the morning I would be able to remember none of them.

In the years that followed I was kept busy staying well through the heat and the cold. I felt no urge to take up the samisen again, and no particular urge to write. Even feelings of grief and anger at the senselessness of my existence seemed to grow fewer over the years.

I am sometimes reminded of a poem by Fernand Gregh:*

> J'ai trop pleuré jadis pour des légères!
> Mes Douleurs aujourd'hui me sont étrangères....
> Elles ont beau parler à mots mystérieux....
> Et m'appeler dans l'ombre leurs voix légères;
> Pour elles je n'ai plus de larmes dans les yeux.

* 1873–1960. The French text is in the original with Kafū's Japanese translation, and the English translation is my own. A slightly different version of Kafū's translation is to be found in his *Coral Anthology*.

Mes Douleurs aujourd'hui me sont des inconnues;
Passantes du chemin qu'on eût peut-être aimées,
Mais qu'on n'attendait plus quand elles sont venues,
Et qui s'en va là-bas comme des inconnues,
Parce qu'il est trop tard, les âmes sont fermées.

I have wept too much over trivial things!
Today My Sorrows are foreign to me. . . .
Let them speak to me in mysterious words. . . .
Let them call from the shadows with their trivial voices.
There are no more tears in my eyes for them.

Today My Sorrows are to me as strangers,
Passers in the street whom one might have loved,
But whom, when they come, one no longer awaits,
And who pass on, still strangers,
For it is too late, hearts have closed.

It is true. Passions have vanished, the heart has dried up. Cries of alarm in the thoughtful world, warning us about the state of affairs with us since the European War, are to me as the flute of the old candy-seller in the street. My greatest pleasure, eating and sleeping and eating again these last few years, has been that the summers have not been too hot and the winters have not been too cold. It is better than laying your head on the lap of a beauty, just being able to digest your food and sleep a dreamless sleep. Once it came to me that I should put things in order, and so avoid complications after my death; and I sold my house and library. As the poem by Mao K'un* in the *Ming Anthology* has it:

Green moss upon the wall, dust on the earthen pots.
In the dawn, house and park are my western neighbor's.
How can I look at the willow before the gate?
Perhaps we will meet tomorrow—but we meet as strangers.

Some day I must write a piece "On Selling My House."†

* 1512–1601.
† It is of some interest that Kafū has slightly misquoted three poems in this essay: that by Tu Hsün-ho, p. 257; the reference to the woman of Shang, by Tu Mu, p. 263; and Chikufujin's elegy to Ranshū, p. 269. Only the second mistake changes the sense in any important way. The correct version, and not Kafū's, has been followed here.

A Strange Tale from East of the River

A Strange Tale from East of the River was written
late in 1936, and serialized in the *Asahi* and published
as a book in 1937. For a discussion, see pp. 148–49.

I almost never go to see a moving picture.

If vague memories are to be trusted, it was toward the end of the
last century that I saw, at a Kanda theater, a moving picture of a San
Francisco street scene. I suppose it must have been about then, too,
that the expression "moving picture" was invented. Today it has almost been discarded. The expression one has learned first comes most
easily, however, and I shall here continue to use the old, discarded one.

A young literary acquaintance, telling me one day shortly after the
earthquake that I had fallen behind the times, dragged me off to a
moving picture in Tameike. It was a moving picture much admired at
the time, and it turned out to be an adaptation of a Maupassant story.
I might better have read the original.

Yet young and old delight in moving pictures and make them the
subject of daily conversation, and even a person like me sometimes
feels inclined to wonder what the conversation might be about. I always make it a special point, therefore, to look at billboards when I
pass moving-picture houses. One can tell from the billboards, without
seeing the pictures themselves, what the general plots are, and what
delights people so.

Asakusa is the part of town where one can see the most moving-
picture billboards at a single viewing. One can see all the several varieties, and compare their virtues and defects. When I am in the vicinity
of Asakusa or Shitaya, I always remember to go to the park and have
a walk around the lake.

It was on a late-summer evening when the wind was getting chilly.
I had looked at all the billboards and was walking from the edge of
the park toward Senzoku. Kototoi Bridge was to the right, Iriya to

the left. Which way should I go, I asked myself. Just then a man, of forty or so, in shabby Occidental clothes, came up beside me.

"How about it? I can introduce you to a good one."

"No, thank you." I walked a little faster.

"You'll never have another chance like this one, Mister. She's a real witch."

"I'm going to the Yoshiwara. Thanks anyway."

I am not quite sure what you would have called him—a pimp, a lady's attendant? In any case, to shake off my tempter, I said quite at random that I was going to the Yoshiwara, and the remark settled the direction of my walk. I remembered as I walked north that I knew a secondhand bookstore below the embankment.

It was on a dark alley leading from the point where the Sanya Canal, having joined the underground stream, flows toward the gate of the Yoshiwara. There were buildings on only one side of the street, and the backs of houses rose above the embankment on the far side of the canal. On the near side wholesale dealers in pipes and tiles and lumber and adobe and the like presented somewhat wider fronts among the ordinary houses. As the canal gradually narrowed, the houses became smaller and smaller, and at night the street was lighted only by the bridges. Where both canal and bridges disappeared, passersby disappeared too. The only lights to be seen fairly late at night were those of the tobacconist and the secondhand bookseller.

I did not know the name of the store, but I knew most of the wares piled inside it. If I came upon the first issue of *Literary Club* or one of the literary supplements to the *Yamato Shimbun* it had to be classified as an unusual find.*

That I should go out of the way all the same to visit the place was not because of the wares but because of the bookseller himself and the flavor of that alley outside the licensed quarter.

He was a diminutive old man with his head shaven smooth. He would have been in his sixties, perhaps even older. His face, his manner, his speech, his dress—they all had in them something of the Edo lowlands, to me rarer and more to be admired than any old book. Before the earthquake you would come upon one or two such old men, children of plebeian Edo, in the dressing rooms of all the theaters and

---

* *Literary Club* (*Bungei Kurabu*) was a literary monthly first published in 1895; the *Yamato Shimbun* was a daily specializing in news of the entertainments.

variety halls. There were, for instance, old Tamé, in attendance on Kikugorō, and Ichizō, who worked for Sadanji; but they are with us no more.

Whenever I opened the glass door, the old man would be kneeling there at the door to the backroom, his round shoulders inclined slightly toward the front of the shop, reading something through spectacles that seemed about to slip from his nose. Since it was always at seven or eight in the evening that I came, his position and his posture were always the same. At the sound of the door, his head, still bowed, would shoot around to see who had come in.

"Good evening." He would then take off his glasses, half raise himself from the floor, beat the dust off a cushion, push it toward me from a sort of crawling position, and make his formal greetings. His words and his manner were always exactly the same.

"As usual, I have nothing at all worth showing you. But wait. I did have the *Hōtan Gazette* somewhere. Not all of it, but then——"

"Tamenaga Shunkō's magazine?"*

"That's right. I did have the first issue somewhere. You might be interested in looking at it. Now where do you suppose I put it?" He took several fascicles from a heap by the wall, and, beating away the dust, pushed them toward me.

"Registered in 1879," I said, taking them up. "It makes you feel young again, reading magazines from those days. I wish I could find a complete run of Robun's *Chimpō*."

"I do see it sometimes, but only an issue here and an issue there. Do you have the *Kagetsu Shinshi*?"†

"Yes."

The door slid open, and the bookseller and I looked around together. The newcomer was also in his sixties, bald and hollow-cheeked and shabby. He laid a dirty kerchief-wrapped parcel on a heap of books.

"Damn these automobiles. They almost got me today."

---

* Tamenaga Shunkō, a disciple of Shunsui, died in 1889, probably in his late seventies. The *Hōtan Zasshi* (*Gazette of Fragrant Tales*) appeared from 1878 to 1884. The suggestion here that the first issue came out in 1879 would seem to be in error.

† A literary magazine published three times monthly, and later semimonthly and monthly, from 1877 to 1884. The *Robun Chimpō* (*Strange Tidings from Robun*) was a magazine edited by Kanagaki Robun from 1877 to 1879.

"Cheap and reliable and convenient, they say. But that's not the way it works. Did you get hurt?"

"No. But this got broken, and saved me." He showed an amulet around his neck. "A taxi ran into a bus ahead of me. I start shaking all over again, just thinking about it. Here. Look at this. I picked it up at the Hatogaya fair. They don't make things this good any more. I don't have a customer in mind just at the moment, but when I saw it, I felt like being a little extravagant."

Baldhead undid his kerchief and took out an unlined woman's kimono and a singlet, its sleeves of a different material from the body. The kimono had a small printed pattern on a gray ground, and the sleeves of the singlet were a bit unusual too. Neither was particularly old, however. I would have judged them to be from about the time of the Restoration.

Then it occurred to me that the singlet might be good for mounting Ukiyoe paintings, or lining one of the book boxes so popular these days, or covering Edo fascicles. I had the bookseller wrap it up with the old magazines.

I thought I would take a bus down Nihonzutsumi toward Asakusa, and waited by the stop at the main Yoshiwara gate. The cab drivers were a nuisance, however, and I started back the way I had come, choosing alleys where there were neither taxis nor streetcars. Soon I could see the lights of Kototoi Bridge through the trees. Having heard that the park along the river was dangerous, I did not go as far as the bank, but, proceeding along a brightly lighted path, sat down on the chain stretched beside it.

On my way to Asakusa I had bought bread and canned goods, which I had in a kerchief. I tried wrapping them up with the old magazines and the singlet, but the kerchief was a trifle small, and hard things and soft things did not go well together. I concluded that it would be best to put the cans in the pockets of my overcoat and wrap the rest in one bundle. I spread the kerchief on the lawn and was contemplating the possibilities.

"What do you think you're doing?" To the rattling of a saber a policeman appeared. He stretched out his long arms and took me by the shoulders.

Silently I retied my bundle and got up. Not one to be kept waiting, he prodded my elbow and ordered me ahead.

Soon the path came out at Kototoi Bridge. He led me across the avenue and handed me over to a policeman at a box, and headed busily off again.

The second policeman began his interrogation.

"Where are you going at this hour of the night?"

"I've been over there."

"Over where?"

"By the canal."

"What do you mean, the canal?"

"The canal that is known as the Sanya Canal, at the foot of Matchi Hill."

"What's your name?"

"Oe Tadasu." The policeman took out his notebook. "You write Tadasu the way it is in the Analects. 'Having unified and rectified the world.' Remember? 'Rectified'—that's the character."

He glowered, ordering me silent. Then he reached and unbuttoned my overcoat.

"No mark," he said, looking inside my suit coat.

"What sort of mark are you looking for?" I laid down my bundle and opened my vest.

"Where do you live?"

"Number 6 Otansumachi 1-chōme, Azabu."

"What do you do?"

"Nothing at all."

"Unemployed? How old are you?"

"I was born in the Year of the Hare, Lesser Earth Sign."

"I asked how old you are."

"Hare, Lesser Earth. 1879." I thought I would say no more, but silence seemed risky. "Fifty-seven years old."

"Pretty young for your age, aren't you?"

I giggled.

"What did you say your name was?"

"Oe Tadasu."

"How many in your family?"

"Three." As a matter of fact I am a bachelor, but I knew from experience that if I told the truth I would come under yet stronger suspicion.

"Your wife and who else?" The policeman took the charitable view.

"The wife and the old woman."

"How old's your wife?"

I had to think for a minute, but then I remembered a woman with whom I had kept company some four or five years before. "Thirty. Born July 14, Year of the Horse, Greater Fire Sign."

I thought if asked her name I would give the name of a woman in a story I was then writing, but the policeman said nothing more. He felt the pockets of my coat and overcoat.

"What's this?"

"Pipe and glasses."

"This?"

"A can."

"This will be your wallet. Take it out."

"There's money in it."

"How much?"

"Twenty or thirty yen, I'd imagine."

He laid it on the telephone stand without looking inside. "What's in that bundle? Come in and open it up."

I did as told. There was no trouble with the old magazines and the bread, but the moment one of the voluptuous sleeves came in sight, the manner of the policeman changed.

"That's a funny thing to be carrying around."

I giggled again.

"A woman's." He took it between his fingers and held it to the light, and glared at me.

"Where'd you get it?"

"I got it from a secondhand dealer."

"How'd you get it?"

"I put down money for it."

"Where was this?"

"By the Yoshiwara gate."

"How much did you pay for it?"

"Three yen and seventy sen."

The policeman threw the singlet down on the table and stared silently at me. Thinking that I was about to be taken to the station and that I would spend the night in a cage, I no longer felt quite so inclined to poke fun at him. I stared back. In silence, he began going through my wallet. In it were an insurance receipt that I had forgotten about, holes worn through at the folds, an excerpt from my family register that I had needed on some occasion or other, my seal, and a certificate of its validity. He unfolded each document in silence, and held the seal to the light. All of this took some time. Still in the doorway, I looked out.

At the police box, the street from Asakusa split into two branches, one fork leading to Minami Senjū, the other to Shirahige Bridge. Intersecting the fork, the avenue from behind Asakusa Park led to Kototoi Bridge and beyond. Traffic was heavy, late though the hour was. For some reason, however, not a single pedestrian had stopped to witness my interrogation. A woman who appeared to be the proprietress of the haberdashery across the way and a young boy, apparently a clerk in her shop, were looking in my direction, but they did not seem especially interested. Presently they began making preparations to close for the night.

"All right. You can put them away."

"Not that I have much need for them," I muttered, replacing the contents of the wallet and retying the kerchief. "Will there be anything more?"

"No."

"You've gone to a great deal of trouble." I lit a gold-tipped Westminster and blew smoke into the box as if to tell him that he could at least have a smell of it. Then I started off, as my feet led me, in the direction of Kototoi Bridge. It occurred to me afterward that if I had not had the family register and the certified seal, I would indeed have spent the night in a cage. Old clothes are strange and ominous objects. That singlet came near being my damnation.

II

I had plans for a novel to be entitled *Whereabouts Unknown*. I had a certain amount of confidence. I thought that if and when I got around to writing it, this new novel would not be among my worst efforts.

The hero's name was Taneda Jumpei. He was in his fifties, a teacher in a private middle school. Several years after the death of his beloved first wife he had taken a second, Mitsuko.

Mitsuko had worked as a maid for the wife of a certain well-known politician. Deceived by the politician, she had become pregnant. The family asked a functionary who managed its affairs, one Endō, to do what had to be done. The conditions were that if Mitsuko was safely delivered of a child, fifty yen a month would be provided toward his support for twenty years. The registration of the child was to indicate no relationship to the father's family. If Mitsuko married, she would be provided with a generous dowry.

Mitsuko was taken into Endō's house and bore a son; and then, before two months had elapsed, she became the second wife of Taneda Jumpei, teacher of English, through the good offices of Endō. At the time, Mitsuko was eighteen, Taneda twenty-nine.

With middle age approaching, Taneda had become a mere shadow of a man. He lived on a meager salary, quite without hope now that his wife was gone. He allowed money and his friend Endō to lure him into a second marriage. The child being so young, nothing had been done about registering it, and Endō entered both mother and child in Taneda's register. If one looked at the register, then, it appeared that Taneda and Mitsuko had lived in common-law marriage, and had formalized the relationship only upon the birth of their first son.

A daughter was born two years later, and then another son.

When Tametoshi, ostensibly Taneda's elder son but actually the baby Mitsuko had brought with her, reached twenty, the money for his education ceased to come. The specified period had elapsed, and the boy's father had died the year before, and his wife soon after him.

As the girl, Yoshiko, and the second son, Tameaki, grew up, expenses increased and increased. Taneda had to take on work at two and three night schools.

Tametoshi, the older boy, became an athlete in a private university and went abroad. The girl became a movie star as soon as she was out of high school.

Mitsuko, who had had a pretty round face at the time of the marriage, was now a fat old woman. Absorbed in the affairs of a certain religious sect, she was elected to its board of governors.

Taneda's house was at times a sort of prayer hall, at times a meeting place for actresses, at times an athletic field. It was so noisy that mice had quite deserted the kitchen.

Taneda had always been a shy, reserved man. As he grew older he found the noise and the confusion scarcely bearable. He disliked everything his wife and children liked. He made a special effort not to think about his domestic affairs. The single revenge the weakling father had was to look upon them all with a cold, contemptuous eye.

He reached fifty, and that spring he retired. On the day he received his retirement allowance, he disappeared.

Earlier, on a streetcar, he had chanced to meet a girl named Sumiko, who had once worked in his house as a maid. He learned that she was now working in a bar at Komagata, near Asakusa. He had visited the place once or twice, and had a drink each time.

On the night he set out with his retirement allowance in his pocket, he went for the first time to Sumiko's room, and, telling her what had happened, spent the night there.

I did not know what I would do with my story thereafter.

The family would ask the police to search. Taneda would be called in and reprimanded. Pleasures learned late in life, however, have been likened to rain late in the afternoon; and I could submit him to whatever disasters I chose.

I thought about the path to his downfall, and his feelings at various stages along the way: his discomfiture when he was taken in by the detective, and his confusion and humiliation when he was handed over to his wife and children, and so on. On my way back from having bought an old singlet in a Sanya alley, I had been apprehended by a policeman and admonished at a police box. There could be no better material than this for describing the feelings of poor Taneda.

The things that most interest me when I write a novel are the choice and description of background. I have from time to time fallen into the error of emphasizing background at the expense of characterization.

Wishing to use for Taneda's hideout a once-famous place that had quite lost its character in the rebuilding of the city, I thought of Honjo or Fukagawa or the outskirts of Asakusa perhaps, or a back alley in the regions beyond, open countryside until but a few years before.

I was familiar, from my walks, with Sunamachi, Kameido, Komatsugawa, and Terajima, but each time I tried to take up my pen I felt that my observations had been inadequate. In the early years of this century I once wrote a story about a prostitute of the Suzaki quarter; and a friend, upon reading it, said: "It is inexcusable, if you are going to write about Suzaki, not to write about August and September, when the typhoons and the tidal waves come up. Why, the tower of the very building you wrote about, sir, has blown over more than once." In background description, one must pay close attention to weather and season. The revered Lafcadio Hearn did so most diligently in his *Chita* and *Youma*.

It was an evening late in June. Although the summer rains were not yet over, the sky had been clear since morning, and was bright even after dinner. When I had finished eating, I set out for the far side of the city, Kameido or Senjū perhaps, wherever my whims might carry me. I first took a streetcar to Asakusa, where, at just the right moment, a bus was leaving for Tamanoi beyond the river.

The bus turned left on the avenue beyond Azuma Bridge, passed the Akiba Shrine, and, after a time, stopped at a railroad track. Numbers of bicycles and taxis were lined up on both sides, waiting for a slow freight train to go by. There were surprisingly few pedestrians. Clusters of children were playing in the shabby streets. I got off at the avenue that runs east from Shirahige Bridge to Kameido. The low lines of houses were broken by an occasional weed-grown lot, and every street looked very much like every other street. Vaguely depressed, I wondered where they all led.

Perhaps, I thought, a back street hereabouts might be a good place for the hero of my novel to hide after abandoning his family. With the busy Tamanoi Licensed Quarter near by, the neighborhood would be appropriate for the denouement I had in mind. I walked on for a hundred yards or so, and tried a side street too narrow for bicycles to pass if the riders happened to have bundles under their arms. Every five or six steps there was a turn. Narrow little alley though it was, however, the neat gates of houses for rent lined it on both sides, and men and women in foreign dress walked by singly and in pairs, on their way home from work. The dogs all had collars and tags, and on the whole seemed well enough cared for. Soon I was at the Tamanoi Station of the Tōbu Railway.

To the left and right of the track were the grounds, heavily shaded, of what appeared to be country villas. All the way from Azuma Bridge there had been no other such growth of old trees. They appeared to have gone long untended, and the bamboo thickets, bent low under the weight of creepers, and the moonflowers blooming in the hedge by the canal formed an elegant composition to make one stop and gaze for a moment.

Reminded that the district around the Shirahige Shrine was known in the old days as Terajima Village, I might once have thought first of the country villa of Kikugorō, the Kabuki actor. Now, at the sight of such a garden in such a place, I was pulled back to graceful artistic pursuits of another day.

Beside the tracks, a wide expanse of native grass, advertised as being for sale or rent, stretched on to an embankment and a steel bridge, the remains of what had until a year or so before been the Keisei Electric. Above the stone steps, already crumbling, the platform of the old Tamanoi Station was overgrown with weeds. It looked very much like a ruined castle.

I climbed through the summer grass to the embankment, from which I had a clear view down over the road I had just taken, over the vacant lots and the newly built houses. The other side of the embankment was a jumble of tin-roofed huts, quite without order, stretching on interminably. The chimney of a public bathhouse rose from the jumble, and at its tip was a half moon. Although the flush of evening still lay across the sky opposite, the moon had taken on the color of night. Among the tin roofs, neon lamps were shining. I could hear radios.

I sat on a stone until it was quite dark. Lights were by now shining in the windows below the embankment, and nothing was hidden in the miserable second-floor rooms. Following a path through the grass, I made my way down. Unexpectedly, I was on the prosperous back street that cuts diagonally across the Tamanoi Licensed Quarter. At entrances to the alleyways among the jammed-in shops there were lamps bearing various legends: Thoroughfare, Safe Transit, Shortcut to Keisei Bus, or perhaps Maiden Lane or Busy Boulevard.

After walking about for a time, I bought a package of cigarettes at a corner shop with a postbox before it. I was pocketing my change when someone shouted: "It's going to rain!" A man in a white smock scurried by, and took shelter in a shop across the way. Next came a woman in an apron, and after her several flustered strollers. An air of expectancy fell over the street. In a sudden gust of wind a reed blind fell clattering to the ground. Paper and rubbish skated down the street like ghosts. A sharp flash of lightning. Then, to a somewhat sluggish clap of thunder, great drops of rain. The sky, so beautiful in the evening, had not prepared us for this.

I had for some years been in the habit of carrying an umbrella whenever I left home; and, however beautiful a day it might be, this was the rainy season. I was therefore not unprepared. I had calmly opened my umbrella and was setting off to inspect the streets and the sky when someone called me from behind. "Let me walk with you. You won't mind—just over to there." A white neck darted under the umbrella.

The high Japanese-style chignon—one knew from the smell of oil that it was freshly dressed—was tied up in long silver threads. I remembered that I had passed a hairdresser's shop with its glass doors open.

It would be a pity to have the silver threads disarranged in the storm. I held out my umbrella to her. "I don't matter myself." My own foreign clothes hardly seemed worth worrying about.

As a matter of fact, the lights from the rows of shops were bright, and even I was a bit bashful about sharing a cozy umbrella with her.

"You don't mind? Just over to there." She took the umbrella, and with the other hand hitched up the skirt of her kimono.

III

There was another flash of lightning and a clap of thunder. "Oh, dear." She turned with a show of surprise and reached for my hand. I was walking a pace behind her. "Come along, now," she said companionably.

"No, go ahead. I'll be following you."

At each alleyway she turned to see that I was not lost. She crossed the canal over a little bridge, and stopped before one of a row of houses shielded by reed awnings.

"You really are wet." She closed the umbrella. Paying no attention to herself, she began slapping the rain from my coat.

"This is your house?"

"Come in. I'll brush you off."

"Don't worry. Foreign clothes don't matter."

"I said I'd brush you off. I know how to be polite, though you might not guess it."

"In what way do you intend to be polite?"

"I keep telling you to come in, don't I?"

The thunder seemed farther off, but the rain only beat down harder, almost like a shower of pebbles. It sent up such a spray even under the awning that I had little margin for refusing her invitation.

The back of the room was screened off by a coarse lattice and a curtain of ribbons from which hung little bells. She wiped her bare feet as I sat below the curtain to untie my shoes. Without bothering to lower her hitched-up skirt, she turned on the light beyond.

"There's no one else here. Come in."

"You're by yourself?"

"There was someone till last night. She moved."

"You manage the house?"

"No, the owner has another place. You know the Tamanoi Variety Hall? He lives behind it. He comes every night at about midnight to check the accounts."

"You have an easy time of it then." I took my place by the long charcoal brazier and watched her make tea, one knee drawn to her breast.

She would be twenty-three or twenty-four. Her features were good. The skin on the round face with its straight, clean nose was dulled from cosmetics, but the outlines of the newly-dressed hair were still very young. The blackish eyes were clear, and the red of her lips and gums showed that her health was not yet seriously damaged.

"Is this well water or tap water?" I asked casually before tasting the tea. If it was well water, I would only pretend to drink. The fact was that I was much less afraid of venereal diseases than of infectious diseases like typhoid fever. Already an old man, and a spiritual wreck before a physical wreck, I worried little about slow, creeping maladies.

"Do you want to wash your hands? The tap is over there." Her manner was light and gay.

"Later."

"Take off your coat, at least. See how wet it is."

"Listen to the rain."

"I hate lightning, much worse than thunder. At this rate I won't be able to go to the bath. You still have time, don't you? I'll just wash my face and make myself up a bit."

She wiped oil from her forehead with a piece of paper, screwing her lips all the while, and went to the wash basin outside the blind. I could see her beyond the ribbons, bowing to wash her face, her kimono pulled over her shoulders. The shoulders and breasts were whiter than the face, and one would have guessed that she had never had a child.

"Here I sit like the husband and master. Dresser, cupboard, everything I need for housekeeping."

"Open the cupboard. You should find a potato or so in it."

"You keep the place in very good order. I'm filled with admiration."

"Every morning I do the housecleaning. I'm a very good housekeeper, even in this business."

"Have you been here long?"

"A year. A year and just a little over."

"This won't be your first place, will it? Have you ever been a geisha?"

Whether she could not hear because she was refilling the basin, or whether she was pretending not to hear, she did not answer. Her kimono still pulled low, she knelt before the mirror, pushed stray hairs up into the chignon, and began powdering her shoulders.

"Where else have you worked? You have to tell me at least that much."

"Well, not in Tokyo."

"Near Tokyo?"

"No. Far away."

"Manchuria?"

"I was in Utsunomiya. All my kimonos are from when I was in Utsunomiya. There, that will do. You needn't ask any more." She stood up and changed to an unlined summer kimono with a pattern printed low on the skirt—it had been draped over the rack beside her. The undersash, in fine reddish stripes, was knotted in front, and the heaviness of the knot seemed to balance the almost too large silver-threaded chignon. At that moment, she was to me the courtesan of thirty years before. Putting the final touches on her dress, she sat beside me, and took a cigarette from the package on the table.

She lighted one and handed it to me. "You can pay whatever you like. Just for congratulations, now that we are here."

I was not unfamiliar with the rules governing the sport in these parts.

"Fifty sen, is it, for the tea?"

"If you're following the rules." She laughed, and left her palm stretched toward me.

"Well, suppose we make it an hour."

"I'm sorry. It seems wrong. It really does."

"But you can pay me back." Taking her hand and pulling her toward me, I whispered my request in her ear.

"I will not!" She glared at me, and gave me a rap on the shoulder. "Be sensible, won't you!"

Those who have read the stories of Tamenaga Shunsui will remember how from time to time Shunsui breaks the narrative to apologize for himself or his characters. Thus a girl in love for the first time forgets all demureness and thrusts herself upon the man whom her heart demands, and Shunsui warns the reader that her acts and words in such circumstances are not grounds for calling her wanton—the cloistered damsel, when she opens her heart, can be voluptuous as not even a geisha can. Or a woman of the licensed quarters encounters a friend from her youth, and Shunsui reminds us that at such times the professional woman can blush and squirm like a maiden. This fact is affirmed by everyone whose experience in such matters is rich, and the reader is not to charge the author with inadequate observation.

After the manner of Shunsui, I should like to make a remark or two here. The reader may feel that the woman was just a little too familiar when she met me there by the road. I merely record the facts of our meeting, however, and add no coloring, no shaping or contriving. Inasmuch as the affair had its beginning in a sudden thunder shower, moreover, certain readers may be smiling at me for having used a well-worn device. Precisely because I am mindful of the possibility, I have refrained from giving the incident another setting. Put in motion by an evening shower, it seemed to me interesting for the very reason that it was so much in the old tradition. Indeed I began this book because I wanted to tell of it.

There are said to be some seven or eight hundred women in the Tamanoi Quarter, and perhaps one in ten still does her hair in the old style. The rest wear Japanese dress of the sort waitresses affect, or Western dress such as dancers might choose. The fact that the woman who took me in from the rain belonged to the old-style minority made me think the tired old device appropriate. I cannot bring myself to do injury to what happened.

Still it rained.

At first the rain had been so fierce that one had to raise one's voice. Now the wind against the door and the thunder had died away, and there remained only the rain striking the zinc roof and dripping from the eaves. For some time I had heard neither voices nor footsteps outside. Then suddenly there was a shriek and a clattering of sandals.

"Terrible, Kii-chan, terrible. Mudfish all over the place."

The woman looked out through the ribbons toward the earth-floored hallway.

"We'll be all right. When the canal overflows, the water comes to here."

"It seems to be letting up a little."

"But when it rains in the evening, business is no good even if it clears later on. Stay awhile. I'm going to have something to eat."

She opened the cupboard, took out a saucer heaped with pickled radish, a bowl, and a little aluminum saucepan, and, sniffing at the contents, put the saucepan on the charcoal embers. I looked to see what was inside. Stewed sweet potatoes.

"I forgot. I have something good." Waiting for a streetcar, I had bought some Asakusa laver.

"A present for your wife?"

"I'm not married. What I eat I have to go out and buy."

"An apartment, then, and a lady with it?" She giggled.

"Do you think I'd be out wandering around at this time of the night? I'd be on my way home, rain and thunder and all."

"That's true." Her expression acknowledged that my defense was completely reasonable. She took the lid from the saucepan, already warm. "Have some?"

"I've eaten."

"Well, look the other way, then."

"You do your own cooking?"

"They bring it from the other house at noon and at midnight."

"Shall I put more water in the tea? This is lukewarm."

"Here I am letting the tea get cold. But listen. It's nice to have some-one to talk to while you eat, isn't it?"

"It's no fun bolting it down by yourself."

"No fun at all. You really are single then? That's very sad."

"You are sorry for me?"

"But don't worry. I'll find you someone."

She gaily made her way through two bowls of rice, gave the chop-sticks a clattering rinse in the bowl, and pushed the utensils into the cupboard. Her chin moved a little as she held back a belch from the pickled radish.

Outside I began to hear footsteps and women's voices. "Well, come right on in. *Do* come in."

"It seems to have stopped," I said. "I'll come again before long."

"Be sure you do. I'm here in the daytime too." She hurried around to help me into my coat, and she pressed her face toward mine over my shoulder. "Be very sure you do."

"What's the name of the house?"

"I'll give you a card."

While I was putting on my shoes, she rummaged through a heap below the little window and handed me a card in the shape of a samisen plectrum: Yukiko, care of Andō Masa, Section 2, 61 Terajimachō 7-chōme.

"Good-bye."

"Be sure you go straight home."

IV.   A Chapter from *Whereabouts Unknown*

Leaning against the railing halfway across Azuma Bridge, Taneda Jumpei looked up at the clock on the Matsuya Department Store and surveyed the stream of people approaching from Asakusa. He was waiting for Sumiko, who would be coming this roundabout way once her establishment had closed for the night.

It was too late for buses and streetcars, but, in the sudden heat of these last few days, men were out taking the cool of evening in their shirtsleeves, and there were women with bundles under their arms, waitresses or barmaids, probably. Taneda meant to go with Sumiko to her room, there to deliberate his future. He had not thought what she might suggest. Indeed he had not had the margin for thinking. He was consumed with anger at having sacrificed twenty years of his life to his family.

"I've kept you waiting." Sumiko came running up, earlier than he would have expected. "I always go across on Komagata Bridge. But Kaneko was with me. She's a terrible gossip."

"There don't seem to be any more streetcars."

"We could walk. It's only three streetcar stops. But let's get a cab from over there."

"I hope there's a vacant room."

"If there isn't, you can spend a night or so in my room."

"Will it be all right?"

"Will what be all right?"

"It was in the papers, wasn't it? About a pair that got picked up in a raid on a rooming house."

"It all depends on the house. I'm sure of that. You can do anything where I live. Why, the women on both sides of me and across the hall are all bar girls, or else they have someone keeping them. I haven't tried to count the men running in and out of the room next door."

Before they had crossed the bridge, they succeeded in hailing a cab that agreed to take them to the Akiba Shrine for thirty sen.

"It's all changed completely. How far does the streetcar track go?"

"Mukōjima—the Akiba Shrine. The bus goes on to Tamanoi."

"Tamanoi—was Tamanoi in this direction?"

"You should know."

"I've been there only once, and then just to have a look at the place. Five or six years ago."

"It's very lively. Night stalls, and shows in the vacant lots, and all sorts of things."

"Oh?" Taneda was gazing at the houses that lined the street. The cab was already at the Akiba Shrine.

"This will be fine." Sumiko pushed the door open and paid the driver. "Let's go in from over there. There's a police box on this side."

They turned along the stone fence of the shrine. On one side was a blind alley lined by the lights of the pleasure quarter. In a corner of a suddenly dark lot was a lighted sign: "Azuma Apartments." It showed the front of a square concrete building. Sumiko went in and put away her sandals in a box marked with her room number.

Taneda started to follow suit, but she stopped him. "Take them upstairs with you. They'll attract attention if you leave them here." She gave him her slippers and went upstairs with his sandals in her hand.

From outside, the building had appeared to be in the Occidental style, but the inside was Japanese, and very flimsy. In a corner at the head of the creaking stairs was a stove, where a woman in a chemise, her bobbed hair in disorder, was heating water.

"Good evening," said Sumiko lightly, unlocking the second door from the end on the right.

It was a medium-sized room with dirty floor-matting. In one corner was a chest of drawers, and opposite it a closet. On the third wall hung a summer kimono and a sheer nightgown.

"It will be cooler here," said Sumiko, opening a window in which were hanging underwear and socks, and laying out a cushion for him.

"It must be pleasant living alone. It makes marriage seem like the worst sort of foolishness."

"My family keeps pestering me to come home. But it wouldn't do. Not any more."

"I only wish I had realized it a little sooner. Now it's too late." Taneda looked out at the sky, past the drying underwear. "Maybe you'd better ask if there's an empty room."

Sumiko went out with a teakettle in her hand. He heard women's voices, and shortly she was back.

"The room across the way at the other end of the hall is empty. But she says the woman who runs the place isn't in tonight."

"So I don't suppose we'll be able to take it?"

"You can stay here a night or two. If you don't mind, I don't."

"Really?" Taneda's eyes were wide. "Of course it's all right with me."

"Maybe I can go to Kimi's next door. If her man isn't there."

"You don't have anyone coming here?"

"Not now. It'll be all right. But you aren't to think I'm trying to tempt you."

Taneda did not answer. It would have been hard to tell from his face whether he wanted to laugh or to cry.

"You have such a nice wife and daughter."

"Oh, I do, do I? No—I may be a little late, but I'm starting over."

"Separate maintenance?"

"Divorce, actually."

"It won't be as easy as all that."

"And so I'm thinking it over. I don't care a great deal what sort of trouble it brings. I'll drop out of sight for a while, and then maybe my chance to break with them will come. Sumiko. I don't want to embarrass you. If we can't get the empty room, suppose I go somewhere else for the night. Maybe I could go have a look at Tamanoi."

"But there's something I want to talk over too. Something I've been wondering what in the world to do about. Suppose we just stay up all night talking."

"At this time of the year it's sunrise before you know it."

"We drove down to Yokohama the other night, and it was already light on the the way back."

"I can imagine the things you'd have to tell about if you wanted to, from before you came to work for us. And then there's all that's happened since."

"I doubt if I could get through it all in one night."

Taneda laughed.

The second floor had been quiet, but now they heard a man and a woman talking. There was a sound of water by the stove again. Sumiko did appear to be prepared to talk the night away. She took off only her obi. Folding it carefully, she laid a pair of socks on it, and put the socks and obi away in the closet. Then she wiped the table and poured tea.

"What do you think got me into this work?" she asked.

"Oh, the pull of the big city, I'd imagine."

"Well, there was that, too. But I didn't like the work my father was in."

"What was it?"

"He liked to think of himself as a sort of Robin Hood." She lowered her voice. "Actually he was an ordinary thug."

v

The rains ended, the hot weather came, and, because the windows were open, sounds not heard in other seasons began to come to my ears. The sound that disturbed me most was that of the radio next door, beyond a thin board fence.

Waiting for the cool of evening, I would turn on the light at my desk; and at exactly that moment it would begin, strident and somehow cracked, and it would not die away until after nine o'clock. I was particularly tormented by political orators with west-country accents, by singers of Naniwabushi, and by readings that made one think of amateur players, broken by snatches of Western music. And the radio alone did not seem to be enough. Morning and night there were phonographs playing popular music. In the summer I would hurry through dinner, or even dine out—I would flee the house at the stroke of six o'clock. Not that there were no radios to listen to even after I went out. The clamor from houses and shops along the way was even more deafening; but it was mixed with the sounds of the city, automobiles and streetcars, and I found less to bother me when I was out walking than when I was alone in my study.

With the end of the rains, the progress of my *Whereabouts Unknown* was interrupted by the neighbors' radio. I had done no work on it for ten days and more. There seemed to be a possibility that I would quite lose interest in it.

Just as in the summer before and the summer before that, I would go out of the house before the sun was down; but the sad fact was that I had nowhere to go. In the days when my old friend, the good Kōjiro, was still alive, I would go to the Ginza every night, and every night I would find more interesting than the night before.* But he is no longer with us, and I have quite wearied of those night streets. And there are reasons why I must be a bit cautious about going to the Ginza. There is a certain ruffian who before the earthquake was a rickshawman for the Shimbashi geisha houses, a man of so evil an aspect, one feels, that a murder or two would mean nothing to him. He loiters around the main Ginza crossing, and when he sees an old acquaintance, pesters him for money.

Once, in front of Kurosawa's, I gave him fifty yen, and the donation proved to have been a mistake. Knowing that his curses would invite a curious crowd if I did not again so favor him, I gave him another fifty. I was not the only one who was buying him drinks, I was sure, and I tricked him one evening into going with me to the police box at the crossing; but the policemen on duty were evidently old friends of his, and they were not prepared to be of service to me. Another day, at the police box at Izumichō—no, the name Izumichō is now gone—I saw him laughing with a policeman. It would appear that the police found him more companionable than the likes of me.

And so I changed the direction of my walks, and went east of the river, and spent the time of the evening with the girl O-yuki, who lived in the house by the ditch.

As I traveled the long route four days and five days running, it came to seem less arduous. As for the changes of cars at Kyōbashi and Asakusa, I became so accustomed to them that my feet moved without guidance from my mind. It became clear that the crowded hours and lines changed with the day of the week, and I learned to avoid them, and so was able to read as I went my way.

I had stopped reading in streetcars ever since I had had to get bifocals, in about 1920; but now, on the long journey to and from Asakusa, I began again. I was not accustomed to reading newspapers or magazines or newly published books, however, and when I first set out for east of the river, I took with me the book my hand fell upon: Yoda Gakkai's *Twenty-four Views of the Sumida.*†

"The long embankment twists and turns. It bends in an arch from

---

* Kōjiro Sōyō, a friend of Kafū's who died in 1935. For more information about him, see the postcript to *A Strange Tale from East of the River,* xvi, 221–49.

† Scholar of Chinese, 1833–1909. The work here quoted is in somewhat eccentric Chinese.

the Mimeguri Inari Shrine on toward the Chōmeiji. Here the cherry blossoms are their thickest. And here, in the age of Kan-ei, Lord Tokugawa released his falcons. Seized with stomach cramps, he drank of the water of the temple well, and was cured. Thereupon he said: 'This is the water of *chōmei,* of longevity.' So it was that the well came to be called the Well of Longevity, and the temple itself the Temple of Longevity. Some years later, again at this spot, Master Bashō wrote a poem praising the snow. It has remained in men's mouths. Ah, how mighty was Lord Tokugawa, his name one to make the earth tremble! That was as it should be. And Master Bashō was a humble man, but one garment to his name, and his fame has come down to us, even as that of Lord Tokugawa. Men are known not by what they are born but by what they do."

It seemed to me that the writings of the old scholar might lend a certain interest to the scenes before me.

Every three days or so, I would have to buy provisions along the way. While I was about it, I would buy a present for the woman. Very soon this practice had a double result.

The woman noted that I bought canned goods, and that there were buttons missing from my shirt and coat; and she concluded that I lived alone in a rented room. There was nothing strange, then, in my coming to see her almost every night. She had no cause to know that I was driven out by a radio, and that not being a devotee of the movies or the theater, I had nowhere else to spend my time. She would have no reason to think I was a person with nowhere to go. So much seemed to be taken for granted. Still, the establishment being what it was, I feared misgivings about my source of income. I casually tried questioning her. It made not the slightest difference, her manner said, as long as the bill for the evening was paid.

"But when they spend they spend, even in a place like this. Once there was a man who stayed one solid month."

"Shouldn't they have called the police?" I looked up surprised. "In the Yoshiwara the very first thing they do is call the police."

"They might here, too, depending on the house."

"And what did he turn out to be? A robber?"

"A dry-goods clerk. Finally the shop owner came after him."

"He'd been collecting bills and decided to run off with the money?"

"Probably."

"Well, I'm all right. I'm all right as far as that goes, anyway." But she looked as if it made little difference one way or another.

I soon came to see that she had determined my occupation for me. The doors upstairs were decorated with Ukiyoe beauties, quarto-size reproductions. I remembered having seen certain of them as magazine illustrations. Utamaro's "Diving Women," Toyokuni's "Women in the Bath," and the like. There was also a print from Hokusai's three-volume erotic work "Virtuous and Felicitous Matches"; but the man had been cut away, leaving only the woman. I explained it to her in some detail. Then, too, after she had seen a customer upstairs, she would sometimes catch a glimpse of me writing in a notebook. She was therefore convinced that I was a writer of "secret" books. She wanted me to bring her a book of my sort when I next came.

I still had the remains of a collection made twenty or thirty years before, and I brought her three or four books as ordered. Thus my occupation was decided, and the nature of my tainted money made clear. The woman's manner became yet freer. She no longer treated me as an ordinary customer.

There are examples enough—and surely no detailed accounting is necessary—to show that women who live in the shade feel neither hostility nor fear, but rather affection and pity, when they encounter men who must shun the public gaze. The Kyoto geisha who helped a man sought by the Shogun's agents, the geisha at the lonely wayside station who did not hesitate to give money to a gambler and smuggler, Tosca who fed the ruined fugitive, Michitose who without the slightest regret gave her love to a desperado.

My only fear was lest, in the vicinity of the quarter or on the Tōbu Railway, I run into a writer or a newspaper reporter. I did not care otherwise when I was encountered or whom I was followed by. I was one who had long before been abandoned by the austere and upright of the world. Since the children of my relatives no longer came to see me, I scarcely had to defer to them. The only people I feared were those who followed the way of the pen. Once, some ten years before, at the time when cafés were springing up all through the Ginza district, I had had a bit too much to drink, and had won the abuse of every newspaper in town. In April 1929, a magazine called *Bungei Shunjū* attacked me as "one whom the world should be spared." Noting such expressions as "seducer of pure maidens," I thought it pos-

sible that the magazine meant to make of me an out-and-out criminal.
It would be difficult to guess what might happen were its reporters
to learn that I was enjoying myself east of the river.

I took great care, of course, at the streetcar stop every night, and
along the main street, lively with night stalls, after I turned into the
Quarter; and even in the alleys, if I came upon numbers of people, I
would look carefully to the right and left, in front and behind. It was
a most useful experience for describing the circumstances of my fugitive hero, Taneda.

VI

I have already said that the house I visited, the house beside the
ditch, was in the Sixties of Terajima 7-chōme. It was toward the
northwest corner of the district, not in a situation that particularly
caught the eye. If one were to seek an analogous spot in the Yoshiwara, it would perhaps be in Kyōmachi off toward the western moat.
And now, since it is something I have recently learned, let me play
the connoisseur and describe the history of the district.

In about 1918 or 1919, when the precincts to the rear of the Asakusa
Temple were cut into for purposes of widening the street, the rows of
archery ranges and dubious drinking houses that had long filled the
place were forced to move. Quite without order or plan, they moved
across the river, to Taishō Avenue, along which the Keisei bus now
runs. Then came a steady succession of similar establishments ex-
pelled from the districts beside the Dempōin Temple and behind the
circus, until virtually every building along Taishō Avenue was a questionable house of some description. A passerby in broad daylight ran
the risk of having his sleeve tugged at or his hat snatched. The police
became stricter, and the houses were forced to move from the main
automobile thoroughfare up into the alleys. Meanwhile, back on the
old Asakusa grounds, the establishments behind the Ryōunkaku
Tower and in the alleys from the northern end of the park into
Senzoku did everything they could to stay where they were; but their
efforts were brought to an end by the earthquake and fire of 1923, and
for a time all of them took refuge in this same district. Some presently
changed their mode of operation, and, upon the reconstruction of the
city, formed a union of geisha houses. The district prospered more and
more, and in the course of time took on the half-permanent aspect it
has today. In the beginning the only link with the rest of the city was

the street across Shirahige Bridge, and until last year, when the Keisei Electric discontinued its service, the liveliest part of the quarter was that near its station.

At about the time of the Reconstruction Festival, in the spring of 1930, a street was put through directly from Azuma Bridge to Terajima. Streetcar tracks were laid as far as the Akiba Shrine, the metropolitan bus route was extended still farther, and a bus garage was put up on the edge of Terajima 7-chōme. Meanwhile the Tōbu Railway built a station in the southwest part of the Quarter, offering transportation from Asakusa until midnight for six sen; and so what had been the front and rear of the Quarter were quite reversed. What had been the most obscure and remote sections now became the easiest of access, and the sections that had been most conspicuous were now at the remote outer edge of things. But such public institutions as the bank, the post office, the bath, the variety hall, the moving-picture theater, and the Tamanoi Inari Shrine remained where they had always been, along Taishō Avenue. On the new street, popularly called the "big little street" or the "redone street," there were rows of taxis and lively night stalls, but there was no police box—there was not even a public latrine. So it is that out-of-the-way districts are caught in the shifting currents of the times. What are we to say then about the fortunes of lone individuals?

Left behind by the times, I seemed to have a bond with the house by the ditch, where I was able to rest, where O-yuki lived. It, too, had been left behind, and now it only brought memories of the first prosperity, when the Quarter was opened. One reached it by turning up an alley off Taishō Avenue, passing the Fushimi Inari Shrine with its dirty banners, and following the canal still farther and deeper. The radios and phonographs on the main street were almost drowned out by the voices of passersby. I was not likely to find a more suitable refuge from the sound of the radio in the summer night.

It seemed to be a rule of the Quarter that from four in the afternoon, when the women took their places at the windows, radios and phonographs were forbidden, and it was also against rules to play the samisen. When a soft rain was falling, the calls of the women to passersby would become more and more infrequent as the evening drew on, and inside the house and out, the humming of mosquitoes would come to the ears, and make one feel, most keenly, the loneliness of the back alley in the unfashionable, out-of-the-way quarter. It was not the humble quarter of the twentieth century; it rather brought the far-off sadness of the past, the sadness one feels in the Kabuki plays of Tsuruya Namboku, for instance.

The figure of O-yuki, her hair always in one of the old styles, and the foulness of the canal, and the humming of the mosquitoes—all of these stirred me deeply, and called up visions of a past now dead some thirty or forty years. I must, if it seems at all possible, state my thanks to her who was the agent for these strange, insubstantial visions. More than the actor in the Namboku play, more than the Shinnai singer, Tsuruga somebody or other, who tells of Ranchō and his tragic love, O-yuki was the skillful yet inarticulate artist with power to summon the past.

In the dim electric light, and in the perpetual hum of the canal mosquitoes, I would watch O-yuki at dinner, a rice cask under her arm, noisily raking in rice; and the figures and the houses of women I knew in my youth would come up in my mind's eye as if they were before me again. I would even be reminded of women who had been the friends of friends. In those ancient times the pretentious forms of address current today had not yet been invented, nor was it fashionable to refer to the humble abode in which a pair lived as "a love nest." Men were altogether more informal in the way they addressed women of their acquaintance, and wives in their speech to husbands.

If one but goes east of the River Sumida, the hum of the mosquitoes by the ditch is even now as it was some thirty years ago, singing the melancholy sweetness of the further reaches of town; and how great, even in these last ten years, has been the change in the speech of the city!

"A clearing in the litter, room for a mosquito net."

"A mosquito net of cotton—and it was hot enough already!"

"Beside a ditch the autumn sun floods into the house from the west."

"A sad house, a shabby house—the heat of autumn, and all the fans are broken!"

"And now, September; the hole in the net has been tied up and tied up again."

"A humming of mosquitoes, even from the garbage can."

"The wall counts the last mosquitoes, and the spots from the leaking roof."

"Autumn comes to a close, and the net will be turned into wine."

These slight epigrams of mine came back to me one evening when I found a mosquito net hanging in O-yuki's backroom. Perhaps half of them were composed on visits to my late friend Inoue Aa, who was then living in a Fukagawa tenement, with a woman not approved of by his family. It would have been in about 1910 or 1911, I suppose.

That night her tooth had begun to ache, and she had just this minute left her place by the window. There being nowhere else to sit, she sat in the doorway beside me.

"You're late. Don't keep me waiting."

Ever since she had concluded that my trade was one to be kept from the world, her manner had tended to go beyond the merely familiar.

"Sorry. A cavity?"

"It came on all of a sudden. I nearly fainted. It's swollen." She turned to show me the swelling. "Watch the place. I'm going to the dentist."

"Is there one near here?"

"Just this side of the clinic."

"By the market?"

"Been everywhere and know everything, don't you. Fickle, that's what you are."

"Ouch. Do you have to be so violent? I'm just trying to make my way in the world, after all."

"Well, take care of the place. I'll come back if there are people ahead of me."

"Waiting and waiting outside the net . . . am I. All right, I'm to wait outside the net."

As the woman's speech became rougher, I made mine rougher, too. I was not only trying to hide my identity. Wherever I go and whomever I am with, I take on the speech of my companion as my own, much as one takes on the speech of a foreign country. When he chooses a rude, rustic manner of address, I find myself doing the same thing. I fear that I am straying from my topic, but I would add that, in my associations with the people of our day, I find it easy enough to choose the proper word of mouth, but when it comes to writing letters the difficulties are enormous. Replies to letters from women are particularly difficult. Just what degree of coyness and intimacy is to go into the contractions? And then there is the modern fashion of changing every adjective into an abstract noun by putting a -ness on the end of it—"inevitableness" and "importantness" and the like. When I am speaking, I am able to imitate the practice half in jest, but when I take up my writing brush, the wave of loathing and revulsion is scarcely endurable. Well, the good things are the things that will not come back. That very day, airing my books, I had come upon an old letter from a graduate of the Yanagibashi geisha quarter who was being kept in Koume, across the river. In those days a certain formality was required in the writing of letters, and even if she did not know how to spell properly, a woman would remember the forms when she reached for her ink and brush. I think I shall copy out the letter here, even at the risk of inviting ridicule:

"Please be advised that I wish to write you a letter. My silence has been of long duration. I'm very sorry, I really am. I wish you to be advised further that I have moved to new quarters, for the ones but recently mine were a mess. It is a matter difficult to give expression to, but there's something I got to talk over with you. I shall be waiting, at your convenience, whenever you choose to call. You must excuse the brevity of this note. I'm in an awful hurry. I'll give you the whole lowdown when I see you. Make it quick.

"You will come upon a boathouse, by over there where the ferry is. Ask the grocery boy there. The weather these days being of a rare order, you might invite Aa to accompany you. I'd love to go to Horikiri with the both of you. Would the morning hours be convenient? This is the question I would ask of you. No need for an answer if you don't feel like it."

Certain passages, it will be noted, carry traces of the woman's downtown speech. The Takeya Ferry is gone, and so is the Makurabashi Ferry. Where am I to search for relics over which to lament my youth?

VII

I half unhooked the old mosquito net and sat on the edge of it. Fanning away the mosquitoes, I occasionally looked at the buried embers and the teakettle. However fierce the heat of the summer night, it was the practice in this Quarter to take tea upstairs to show that a customer had come. No house was without charcoal embers and hot water.

There was a low voice and a tapping at the window.

Sure that it would be an old customer, I was debating whether or not to go out, when a man reached through the window, unfastened the door, and came in. About fifty years old, he wore a whitish summer kimono tied with a soft obi, and there was a mustache on the round, countrified face. He carried a bundle done up in a kerchief. I guessed immediately that it was the master of O-yuki and her house.

"I met O-yuki outside," I said without waiting for him to speak. "She said she was going to the dentist or somewhere."

Apparently he already knew it. "She'll be right back. Just wait here." Without a sign that he found my presence suspicious, he undid the bundle and put a little aluminum saucepan inside the cupboard. Clearly he was the master—he had brought O-yuki's dinner.

"Isn't it fine that O-yuki keeps busy?" said I, thinking that I should offer a little flattery in place of the more usual greetings.

"I beg your pardon? Oh, yes." He seemed troubled for an answer. The words said very little. His attention was on the embers and the hot water, and he avoided looking at me. He looked away, rather, as if he wanted to avoid conversation. I, too, fell silent.

Such encounters are exceedingly uncomfortable both for customer and for proprietor. Meetings between customers and the owners of houses of assignation are all alike, probably because they are usually the result of a highly unpleasant disagreement involving a lady.

The mosquito repellent that O-yuki generally lighted in the doorway did not seem to have been set out this evening, and the roaring mosquitoes attacked one's face and even threatened to fly inside one's mouth. Accustomed though he should have been to mosquitoes, he could endure but a few minutes of them. He tried to switch on the electric fan below the lattice, but evidently it was broken. When he found a bit of repellent in the drawer of the brazier, we both looked up, rescued. I saw my opportunity.

"The mosquitoes are bad everywhere this year. The heat has been much worse than usual."

"Oh? But this is reclaimed land, and it has never been properly drained." He spoke hesitantly.

"The roads have improved, though. It's much more convenient than it used to be."

"And to make up for it, the regulations are worse. A regulation for everything."

"That seems to be true. Two or three years ago you usually had your hat snatched when you went by."

"That was a real problem. People wouldn't come by, even if they had business. We warned the women, but we couldn't keep watch over them every single minute. Finally we had to fine them. Forty-two yen for running out in front and trying to catch a customer. And we made a rule against sending men to the park after customers."

"You fine them for that, too?"

He nodded.

"How much?"

I meant in a circumspect, unobtrusive way to ask him about the Quarter, but just then someone called "Mr. Andō" and slipped a piece of paper through the window. A moment later O-yuki came in, picked up the paper, and laid it on the edge of the brazier. I saw that it was a mimeographed lookout notice for a fugitive robber.

O-yuki did not even glance at it. "Papa, he says I'll have to have my tooth pulled. This one." She thrust her open mouth at him.

"You didn't need anything to eat tonight, then." The man started to get up. For his special benefit, I handed money to O-yuki and went upstairs ahead of her.

Besides a small room with a window and a low table, there were two slightly larger rooms. What had originally been one house seemed to have been partitioned, front and back, and downstairs there was neither kitchen nor back door. On the second floor the rear wall was no more than paper over thin boards, and the voices in the house behind were as clear as if in the same room. I often entertained myself by pressing my ear to the wall.

"There you go again. Even in this hot weather." O-yuki came up and immediately went into the room with the window. She pulled back the faded chintz curtain. "Come in here. There's a fine breeze. Oh, look. Lightning still."

"It's getting a little cooler. A very fine breeze indeed."

The street immediately below was blocked off by the awning, but one could see, for a surprising distance, the second floors across the canal, the faces of the women in the windows, people coming and going. The sky above the roofs was heavy and leaden, starless, lighted a faint red halfway from the horizon by neon lamps on the main street. It made the hot night seem even hotter. O-yuki laid a cushion on the window sill and sat down. She looked at the sky for a time, and reached for my hand.

"Listen. Suppose we paid off my debts. Would you let me live with you?"

"Me? What good would I be?"

"You mean you aren't fit to be a husband?"

"If a man can't feed you, he's hardly fit to be your husband."

O-yuki said nothing more. She began humming a nasal tune to the accompaniment of the violin we could just then hear at the end of the street. I tried to glance at her face, but suddenly she stood up, grasped the window sash with one hand, and leaned out.

"If I were ten years younger." I sat before the table and lighted a cigarette.

"How old are you, anyway?"

She had turned to me, and I felt that I was saved. There was as usual a dimple on one cheek.

"I'll be sixty in no time."

"Papa! Sixty? You're very healthy for your age." She gazed into my face. "No, you're not even forty. Thirty-six, maybe, or thirty-seven."

"My mother was my father's mistress. I don't really know how old I am."

"You're young even for forty. Look at your hair. I never would take you for forty."

"That would make it 1897, then, when I was born. If I'm forty now."

"How old do you think I am?"

"You look twenty-one or so. Twenty-three, possibly?"

"Flatterer. I'm twenty-five."

"O-yuki. You said you were a geisha in Utsunomiya."

"Yes."

"How did you happen to come here? How did you happen to know about this?"

"I was in Tokyo for a while."

"And needed money?"

"If I didn't, why would I ... the man got sick and died, and I was a little ..."

"It must have shocked you at first. Geishas don't do things quite this way."

"It didn't, really. I knew what I was doing. Geishas never earn what they have to spend, and never work themselves out of debt. And then, well, if you're going to take the plunge, you might as well plunge the whole way. That's how to do it."

"You thought things through? All by yourself?"

"A woman in a teahouse back in the days when I was a geisha had a business here. I heard about it from her."

"Even so, it's remarkable. Work on your own when your term is up, and put aside what you can."

"People my age are meant for this sort of thing, or so she said. But you never know what will happen afterward, do you."

At this unblinking gaze, I felt a strange uneasiness come over me again. I could not accept the possibility that—still, there it was to bother me, like a particle lodged between two back teeth. This time it was I who wanted to look out at the sky.

From time to time, along the horizon where the neons reflected, there had been flashes of lightning; and just then a particularly sharp flash came at us. There was no thunder, however, and the wind had quite stopped. All the sultriness of late afternoon seemed to come back.

"It looks like another shower."

"I was on my way back from the hairdresser's. It's been three months... *hasn't* it."

"It's been three months," and, slightly protracted, "*hasn't* it": the words seemed to carry a vague, broad appeal, as of calling something up from the very distant past. If she had said "It's been three months," or "It's been three months, hasn't it," with a clear break at the end of the sentence, it would probably have sounded like a most ordinary statement. But the protracted "*hasn't* it" had the ring less of an exclamation than of a device for drawing out an answer. I found even the word "yes" falling back in my throat, and I answered only with my eyes.

Each evening O-yuki received numberless men who made their way into the alleys. Why, then, had she not forgotten the day she first met me? The question came to me like a glimpse of something that could not be. To recall the day we first met gave her pleasure. I would not have dreamed that a woman of the Quarter could feel a liking, love, any soft, warm emotion of the kind, for an old man, even though she had taken him for a man of forty.

I have said that I had many reasons for coming here almost every night. To reconnoiter the ground for my novel *Whereabouts Un-*

known. To flee the radio. To avoid Marunouchi and the Ginza and the other busy centers of the city, for which I had a deep dislike. There were other reasons, too, but none that I could tell the woman. I had made O-yuki's house a resting place on my nocturnal walks, and to suit my purposes I had told her lies quite as they came to me. Though I had not intentionally set out to deceive her, I had not corrected her first error, and giving myself up to the game, I had hidden my identity by words and deeds that deepened the misunderstanding. For this much I suppose that I cannot escape responsibility.

In Tokyo, and even in the Occident, I have known almost no society except that of courtesans. I do not wish to state the reasons here, and there is no need to. The inquisitive reader who has wanted to know more about the person I am will have found his wishes only too well satisfied by a reading of certain inadequate works from my middle years: among them the dialogue "Early Afternoon," the fugitive essay "House for a Mistress," and the story "Unfinished Dream." They are all wordy and badly written, however, and since it would be a great demand upon the reader to ask that he look into them all, I might here quote a passage from "Unfinished Dream": "He frequented the pleasure quarters with such enthusiasm that ten years were as a day; for he knew only too well that they were quarters of darkness and unrighteousness. And had the world come to praise the profligate as loyal servant and pious son, he would have declined, even at the cost of selling his property, to hear the voice of praise. Indignation at the hypocritical vanity of proper wives and at the fraud of the just and open society was the force that sent him speeding in the other direction, toward what was from the start taken for dark and unrighteous. There was more happiness in finding the remains of a beautifully woven pattern among castaway rags than in finding spatters and stains on a wall proclaimed immaculate. Sometimes in the halls of the righteous droppings from crows and rats are to be seen, and sometimes in the depths of corruption flowers of human sympathy and fruits of perfumed tears are to be found and gathered."

Whoever reads this will at least see why I felt no deep fear of or revulsion from the foul ditch, and the women who lived among the mosquitoes—why, indeed, from before I saw them I felt a certain nearness to them.

So that I might become friends with them, so that they would not draw back in awe of me, I thought it best to hide my identity. It would have been most cruel to have the women think that I was one who had no reason to come, and might better stay away. I wanted at all costs to avoid being taken for one who looked down upon them and their wretched lives, as if watching them act a play. There was no help for it but to hide my identity.

I had in fact had the experience of being told that I was not the sort of person to be coming to the Quarter. One evening, near the metropolitan bus garage on the new street, I was stopped and questioned by a policeman. I greatly dislike announcing myself as a writer and man of letters, and dislike even more being taken as such; and so, as was my usual practice, I told him that I was unemployed, a vagrant. He stripped off my coat and went through my pockets. As a precaution against just such interrogations, I always carry my seal and a certificate of its validity, together with an extract from my family register. That night I happened to have three or four hundred yen in cash, since I had to pay the carpenter, the gardener, and the bookseller the next day. Startled, the policeman labeled me a man of property.

"This isn't the sort of place men of property should be wandering around in. Go on home, go on home, before you get in trouble. If you have to come, come some other time."

Seeing that I hesitated, he hailed a cab and even opened the door for me.

I had the driver go down the new street and do a round of what is called "The Loop" or something of the sort. I made a circuit of the warren, in other words, and got off near the Fushimi Inari Shrine. Afterward I bought a map and studied the streets, and was careful never to pass a police box.

Now, at the strange, plaintive note in O-yuki's voice as she spoke of the night we met, I could find no words for an answer. Wanting at least to hide my face in the smoke, I reached for another cigarette. O-yuki still gazed at me with those near-black eyes.

"You do look so much like him. When I saw you that night from behind, you took my breath away."

"Oh? Strangers will look like people you know, won't they." I tried to hide my relief. "Who do I look like? The man who died?"

"No. I had just become a geisha. I thought I'd die if I couldn't be with him."

"Just let the excitement get the best of you, and you're sure to feel that way one time or another."

"And you? Not you, I'll bet."

"You're saying I'm cold, are you? Don't judge by appearances. And don't pretend that you're better than I am."

O-yuki showed her one dimple, and said nothing. That dimple, carved deep to the right of her slightly out-thrust lower lip, gave her face the freshness of a very young girl's; but tonight it was inexpressibly sad, a dimple made by sheer force of will. To gloss over the moment, I said:

"Does it ache again?"

"It's nothing. He gave me an injection."

The conversation broke off; and soon an old customer was good enough to come tapping at the door. O-yuki got up in haste and leaned over the blind that closed off the lower part of the window.

"Well, Take-san. Do come in."

She ran downstairs and I followed her. Hiding in the toilet until the man had gone upstairs, I stole quietly out.

VIII

There was still no rain. Fearful of the heat in that sitting room, its charcoal embers aglow, and of the mosquitoes, I went outdoors. It was too early to go home. Following the canal to the end of the alley, I crossed over to a busy street by a wooden bridge. Festival stalls lined both sides of the street, too narrow in any case for automobiles, and I had to force my way through the night throngs. To the right of the bridge was an intersection, one corner of which was occupied by a seller of horse meat. Beyond the crossroad were the gate of the Tamanoi Inari Shrine, a public telephone, and a stone tablet bearing the name of a Zen temple. I remembered having heard from O-yuki that shrine fairs came on the second and twentieth of the month, and that because on those nights the main streets were crowded and few people pushed their way into the lanes and alleys, the shrine was known to the women in the windows as "the pauper Inari." I started toward it, for I had not yet paid my respects.

I have neglected to say that since I had taken to spending my nights

in the Quarter, since I had come to feel at home there, I had made it
a practice to remodel myself before I left home, and follow the fash-
ions of the people I saw strolling among the night stalls. The change
required no great effort. A striped shirt, collar open, no necktie; a
coat carried in one hand; no hat; hair so matted that one wondered
if it had ever seen a comb; trousers as thin at the seat and knees as
possible. No shoes, in their place sandals with the rear clog worn
away. Only the cheapest cigarettes. And so on and so on. It was no
trouble at all. I had only to change from the clothes I wore when I
was in my study or when I received guests to the clothes I wore when
I raked the garden or cleaned away soot, and borrow a pair of old
sandals from the maid.

Put on a pair of old sandals and a pair of old trousers, find an old
towel and tie it carelessly around your head, and you can walk
through the eastern flats from Sunamachi on the south to Senjū on
the north and Kanamachi on the northeast, and never have to worry
that passersby will turn to stare. You might be someone from the
neighborhood out shopping, you can walk the side streets and push
your way up the alleys in complete security. This careless dress ("the
messier the dress," says the epigram, "the cooler the second-floor
breeze") is suited to the Tokyo climate, especially in the worst of
the heat. If you dress like a dubious taxicab driver, you can spit wherever you like, on the street, in a streetcar, anywhere, and you can
throw cigarette butts and matches and paper and banana peels wherever you like. When you come to a park—again it is quite up to you—
you can fling yourself on a bench or the grass and throw out your
arms and legs and snore or growl out Naniwabushi. The dress fits
the Tokyo climate admirably, and Tokyo architecture, too. You can
abandon yourself to the consciousness of dwelling in a rebuilt city.

Of the strange summer custom women have taken to of going out
in a single nightgownlike garment, my good friend Satō Yōsai has
already written, and I shall add nothing more.*

Dragging along the unfamiliar sandals, taking care not to stumble
or get stepped on or otherwise injure myself, I pushed my way
through the crowds and on to the shrine, at the head of the alley
opposite. Night stalls lined the alley, and in a somewhat wider space

---

* The poet and novelist Satō Haruo.

beside the shrine, pots of roses and lilies and summer chrysanthemums for sale made an unseasonal flower garden. In a corner, plaques bearing the names of people who had donated money toward rebuilding a temple hall were lined up like a picket fence. Perhaps the temple had burned down, or perhaps, as was the case with the Inari, it had been moved from another site.

I bought a potted carnation and made my way past the Tamanoi Inari Shrine and out by another alley to Taishō Avenue, from which I had come. On the right just ahead there was a police box. Tonight I was dressed like a native of the district, and since I even had a potted plant from the festival stalls, I thought I should be safe. Still, police boxes were to be avoided when possible. I reversed my course, and turned in between a wine shop and a fruiterer.

Behind the shops on one side stretched the labyrinth known as the First Section. The ditch running through the Second Section, where O-yuki lived, emerged beside a road at the edge of the First Section, passed a public bath whose curtain said "Nakajima Waters," and lost itself among the dark tenements outside the Quarter. I thought of the canal, even dirtier than the "Moat of the Black-toothed Beauties" that once surrounded the North Quarter,* and I thought how, in the days when this Terajima was open fields, it was a clear stream with dragonflies playing among water flowers; and I could not keep back sentiments unbecoming to an old man. There were no festival stalls on this street. As I passed a Chinese restaurant with a tall neon sign announcing it as "Kyushu House," I could see the lights of automobiles on the new avenue, and hear phonographs.

The potted carnation was heavy. Turning at Kyushu House, I found myself on the narrowest, most prosperous street of all, along which ran the boundary between the First and Second Section of the labyrinth on the right and the Third Section on the left. Here there were kimono shops and Western dry-goods stores and Western restaurants. And there was a postbox. It must have been in front of this postbox that O-yuki, on her way back from the hairdresser's, fled to the shelter of my umbrella.

Deep in my heart, the uneasiness of the moment when O-yuki had given that brief, flickering hint of her emotions was still with me.

* The Yoshiwara. Courtesans traditionally blackened their teeth.

I had learned almost nothing of O-yuki's past. She said that she had been a geisha somewhere, but since she knew none of the old music, neither Nagauta nor Kiyomoto, one could not take the fact for certain. My first impression, based on no concrete evidence, had been that she was a woman from a not-too-cheap house in the Yoshiwara or Suzaki. Had I perhaps been right?

There was no trace of a provincial accent in her speech, but her features and the smoothness of her skin suggested that she was not from Tokyo or near it. I took her for the child of parents who had moved to Tokyo from afar. Her nature was bright and lively, and she did not seem to be especially disheartened at the surroundings in which she found herself. She seemed rather to have the spirit and with it the ability to make a living on the capital the experience of those surroundings had given her. And her feelings toward men: she listened without suspicion to the lies that slipped from my mouth, and it was therefore clear that she was not yet completely jaded. If she could make me think so, then she must be called simple and honest by comparison with veteran waitresses from big Ueno or Ginza cafés.

Were I to gather my courage and compare the women in the windows with the barmaids up and down the Ginza, I would find the former altogether more lovable, more alive to ordinary human sympathies. And if I were then to compare the two districts themselves, I would note that Tamanoi, with its want of shallow display, its unassertiveness, gives far less cause for displeasure than the Ginza. In both places night stalls line the streets, but in Tamanoi one does not come upon clusters of drunkards, and almost never upon the bloody quarrels that are common enough on the Ginza. And there is another sight one sees on the Ginza: a middle-aged person, evil of countenance, his foreign clothes splendid enough but his occupation difficult to identify, swaggering along, brandishing his cane, singing a song and berating women and children who happen to get in his way. If one but puts on old sandals and an old pair of trousers and comes to these far reaches of the city, one is in far less danger, however crowded the night may be, than on a back street of the Ginza, and there is much less of this constantly having to yield the way.

The lively street with the postbox was at its brightest by the haberdashery, and grew darker beyond. A rice store and a greengrocery caught the eye, and presently, from the lumberyard down the street,

my steps, quite trained by now to the Quarter, took me up the alley
between the bicycle garage and the hardware store.

Immediately beyond were the dirty banners of the Fushimi Inari
Shrine. The reveling strollers appeared not to notice the shrine or the
banners. The alley attracted far fewer than most. Taking advantage
of the fact, I always stole in past the shrine, and after glancing back
at the thick growth of figs behind the houses on the main street and
at the grapevines along the canal railing as at a scene most unexpected
in this Quarter, I would look over at O-yuki's window.

There still seemed to be a customer upstairs. A light was shining
through the curtain, and the first-floor window was open as before.
The radios on the main street seemed to have stopped. Leaving the
carnation at the window, I started toward Shirahige Bridge. A Keisei
bus came up behind me, but I was not sure where the stop would be.
I walked along looking for it, and soon the lights of the bridge were
before me.

I had not yet finished my *Whereabouts Unknown,* which I had begun in early summer. It had been three months, said O-yuki, reminding me that it had been even longer since I had begun writing. I had
left Taneda Jumpei and the girl Sumiko, with whom he shared lodgings, out walking on Shirahige Bridge, refugees from the heat of their
rented room.

Ordinarily I would have turned down the river, but tonight I
walked on to the bridge, and stood leaning against the railing.

My first plans for the novel had had the girl Sumiko, in her early
twenties, falling easily into the deepest of relationships with Taneda,
then already fifty; but I had come to feel that there was something
unnatural about the relationship. That fact, and the blistering heat,
had made me stop writing.

But now, as I leaned against the railing and listened to the music
and the singing from the park downstream, and thought of O-yuki
in the upstairs window, and her tone and manner as she had spoken
of those three months—I knew that there was nothing at all unnatural about the relationship. There was no need whatsoever to dismiss
it as a forced contrivance, a trick of an inept novelist. Indeed I had
come to feel that the results would be unfortunate if I were to change
my original plans.

I took a cab home from Asakusa, and when, as always, I had
washed my face and combed my hair, I lighted incense in the burner

at my desk. Then I glanced over the last part of the interrupted manuscript.

"What's that over there? A factory?"

"A gashouse or something of the sort. They say the view used to be good off in that direction. I read about it in a book."

"Shall we walk on? It isn't very late."

"There's a police box on the other side."

"Oh? Let's go back, then. I feel like a criminal. A real fugitive."

"You shouldn't say it in such a loud voice."

Taneda did not answer.

"You never know who might be listening."

"You're right, I suppose. But this is my first experience as a fugitive. I'm not likely to forget it soon."

"Running away from it all—isn't there a song that goes something like that? Running away from it all, way up high in the mountains."

"Sumiko. All of a sudden I feel much younger. Last night gave me something to live for."

"People are as young as they feel. You can't let it get you down."

"I suppose not. But the fact is that I'm not young any more. You'll be getting rid of me in no time."

"There you go again. Haven't I told you not to say such things? I'll be thirty soon myself. I've done the things I've wanted to do, and now I'll settle down and earn a little money."

"So you think you'll open a shop?"

"Aki will be coming tomorrow, and I'll give her the down payment. So I won't need your money yet. Just keep it—the way we decided last night. All right?"

"But somehow—"

"No, it's the best way, I tell you. I'll feel much better if you have money in the bank. I'll take out all I have, and pay her. That really seems the best way, now that I've made up my mind."

"But is Aki all right? After all, there's money involved."

"Oh, she's all right. She has plenty of money of her own. The man that owns the Tamanoi Palace is behind her."

"Who's he?"

"He has several shops and houses in Tamanoi. He's already in his seventies, but he's very energetic still. He really is. I used to see him sometimes in the café."

"Oh?"

"Aki said if I was going into business, that was the business I ought to get into. She said she'd have him find me a house and some girls, too. But I didn't have anyone to talk it over with, and then I wouldn't have been able to run it by myself. So I'll open a stall. I can manage that by myself."

"And you've decided on Tamanoi?"

"Aki's mother runs a pawnshop. Aki set her up in it."

"A real business woman."

"Oh, she has a head on her shoulders. She's not the kind to cheat a person, though."

IX

In mid-September, the heat was if anything worse than in mid-August. The wind striking the reed blinds sometimes had the sound of autumn, but always in the evening it would stop, and the nights would be as still as in the Kansai. For nights on end it would only seem to grow sultrier as the hours passed.

With writing and with airing my books, I was unusually busy. For three days I did not go out.

Airing my books in the sun of early fall, and burning leaves on an early winter afternoon, were among the chief pleasures in my solitary life. Airing my library gave me a chance to take down books long stored away on high shelves, look back on the days when I had read them with eagerness, and think upon changes in times and in tastes. Burning leaves let me forget for a little while the world of which I was a part.

When, at length, I had gone through the books, I waited only for dinner to be over. Changing into old trousers and worn sandals, I went outside. There was already a light at the gate. For all the heat of the still nights, the days had somehow grown shorter.

Though it had been but three days, I felt for no reason at all, once I was outside, that I had taken too long in going where I must go. Thinking to cut the time by even a few minutes, I changed at Kyō-bashi to the subway. I had known the pleasure quarters from my youth, and yet it would be no exaggeration to say that I was feeling something that had left me for thirty years, this impatience to visit a woman. From Asakusa I took a cab to my alleyway. The same Fushimi Inari Shrine. The dirty old votive banners, four or five of them, had been changed for new, and there were only white banners now. The red ones had been discarded. The same canal, the same figs, the same grapevines. The leaves were a little thinner, to tell one that however hot it might be, however reviled these alleys might be, here, too, autumn was creeping up night by night.

The same O-yuki at the same window, but the usual coiffure was changed. A new chignon and ribbon, "peony" or something of the sort the style is called. I walked toward her noting in astonishment the difference it made. She flung the door roughly open.

"Well!" Then, after the one sharp word, her voice dropped. "I was worried. So it wasn't you after all."

I found it hard to guess what she meant. I sat in the doorway without taking off my sandals.

"I saw in the papers. It didn't quite match, though, and I thought probably it wasn't you. But I was worried just the same."

"Oh." At length understanding, I, too, lowered my voice. "I hope you don't think I'd be such a fool. I'm very, very careful."

"But what happened? Where were you? Now that you're here, it doesn't seem so important, but it's very lonely when someone ought to come and doesn't."

"I suppose you've been as busy as ever."

"You know how it is in this heat."

"It doesn't seem to get any cooler, does it."

"Hold still." She crushed a mosquito on my forehead with the palm of her hand. There seemed to be even more mosquitoes in the house than before, and their needles were thicker and sharper. O-yuki took out a piece of paper and wiped the blood from her hand and my forehead. "Look at that, will you." She showed me the paper, then threw it away.

"It will be the end of the year before they're gone."

"It really will. We must have had them last year through November. As late as the Otori Fair, anyway."

"The Paddies?" But I remembered that times had changed, and the expression would mean nothing to her.* "You people go to the fair behind the Yoshiwara?"

"Yes." Hearing a bell in the street, she stood up and went to the

---

* Until the Meiji Period, the Yoshiwara, on the northern outskirts of the city, was known as "The Paddies."

window. "Ken-chan. Over here. What are you staring at? Bring two ices. And while you're at it, get me some mosquito repellent. There's a good boy."

She sat by the window, now being heckled by sightseers, now heckling them back. Then again she would turn to me, beyond the lattice. The boy came with the ices.

"You'll have one, won't you? Today the bill is mine. I know you like ice."

"How did you remember? A trivial thing like that."

"Oh, I remember. See how serious I am? That's why you have to stop misbehaving."

"You think when I don't come here I'm going to another house?"

"But that's generally the way with men."

"Let's be friends at least while we eat."

"We'll see." Raising a violent clatter with her spoon, O-yuki stirred at the heaped-up ice.

A passerby looked in. "Well, madame. Is it good?"

"Open your mouth and I'll give you a bite."

"With cyanide in it? I'd like to live a while yet."

"Oh, you would, would you? And you without two cents to rub together."

"Says the canal mosquito."

"To the garbage-can blowfly." O-yuki was not to be bested. The next group of hecklers laughed and walked on.

O-yuki would have a spoonful of ice and look up, and call out mechanically "Sa-a-ay, there," giving it a seductive lilt. When someone stopped and looked in the window, she would add, sweetly and coaxingly: "Well, *do* come in. First this evening. *Do* come in." Or sometimes, expansively: "It doesn't matter a bit. Come on in, and if you aren't satisfied you can just leave. You can just go straight home." She would talk to the man for a time, and she did not seem especially dejected when he, too, went away. As if just remembering, she would return to the melting ice, attack it noisily, and have herself a cigarette.

In describing O-yuki, I have said that she was bright and lively, and I have said that she did not seem especially depressed by her surroundings. These conclusions, it is true, are based only on glimpses through the curtain as I sat in a corner beyond, fanning away mosquitoes and trying to still the flapping of the broken fan. They are perhaps inadequate conclusions. Perhaps I was seeing but one side of a complex person.

But in a sense it is possible for me to affirm that my conclusions were not mistaken. Quite aside from O-yuki's nature, there was a gossamer thread that tied her to the passers outside. If I am wrong in saying that O-yuki had a bright and lively disposition and was not particularly depressed, then I should like to apologize for myself by explaining that the mistake had its origins here. Outside were the masses. The world. Inside was one individual. Between the world and the individual there was harmony. Why should this have been so? Because O-yuki was still young. Because she had not yet lost her feeling for the masses, the world outside. Seated at the window was a lowly O-yuki, while in her heart there lay hidden another O-yuki. And the men who came into the alley had taken off their masks and left behind their pretensions.

From my youth I had been making my way into the streets of the heavily painted, and even now I had not awakened to the evils of the practice. Under the pressure of circumstances, I had more than once followed the wishes of a woman and brought her into my house and set her at broom and dustpan. Always the experiment had been a failure. When such a woman leaves behind her old surroundings and no longer thinks herself lowly, she soon becomes unmanageable, either the slovenly wife or the fiery wife.

O-yuki had, as time passed, come to think of leaving her old surroundings, with my help. She was by way of becoming the slovenly wife or the fiery wife. To make her neither the one nor the other in her later years, to make her an ordinary, happy housewife, must be the work not of me, whose experience was rich only in failure, but of someone who still had months and years before him. If I were to say as much to O-yuki, it was not likely that she would understand. She knew but one side of my double nature. It would be very easy to reveal the side she had not guessed, to show her where it was inadequate. Still I hesitated, less for my own sake than because I feared the terrible disappointment when O-yuki saw her mistake.

O-yuki was the muse who had accidentally called back into a dulled heart shadows of the past. If she had not been drawn to me, or if I had not thought she was, I would without doubt have torn up the manuscript that had long been waiting on my desk. O-yuki was the strange force to make a forgotten old author finish a work, in all probability his last. Each time I saw her I wanted to thank her from my heart. Perhaps I had deceived her, poor as she was in experience of the world, and perhaps I had toyed with her body and her honest emotions. Deeply though I might want to apologize for a wrong difficult to forgive, however, I could only lament that events had gone against me.

At O-yuki's words in the window that evening, the pain became more intense. There could be no better solution than not to see her again. If the separation were to come now, the wound would be easier to heal. I had not yet asked her real name or the circumstances of her birth, and she had had no occasion to reveal them. For no special reason, the feeling grew, as the hours passed, that this was the night to say good-bye, that if I let the chance pass, the sorrow would be past remedying.

A breeze came up, passed from the main street into the alleys, struck here and there, blew in through the little window, shook the ribbons on which the bells hung; and at the sound, this sense of being pursued to a decision became even stronger. The sound, different from the tinkling when a seller of bells passes one's latticed window, is to be heard only in such unusual places. With the heat unrelieved each night as late summer moved into autumn, one had somehow not noticed; and because one had not noticed, the sound brought a stabbing awareness that the long, deep nights had come. Perhaps it was only in my imagination that the footsteps outside were softer and clearer. A woman sneezed in a window somewhere.

O-yuki left her window. Lighting a cigarette, she seemed to remember something. "Will you come early tomorrow?"

"Early? Before dark?"

"Earlier. Tomorrow is Tuesday and I have to be examined. I'll be finished at eleven. Will you take me to Asakusa afterward? I don't have to be back till around four."

I thought there would be no harm in it. I thought it would be good to drink a farewell cup. But I was afraid I might meet a reporter or a gentleman of letters and again be assassinated by pen.

"There are reasons why I don't want to be seen in the park. Do you have something to buy?"

"I need a watch. And then it's time to change to winter kimonos."

"We complain about the heat, but before long the equinox will be here. How much of a winter kimono? Do you wear them at work?"

"Yes. It would have to cost at least thirty yen."

"If that's all, I have it here." I took out my wallet. "Go and order yourself one."

"Really?"

"The money's all right. You have nothing to worry about."

I gazed at her, to remember the eyes fixed on me in such astonishing pleasure. I put the notes on the table.

There was a knock on the door, and O-yuki's master called in. Cutting off whatever she was about to say, she pushed the notes inside her obi. I stood up abruptly and passed the man as he came in.

The wind, full from the main street, lashed at my hair as I came to the Fushimi Inari Shrine. In the habit of wearing a hat wherever else I went, I raised my hand to my head at the first gust, and smiled wryly upon realizing that I was hatless. The votive banners were bent almost to breaking, and, with the curtains of the little night stalls along the alley, they whipped in the wind as if about to fly off. In the darkness behind an abandoned house, at a bend in the canal, figs and grapes sent up a dry rustling. The Milky Way, and every star in the suddenly open sky over the main street, shone before me in crystalline majesty, infinitely sad and lonely. The loneliness was only intensified by streetcars beyond the row of houses, and by honking taxicabs, deadened in the harsh wind. Generally when I went home by way of Shirahige Bridge, I would turn into some side street at random, from the vicinity of the Sumida post office or the moving-picture house known as the Mukōjima Theater. Making my way through the alleys, I would come out behind the Shirahige Shrine. Sometimes, from late August into September, when there was a shower in the night and when, afterward, the moon was bright, I would think of old scenes and find that I had walked all the way to Kototoi Hill. Tonight there was no moon. The wind from the river was cold. Huddling between the shelter and the temple, I waited at the Jizō Hill bus stop.

x

Four or five days passed. Though I had left money for the winter kimono, meaning that night to be the last, I found myself wanting to see O-yuki again. How would she be? I knew that she would be at the window as always; but the desire at least to see her face was irresistible. I would go for a secret look at her. By the time I had had a walk about the Quarter, the radio next door would have stopped. Thus I laid the blame on the radio, and set off for a walk east of the river.

Before starting up the alley, I bought a hunting cap to hide my face. I waited for sightseers to come by, and hid myself in their shadow; and, looking across at O-yuki's house beyond the canal, I saw her in the window, the "peony" chignon changed for the earlier style. And I saw, too, that the right-hand window under the same eaves, a window that had until then been closed, was bright, and a face surmounted by a round chignon was moving in it. A new girl had come —"a debutante" I believe they would call her in the Quarter. Though I could not really tell, she seemed older than O-yuki, and not very attractive. Losing myself in the crowd, I turned into another alley.

Perhaps because the wind had again stopped at sunset and the night was sultry, the crowds in the alleys were as thick as during the summer. I could make my way around the corners only by turning sideways. The pouring sweat and the tightness of the air were intolerable. Seeking an exit to an automobile thoroughfare, I walked along a shopping street in which there were no night stalls. At the 7-chōme bus stop I stood wiping the sweat from my forehead, with every intention of going straight home. Since the stop was but a hundred or two hundred yards from the garage, an empty bus pulled up as if especially for me. I started forward, then felt a surge of regret and walked off toward the 6-chōme bus stop, beside a postbox and a corner wineshop. There several people were waiting. Three or four buses went by, and I stood looking absently down the willow-lined street, and across the wide vacant lot at the corner.

From summer into autumn, until but a very short time before, there had been a phonograph blaring there each night, first for an equestrian show, then for a monkey show, finally for a ghost show. Now it had become a vacant lot again, and the dim lights around it were reflected in mud puddles. Well, I would see O-yuki once more, and tell her I was going on a trip. I did not mean to come again in any case, and the unhappiness would linger more stubbornly if I were to disappear like a weasel in the night. I wanted to tell her the whole truth. When I was in the mood for a walk, I had nowhere to go. The people

I would like to see had all died before me. The stylish quarters of samisen and song were now places where musicians and dancers vied with one another for fame, and not places where an old man could go for a talk of old times and a cup of tea. Quite by accident, I had learned, in a corner of the labyrinth, to steal half a day of calm from the world. Late though it was, I would like to explain, I hoped that with these facts in mind she would continue to receive me when I came, even though it might be a trial. I went into the alley, and stopped before O-yuki's house.

"Well, come on in." Her manner and tone said that someone who should come had at length come; but instead of taking me into the sitting room below, she led the way upstairs. I guessed what had happened.

"The master is here?"

"And his wife, too."

"I see you have a new one."

"And an old woman to do the cooking."

"It's very lively all of a sudden."

"When you've been living alone, it's a nuisance to have so many people around." She seemed to remember: "Thank you very much for the other day."

"Did you buy a good one?"

"A very good one. It should be coming tomorrow. I bought an obi too. See how this one is worn. Afterward I'll show it to you."

She went below for tea. We sat on the windowsill for a time, talking of nothing in particular. There was no sign yet that the master and his wife were leaving. The bell at the head of the stairs rang. It was to tell O-yuki that an old customer had come.

Because the air of the house had changed from the days when O-yuki was alone, because I found it hard to compose myself and O-yuki seemed to be thinking about the master, I left unsaid what I wanted to say, and went out the door before a half hour had passed.

Soon we had entered the season of the equinox. The skies changed, and when low, black clouds would scuttle past, driven by the south wind, showers would come like a scattering of gravel, and as suddenly stop again. Sometimes, however, the rain would continue the whole night through. The amaranth in my garden fell over, broken at the base. The other autumn flowers fell with it, leaves and all. The red stems of the begonia, already in seed and stripped of leaves, were sadly faded. The surviving locusts and crickets, during lulls in the rain, seemed to mourn the confusion of moist leaves and dead stems that was the garden. Always, after the autumn winds and rains, when I would look out over my garden, I would remember the poem about the stormy evening at the autumn window, from *The Dream of the Red Chamber*:

> The autumn flowers are faded, the autumn grasses sere.
> The autumn lamp burns brightly through the long, long
> autumn night.
> We have praised the autumn window, autumn has seemed
> without end.
> How then shall we bear the tempest, speeding the desolation?
> It has come so quickly, the autumn storm, to speed the
> autumn on,
> To break the green of the autumn dream, beside the autumn
> window.

And always, knowing well the futility, I would search for a way to translate it into Japanese.

It rained through the equinox. When the weather cleared, there was little left of September. The harvest moon came for this year, too.

The moon had been good from late the night before, and from early on the evening of the full moon, the last of the clouds disappeared.

That night I learned that O-yuki was ill and in the hospital. I heard it from the old woman at the window, and had no way of knowing the illness.

With October came the cold, earlier than usual. On the night of the harvest moon, did I not already see a sign near the Tamanoi Inari Shrine? "The time has come to paper the cracks in your doors. As a special service we offer good paste free." It was no longer the season for slipping bare feet into old sandals and walking the night streets hatless. That radio, now behind shutters, no longer tormented me as it once had. I managed to keep busy under the lamp in my study.

I must now lay down my brush, my strange tale from east of the river finished. To give it an ending in the old style, I should perhaps add a chapter describing how, quite by accident, six months or a year later, I met O-yuki in a wholly unexpected place. She had changed her profession. And if I wished to make the scene yet more effective, I could have the two of us see each other from the windows of passing automobiles or trains, unable to speak, however intense the longing. My scene would have a very special power if we were to pass on ferries, on, say, the murmuring River Toné, in the time of the autumn leaves and flowers.

In the end, neither O-yuki nor I knew the other's name or home. We became friends in a house by a canal east of the river, amid the roar of mosquitoes. We were such that once we parted, there would be neither chance nor means to bring us together again. One might say that we played frivolously at love. Still, there was a particular warmth in knowing from the outset that we would part and not meet again. If I try to describe it, I will only exaggerate, and if on the other hand I toss it off lightly, I will know the distress of having been unworthy of the occasion. The power with which just such feelings are described at the end of Pierre Loti's *Madame Chrysanthemum* is enough to bring tears to one's eyes. If I were to attempt that particular shading of fiction for my strange tale, I would bring ridicule upon myself as an imitator of Loti who has not imitated well enough.

I had known that O-yuki would not long be living in that house by the ditch, her charms for sale at an exceedingly low price. Once when I was young, I was told by an old man well versed in the ways of the Quarters that a person drawn to a woman as he has not been drawn before, and convinced that unless he takes her immediately someone else will have her, can be quite certain that she will fall ill and die, or marry some disagreeable man and go off to the far provinces. Strange and vague forebodings, he said, have a way of being right.

O-yuki was too intelligent and too pretty for that Quarter. She was the heron in the flock of chickens. But times have changed. There seemed little likelihood that she would fall ill and die. Nor did it seem likely that, pressed by a sense of duty, she would give herself to a man she did not care for.

The roofs of the dirty, jammed-in houses, on and on. O-yuki and I, in the black upstairs window, looking up at lights reflected in a sky heavy before a storm, one damp hand in the other. Suddenly, as we sat talking in conundrums, a flash of lightning, and her profile. The picture is here before my eyes, and will not leave. I lost myself in the sport of love when I was twenty; and now, past the border of old age, to have to tell of this foolishness! The jokes of fate can be cruel.

There remain a few blank lines on the back of my page. So let my brush go where it will, to console the night with a few lines of poetry or prose, I scarcely know which:

> Blood on the temple, from one of the last mosquitoes.
> You dried it and threw it away
> In a corner of a garden
> Where a single stem of amaranth remains.
> It does not know that it must fall and die,
> Not to feel the harsher winds of winter.
> For night by night the frost is whiter, thicker,
> And the rich brocade of leaves but seems the sadder
> That it must deepen even as it fades.
> There in the corner a stricken butterfly
> Wavers on broken wings
> In the shade of a dying stem of amaranth
> Which it takes to be a flower, a return of spring.
> A corner of a garden in gathering twilight
> Of the end of autumn, all too brief
> For vagrant dreams to form.
> I too am now alone, I have taken my leave.
> And to what shall I liken my heart, by an amaranth,
> A single amaranth that must fall and die?

The Decoration

"The Decoration" was written in 1942, but not
published until 1946, when it appeared in
the magazine *Shinsei*. It became the title of a
collection in 1947. For a discussion, see p. 160.

Theaters, variety halls—in and out of the dressing rooms of all such
places, their eyes on possible customers among the actors and among
those who see to the needs of actors, go numbers of people whose lives
are even more fleeting and precarious than those of the actors themselves.

In a place that I once frequented, the Opera House, on a corner in
Asakusa Park, there was an old man, caterer of short orders, a snapshot of whom I chanced to take in his last healthy days. I do not know
his name or where he came from.

"Never had my picture taken, not even once," he said, the happiness
on his face quite belying his usual taciturnity. He thanked me again
and again, and that wave of gratitude, I suspect, was the last bit of
emotion in his life. By the time the picture was developed and printed, he had disappeared, probably died, no one knew where. Until I
asked about him, no one backstage had even noticed that he was gone.

I remember why I was carrying a camera that day. A certain cemetery in Minowa, north of Asakusa, was about to be moved, and there
were tombstones that I desperately wanted to have pictures of before
they disappeared. On my way back I walked briskly through the park
and on to the Opera House, by the shore of the pond.

"After the performance tonight, rehearsal will begin on the second
and third scenes of the new review." A jumble of such notices was
pasted on the board wall just inside the stage door. Beyond was a
steep, dirty, creaky stairway. Off the cramped hall at the head of the
stairway was the dressing room of the dancing girls, its battered doors
open even in the coldest part of winter. The dressing room of the star

performer and that of the singer of popular songs opened from corners opposite. On the next level was the common room of the male performers. This last was called "the youth department," and the quarreling and fisticuffs never stopped. The place where I chose to pass my time was neither the star's room nor the singer's. It was rather the big room where the dancing girls lay sprawled about.

There had been a warning from the police that men who had no business there were to be seen in the room under no circumstances. I alone had complete freedom of access. No one in the company ever challenged me, or seemed to find my presence strange. There ought to be elaborate reasons that this should have been the case. I see no need, however, to explain in proud and lofty tones and great detail the relationship between me and the theater that had led to these very special rights. Perhaps it would be simplest to say that when I first visited the dressing room, I had reached what might be described as a most advanced age of discretion, and was therefore seen as one who no longer had the physical capacity to do damage to the public morals, in whatever numbers and whatever postures of abandon naked women might surround him. I do not wish to speak smugly of relations with men of letters and the theater over the years, relations such as to make this trust in me quite natural. I wish to get on with more important business: to describe for the curious who have not themselves seen this world apart what the dressing room of the dancers was like.

One would have been hard put, from a glance at the room, to judge its exact dimensions. There were on occasion twenty and more girls, however, and it was large enough to squeeze them all in, albeit like a flock of starlings. The room was not rectangular, but warped into a sort of triangle. Just inside the opening where the door should have been, there was a wooden floor perhaps three feet wide by nine or ten feet deep. The rest of the room was carpeted with reed matting, but only once or twice in the four or five years I frequented the place did I see the matting other than battered and torn.

There were usually some fifteen girls, on battered cushions laid on the battered matting. Some were as good as naked in their review costumes, others in dressing gowns and bathrobes, careful only to conceal their private parts. Sprawled on their backs, sitting cross-legged, they cared not in the least who saw them. Four and five would sit playing cards, their foreheads almost pressed together. One would be nursing a baby, another making up at a mirror, another, apart from the rest, absorbed in applying false eyelashes. Still others would be knitting, or reading popular magazines.

The wooden floor at the entrance was sometimes such a clutter of footwear that one could find nowhere to step: high-heeled dancing shoes and sandals of silver, some of the former with broken heels and straps, in among slippers for use backstage and sandals of felt and wood for out of doors. Although two girls each day were charged with sweeping, their ministrations, however constant, had little chance of keeping up with the litter being ground into the matting, the peanut and chestnut shells, the paper, the fruit peels, the cigarette butts.

On the narrow strips of dirty, flaking wall between the mirror stands, one for each girl, were layer after layer of scribbled remarks and sketches. There were pictures of movie actors and actresses pinned up in complete disorder. In cigar boxes, also fastened with pins, would be two and three cosmetics brushes, their tips frayed and tattered. Review costumes heaped upon review costumes, one did not know how many layers of them, blocked the narrow windows even in the hottest of the summer. When the windows were open or broken, you had glimpses through the costumes of the treetops around the pond, and the roofs of the theaters beyond.

Such was the dressing room of the dancers in the Opera House. It was given over to clutter, such a clutter that you wondered how anything more could possibly be added. An indescribable disorder—it might be likened to a laundry or a used-clothes house on moving day. What first caught the eye, however, was not the violent jumble of colors, or even the faces of the girls as they sprawled about on the floor and then sat up again. It was the powerful flesh of their arms and legs. The effect was therefore wholly different from the dirt and clutter of a tenement house. One might say that it called to mind the earthen hallway of a florist's shop, where a litter of torn-off petals and withering leaves is left unswept and trampled into shapelessness.

A mixed odor overwhelmed the nostrils, an odor compounded of cheap perfume and oil and skin and dust. From far down the stairs came voices and the sour notes of the orchestra. The pounding of sandals never stopped for a moment as people ran up and down the wooden stairs. These noises mingled with the noises from the park

outside, and with the shrill voices and laughter of the women rever-
berating from the low ceiling, and the humming that had become
habitual of songs for the new review. But when one was used to it,
the din did not seem completely overpowering.

In the dancers' room, with its darkness and noise and confusion, I
felt once again the mild, bland melancholy I knew on occasion in
out-of-the-way pleasure quarters. The nostalgia was intensified by
the tired faces and the worn figures of the peddlers and caterers who
frequented the place, hoping to sell to the girls.

That day, when as usual I marched up the stairs, I saw a young
man in Occidental clothes, his pockmarked face suggesting that he
might be a Korean, beginning to put cosmetics away in a suitcase.
As he took his money and started out, a woman in her forties, something about her suggesting that she was a tenement wife from one
of the back alleys, began taking out her wares, shirts and towels and
handkerchiefs, women's and men's too, all for the summer, to remind
one that young leaves were coming out in the park and that the heat
was getting worse day by day.

"Come and look, everybody. Pure cotton. You'd be paying taxes if
you bought at the regular price."

At the mention of pure cotton, even the girls who had been lying
on the floor hurried over for a look. Men from the "youth department," passing in the hall after having washed away makeup from
the first act, some naked to the waist, pushed their way in among the
girls. Very cheap, said one, very expensive, said another—and in upon
the confusion came a large, red-faced old man, making his way heavily to the top of the stairs, a battered hamper in his hand.

"You're late. I'm starved," said a girl who had taken a handkerchief
over to examine it by the window. Her voice was shrill and scolding,
but the old man did not answer. Sluggishly he took the lid from the
hamper.

"And what was it you ordered? No trimmings today," he added,
handing her a bowl.

He would have been in his fifties, perhaps even past sixty. He was
dressed in the old manner, dark blue tights and a bib over a shabby
knitted undershirt, his frame so sturdy even now that the bib seemed
to eat into it. Although a thick, greasy sweat covered his round face
and filled the deep furrows on his forehead, the small, good-natured

eyes went on blinking through it, and he made no motion toward wiping it away with the towel knotted around his head.

This was the old man I made so happy with my camera.

Every day, choosing his time carefully, he would come for orders, and again choosing a likely time, he would come around to deliver them in his hamper. It was losing its handle, and one would have judged that it had never been washed or polished. I had been told that he rarely missed a day's work; but no one in the theater knew where he lived, or whether he was married and had children. Although the girls called him "the old man from the Sameya," there did not seem to be a restaurant called the Sameya anywhere in the park or its environs. Apparently persons of some influence, rather like local bosses, had monopolies on the purveying of various commodities to the Opera House and other places of entertainment. It seemed clear that the old man had not attained to such a status, however, and that, at his advanced years, he eked out a day-to-day living as a sort of delivery boy for one of the bosses. Not one of the dishes he delivered, even with the "trimmings," could have cost more than twenty sen; and with a share of the tiny profits he was seeing himself through his last years.

He would deliver his orders to the dancing girls and to the youth department above, and come sluggishly back with late orders. By that time the long summer day would be drawing to a close, and the lights of the entertainment district would be flashing on.

All of the girls left their upstairs room and went on stage to prance and kick. Afterwards they fell exhausted on the matting before the mirrors, waiting for the evening performance, the last one of the day. There were two or three hours between performances.

I went down, and from behind the scenes observed the art with which they flung their legs into the air simultaneously. Then I went out into the alleys with certain of the theater people, and, in the shooting stalls thereabouts, had a try at shooting down the Hakata dolls that were the prizes. Finally, tired of such sports, I went back to the dancers' room.

The old man had come and gone several times, it would seem, and now he was clearing away the dirty dishes, finishing his day's work. He had taken a cigarette stub from behind his ear and was talking to an actor in a soldier's uniform.

"So you were in a war yourself?" the youth was saying. "When was that?"

"Haven't I already told you? The big war. The war with the Russians. In Manchuria." He retied the towel that seemed about to slip from his bald head. "How many years ago was it, I wonder. I'm not the man I used to be." He sighed as if remembering something. The narrow eyes, blinking as always, were fixed dully on the uniform.

"How old are you, anyway?"

"It would have been 1904. A long time ago. A long, long time ago." The occasions for thus taking a quiet look back over the years were not common, it seemed, and, on such short notice, the old man had trouble counting them up.

"I was young and healthy in those days myself," he said, taking a puff on his cigarette. He wiped the sweat from his forehead with the palm of his hand and fell silent.

"Did you get a decoration?" asked the uniformed actor, leaning toward a dancer who lay on the matting beside him.

"That I did. You think I'm joking? I'll show it to you." Pride seemed to flow up from deep within him. "I'll show it to you. It's at the boss's."

"Oh, do. Do show it to us," said the girl, pushing away the heavy soldier. "You can borrow Shin-chan's uniform and pin it on."

The old man laughed. It was unusual to see him laughing. Then, abruptly, he got up and went out with his hamper and dirty dishes.

As always, the girls pressed me to take their pictures, and I obliged. It was already dark outside, but the fairly bright lights at the mirrors were enough for my purposes.

Presently the old man came back, this time without his hamper. He sat down heavily in the same place and took a dirty cloth bundle from his bib. It was the decoration. The actor with whom he had been talking had gone on stage, however, and other actors in army uniforms were running up and down the stairs. Apparently a military drama of some sort was being staged. There was a booming of cannon, and the smell of powder drifted up to the dressing room. Voices were raised in a war song.

The girls swarmed around to look at the medal and citation. One of them said that he must have his picture taken, and ran off to sew the medal on a uniform. The old man took off his bib and put on the army jacket and cap, and, with a stage sword and pistol at his belt, stood for his picture. The chattering and cheering of some twenty girls had put him in a festive mood.

He had never exchanged words with me before, but now, sweat dripping from his face, he thanked me over and over again.

That night I developed the film. The lighting had been better than I thought, but I noticed that the decoration was over the right pocket, not the left as regulations required. The girl had sewn it as the spirit moved her, apparently, on a jacket discarded by an actor. Perhaps the old man himself had in the course of time forgotten the correct way.

I printed an enlargement all the same, reversing the negative to make things seem in order. Some ten days later I took it to the dressing room.

"The old man from the Sameya doesn't seem to be coming today," I said to one of the girls after I had waited for a time.

"He hasn't come since."

"Oh? You must be having a bad time of it, then, with no one to feed you."

"Someone brings things from someplace else."

That was the end of our conversation.

I went to the dressing room again a week later, but by that time no one had an answer when I asked about the old man from the Sameya. No one seemed inclined to remember that there had been such a person.

He had always had oily beads of sweat on a face that was flushed as if from drink, and he had always climbed the stairs with great difficulty. I took it that he had had an attack of apoplexy or something of the sort. Had I known of surviving relatives, I would have liked to deliver the picture, but of course I had no way of tracing them.

If I were to look for the snapshot, I think I would probably find it in a box labeled "Asakusa customs." It would be in with all sorts of photographs and scraps of paper, programs and popular songs and the like.

The Dancing Girl: Chapter 10

The Dancing Girl was written in 1944 and published
in the magazine *Tembō* in 1946. It was included
in the 1947 collection called *The Decoration*. For a
discussion, see pp. 160–62. Chiyomi is the sister, Hanae
the mistress. The baby, it will be noted, has arrived.

On rehearsal nights neither Hanae nor I reached home before dawn. One evening Hanae went out after leaving instructions with Chiyomi about the baby's bottle and the like.

When the rehearsal was over, seven or eight of us who lived in the same direction started out together, talking as we headed from the theater district toward the main street. A third-quarter moon hung over the end of the straight, narrow street that leads from Kappa Bridge to Iriya. Street lights were still on. Under the eaves it was pitch dark, but back toward the park, from which we had come, the sky was already faintly red. The dawn lighted the theaters from the east, so that the angles of the buildings were clear and sharp, and the boundary between night and day cleanly marked off.

The women were intent on getting home as soon as possible, and no one had an eye for the streets around us; but with me it was different. The very fact that the scene was so familiar meant that changes brought back the months and the years spent in Asakusa, and filled me with a soft sadness, a nostalgia beyond description. It was therefore when we were making our way home after rehearsal, not at night but in the early dawn, that I would feel as if I were having the experience for the first time, and would want to think not only of our lives, Hanae's and Chiyomi's and mine, but of the lives of the others too, as something from a novel. A stupid thought, perhaps, a bit of common, vulgar sentimentality. But it was precisely because of the sentimentality that I had, for a whole decade of months and years, been able to go on with it, the brassy music in dust from the stage, and not miss a single day.

I looked up. The street lights were out, and a streetcar came around the Tamurachō corner. The roofs of the buildings in the park were already bright, and the street in the direction of Kappa Bridge, dark but a moment before, was so light that we could see our destination. Not a single milkman or delivery boy was to be seen, however, and drivers were asleep in their cabs.

There were cheap all-night restaurants along the way that catered to drivers. I suggested that we go in and have a bowl of clam soup or something of the sort, but Hanae was worried about the baby. We left the others and turned up the alley to our room.

All by itself, the baby was sound asleep in its blankets. Chiyomi was nowhere in sight. Hanae made some toast over the gas range, and we had it as a token breakfast, and still Chiyomi was not back. We went to bed immediately, setting the alarm for eleven-thirty, since on opening day we did not have to be at the theater until afternoon. Even then Chiyomi had not come back. We thought of asking the landlady to take care of the baby, but we were not really sure that we trusted her. So finally we set out for the theater, Hanae carrying the baby all bundled up in a padded kimono, I with a bottle of milk in my hand.

We stepped through the door of the dancers' dressing room, left wide open even in the middle of winter.

"A baby! Isn't it sweet!"

Thirty girls were lined up at the mirror stands. They jumped up to greet us. They had known that the baby was not Hanae's but that of her younger sister, who had been with the troupe for a time the year before. There had been some doubt about the father, but, seeing me thus with a bottle of milk, they appeared to think that the answer to that question was as they had suspected. One of the girls took the milk over to heat it on the hand warmer by her mirror. I had wondered which of the candidates for paternity they might think the baby resembled, and meant to keep my ears open for rumors; but it began to seem that I had little hope of hearing anything.

This, perhaps, is the way with the world: people are interested in gossip while a doubt remains, but once the doubt is gone they accept the conclusion and see no need for further inquiry. Perhaps, too, the dancing girls in Asakusa Park, thinking of their own origins, were not disposed to inquire too deeply into the lineage and parentage of the baby before them. Affairs between a man and his stepdaughter, a man and his foster daughter, father-in-law and daughter-in-law—

such affairs were likely to be common enough in the neighborhoods from which they had come, in the houses right next door to their own. My relationship with Chiyomi did not therefore seem especially remarkable. These girls were for the most part products of tenements. If they had not become dancers, they would have had to go to work as factory girls, waitresses, nursemaids, or bus conductors, to contribute to the family income. And they were very practiced tenders of babies. While Hanae was on stage, one of the others who happened to be free would give the baby its bottle with one hand and repair her makeup with the other, or cover it with the still-warm clothes she had just taken off. There were some who, whatever the reason—it was as if they wanted children of their own, and were seeking consolation, knowing that they could have none—would lie down beside the baby, and, gazing into its face, sing it a lullaby. Every Asakusa theater had mothers and daughters in the same troupe, the latter born and reared backstage. I wondered if such would be the fate of Yukiko, the child Chiyomi had borne and Hanae was to rear.

The Scavengers

"The Scavengers" was written late in 1948 and
published in the magazine *Chūō Kōron* the following
year. In 1950 it was included in a collection entitled
Gift from Katsushika. For a discussion, see p. 176.

The branch of the Sōbu Line between Noda and Funabashi carries so
few passengers other than those out hunting rice and sweet potatoes
that it has come to be known as "the scavenging line." The trains generally have but two or three cars, battered and dirty to the point that
they seem to be meant not for passengers but for freight. There is not
a pane of glass in the window frames, and old boards nailed together
serve as doors. The state of the uncushioned benches is such that a person in ordinary dress has trouble finding a place fit for sitting. The few
trains each day, no more than three or four, are always so crowded that
on dark days one can scarcely make out what is baggage and what
passengers.

It was about ten o'clock on the morning of a day when the scavenging train was even more crowded than usual. Because of floods on the
Toné River, service to the north, and even between Tokyo and Ichikawa, had been out for several days, and the tracks had only just been
reopened. The train was about to enter a station some two or three
stops before Funabashi when a rumor began to circulate to the effect
that policemen were waiting in Funabashi Station to look for black-
market food. It spread through the scavenging train like a flash fire.

All of the scavengers had gone out that morning before daylight to
make the rounds of farms with which they were acquainted, and now
they were in a hurry to get back to Tokyo and sell what they had in
their knapsacks. Well, they would get off at the next stop, no matter
what village it proved to be. If things seemed in order, they would get
back on the train. Otherwise they would walk to Funabashi, there to
catch a train for Tokyo. Some suggested that it might be better to turn
back to Kashiwa, and there catch a train for Ueno. Someone reached

for the knapsack at his feet. As if that were the signal, the flood toward the doors began, like an army in rout. Almost no one was left behind. The train was still in motion when the flood began spilling out on the platform.

"So this is where we are," said those who knew the land, starting briskly for the gate.

Those who were strangers followed.

"I have a feeling I've been here before."

"A bad place to do any buying. The farmers know they have you where they want you."

"They won't take money. If you want to get anything out of them you've got to bring shoes or towels."

"There should be a bus to Nakayama from a little farther down."

Such were the remarks they exchanged as they trudged along.

It was a pleasant October day, not a cloud in the sky. The rice, already cut, hung on frames among the paddies. Cabbages and radish leaves were spread out like carpets. The tips of the branches, in which shrikes were calling back and forth, carried traces of autumn color, and the persimmons in farmyards where chrysanthemums and camellias were just coming into bloom were a bright vermilion. It was good weather for walking. Weighted down by their bundles, the scavengers fell into a column as they started for their several destinations. The men were in sweaters or civil-defense uniforms that were no better than rags, and old yellow caps and battered shoes or straw sandals. Most of them seemed to be in their forties. The women, too, seemed for the most part to be about forty. They had dirty towels tied around their faces to keep off the sun, and they wore baggy trousers over their skirts. Some were barefoot.

Gradually the column began to break up, the good walkers pushing ahead, the weaker ones falling behind in groups of three and four. Presently some stopped to rest, laying their packs on the grass. It became difficult to know which were from the scavenging train and which were residents of the district. Everyone was dressed very much like everyone else, and all of the bundles were similar.

At a curve in the road where flaming daisies were in bloom, an old woman was the very first to put down her pack. She propped it against a milestone, under a nettle tree. Vacantly, she turned her eyes on the backs of those who had gone on.

A woman perhaps in her forties came up. They appeared to be acquaintances from the train.

"It's a real nuisance, isn't it. I think I'll have a rest too."

"What time do you suppose it is?" The old woman squinted up at the bright autumn sun.

"It'll soon be twelve. If we don't hurry, we might miss out."

"Maybe we should have gone on down the tracks to Funabashi."

"I don't know the roads around here. Do you?"

"I have a feeling I've been here before. Only once, though, and then with someone from the neighborhood. I have no idea where anything is. It was a long time ago. The war had started, I think, but not the air raids."

"It'll soon be ten years. And even now that it's over, you don't know where it will all end. It's a hard life, I say, when you have things like this happening to you."

"A hard life it is, all right. Bad enough for people like you. And what am I to do at my age?"

"How old are you?"

"Sixty-seven. I'm no good any more. It seems like just yesterday that I could carry sixty and seventy pounds with no trouble. But you can't fight the years."

"You do pretty well, whatever you say. I'm beginning to wonder how long I'll hold out myself."

"Oh, you'll have the young ones to look after you. They won't let you starve."

"I only hope you're right. But you can't depend on them these days. Well, it doesn't do a person much good to sit here grumbling. We've had quite a rest. Shall we move on?"

The younger woman, who appeared to be a housewife, hitched up her pack. The older woman, too, shouldered her rice, done up in a large, greenish kerchief, and the two of them started down the unfamiliar road.

"Where do you live in Tokyo? Honjo?"

"Nihombashi. Hakozaki."

"You're lucky. Hakozaki wasn't bombed. I was in Kinshichō myself, and I was lucky to get away with the clothes on my back. Couldn't take a thing with me."

"It was the same with me. I was working in Sagachō, cooking for a man by the upper bridge, a wholesale dealer in china. Both the old master and the young master were killed in the raid. It's funny, isn't it. It doesn't matter about someone like me, and I come through without a scorch. And the young master gets killed, and him with so much to live for. You never can tell. That's what I always say."

"Listen—the siren. Noon." The younger woman turned to look in the direction of the siren, which seemed fairly near. The old woman paid no attention. Untying the towel around her face and wiping the sweat from her forehead, she fell a step and two steps behind.

"Suppose we have lunch over there. It doesn't matter how much of a hurry you're in, you can do just so much walking." Seeing a dilapidated little wayside shrine under a great camellia tree, the younger woman unloaded her pack on the stone platform. Cocks were crowing busily. The old woman laid down her cloth bundle beside the other, and watched in silence as the housewife undid her lunch.

"Aren't you eating?" asked the latter.

"I'm not hungry yet."

"Well, you'll have to excuse me, then. I'm starved."

"Please go right ahead. I'll just rest here a while."

The housewife took a large ball of rice in both hands and plunged into it without looking up. Then she saw that the old woman was squatting as if in pain, her knees hugged in her arms.

"What's the matter? Don't you feel well?"

There was no answer. Perhaps the old woman was hard of hearing, perhaps she did not want to talk. The housewife attacked a second ball of rice, and, crunching away at a pickle, licked her fingers. The old woman was teetering forward, her head between her knees. There was a loud snore. No one like a child or an old person for snoring, no matter where you are, the housewife seemed to be thinking.

"Wake up. It's time we got started."

There was no answer.

"Well, I'll be on my way, then," she said, hoisting up her pack.

Just then the old woman fell forward, and the housewife sensed for the first time that something was desperately wrong. Lifting the other from behind, she saw that the eyes were closed and there was foam at the mouth.

"What's the matter? What's the matter? Come on, now, pull yourself together." She shook the old woman. There was no answer. The old woman slipped from her arms and rolled over.

The housewife looked around. As far as the eye could reach, over fields of radish and spinach and onions, there was not a person, not a farmhouse, in sight. There was only the shimmering autumn sunlight. A horse cart approached and went off again, paying no attention to the two. The housewife thought of an old person who had lived next to her, and who, while talking of this and that after a bath one evening, had fallen over dead.

"So she's gone and done it."

She looked around. Then she took off her knapsack again. Dragging it and the woman's bundle in under the eaves, she quickly changed her sweet potatoes for the polished rice the old woman had been carrying. By weight, rice brought more than sweet potatoes.

She retied the old towel around her face, and, without a glance backward, started off down the road.

It dipped and gradually rose again, to disappear in a pine grove atop a distant hill. There was a lowing of cattle from generally that direction. Panting desperately and bathed in sweat, the woman hurried along as if someone were chasing her. However often she wiped her forehead, sweat came pouring into her eyes an instant later. She had to rest. If she overtaxed herself she would meet the old woman's fate. But, stumbling in a rut from time to time, she was determined to get as far as that pine grove. She was terrified at the thought of being left anywhere along the road she had come. She would get beyond the pine grove, even if she had to crawl.

Once there, once beyond the pine grove, she would somehow have passed a boundary. She would somehow be at a sufficient distance that the scene of the crime no longer concerned her. She felt that if only she could get beyond the grove, then no one walking in the same direction would know where she had come from.

She was not wrong. Perhaps it was her imagination, but when she climbed the rise, shoulders heaving, and entered the pine grove, the scenery ahead beyond the trees and the dwarf bamboo, the aspect of the trees themselves, seemed completely different. The crops in the fields were different. Here and there among the thatched roofs was the tiled roof of a two-story house with glass doors and an imposing gate. The grove was shady and the breeze cool. She heaved a sigh, and as she squatted down to rest, the weight of the rice threw her forward. She was not able to get up for a time.

A middle-aged man came up the rise on a bicycle. Stopping near her to wipe away the sweat, he lighted a cigarette. She glanced at him. He would be a scavenger himself, on the way back from looking for food. On the luggage stand of his bicycle was what appeared to be a folded knapsack.

"Are you out buying?" the woman asked timidly.

"No luck at all. Things are completely out of sight."

"It's not easy, is it, when they don't want to sell."

"It's not easy at all. With rice you don't get anywhere. They ask whatever comes into their heads and aren't satisfied with just money."

"They put the squeeze on me, too, but I was finally able to get a little."

"Women seem to do better than men. Two hundred yen a quart they want. Can you believe it?"

"But there are places in Tokyo where you can get more than that. If you make me a good offer, I might let you have some of mine here."

"Thank you. That would be very kind of you. How much do you have?"

"Maybe half a bushel. It's pretty heavy, and I'm afraid I'm coming down with a cold. You can have it if you want it."

"How would one eighty a quart be?"

"That's what I bought it for. You ought to let me make a least five a quart."

The man felt the weight of the pack. Then, looking to see that no one was coming, he untied his knapsack and took out scales.

The transaction was soon finished.

Freed of her burden, the woman tucked the roll of bills into the breast of her kimono. She looked at the man's receding back as she left the grove. Birds were singing in the trees, and insects in the grasses.

Appendix, Bibliographical Note, Index

Appendix: A Postscript on the Diary

Volume xxiv, 1964, of the Iwanami collected works (see the Bibliographical Note, pp. 351–52) contains the text of Kafū's diary from January 1, 1945, to April 29, 1959, the eve of his death. It contains additional fragments of great interest to students of the diary: clean copies of the entries for the first two weeks of 1946 and the first two weeks of 1947; and variant drafts for most of 1946 (January 19 to the end of the year) and almost all of January, 1947. By "clean copy" is meant a text in a form comparable to that of the earlier, bound portions of the diary. The whole of the diary after January 14, 1947, was by this definition in draft form at the time of Kafū's death.

When the fragments are combined with what is run as the main Iwanami text, the following duplications are found: two texts, both clean copies, for the first two weeks of 1946; two texts, one clean and one a draft, for the entries from January 19, 1946, to the end of the year; three texts, two drafts and one clean copy, for the first two weeks of 1947; and two texts, both drafts, through January 30.

Close perusal of the duplications does not answer important questions about the diary with finality, but it does suggest possibilities. Two very important questions cannot be answered: whether or not distortions and even downright lies were present in early drafts; and whether or not the process of revision evident in the 1946 and 1947 texts was followed for the diary as a whole. The testimony of those who knew Kafū continues to argue, unfortunately, that he was not above setting down an untruth from time to time.

Yet the evidence from these fragmentary duplications strongly suggests that once something was in draft it was not altered significantly, and that not a great deal was added to a draft. It seems more than possible, therefore, that this study has been unfair to Kafū in at least one respect: the implication that some of the anti-military remarks for which he became such a hero after the war might have been added when the pro-military view was no longer fashionable. The variant texts give no reason for doubting Kafū's integrity in this larger matter, whatever fibs he may have set down about friends and colleagues.

The two clean copies for early 1946 are identical but for minor changes in wording. The revisions for the rest of 1946 are also largely matters of wording and orthography. One can see the stylist at work, polishing and shaping. A translation from the draft entry for May 19, 1946, for instance, would amount to virtually the same thing in English as the translation already offered from the clean copy (see page 173). The words "early in the morning" would become "on my way home in the morning," and the rest would remain very much the same.

Occasionally a bit of information is shifted from one day to another, but not in such a fashion as to give a dishonest suggestion of prescience. It is curious that small deletions should be considerably more frequent than small additions for the first half of the year, and the reverse the case for the second. Kafū evidently had his ups and downs.

More interesting is the nature of such changes. A scattering of examples should show that they are of no crucial importance.

Here are some deletions (items present in the draft but not in the clean copy): a complaint about the loss of a writing brush on January 19; a description on January 31 of certain truths that an almanac has revealed about the amorous affairs of those born in the Year of the Hare (1879, when Kafū was born, was such a year); the whole of the entry for April 9, largely a complaint about a stomachache and a word of gratitude for a gift of underwear; the record of a pair of baths on April 23 and April 30; on June 11, the information that the professional ladies along the railway line to Ichikawa charge five yen extra per condom; and a complaint about photographers on June 15.

And a few additions: on May 10, some haiku not in the draft; on May 12, a few details about a stroll through the Ichikawa countryside; on October 2, mention of a crescent moon seen through a pine grove; on November 10, a description of a Shokusanjin manuscript; and on December 26, an ill-tempered remark about Kineya Gosō's children. The last item cannot be taken as evidence of a later change of heart, since rancor at the whole family, with whom Kafū was then living, runs through the main 1946 text and the variants as well.

The 1947 fragments are interesting chiefly for the evidence they give of the care Kafū lavished on his diary. Again the changes are of little substantial importance. Close examination of the threefold overlap reveals that, where the three texts differ, the month-long draft has far more in comon with both the fortnight of clean copy and the main (year-long) Iwanami text than either of the latter two has with the other. One may conclude, therefore, that Kafū did a preliminary revision of the entries for most of January, but only got around to beating two weeks' worth into a shape that really satisfied him.

Bibliographical Note

Far the most important source for this book has been the writings of Kafū himself. Three editions of his "complete writings" had been completed at the time the manuscript was finished: one, in six volumes, brought out by Shunyōdō before the 1923 earthquake; a reissue, also in six volumes, by the same company after the earthquake; and the Chūō Kōron version, in twenty-four volumes, published between 1948 and 1953. This last collection has been indispensable, and when there has been significant variation among texts, as with *A Strange Tale from East of the River,* the Chūō Kōron text has been followed. (It would not have sufficed for a complete translation of *Rivalry,* since Chūō Kōron did not make bold to publish the more indecent parts of that novel; but the problem did not arise in the only lengthy section translated here.)

There are at least three shortcomings in the Chūō Kōron "complete works": the failure to include letters; the fact that the diary breaks off at 1945, and is expurgated for the earlier years; and the omission of Kafū's postwar writings, which have appeared in three separate volumes, all published by Chūō Kōron. The diary through 1948 has since appeared, published in magazines and by the Tōto Shobō. Nothing for the later years had appeared at the time this manuscript was completed.

Presumably most of these defects will be remedied when the Iwanami version of the complete works is finished. It had begun to come out when I was getting to the end of this study, and one of the defects was already by way of being remedied, the omission of certain passages from the earlier years of the diary. The temptation was strong to go back and rewrite each time a new bit of the Iwanami diary appeared, but it soon became apparent that a halt would have to be called, and the Chūō Kōron edition considered final. It seems clear, in any case, that the passages deleted from the Chūō Kōron version have to do in the main with chitchat of a vaguely malicious nature about persons still living, and would not, even if taken into consideration one by one, have altered the manuscript in any significant fashion. A bit of color may have been lost, since some of the deleted passages are a trifle indecent, but the manuscript seemed to contain enough indecency already.

Critical writings on Kafū began to appear almost as soon as Kafū began writing. At the head of the list is an essay on *Hell Flowers* by Takayama Chogyū, published in the magazine *Taiyō* for November 1902. Other critical comments have been referred to from time to time in the text. One may safely say, however, that the critics did not really get down to work until the postwar Kafū revival. Two collections of critical and biographical essays are extremely valuable: the special Kafū edition (1956) of the magazine *Bungei*; and *Studies of Nagai Kafū* (*Nagai Kafū Kenkyū*), edited by Nakamura Shinichirō and published by Shinchōsha in 1956. At least three book-length studies, varying mixtures of biography and criticism, deserve to be mentioned: *Nagai Kafū* by Yoshida Seiichi, the revised edition of which was published by Hanawa Shobō in 1953; *Random Thoughts on Kafū* (*Kafū Zakkan*) by Satō Haruo, published by Kokuritsu Shoin in 1947; and *The Writings of Kafū* (*Kafū Bungaku*) by Hinatsu Kōnosuke, published by Mikasa Shobō in 1950.

Satō's *Fictional Account of the Life of Nagai Kafū* (*Shōsetsu Nagai Kafū Den*) was published by Shinchōsha in May 1960, just a year after Kafū's death. A mixture of fact and fiction, as the title suggests, it is valuable for psychological insights and for an account of Kafū as seen by a sensitive colleague. For biographical minutiae, the essays of the *Mainichi* reporter who was among Kafū's companions in the postwar years and whose pen name is Okado Katsuji are very useful. The most accurate and detailed chronology of Kafū's life was compiled by Aiso Ryōsō, another friend of his last years, and is to be found in Volume XVI of *A Complete Collection of Modern Japanese Literature* (*Gendai Nihon Bungaku Zenshū*), Chikuma Shobō, 1956.

Another translation of *The River Sumida* will be found in *Modern Japanese Literature*, edited by Donald Keene, Grove Press, 1956. The fact that I have not used the earlier translation, by Dr. Keene himself, indicates not a want of admiration for that translation but rather an abundance of admiration for the work itself, such as to make me wish to have a try at a translation of my own. A complete translation of what I have called *Rivalry* (or, rather, of the prewar expurgated version of that novel) was published in 1963 by the Charles E. Tuttle Company under the title *Geisha in Rivalry*. Again the translation in this book is my own, and again that fact is not to be interpreted as hostile criticism of the other translators, Messrs. Kurt Meissner and Ralph Friedrich. My translation of "Quiet Rain" first appeared in the *Japan Quarterly* for January–March 1964, and about half of my translation of *A Strange Tale from East of the River* appeared in the same magazine for April–June 1958. There is a French translation, by Serge Elisséeff, of "The Peony Garden."

Index